Sustainable Welfare in the Asia-Pacific

ADVANCES IN ECOLOGICAL ECONOMICS

Series Editor: Jeroen C.J.M. van den Bergh, *ICREA Professor, Universitat Autònoma de Barcelona, Spain and Professor of Environmental and Resource Economics, Vrije Universiteit, Amsterdam, The Netherlands*

Founding Editor: Robert Costanza, *Gund Professor of Ecological Economics and Director, Gund Institute for Ecological Economics, University of Vermont, USA*

This important series makes a significant contribution to the development of the principles and practices of ecological economics, a field which has expanded dramatically in recent years. The series provides an invaluable forum for the publication of high quality work and shows how ecological economic analysis can make a contribution to understanding and resolving important problems.

The main emphasis of the series is on the development and application of new original ideas in ecological economics. International in its approach, it includes some of the best theoretical and empirical work in the field with contributions to fundamental principles, rigorous evaluations of existing concepts, historical surveys and future visions. It seeks to address some of the most important theoretical questions and gives policy solutions for the ecological problems confronting the global village as we move into the twenty-first century.

Titles in the series include:

Joint Production and Responsibility in Ecological Economics
On the Foundations of Environmental Policy
Stefan Baumgärtner, Malte Faber and Johannes Schiller

Frontiers in Ecological Economic Theory and Application
Edited by Jon D. Erickson and John M. Gowdy

Socioecological Transitions and Global Change
Trajectories of Social Metabolism and Land Use
Edited by Marina Fischer-Kowalski and Helmut Haberl

Conflict, Cooperation and Institutions in International Water Management
An Economic Analysis
Ines Dombrowsky

Ecological Economics and Sustainable Development
Selected Essays of Herman Daly
Herman E. Daly

Sustainable Welfare in the Asia-Pacific
Studies Using the Genuine Progress Indicator
Edited by Philip Lawn and Matthew Clarke

Managing without Growth
Slower by Design, Not Disaster
Peter A. Victor

Sustainable Welfare in the Asia-Pacific

Studies Using the Genuine Progress Indicator

Edited by

Philip Lawn

Flinders University, Adelaide, Australia

and

Matthew Clarke

Deakin University, Melbourne, Australia

ADVANCES IN ECOLOGICAL ECONOMICS

Edward Elgar

Cheltenham, UK • Northampton, MA, USA

Published by
Edward Elgar Publishing Limited
The Lypiatts
15 Lansdown Road
Cheltenham
Glos GL50 2JA
UK

Edward Elgar Publishing, Inc.
William Pratt House
9 Dewey Court
Northampton
Massachusetts 01060
USA

A catalogue record for this book
is available from the British Library

Library of Congress Control Number: 2008927957

ISBN 978 1 84720 501 8

Printed and bound in Great Britain by MPG Books Ltd, Bodmin, Cornwall

Contents

Figures

Tables

Contributors

Matthew Clarke, School of International and Political Studies, Deakin University, Melbourne, Australia

Vicky Forgie, New Zealand Centre for Ecological Economics, Massey University, Palmerston North, New Zealand

Derrylea Hardy, New Zealand Centre for Ecological Economics, Massey University, Palmerston North, New Zealand

Vu Xuan Nguyet Hong, Central Institute for Economic Management, Hanoi, Vietnam

Philip Lawn, Faculty of Social Sciences, Flinders University, Australia

Matsuyo Makino, School of Economics, University of Hyogo, Japan

Garry McDonald, New Zealand Centre for Ecological Economics, Massey University, Palmerston North, New Zealand

Murray Patterson, New Zealand Centre for Ecological Economics, Massey University, Palmerston North, New Zealand

Judith Shaw, Monash Asia Institute, Monash University, Australia

Yan Yang, Department of Environmental Science and Engineering, Tsinghua University, China

Yanjiao Zhang, New Zealand Centre for Ecological Economics, Massey University, Palmerston North, New Zealand

Zonggou Wen, Department of Environmental Science and Engineering, Tsinghua University, China

Preface

It is no small thing to shift the burden of proof. Yet that is what Lawn and Clarke, and their colleagues, have done in this remarkable study. The presumption in the 'empty world' has been that growth in Gross Domestic Product (GDP) is 'economic' in the sense that it increases benefits faster than costs, as well as in the sense that this thing we call the economy is getting physically bigger. It was not previously considered necessary to distinguish the two meanings of 'economic' growth. Lawn and Clarke have shown that, in a large part of today's 'full world', growth in GDP often costs more than it is worth at the margin, and thus should be called 'uneconomic' growth. In this book's language uneconomic growth occurs after a threshold at which the Genuine Progress Indicator (GPI) levels off or declines while GDP keeps on increasing. Advocates of GDP growth, who generally point to Asia as their best success story, heretofore were never asked to prove that such growth was in truth economic. Now, after the theoretical demonstration that uneconomic growth in the macroeconomy is quite possible, followed by the empirical demonstration that it is in fact often the case, the burden of proof in policy arguments must shift from the shoulders of growth critics to the shoulders of growth advocates. This is quite an accomplishment and needs to be strongly claimed and emphasised.

For many years I have worked with ideas that are used in this book – the steady-state economy, the Index of Sustainable Economic Welfare, contradictions between comparative advantage and international capital mobility, and others. It is a pleasure to see these ideas not only applied, but sharpened and polished as well. Although I have very little knowledge of Asia, I cannot resist recounting one relevant episode out of my limited experience. Around 1992 I was part of a World Bank mission to Thailand. This was at the end of a decade in which Thailand's GDP had doubled. Now doubling is a big change, and ten years was within the easy memory of most adult Thais. In conversations I began to ask people how much their lives had been improved over that decade. Many said that life had been better ten years ago. I suggested that maybe life always feels better when you are ten years younger. They assured me that they had corrected for that! Some thought things were a little better, but the suggestion that life might be twice as good was considered laughable by all. This experience led me to suggest to my bosses at the World Bank that we finance a study – a scientific survey asking people how much life had improved over the decade in which GDP doubled, and to give the main reasons for their answer. History had given us a unique experiment, and we should take advantage of it and learn something. My proposal was turned down, I think because the World Bank, the prime pusher of growth, was worried that it might learn an 'inconvenient truth'. In 1992 the burden of proof was on me. Now, with Lawn and Clarke to appeal to I think the burden of proof will be on the World Bank.

The study I had proposed to the World Bank was to look at what is now called 'self-evaluated happiness', whereas Lawn and Clarke look at a more objective index of welfare, the GPI. Studies of self-evaluated happiness have now come into fashion, and generally support the same conclusions that Lawn and Clarke reach on the basis of more objective data. The finding is that self-evaluated happiness rises with absolute income up to a threshold beyond which increases in absolute income do not increase happiness. The emphasis in these studies is on the psychological phenomena of 'satiation and relative position' with its self-cancelling effects, rather than biophysical phenomena of rising external costs imposed by a full world. The two approaches are not in conflict but in fact are quite complementary. The fact that they yield broadly similar conclusions regarding the futility of growth to increase welfare beyond a threshold is a devastatingly important point worthy of intense study and reflection. But beware; we may have to conclude that growth is becoming uneconomic and that we need a new principle and new policies by which to organise our separate national commonwealths and their international federation. That is a very big problem. Thanks to Lawn and Clarke for suggesting many specific policies rooted in a clear analysis of that very big problem.

Herman E. Daly
Professor, School of Public Policy
University of Maryland, USA

Acknowledgments

We are grateful for the research support provided by Flinders and Deakin Universities and the various institutions that assisted the contributors to calculate the Genuine Progress Indicator (GPI) and participate in a GPI workshop. In regard to the latter, we would like to thank the organisers of the International Society for Ecological Economics conference held in Delhi in December 2006 for enabling us to hold a pre-conference workshop on the Asia-Pacific region. This book benefited greatly from the presentations made at the workshop and the open discussion that followed on GPI comparisons, trends, and major influences.

Finally, and most importantly, we would like to thank each of the chapter contributors for the effort involved in calculating the GPI for their respective country (by no means a simple task), their co-operation and willingness to meet chapter requirements, the promptness of both their chapter writing and response to subsequent feedback, and the overall quality of their work.

PART I

Introduction to the Asia-Pacific Region and the Genuine Progress Indicator

1. An introduction to the Asia-Pacific region

Philip Lawn and Matthew Clarke

THE AIMS OF THE BOOK

Frequent references are made in financial journals to the 'Asian economic miracle' that has occurred over the last 20 years. In the process, considerable attention has been drawn to the fact that Asia is experiencing the fastest rate of growth in Gross Domestic Product (GDP) of any region in the world.[1] At the same time, the GDP of Oceania has also grown steadily. Indeed, since the mid-1990s, it has grown at a much faster rate than in North America and most European countries (WRI, www.earthtrends.wri.org).

In view of the high growth rates in the Asia-Pacific region, it is commonly assumed that the region has progressed rapidly since the mid-1980s and that the rate of genuine progress is accurately reflected by the extent of the recent increases in real GDP. But is this really the case? Just over 20 years ago, various governments in the Asia-Pacific region – both national and provincial – acknowledged that sustainable welfare does not rest solely on the rate of GDP growth. In recognition of the important role played by non-economic goods and services in achieving a more prosperous, equitable, and fulfilling life, the following was declared:

> The principal aim of governments is to develop a community which possesses prosperity and a high standard of living. The prosperity should be based not only on the acquisition of goods but also on participation in a vigorous intellectual, social, and cultural life within the community. Governments should also seek to facilitate an equitable access to this prosperity .... so that each member of the community can achieve both economic security and personal fulfilment. (Victorian Department of Budget and Management, 1984, p. 1)

Whilst the social and environmental dimensions of sustainable welfare were somewhat overshadowed by growth considerations during the 1990s – particularly following the early 1990s global recession and the Asian financial crisis of the mid-1990s – they are again receiving the attention they deserve. Continuing high levels of absolute poverty, deforestation, climate change, rising oil prices, fish stock depletion, war, and the threat of terrorism have realigned people's major concerns and priorities. Indeed, it is the re-emphasis on non-economic goods and services that has led to the calculation of a Genuine Progress Indicator (GPI) for seven countries in the Asia-Pacific region.

From the seven case studies specifically conducted for this book, our aim is to reveal the extent to which sustainable welfare has genuinely progressed in the Asia-Pacific region. Furthermore, we hope to establish what factors have had the greatest impact on the GPI calculated for each country and on the genuine progress experienced across the Asia-Pacific region as a whole. In the process, we will also determine whether the GPI is tapering off in many Asian nations as it has in a number of European and North American countries. Should we be successful, it is our belief that this collaborative study will lead to the identification of policy concerns that, if urgently and appropriately addressed, would boost the sustainable welfare of the Asia-Pacific region both now and into the future.

Four motivating factors have led to this Asia-Pacific project on genuine progress. The first is our concern that conventional macroeconomic indicators, such as GDP, fail to expose the full impact of a growing economy on the welfare of the average citizen. Secondly, we are also fearful that GDP does not reveal the potential impact that growth has on the capacity of the natural environment to sustain economic welfare into the future.

Thirdly, we believe that an absolute reliance on conventional macroeconomic indicators as a means to designing current and future policies may prove perilous. Without indicators to account for the full impact of GDP growth on sustainable welfare, future policy measures are likely to lead a nation down an undesirable pathway where extrication will be both difficult and costly.

Our fourth motivating factor is the plethora of conflicting information relating to the economic, social, and environmental well-being of people across the Asia-Pacific region. Whilst various statistics paint an apparently favourable picture of recent developments, there are many statistics that indicate otherwise or, alternatively, suggest that a range of problem areas are likely to emerge in the near future. The contrasting nature of the economic, social, and environmental data renders any assessment of genuine progress extremely difficult. Despite some weaknesses, we believe the GPI can greatly facilitate a more accurate assessment of the general advancement being made across the Asia-Pacific region.

POSITIVE DEVELOPMENTS IN THE ASIA-PACIFIC REGION

In order to demonstrate why a piecemeal assessment of genuine progress in the Asia-Pacific region is likely to be fruitless, we begin by detailing recent examples of the positive outcomes emerging in the region. To this end, we have selected a range of economic, social, and environmental factors to avoid the presentation of a narrow development perspective of the Asia-Pacific region.

Rate of Growth in Real GDP

From a macroeconomic standpoint, Table 1.1 reveals that the real GDP of virtually every country across the Asia-Pacific region increased over the 20-year period from 1985 to 2004. Indeed, the annual rate of GDP growth for Asia averaged 4 per cent during this 20-year period and 3.3 per cent in the decade from 1995 to 2004. This constitutes a doubling in real GDP across Asia over the past 20 years and occurred despite the Asian financial crisis in the late 1990s that resulted in Asia's real GDP declining by 0.2 per cent in 1998. Moreover, the average rate of GDP growth in Asia from 1985 to 2004 was higher than any other region in the world (Table 1.1).

Not to be outdone, the average rate of GDP growth in Oceania between 1995 and 2004 was 3.7 per cent per annum, which was higher than the rate of GDP growth in Asia (Table 1.1). Although the average annual growth rate over the 20-year period from 1985 to 2004 was, at 3.3 per cent, lower in Oceania than in Asia, it was bettered only by the Middle East and North Africa.

Table 1.1 *GDP growth rates of selected Asia-Pacific countries and world regions*

Country/region	Average annual growth rate (%) 1985–2004	Average annual growth rate (%) 1995–2004
Asia	4.0	3.3
Cambodia	N.A.	6.9
China	9.8	9.2
India	5.8	6.1
Indonesia	5.1	3.2
Japan	2.4	1.2
Malaysia	6.1	5.2
Pakistan	3.8	4.6
Philippines	3.1	4.0
Singapore	6.5	5.1
South Korea	6.8	5.1
Thailand	6.2	3.3
Vietnam	6.6	7.3
Oceania	3.3	3.7
Australia	3.5	3.8
Fiji	N.A.	2.4
New Zealand	2.4	3.3
Papua New Guinea	0.5	3.1
World	3.0	3.0
Europe	2.3	2.4
North America	3.2	3.3
C. America & Caribbean	2.8	3.0
South America	2.7	2.2
Middle East & North Africa	3.9	4.0
Sub-Saharan Africa	2.8	3.8

Source: World Bank (1996).

As for individual countries in the Asia-Pacific region, annual rates of GDP growth for the period 1995 to 2004 averaged 9.2 per cent in China, 7.3 per cent in Vietnam, 6.9 per cent in Cambodia, 6.1 per cent in India, 5.2 per cent in Malaysia, and 5.1 per cent in both Singapore and South Korea (Table 1.1). These rates of growth far exceeded the world average

(3 per cent) as well as the average growth rates of Central America and the Caribbean (3 per cent), South America (2.2 per cent), Sub-Saharan Africa (3.8 per cent) and the Middle East and North Africa (4 per cent). Even Australia and New Zealand – two industrialised countries in the Asia-Pacific region that began the period with a much larger real GDP base – respectively averaged growth rates of 3.8 per cent and 3.3 per cent per annum between 1995 and 2004.

External Debt

Debt is often highlighted as a major development obstacle for newly industrialising countries. With this in mind, Table 1.2 reveals the external debt and the debt-GDP ratio of a number of Asia-Pacific countries in 1986, 1992, 1998, and 2004. Although the external debt of most countries in Table 1.2 increased significantly between 1986 and 2004 (e.g., China by 586.9 per cent, Indonesia by 114.5 per cent, Thailand by 81.6 per cent, India by 66.9 per cent, Pakistan by 56.2 per cent, and Malaysia by 56 per cent), the right-hand side of Table 1.2 reveals a more positive picture in terms of the ratio of external debt to GDP. In theory, the debt-GDP ratio provides an indication of a nation's capacity to service its external debt. Presumably a lower debt-GDP ratio suggests that a country is better positioned to service its external debt, even if the magnitude of the debt has itself increased.

Despite increases between 1986 and 1992 in the debt-GDP ratio for the majority of countries listed in Table 1.2, every country experienced a decline in the ratio between 1998 and 2004. All nations but Indonesia, Malaysia, the Philippines, and Thailand – the countries most affected by the Asian financial crisis of 1997 – enjoyed a fall in their debt-GDP ratio between 1992 and 1998. This suggests that the poorer Asia-Pacific countries have, potentially at least, increased their capacity over the past decade to service their external debts. Having said this, the debt-GDP ratio in 2004 remained at levels many observers would regard as dangerously high for Cambodia at 0.69, Indonesia at 0.55, Papua New Guinea at 0.55, and Malaysia at 0.44.

We have used the term 'potentially' in relation to debt serviceability because the capacity to service external debt depends ultimately on whether current levels of real GDP are sustainable. This is of particular importance if the growth in real GDP has been financed by the depletion of income-generating natural capital. We will have more to say about the

Table 1.2 External debt of selected Asia-Pacific countries

Millions of constant US$ (2000 prices)						Debt-GDP ratio			
Country	2004	1998	1992	1986	% change in debt 1986–2004	2004	1998	1992	1986
	a	*b*	*c*	*d*	*e*	*f*	*g*	*h*	*i*
Asia									
Cambodia	3 103.6	2 554.7	2 118.7	N.A	N.A	0.69	0.79	0.92	N.A.
China	228 784.7	149 272.1	83 826.5	33 305.7	586.9	0.13	0.14	0.17	0.08
India	112 789.4	101 207.0	104 469.9	67 574.2	66.9	0.18	0.24	0.37	0.20
Indonesia	129 264.9	156 765.3	101 851.8	60 261.5	114.5	0.55	1.58	0.63	0.54
Malaysia	47 924.7	43 959.8	23 168.3	30 722.5	56.0	0.44	0.59	0.34	0.77
Pakistan	32 798.6	33 442.1	28 839.4	20 998.4	56.2	0.37	0.52	0.51	0.47
Philippines	55 649.3	55 568.3	38 446.9	39 603.2	40.5	0.72	0.82	0.63	0.94
Thailand	47 153.8	108 753.3	48 359.7	25 966.2	81.6	0.32	0.94	0.37	0.43
Vietnam	16 382.5	23 279.1	28 161.1	N.A	N.A	0.39	0.83	2.47	N.A.
Oceania									
Fiji	185.5	196.4	383.9	619.4	-70.1	0.08	0.11	0.22	0.34
Papua NG	1 975.1	2 811.3	4 385.2	2 786.0	-29.1	0.55	0.72	0.87	0.75

Source: World Bank (2006).

role of natural capital and its link to sustainable income and external debt serviceability in Chapters 2 and 3.

Average Life Expectancy

Perhaps the clearest example of significant progress in the Asia-Pacific region relates to the dramatic increase in average life expectancy between 1965 and 2005 (see Table 1.3). In Asia, it rose from 54.8 years in 1965–70 to 67.8 years by 2000–05. Moreover, having begun 1.4 years below the world average in 1965-70 (56.2 years), life expectancy in Asia by 2000–05 was 2.4 years higher than the world average (65.4 years). In all, life expectancy in Asia increased by 13 years between 1965–70 and 2000–05 compared to the increase in the world average of 9.2 years over the same period.

Whilst the increase in average life expectancy in Oceania was slightly less than the rise in the world average between 1965–70 and 2000–05 (8.4 years compared to 9.2 years), it was, at 74.7 years in 2000–05, 9.3 years higher than the world average (Table 1.3). In addition, it was 0.5 years higher than in Europe, and second only to North America. Nonetheless, it should be recognised that Australia and New Zealand, with three-quarters of the Oceanic population and average life expectancies of 80.2 and 79 years respectively, have a strong upward influence on the region's average. This can easily mask the fact that the average life expectancy of Fiji, at 67.8 years, is much lower than the Oceanic average, and that the average for Papua New Guinea, despite its considerable rise between 1965–70 and 2000–05, was the lowest in 2004 of all the countries listed in Table 1.3. Furthermore, at 55.1 years, it was exceeded by the average life expectancy of all the world's major regions except Sub-Saharan Africa (46.6 years).

The most spectacular increases in average life expectancy across the Asia-Pacific region occurred in a number of Asian countries. In Vietnam, for example, life expectancy increased by a massive 22.6 years from 1965–70 to 2000–05, by 20.5 years in Indonesia, 19.3 years in South Korea, 15.1 years in India, 13.8 years in the Philippines, 13.6 years in Malaysia, and 13.1 years in Pakistan. Of the Asian countries listed in Table 1.3, the lowest increase in life expectancy over the 35-year period was 10.6 years in Cambodia, Thailand, and Singapore. In defence of Singapore, its average life expectancy of 78.6 years in 2000–05 was 10.8 years above the Asian average and exactly one year higher than the average of North America. No doubt the rise in average life expectancy

Table 1.3 Average life expectancy of selected Asia-Pacific countries and world regions

Country/region	2000–05 (years)	1965–70 (years)	Increase (years)
Asia	67.8	54.8	13.0
Cambodia	56.0	45.4	10.6
China	71.5	59.6	11.9
India	63.1	48.0	15.1
Indonesia	66.5	46.0	20.5
Japan	81.9	71.1	10.8
Malaysia	73.0	59.4	13.6
Pakistan	62.9	49.8	13.1
Philippines	70.2	56.4	13.8
Singapore	78.6	68.0	10.6
South Korea	76.9	57.6	19.3
Thailand	69.7	59.1	10.6
Vietnam	70.4	47.8	22.6
Oceania	74.7	66.3	8.4
Australia	80.2	70.9	9.3
Fiji	67.8	58.6	9.2
New Zealand	79.0	71.3	7.7
Papua New Guinea	55.1	42.2	12.9
World	65.4	56.2	9.2
Europe	74.2	70.5	3.7
North America	77.6	70.5	7.1
C. America & Caribbean	72.5	59.6	12.9
South America	71.4	58.9	12.5
Middle East & North Africa	67.8	51.1	16.7
Sub-Saharan Africa	46.6	43.7	2.9

Source: Population Division of Dept of Economic and Social affairs of the UN Secretariat (2005).

can be attributed in part to the widespread increase in real GDP, improved sanitation and hygiene, and the boost in public and private expenditure on health and education.

Table 1.4 Adult literacy rates of selected Asia-Pacific countries and world regions

Country/region	2004 (15 years +) (%)	1990 (15 years +) (%)	Absolute change in % (% points)
Asia	78.0	N.A.	N.A.
Cambodia	73.6	62.0	11.6
China	90.9	78.3	12.6
India	61.0	49.3	11.7
Indonesia	87.9	79.5	8.4
Japan	99.0	99.0	0.0
Malaysia	88.7	80.7	8.0
Pakistan	48.7	35.4	13.3
Philippines	92.6	91.7	0.9
Singapore	92.5	88.8	3.7
South Korea	99.0	99.0	0.0
Thailand	92.6	92.4	0.2
Vietnam	90.3	90.4	-0.1
Oceania	92.6	N.A.	N.A.
Australia	99.0	99.0	0.0
Fiji	92.9	88.6	4.3
New Zealand	99.0	99.0	0.0
Papua New Guinea	57.3	56.6	0.7
World	81.8	N.A.	N.A.
Europe	98.7	N.A.	N.A.
North America	99.0	N.A.	N.A.
C. America & Caribbean	87.2	N.A.	N.A.
South America	90.8	N.A.	N.A.
Middle East & North Africa	72.5	N.A.	N.A.
Sub-Saharan Africa	60.3	N.A.	N.A.

Source: UNESCO, Institute for Statistics (2005).

Adult Literacy

The latter of the aforementioned expenditures – namely, the increase in education spending – also had a positive impact in terms of the increase in adult literacy rates in the Asia-Pacific region. Table 1.4 reveals that the adult literacy rates of many Asian countries increased by between 8 and 13.3 percentage points between 1990 and 2004. As for the countries that experienced much smaller or negligible rises, all were enjoying relatively high literacy rates by 1990. The only exception was Papua New Guinea, in Oceania, which possessed an adult literacy rate in 2004 of just 57.3 per cent and enjoyed a negligible 0.7 percentage point rise between 1990 and 2004.

Interestingly, apart from Japan and South Korea, Asian countries appear to be having difficulty surpassing the low-90 per cent literacy rate. This can be attributed to the continuing disparity between male and female literacy rates throughout most of the Asia-Pacific region. This gender gap will need to be bridged in future if the aggregate adult rate of Asian countries is to ever reach the high-90 per cent rate being experienced in Japan, South Korea, Australia, and New Zealand.

Reduced Percentage of Undernourished Citizens

Another indicator of genuine progress, particularly in the case of developing nations, is the reduction in the percentage of undernourished citizens. Table 1.5 indicates that the proportion of undernourished citizens of all the selected countries in the Asia-Pacific region declined over the period 1990–92 to 2000–02.[2] The most dramatic improvements were made in Vietnam (down from 31 per cent of the population to 19 per cent), Cambodia (43 per cent to 33 per cent), and Thailand (28 per cent to 20 per cent). In most cases, rates of undernourished citizens were low in 2000–02, however, they remained very high in the countries just mentioned as well as in the Philippines (22 per cent), India (21 per cent), Pakistan (20 per cent), and China (11 per cent) (Table 1.5). While progress in terms of nourishment has obviously been forged in the Asia-Pacific region, there is still considerable room for improvement.

The Human Development Index (HDI)

The Human Development Index (HDI) is a composite index that measures the average achievements by a country in relation to: (a) average life expectancy; (b) knowledge, as reflected by the adult literacy rate and the combined gross enrolment ratio for primary, secondary, and tertiary education institutions; and (c) per capita GDP.[3] The final value of the HDI, which must lie somewhere between zero and one, is

Table 1.5 *Proportion of undernourished citizens in the Asia-Pacific region*

Country	1990–92 (% of population)	2000–02 (% of population)
Asia		
Cambodia	43	33
China	16	11
India	25	21
Indonesia	9	6
Japan	0	0
Malaysia	3	2
Pakistan	24	20
Philippines	26	22
Singapore	0	0
South Korea	2	2
Thailand	28	20
Vietnam	31	19
Oceania		
Australia	0	0
Fiji	0	0
New Zealand	0	0
Papua New Guinea	N.A.	N.A

Source: United Nations Development Programme (2005).

effectively an indicator of 'deprivation' (UNDP, 2006a). As a means of illustration, if the HDI of a nation is equal to the highest possible value of one, it effectively implies that its citizens suffer no deprivation both in an absolute sense and in relation to the citizens of other nations.

The HDI is not nearly as comprehensive as the Genuine Progress Indicator to be revealed in upcoming chapters in this book, since its calculation overlooks a range of critical economic, social, and environmental factors. However, the HDI can provide some basic insight into how well a nation is performing across three basic human development dimensions.

The HDI from 1975 to 2003 of selected Asia-Pacific countries is revealed in Table 1.6. Also provided in Table 1.6 (column *h*) is the net increase in the HDI over this 28-year period. Every Asia-Pacific country

Table 1.6 Human Development Index (HDI) and rankings of selected Asia-Pacific countries

Country	1975	1980	1985	1990	1995	2000	2003	Increase 1975–2003	HDI ranking 1998	HDI ranking 2003	Change in rank 1998–2003
	a	*b*	*c*	*d*	*e*	*f*	*g*	*h*	*i*	*j*	*k*
Asia											
Cambodia	N.A.	N.A.	N.A.	N.A.	0.533	0.541	0.571	N.A.	136	130	+6
China	0.525	0.558	0.594	0.627	0.683	0.720	0.755	0.230	99	85	+14
India	0.412	0.438	0.476	0.513	0.546	0.577	0.602	0.190	128	127	+1
Indonesia	0.468	0.530	0.583	0.625	0.663	0.680	0.697	0.229	109	110	-1
Japan	0.857	0.882	0.895	0.911	0.925	0.936	0.943	0.086	9	11	-2
Malaysia	0.615	0.659	0.695	0.721	0.760	0.790	0.796	0.181	61	61	0
Pakistan	0.363	0.386	0.419	0.462	0.492	N.A.	0.527	0.164	135	135	0
Philippines	0.654	0.687	0.693	0.720	0.736	N.A.	0.758	0.104	77	84	-7
Singapore	0.725	0.761	0.784	0.822	0.861	N.A.	0.907	0.182	24	25	-1
South Korea	0.707	0.741	0.780	0.818	0.855	0.884	0.901	0.194	31	28	+3
Thailand	0.614	0.652	0.678	0.714	0.749	N.A.	0.778	0.164	76	73	+3
Vietnam	N.A.	N.A.	N.A.	0.617	0.660	0.695	0.704	N.A.	108	108	0
Oceania											
Australia	0.848	0.866	0.879	0.893	0.933	0.960	0.955	0.107	4	3	+1
Fiji	0.663	0.686	0.702	0.724	0.741	0.750	0.752	0.089	66	92	-26
New Zealand	0.848	0.854	0.868	0.875	0.905	0.924	0.933	0.085	20	19	+1
Papua NG	0.425	0.445	0.467	0.481	0.515	0.529	0.523	0.098	133	137	-4

Source: United Nations Development Programme (UNDP) (various).

listed in Table 1.6 experienced a net rise in its HDI over this period. In fact, Australia and Papua New Guinea were the only nations to suffer an inter-period decline in the HDI. This occurred between 2000 and 2003 where, in Australia's case, it came after achieving the highest HDI value in the world in 2000. The decline in the HDI to 2003 resulted in Australia slipping to third position in the overall world rankings.

The largest rises in the HDI between 1975 and 2003 were achieved by China (0.230), Indonesia (0.229), South Korea (0.194), India (0.190), Singapore (0.182), and Malaysia (0.181). These are considerable achievements given that a 0.200 rise in the HDI represents a reduction in deprivation equal to 20 per cent of total deprivation eradication.

In the overall world rankings, most Asia-Pacific countries made enormous gains between 1975 and the mid-1990s (UNDP, various). However, between 1998 and 2003, the only significant positive mover was China, up from a ranking of 99th in 1998 to a ranking of 85th in 2003. Although Cambodia progressed by six places between 1998 and 2003 and South Korea and Thailand moved up three places over the same five-year period, most Asia-Pacific nations remained stationary in the rankings or moved one place, generally in a positive direction. The three exceptions were Fiji (down from 66th in 1998 to 92nd in 2003), the Philippines (77th to 84th), and Papua New Guinea (133rd to 137th).

Environmental Factors: Industrial Water Pollution and Land Conservation

From an environmental perspective, two positive developments have taken place in the Asia-Pacific region over recent times. The first, as revealed in Table 1.7 (columns *l* and *m*), relates to industrial water pollution (organic water pollutant emissions). Although emissions levels are still very high in China, India, Japan, and Indonesia, the trend change in emissions of the countries listed in Table 1.7 either fell or remained steady. What's more, only one of the heavy polluters – Indonesia – failed to experience a decline in the rate of industrial water pollution.

The second positive environmental factor is the percentage of the total land area devoted to conservation. In Asia, protected areas constitute 9.9 per cent of the total land area, while in Oceania, 9.7 per cent of the total land area is set aside for conservation (Table 1.7, column *p*). Although both percentages are slightly less than the world average of 11.4 per cent, they exceed the percentages of Europe, Central America and the Caribbean, and the Middle East and North Africa. More heartening is the

Table 1.7 Economic, social, and environmental data and trends of selected Asia-Pacific countries and world regions

Region/ country	Pop. 2004 (mill.)	Pop. 2050 (projected) (mill.)	Per capita GDP 2004 (Int.$)	Poverty rate (% below US$2 per day)	Unemp. rate (% per year)	Adult literacy rate (15+) (% in '04)	Life exp. at birth (years)	CO_2 emissions 2002 (million tonnes)
	a	*b*	*c*	*d*	*e*	*f*	*g*	*h*
Asia	3 568.6	4 649.8	5 554	N.A.	N.A.	78.0	67.8	8 328.7
Cambodia	13.3	26.0	2 423	77.7	1.8 ('01)	73.6	56.0	0.6
China	1 299.9	1 392.3	5 896	46.7	4.2 ('05)	90.9	71.5	3 783.2
India	1 087.1	1 592.7	3 139	79.9	4.3 ('00)	61.0	63.1	1 105.6
Indonesia	220.1	284.6	3 609	52.4	9.1 ('02)	87.9	66.5	332.3
Japan	127.9	112.2	29 251	0.0	4.4 ('05)	99.0	81.9	1 213.5
Malaysia	24.9	38.9	10 276	9.3	3.6 ('03)	88.7	73.0	133.1
Pakistan	154.8	304.7	2 225	73.6	7.7 ('05)	48.7	62.9	107.5
Philippines	81.6	127.1	4 614	47.5	7.4 ('05)	92.6	70.2	74.1
Singapore	4.3	5.2	28 077	0.0	5.3 ('04)	92.5	78.6	54.7
South Korea	47.6	44.6	20 499	0.0	3.7 ('05)	99.0	76.9	499.5
Thailand	67.3	74.6	8 494	25.2	1.4 ('05)	92.6	69.7	203.3
Vietnam	82.0	116.7	2 470	N.A.	2.1 ('04)	90.3	70.4	67.0
Oceania	32.6	47.5	22 898	N.A.	N.A.	92.6	74.7	375.8
Australia	20.1	27.9	30 331	0.0	5.1 ('05)	99.0	80.2	337.4
Fiji	0.8	0.9	6 066	N.A.	N.A.	92.9	67.8	1.4
New Zealand	4.0	4.8	23 413	0.0	3.7 ('05)	99.0	79.0	33.6
Papua NG	5.8	10.6	2 543	N.A.	2.8 ('00)	57.3	55.1	2.5
World	6 389.3	9 075.9	8 908	N.A.	N.A.	81.8	65.4	24 756.7
Europe	728.6	653.3	20 425	0.0	N.A.	98.7	74.2	6 118.0
N. America	327.5	438.0	38 855	0.0	N.A.	99.0	77.6	6 291.4
C. America	183.7	256.0	8 377	23.4	N.A.	87.2	72.5	532.6
S. America	370.1	526.9	8 053	N.A.	N.A.	90.8	71.4	787.8
M.E. & N.Af.	443.6	812.6	6 621	19.8	N.A.	72.5	67.8	1 698.4
Sub-S Africa	734.6	1 691.8	1 951	74.9	N.A.	60.3	55.1	573.8

Table 1.7 (continued)

Region/ country	CO_2 emiss. (trend)	Total energy cons. 2001 (Mtoe)	Total energy cons. (trend)	Indust. water pollution 2000 (Ktonne)	Indust. water pollution (trend)	Forest area % of orig. forest (% in '96)	Forest area % of orig. forest (trend)	Protected areas as % of total area (%)
	i	*j*	*k*	*l*	*m*	*n*	*o*	*p*
Asia	rising	3 145.5	rising	N.A.	N.A.	N.A.	N.A.	9.9
Cambodia	rising	N.A.	N.A.	N.A.	N.A.	65.1	falling	22.7
China	rising	1 139.4	rising	2 222.4	falling	21.6	rising	11.8
India	rising	531.4	rising	553.2	falling	20.5	steady	5.1
Indonesia	rising	152.3	rising	275.1	steady	64.6	falling	13.6
Japan	steady	520.7	rising	466.9	falling	58.2	steady	14.0
Malaysia	rising	51.6	rising	62.3	steady	63.8	falling	30.5
Pakistan	rising	64.5	rising	N.A.	N.A.	5.8	falling	8.3
Philippines	steady	42.2	rising	N.A.	N.A.	6.0	falling	8.2
Singapore	steady	29.2	rising	10.6	steady	3.2	steady	5.2
South Korea	rising	194.8	rising	113.0	falling	16.5	falling	3.6
Thailand	rising	75.5	rising	N.A.	N.A.	22.2	falling	15.6
Vietnam	rising	39.4	rising	N.A.	N.A.	17.2	rising	4.2
Oceania	rising	N.A.	N.A.	N.A.	N.A.	64.9	falling	9.7
Australia	rising	115.6	rising	40.8	steady	64.3	falling	9.7
Fiji	rising	N.A.	N.A.	N.A.	N.A.	49.9	steady	15.9
New Zealand	steady	18.3	rising	16.8	falling	29.2	rising	24.3
Papua NG	steady	N.A.	N.A.	N.A.	N.A.	85.4	falling	1.6
World	rising	10 029.1	rising	N.A.	N.A.	53.4	falling	11.4
Europe	falling	3 606.4	rising	N.A.	N.A.	58.4	rising	8.4
N. America	rising	2 529.6	rising	N.A.	N.A.	77.3	steady	10.9
C. America	rising	214.2	rising	N.A.	N.A.	54.5	falling	8.5
S. America	steady	382.2	rising	N.A.	N.A.	69.1	falling	20.8
M.E. & N.Af.	rising	577.3	rising	N.A.	N.A.	N.A.	N.A.	9.6
Sub-S Africa	rising	N.A.	N.A.	N.A.	N.A.	N.A.	N.A.	10.9

Sources: (*a*, *b*, *g*) Population Division of Dept of Economic and Social Affairs of the UN Secretariat (2005); (*c*, *d*, *l*, *m*) World Bank (2006); (*e*) ILO (2006); (*f*) UNESCO (2005); (*h*, *i*) WRI (2005); (*j*, *k*) IEA (2004); (*n*, *o*) Bryant et al. (1997); (*p*) UNEP-WCMC (2004).

fact that the heavily forested countries of Malaysia, Cambodia, Thailand, and Indonesia have conservation percentages over and above the world average (30.5 per cent, 22.7 per cent, 15.6 per cent, and 13.6 per cent respectively). The low rates of conservation in South Korea, India, Vietnam, and Papua New Guinea is, nevertheless, cause for much greater concern.

NEGATIVE FACTORS TO EMERGE IN THE ASIA-PACIFIC REGION

We now turn to some of the negative factors that blur the picture in terms of how well the Asia-Pacific region has progressed in recent times. Again, we have focused on a range of economic, social, and environmental factors and begin with the population numbers of Asia.

Human Population

While population numbers do not, by themselves, constitute a negative statistic, it is difficult to believe that the projected increase in Asia's population from 3.57 billion in 2004 to 4.65 billion by 2050 will not seriously undermine the capacity of many Asian countries to eradicate poverty and limit environmental stress (Table 1.7, columns *a* and *b*). Of significant concern is the fact that five Asian countries with the highest projected percentage increases in their population – namely, Cambodia, India, Indonesia, Pakistan, and the Philippines – all have per capita levels of GDP less than the Asian average. The same can also be said of Papua New Guinea in Oceania. Most serious of all, however, is the potential dilemma confronting India given the prospect of having to support an extra half a billion people by 2050.

Relative Per Capita GDP

It has already been explained that the Asia-Pacific region experienced some of the highest rates of GDP growth in the world between 1985 and 2004 (see Table 1.1). Despite this, Table 1.7 (column *c*) reveals that the per capita GDP of Asia remained considerably below the world average in 2004 (Int$5554 compared to Int$8908).[4] While a number of the listed countries in Table 1.7 had a per capita GDP well above the world average – e.g., Japan (Int$29 251), Singapore (Int$28 077), South Korea (Int$20 499), and Malaysia (Int$10 276) – the great majority of Asian nations experienced per capita GDP levels in 2004 that were less than half the world average. Even the rapidly growing nations of China and India could only manage per capita GDP levels in 2004 that were respectively 66.2 per cent and 35.2 per cent of the world average.

In contrast to Asia, the per capita GDP of Oceania in 2004 was well above the world average at Int$22 898 and was second only to North America. However, this average is altogether superfluous given the enormous disparity in per capita GDP across the Oceanic region. Australia, for example, had a per capita GDP of Int$30 331 in 2004 whilst its nearest northern neighbour, Papua New Guinea, could manage a per capita GDP of just Int$2543. Of all the countries listed in Table 1.7, only Pakistan (Int$2225) and Cambodia (Int$2423) had a lower per capita GDP than Papua New Guinea. Furthermore, although Fiji enjoyed a per capita GDP in 2004 higher than the Asian average, it was, at Int$6066, less than the world average. It was also lower than the averages of Central America and the Caribbean (Int$8377), South America (Int$8053), and the Middle East and North Africa (Int$6621).

Absolute Poverty

In view of the relatively low levels of per capita GDP being enjoyed by a large number of Asia-Pacific nations, it is not surprising that a high rate of absolute poverty is prevalent throughout much of the Asia-Pacific region (Table 1.7 column *d*). The percentage of the population living on less than US$2 per day remained very high in many countries over the period from 1989 to 2004. Whilst no percentage figure can be given for the region as a whole, the absolute poverty rates averaged 79.9 per cent in India, 77.7 per cent in Cambodia, 52.4 per cent in Indonesia, 47.5 per cent in the Philippines, and 46.7 per cent in China. This compares with 74.9 per cent for Sub-Saharan Africa, by far the world's poorest region in terms of per capita GDP. Since the percentages represent the average poverty rates for each country over a 15-year period, there is a high probability that the respective rates in 2004 would be lower than the average rates presented in Table 1.7.[5] Nevertheless, given the exceedingly high average rates in most countries, there is little doubt that the absolute poverty rates in 2004 would still be unacceptably high in most instances.

Income Inequality

Perhaps one of the more alarming features of the economic transition that has taken place in the Asia-Pacific region in recent decades has been general increase in income inequality (UNDP, 2006b). The commonly used indicator of income inequality is the so-called Gini coefficient. The value of the Gini coefficient can range from zero (absolute income equality) to a value of one (where one individual receives the entire nation's income).

Trends in the Gini coefficient of selected Asian countries suggest that the faster-growing economies of China and India have experienced a dramatic shift in the distribution of income from poor to rich. For example, China's Gini coefficient rose from 0.315 in the 1980s to 0.403 by the late 1990s, whilst India's Gini coefficient rose from 0.293 to 0.325 over the same period (Table 1.8). Other countries listed in Table 1.8 that also experienced a rise in the Gini coefficient include Laos, Malaysia (during the 1990s), the Philippines, Vietnam, Bangladesh, Pakistan (during the 1990s), and Sri Lanka. The exceptions were South Korea (early 1990s) and Thailand. Indeed, Thailand enjoyed a significant fall in its Gini coefficient from 0.488 in the early 1990s to 0.432 in the late 1990s.

There has long been a theory suggesting that income inequality typically rises in the initial stages of a nation's industrialisation process (i.e., as its per capita GDP steadily increases for the first time) and later declines as concerns for non-economic factors emerge more prominently in the consciousness of the nation's citizens (Kuznets, 1955). Whether greater income equality will eventuate amongst Asian countries simply through continued growth in real GDP is a moot point since the circumstances surrounding the Asian growth phenomenon differ entirely to those experienced in the 1950s and 1960s by North American and European countries. What's more, the Gini coefficient has increased for a number of wealthy nations since the mid-1990s, thereby indicating that increasing income inequality is not simply the preserve of developing nations (e.g., Australia up from 0.292 in 1997 to 0.311 in 2001 (ABS, 2007); and the USA up from 0.394 in 1970 to 0.469 in 2005 (US Census Bureau, 2005). In any case, the trend towards increasing income inequality in the Asia-Pacific region implies that recent economic benefits are bypassing many needy people and thus falling into the hands of those already economically endowed.

Table 1.8 Gini coefficient of selected Asian countries

Country	1980s (average)	Early 1990s	Late 1990s
North-East Asia			
China	0.315	0.335	0.403
South Korea	0.359	0.294	0.300
South-East Asia			
Indonesia	0.317	0.317	0.317
Laos	N.A.	0.296	0.365
Malaysia	0.469	0.429	0.443
Philippines	0.409	0.438	0.462
Thailand	0.460	0.488	0.432
Vietnam	N.A.	0.357	0.361
South & SW Asia			
Bangladesh	0.260	0.266	0.315
India	0.293	0.315	0.325
Pakistan	0.350	0.348	0.410
Sri Lanka	N.A.	0.301	0.344

Source: World Bank (2006).

Unemployment

The trend in the next progress factor – unemployment – is a little more difficult to interpret due to the varying employment performances across the Asia-Pacific region. Table 1.7 (column *e*) reveals the unemployment rates of selected Asia-Pacific countries during various stages between 2000 and 2005. It can be plainly seen that the unemployment rate of some countries was quite high (e.g., Indonesia 9.1 per cent, Pakistan 7.7 per cent, and the Philippines 7.4 per cent), while other countries enjoyed a low unemployment rate (e.g., Thailand 1.4 per cent, Cambodia 1.8 per cent, and Vietnam 2.1 per cent).

In a United Nations report on the Asia-Pacific region, it has been shown that, despite the rapid rate of GDP growth in many Asia-Pacific countries, employment growth has been modest at best (UNDP, 2006a). Indeed, in many instances, employment growth has not kept pace with the expansion of the labour force such that, in South-East Asia, the unemployment rate increased from 3.9 per cent in 1993 to 6.3 per cent in

2003. Worse still, youth unemployment (unemployment of 15–24 year olds) stood at 17 per cent in 2004 (UNDP, 2006a).

Much of the unemployment problem can be attributed to a fall in the employment elasticity of East Asia. The employment elasticity measures how sensitive employment growth is to increases in real GDP. A fall in the employment elasticity statistic implies that a given rise in real GDP generates fewer jobs. In East Asia, the employment elasticity declined from 0.56 in the 1980s to 0.15 in the 1990s. This very low value for employment elasticity has continued beyond the 1990s. In South Asia, however, the employment elasticity increased slightly over the same period from 0.28 to 0.31. As a consequence, the 8.2 per cent annual rate of output growth in East Asia in the 1990s resulted in employment growth of just 1.2 per cent per annum. Conversely, a much smaller 5.2 per cent rate of output growth in South Asia led to an annual employment growth rate of 1.6 per cent (UNDP, 2006a). It is therefore imperative that more is done to increase the employment elasticity of many countries, particularly in the burgeoning manufacturing sector where the employment elasticity of East Asia slumped to 0.07 in the 1990s. Only then will it be possible to maximise employment gains across the Asia-Pacific region.

Environmental Factors

Carbon dioxide emissions

Moving from economic and social factors to environmental concerns, Asia overtook Europe and North America between 1985 and 2002 to become the highest CO_2-emitting region in the world. In 2002, Asia emitted 8329 million tonnes of carbon dioxide (Table 1.9, column *a*). This constituted 33.6 per cent of total world CO_2 emissions – up considerably from 23.3 per cent of world emissions in 1985 – and compares with the emission of 6291 million and 6118 million tonnes of carbon dioxide in North America and Europe respectively. Alarmingly, CO_2 emissions in Asia rose by 83 per cent between 1985 and 2002 or an average of 3.4 per cent per annum. By comparison, the total CO_2 emissions of the world increased by a significantly lower 27 per cent over the same period or 1.4 per cent per annum (Table 1.9, columns *c* and *d*).

Table 1.9 *Carbon dioxide emissions of selected Asia-Pacific countries and world regions*

Country/ Region	2002 (mill. tonnes)	1985 (mill. tonnes)	Emissions rise (%) 1985-2002	Average annual rise (%)	% of world emissions 2002	% of world emissions 1985	Per capita emissions (t/person) 2002	Per capita emissions (t/person) 1985	Per capita rise (%) 1985-2002	Average annual rise (%)
	a	*b*	*c*	*d*	*e*	*f*	*g*	*h*	*i*	*j*
Asia	8 328.7	4 550.2	83.0	3.4	33.6	23.3	2.32	1.66	39.8	2.0
Cambodia	0.6	0.4	42.8	2.1	0.0	0.0	0.05	0.05	0.0	0.0
China	3 783.2	1 920.1	97.0	4.1	15.3	9.9	2.93	1.79	63.7	2.9
India	1 105.6	463.3	138.6	5.2	4.5	2.4	1.05	0.61	72.1	3.2
Indonesia	332.3	104.8	217.2	7.0	1.3	0.5	1.55	0.63	146.0	5.4
Japan	1 213.5	930.6	30.4	1.6	4.9	4.8	9.52	7.70	23.6	1.3
Malaysia	133.1	41.7	219.5	7.1	0.5	0.2	5.55	2.66	108.6	4.4
Pakistan	107.5	43.0	150.0	5.5	0.4	0.2	0.72	0.45	60.0	2.8
Philippines	74.1	28.2	162.8	5.8	0.3	0.1	0.94	0.52	80.8	3.5
Singapore	54.7	17.1	219.9	7.1	0.2	0.1	13.14	6.32	107.9	4.4
South Korea	499.5	167.3	198.6	6.6	2.0	0.7	10.57	4.1	157.8	5.7
Thailand	203.3	44.7	355.2	9.3	0.8	0.2	3.25	0.88	269.3	8.0
Vietnam	67.0	17.4	284.1	8.2	0.2	0.1	0.83	0.30	176.7	6.2
Oceania	375.8	249.6	50.6	2.4	1.5	1.3	12.18	10.38	17.3	0.9
Australia	337.4	223.6	50.9	2.5	1.4	1.1	17.29	14.27	21.2	1.1
Fiji	1.4	0.6	125.1	4.9	0.0	0.0	1.69	0.88	92.0	3.9
New Zealand	33.6	22.5	49.4	2.4	0.1	0.1	8.62	6.93	24.4	1.3
Papua New Guinea	2.5	2.1	16.6	0.9	0.0	0.0	0.45	0.58	-22.4	-1.5
World	24 756.7	19 492.7	27.0	1.4	100.0	100.0	3.97	4.02	-1.2	-0.1
Europe	6 118.0	7 440.5	-17.8	-1.1	24.7	38.2	8.40	10.55	-20.4	-1.3
North America	6 291.4	5 072.7	24.0	1.3	25.4	26.0	19.59	18.87	3.8	0.2
C. America & Carib.	532.6	362.3	47.0	2.3	2.2	1.9	3.07	2.82	8.9	0.5
South America	787.8	513.0	53.6	2.6	3.2	2.6	2.19	1.90	15.3	0.8
M. East & N. Africa	1 698.4	858.4	97.9	4.1	6.9	4.4	4.02	3.01	33.6	1.7

Sources: World Resources Institute (WRI) (2005). The WRI calculates carbon dioxide emissions from three sources: (a) IEA (2002),(b) IEA (2004), CO_2 Emissions from Fuel Combustion (2004 edition); (c) Marland et al. (2005).

In terms of individual nations, a number of high-emitting countries in the Asia-Pacific region stand out. China, Japan, and India, for instance, respectively emitted 3783 million, 1213 million, and 1106 million tonnes of carbon dioxide in 2002. Whilst China's CO_2 emissions increased by 97 per cent between 1985 and 2002 (average rise of 4.1 per cent per annum), India's emissions grew by 138.6 per cent (average rise of 5.2 per cent per annum). The increase in Japan's CO_2 emissions was much lower at 30.4 per cent and had effectively stabilised by 1996. Altogether, the emission levels of China, Japan, and India respectively equated to 15.3 per cent, 4.9 per cent, and 4.5 per cent of total world emissions (Table 1.9, column *e*). This was up from 9.9 per cent, 4.8 per cent, and 2.4 per cent of world emissions in 1985 (Table 1.9, column *f*).

The CO_2 emissions of other Asia-Pacific nations were considerably smaller than these three Asian heavyweights with only Australia, Indonesia, and Thailand making any noteworthy contribution to total world emissions. Having said this, the growth in emission levels of some Asia-Pacific countries between 1985 and 2002 was extraordinarily rapid. For example, the respective increases in the CO_2 emissions of Thailand, Vietnam, Singapore, Malaysia, Indonesia, South Korea, and the Philippines were 355.2 per cent, 284.1 per cent, 219.9 per cent, 219.5 per cent, 217.2 per cent, 198.6 per cent, and 162.6 per cent. This constituted average rises of 9.3 per cent, 8.2 per cent, 7.1 per cent, 7.1 per cent, 7 per cent, 6.6 per cent, and 5.8 per cent per annum (Table 1.9, columns *c* and *d*).

In Oceania, Australia was by far the most prominent emitter with 337.4 million tonnes of carbon dioxide in 2002, although Fiji experienced the largest percentage increase between 1985 and 2002 at 125.1 per cent (average rise of 4.9 per cent per annum). The most concerning feature about the increase in CO_2 emissions of Australia and New Zealand (50.9 per cent and 49.4 per cent respectively) is that both countries were already heavily industrialised by 1985. The rise in emissions of these two countries far exceeded the world average (27 per cent) as well as that of industrialised North America (24 per cent) and Europe (−17.8 per cent).

On a per capita basis, Australia was by far the worst performing nation in the Asia-Pacific region with a CO_2 emissions level of 17.29 tonnes per person in 2002. This compares with 13.14 tonnes per person in Singapore, 10.57 tonnes per person in South Korea, 9.52 tonnes per person in Japan, and 8.62 tonnes per person in New Zealand, four other major per capita emitters in the Asia-Pacific region (Table 1.9, column *g*). Disconcertingly, the per capita CO_2 emissions of these countries rose between 1985 and 2002 during which time the per capita average of the world fell (4.02 to 3.97 tonnes per person). In addition, the per capita CO_2 emissions of Singapore, South Korea, Japan, and New Zealand overtook that of Europe (8.40 tonnes per person in 2002).[6]

Although the majority of Asian countries have low per capita emissions levels – indeed, almost all nations were below the world average in 2002 – they are steadily rising. China's per capita CO_2 emissions rose between 1985 and 2002 by 63.7 per cent (average rise of 2.9 per cent per annum), whilst India's increased by 72.1 per cent (average rise of 3.2 per cent per annum) (Table 1.9, columns *i* and *j*). These two countries by no means experienced the most rapid per capita rises in the Asia-Pacific region; however, their impact should be seen in light of the fact that: (a) both countries are already among the world's heaviest CO_2 emitters; and (b) India's population, as from now, is projected to increase by half a billion people by 2050. China's population is not expected to rise significantly between now and 2050. Nevertheless, the sheer weight of its population implies that any increase in China's per capita CO_2 emissions will have a significant aggregate impact.

Energy consumption

As far as energy consumption is concerned, another important environmental variable, the evidence provided in Table 1.7 (column *k*) is perhaps more alarming than the trend change in carbon dioxide emissions. In 2001, Asia's energy consumption of 3145.5 megatonnes of equivalent oil barrels (Mtoe) was higher than North America (2529.6 Mtoe) and second only to Europe (3606.4 Mtoe). Not unlike CO_2 emissions, China, India, and Japan were again the largest energy consumers in the Asia-Pacific region. Indeed, China's energy consumption in 2001 constituted 11.4 per cent of the world's total consumption of energy.

Whereas the CO_2 emissions of some Asia-Pacific countries have recently stabilised, the same cannot be said of energy consumption. The rate of energy consumption of every nation listed in Table 1.7 – where appropriate data is available – was on the rise in 2001. In the case of India and China, energy consumption was rising at an astonishing rate. Between 1990 and 2001, energy consumption in India and China increased by 46.3 per cent and 30.8 per cent respectively (own calculations) (IEA, 2003).[7] Of course, at least for some period of time, it is possible for a nation to simultaneously consume more energy and reduce its impact on the environment by substituting towards renewable energy sources. However, there are constraints to this form of substitution. In addition, the capacity to minimise the environmental impact of increased energy consumption is ultimately limited by the ecosphere's non-growing waste assimilative capacity. Given the prospect of higher per capita levels of real GDP in the Asia-Pacific region, it is difficult to envisage any major slowdown in the rate of energy consumption in the foreseeable future. This will almost certainly contribute towards increased CO_2 emissions and greater levels of air pollution in the major cities of the Asia-Pacific region. The latter is already raising serious health concerns in China, Thailand, and Indonesia.

Remnant forest

Table 1.7 (column *n*) reveals the percentage of original forest in existence in 1996. In the case of Papua New Guinea (85.4 per cent), Cambodia (65.1 per cent), Indonesia (64.6 per cent), Malaysia (63.8 per cent), Australia (64.3 per cent), and Japan (58.2 per cent) most of the original forest area remains. It should, nevertheless, be understood that some forest areas incorporated into this statistic include plantation and regrowth timber. Thus the forest area existing in 1996 does not indicate the extent to which the ecological integrity of forests has been maintained.

Countries with little of their original forest remaining include the Philippines (6 per cent), Pakistan (5.8 per cent), Vietnam (17.2 per cent), India (20.5 per cent), and China (21.6 per cent). The percentage of remaining forest area in these countries is far less than the world average of 53.4 per cent as well as the average of South America (69.1 per cent) and Central America and the Caribbean (54.5 per cent).

The most damning aspect of the data on the Asia-Pacific region is the trend change in forest area. As column *o* of Table 1.7 shows, the majority of nations were experiencing a fall in forest stocks as of 1996, with only China, Vietnam, and New Zealand enjoying an increase in forest area. Of greatest concern is the fact that countries with the largest percentages of remaining forest areas also possessed some of the highest rates of decline over the past 15 years. For example, the average annual percentage change in total forest area of Cambodia, Indonesia, Malaysia, and Papua New Guinea was –2 per cent, –1.7 per cent, –0.4 per cent, and –0.5 per cent respectively during the 1990–2000 period, and –1.1 per cent, –2 per cent, –0.7 per cent, and –0.5 per cent between 2000 and 2005 (WRI, www.earthtrends.org) It is highly probable that the high rate of deforestation throughout much of the Asia-Pacific region constitutes an example of natural capital depletion that is being used to finance recent increases in consumption and boost real GDP. As we shall see in the next chapter, while deforestation of this type augments national income in the conventional sense, it may not do so if national income is viewed from a more logical theoretical perspective.

Ecological footprint, biocapacity, and ecological surplus/deficit

A biophysical indicator receiving considerable attention of late is the so-called Ecological Footprint (EF). A country's EF is the equivalent area of land required to both generate the renewable resources and to absorb the high entropy wastes needed to sustain economic activity at the current level (Wackernagel and Rees, 1996). To determine whether a nation is depleting its natural capital, the EF is compared with its biocapacity. The biocapacity refers to the amount of available land a nation has to both generate an ongoing supply of renewable resources and absorb its own and other nations' spillover wastes. Unsustainability occurs if a nation's ecological footprint exceeds its biocapacity (ecological deficit).

Table 1.10 reveals the EF, biocapacity, and ecological surplus/deficit of selected Asia-Pacific countries and world regions. Worryingly, Table 1.10 shows that the great majority of Asia-Pacific nations are already in ecological deficit. Countries with the largest ecological deficits are Japan (–3.7 hectares/person), South Korea (–3.6 hectares/person), China (–0.8 hectares/person), the Philippines (–0.5 hectares/person), and India and Thailand (–0.4 hectares/person). Although improved resource use efficiency can reduce a nation's per capita EF, the projected increase in the populations of most Asian countries, in particular India, suggests that the aggregate footprints and deficits of these nations are likely to magnify by the year 2050. This is cause for great concern given that the countries in ecological deficit are predominantly those with the lowest per capita GDP and the highest poverty rates.

Table 1.10 Ecological footprint, biocapacity, and ecological surplus/ deficit of selected Asia-Pacific countries and world regions

Region/ country	Ecological Footprint 2003 (global ha/person)	Biocapacity 2003 (global ha/person)	Ecological surplus (+) or deficit (–) (global ha/person)
Asia	N.A.	N.A.	N.A.
Cambodia	0.7	0.9	0.2
China	1.6	0.8	-0.8
India	0.8	0.4	-0.4
Indonesia	1.1	1.0	-0.1
Japan	4.4	0.7	-3.7
Malaysia	2.2	3.7	1.5
Pakistan	0.6	0.3	-0.3
Philippines	1.1	0.6	-0.5
Singapore	N.A.	N.A.	N.A.
South Korea	4.1	0.5	-3.6
Thailand	1.4	1.0	-0.4
Vietnam	0.9	0.8	-0.1
Oceania	N.A.	N.A.	N.A.
Australia	6.6	12.4	5.8
Fiji	N.A.	N.A.	N.A.
New Zealand	5.9	14.9	9.0
Papua New Guinea	2.4	2.1	-0.3
World	2.2	1.8	-0.4
Europe (EU25)	4.8	2.2	-2.6
North America	9.4	5.7	-3.7
C. America/Caribbean	N.A.	N.A.	N.A.
South America	N.A.	N.A.	N.A.
M. East & North Africa	N.A.	N.A.	N.A.
Sub-Saharan Africa	N.A.	N.A.	N.A.

Source: Global Footprint Network (2006).

INDICATORS OF SUSTAINABLE WELFARE

In view of the conflicting statistics presented above, we believe it is reasonable to ask whether the sustainable welfare of people in the Asia-Pacific region has been rising and, if so, to what extent it has advanced in recent times. In considering this question, we believe two further questions need to be posed and adequately answered:

- To what extent does a rise in real GDP reveal the genuine progress of people living in the Asia-Pacific region?
- Why is it that real GDP, inflation rates, stock market indices, and other economic data are invariably regarded as statistical 'fundamentals' but not the social and environmental impacts of a growing economy?

Similar questions have already been raised in the past. Efforts undertaken to answer them have led to various studies on the sustainable welfare of nations. Almost all such studies involve the calculation of the GPI at the national level.[8] Examples include GPI estimates of the USA, Canada, the UK, most European and Scandinavian countries, but only one or two developing nations. As yet, no GPI study has been specifically conducted on a particular region in the world comprising countries at various stages of industrialisation and with vastly different political, social, and cultural characteristics. This book constitutes the first attempt at such a study.

Figure 1.1 compares the GPI and GDP of six individual countries. As the figure indicates, there is a tendency, at first, for the GPI to closely follow the upward trend of GDP. However, once GDP reaches an apparent 'threshold' level, the GPI ceases to rise and, in some cases, begins to decline (Max-Neef, 1995). For virtually all developed countries, this countermoving trend occurred in the 1970s or early 1980s.

The most significant message conveyed by Figure 1.1 is the notion that indiscriminate growth or growth in real GDP beyond a certain level may be detrimental to sustainable welfare. We therefore believe it is vital to know whether a similar trend movement of the GPI exists for Asia-Pacific countries and, more importantly, if the threshold hypothesis posited by Max-Neef is occurring at much lower levels of per capita GDP than in the industrialised nations of Europe and North America. If the answer in both instances is yes, it may be necessary for some Asia-

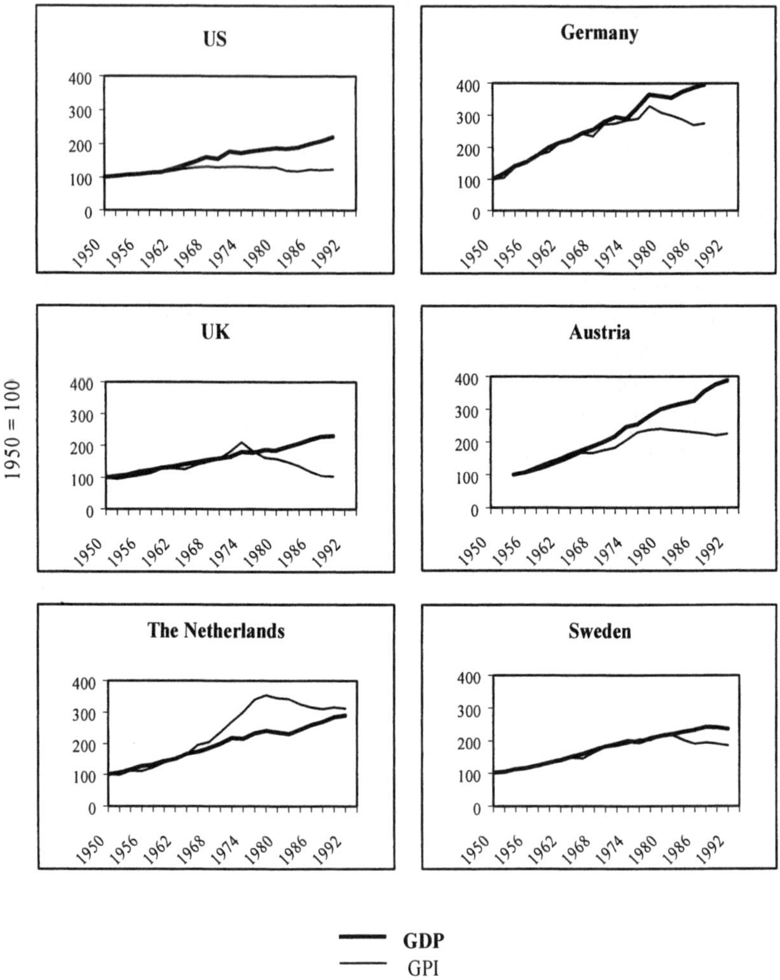

Source: Jackson and Stymne (1996).

Figure 1.1 *Comparison of GDP and GPI for the USA, Germany, UK, Austria, the Netherlands, and Sweden*

Pacific nations to begin the transition to a lower rate of GDP growth or a steady-state economy – the latter involving a national economy that does not physically grow but qualitatively improves in terms of its content of physical goods, the means by which the goods are produced and maintained, and the purpose for which the goods are intended.[9] Whether it be a low-growth or a steady-state economy, advancing the GPI may therefore require a greater policy focus on production excellence, greater resource use efficiency, distributional equity, and natural capital maintenance.

THE STRUCTURE OF THE BOOK

To achieve our aims, this book is structured as follows. In Chapter 2, we explain why the commonly used economic statistic of GDP is an inadequate indicator of sustainable welfare. Following this, in Chapter 3, we explain why the GPI is a far superior welfare indicator. In this chapter we outline fully both the rationale for the GPI and the methodology typically used in its calculation.

Of course, some degree of caution should always be adopted when a study relies so heavily on one specific indicator. With this in mind, we point out some of the weaknesses of the GPI in Chapter 4 and, in the process, defend the use of the GPI as an indicator of sustainable welfare. Since the weaknesses of the GPI relate primarily to the lack of comprehensive data sources on social and environmental factors, we put forward some suggestions to facilitate the establishment of a more informative indicator framework.

The results of seven GPI studies in the Asia-Pacific region are presented and analysed in Chapters 5–11. In each case, the contributors provide a summary of the items used to calculate the GPI and the valuation methods employed. All the chapters conclude with identification of the major items influencing the studied nation's GPI and, in some instances, what is required of policy-makers to advance the nation's genuine progress into the future.

Finally, in Chapter 12, we compare the GPI results across the Asia-Pacific region to investigate whether there are consistent factors affecting the genuine progress of all the studies countries and/or if there are concordant factors affecting nations with similar features and characteristics. From such a comparison, we firstly outline a new hypothesis regarding the relationship between per capita GDP and sustainable welfare. Secondly, we put forward an overall course of action that we believe is necessary to facilitate future increases in sustainable welfare across the Asia-Pacific region.

In all, we hope that this book will increase our understanding of the genuine progress being made in what is a rapidly growing region with increasing global importance. We are confident the book will serve as a valuable template for genuine progress studies in other world regions and assist policy-makers and non-governmental organisations to lay the foundations necessary to increase sustainable welfare throughout the Asia-Pacific region and other regions of the world.

NOTES

1. For the purposes of this book, Asia refers to all countries on the Asian continent except those in the Middle East.
2. In the case of Japan, Singapore, Australia, Fiji, and New Zealand, the rate of undernourishment was zero per cent in both 1990–92 and 2000–02.
3. See the United Nation's *Human Development Report 2006* (UNDP, 2006a) for a technical explanation as to how the HDI is calculated.
4. An International dollar (Int$) adjusted for purchasing price parity has the same purchasing power as a US dollar in the USA and therefore buys an equivalent quantity of goods and services irrespective of the country. Purchasing price parity rates provide a standard measure allowing comparisons of real price levels between countries, just as conventional price indexes allow comparisons of real values over time.
5. Of course, it is also likely that the average poverty rates for each country over the 1989–2004 period would have been lower than the respective poverty rates for each country in 1989.
6. Australia's per capita CO2 emissions already exceeded the European average in 1985 (14.27 versus 10.55 tonnes per person).
7. Other relatively large energy consumers experienced even greater increases in energy consumption between 1990 and 2001 (e.g., South Korea 100.4 per cent, Indonesia 64.1 per cent, and Australia 32.1 per cent) (IEA, 2003).
8. To our knowledge, the GPI has only been calculated at the state or provincial level in three separate cases – for the American State of Vermont (Costanza et al., 2004), the Canadian province of Alberta (Anielski, 2001), and the Australian state of Victoria (Lawn and Clarke, 2006).
9. For more on the notion of a steady-state economy, see Daly (1991) and Lawn (2007).

REFERENCES

Anielski, M. (2001), *The Alberta GPI Blueprint: The Genuine Progress Indicator (GPI) Sustainable Well-Being Accounting System*, Pembina Institute for Appropriate Development, Alberta.

Australian Bureau of Statistics (ABS) (2007), *Household Income and Income Distribution 2005–06*, Catalogue No. 6523.0, Canberra: AGPS.

Bryant, D., Nielsen, D. and Tangley, L. (1997), *The Last Frontier Forests: Ecosystems and Economies on the Edge*, Washington, DC: World Resources Institute.

Costanza, R., Erickson, J., Fligger, K., Adams, A., Adams, C., Altschuler, B., Balter, S., Fisher, B., Hike, J., Kelly, J., Kerr, T., McCauley, M., Montone, K., Rauch, M., Schmiedeskamp, K., Saxton, D., Sparacino, L., Tusinski, W. and Williams, L. (2004), 'Estimates of the Genuine Progress Indicator (GPI) for Vermont, Chittendon County, and Burlington from 1950 to 2000', *Ecological Economics*, **51**, 139–155.

Daly, H. (1991), *Steady-State Economics: Second Edition with New Essays*, Washington, DC: Island Press.

Global Footprint Network (2006), *Ecological Footprint and Biocapacity*, Oakland, CA: Global Footprint Network.

International Energy Agency (IEA) (2002), *International Energy Annual*, http://www.iea.doe.gov/iea/carbon.html.

International Energy Agency (IEA) (2003), *Energy Balances of OECD Countries and Energy Balances of non-OECD Countries*, Electronic database, http://data.iea.org/ieastore/default.asp, Paris: OECD.

International Energy Agency (IEA) (2004), *CO_2 Emissions from Fuel Combustion*, http://data.iea.org/ieastore/co2_main.asp.

International Labour Organization (ILO) (2006), *Labour Statistics Database (1998–2006)*, Geneva: ILO.

Jackson, T. and Stymne, S. (1996), *Sustainable Economic Welfare in Sweden: A Pilot Index 1950–1992*, Stockholm: Stockholm Environment Institute, The New Economics Foundation.

Kuznets, S. (1955), 'Economic growth and income inequality', *American Economic Review*, **49**, 1–28.

Lawn, P. (2007), *Frontier Issues in Ecological Economics*, Cheltenham, UK and Northampton, MA, USA: Edward Elgar.

Lawn, P. and Clarke, C. (2006), *Measuring Genuine Progress: An Application of the Genuine Progress Indicator*, New York: Nova Science Publishers.

Marland, G., Boden, T. and Andres, R. (2005), 'Global, regional, and national fossil fuel CO_2 emissions', in US Department of Energy, *Trends: A Compendium of Data on Global Change*, Carbon Dioxide Information

Analysis Center, Oak Ridge, TN: Oak Ridge National Laboratory, US Department of Energy, http://cdiac.esd.ornl.gov/trends/emis/meth_reg.htm.

Max-Neef, M. (1995), 'Economic growth and quality of life', *Ecological Economics*, **15**, 115–118.

Population Division of the Department of Economic and Social Affairs of the United Nations Secretariat (2005), *World Population Prospects: The 2004 Revision*, Dataset on CD-ROM, New York: United Nations.

United Nations Development Programme (UNDP) (2005), *Human Development Report 2005*, New York: UNDP.

United Nations Development Programme (UNDP) (2006a), *Human Development Report 2006*, New York: UNDP.

United Nations Development Programme (UNDP) (2006b), *Trade on Human Terms: Transforming Trade for Human Development in Asia and the Pacific*, Asia-Pacific Human Development Report 2006, New York: UNDP.

United Nations Development Programme (UNDP) (various), *Human Development Report*, New Delhi: Macmillan India.

United Nations Educational, Scientific, and Cultural Organization (UNESCO), Institute for Statistics (2005), *World Education Indicators, Literacy and Non-Formal Education Section*, Statistical Tables, Paris: UNESCO.

United Nations Environment Programme-World Conservation Monitoring Centre (UNEP-WCMC) (2004), *World Database on Protected Areas (WDPA)* http://sea.unep-wcmc.org/wdbpa/download/wdpa2004/index.html.

United States Census Bureau (2005), *Income, Poverty, and Health Insurance Coverage in the United States: 2005*, Washington, DC: US Government Printing Office.

Victorian Department of Budget and Management (1984), *Victoria: The Next Step*, Melbourne: DBM.

Wackernagel, M. and W. Rees (1996), *Our Ecological Footprint: Reducing Human Impact on the Earth*, Gabriola Island: New Society Publishers.

World Bank (2006), *2006 World Development Indicators*, Washington, DC: World Bank.

World Resources Institute (WRI), *Earthtrends*, www.earthtrends.wri.org.

World Resources Institute (WRI) (2005), *Climate Analysis Indicators Tool (CAIT) Version 3.0*, Washington, DC: WRI.

2. Why is Gross Domestic Product an inadequate indicator of sustainable welfare?

Philip Lawn and Matthew Clarke

WHAT IS GROSS DOMESTIC PRODUCT?

Gross Domestic Product (GDP) is a monetary measure of the goods and services annually produced by domestically *located* factors of production (i.e., by the natural and human-made capital located in a particular country). By natural capital, we mean forests, sub-soil assets, fisheries, water resources, and critical ecosystems. Human-made capital, on the other hand, includes the stock of producer goods (e.g., plant, machinery, and equipment) that are used to produce consumer goods and replacement producer goods.

GDP can be measured in *nominal* or *real* values. If GDP is measured in nominal values, it is measured in terms of the prices at the time of production. On the other hand, if GDP is measured in real values, it is measured in terms of the prices of all goods and services in a particular year – often referred to as the *base* year.

In order to clarify the difference between real and nominal GDP, consider the following basic identity to describe a nation's nominal GDP in 2001/02:[1]

$$nominal\ GDP_{2001/02} = P_{2001/02} \times Q_{2001/02} \qquad (2.1)$$

where P = the price index of goods and services as at June 2002 and Q = quantity of goods and services produced during the 2001/02 financial year.

As can be seen from (2.1), the nominal GDP in 2001/02 involves the multiplication of the quantity of goods and services produced during the

2001/02 financial year by their prices at the time of production. Assume, now, that the 2003/04 financial year was chosen as the base year to calculate the real GDP in any particular financial year. The real GDP of 2001/02 would subsequently be measured in terms of the prices of all goods and services as at June 2004. It would thus be:

$$real\ GDP_{2001/02} = P_{2003/04} \times Q_{2001/02} \tag{2.2}$$

where P = the price index of goods and services as at June 2004 and Q = quantity of goods and services produced during the 2001/02 financial year.

Imagine now that we wish to compare the real GDP for each year over a three-year period from 2001/02 to 2003/04. The real GDP for each year would be:

$$real\ GDP_{2001/02} = P_{2003/04} \times Q_{2001/02} \tag{2.3}$$
$$real\ GDP_{2002/03} = P_{2003/04} \times Q_{2002/03} \tag{2.4}$$
$$real\ GDP_{2003/04} = P_{2003/04} \times Q_{2003/04} \tag{2.5}$$

Note that the only 'flexible' variable in each case is the quantity of goods and services produced during the financial year (Q). The prices used to value the goods and services (P) remains constant at $P_{2003/04}$. By keeping all prices fixed in terms of a base year, annual changes in real GDP reflect differences in the quantity of goods and services produced from year to year. It is for this reason that real GDP is often preferred to nominal GDP in discussions relating to national welfare. It should also be noted that real GDP and nominal GDP are only the same in the base year since, unlike other years, both are measured in terms of the prices of goods and services during that year.

Why is it important to make a distinction between real and nominal values? In simplistic terms, imagine that the price index for the 2003–04 financial year was \$10 (i.e., $P_{2003/04}$ = \$10) and the quantity of goods and services produced during the 2003/04 financial year numbered 10 million (i.e., $Q_{2003/04}$ = 10 million). The nominal GDP for the 2003–04 financial year would be:

$$nominal\ GDP_{2003/04} = P_{2003/04} \times Q_{2003/04} \tag{2.6}$$
$$nominal\ GDP_{2003/04} = \$10 \times 10\ \text{million} \tag{2.7}$$
$$nominal\ GDP_{2003/04} = \$100\ \text{million} \tag{2.8}$$

Let's assume that over the next financial year, 2004/05, 11 million goods and services were produced ($Q_{2004/05}$ = 11 million). At the same time, inflation was 5 per cent such that the price index for the 2004/05 financial year was \$10.50 (i.e., $P_{2004/05}$ = \$10.50). We shall assume that the 5 per cent inflation rate was caused by monetary policy settings by a nation's central bank and had nothing to do with the nature of the goods and services produced during the 2004/05 financial year. The nominal GDP for 2004/05 would be:

$$nominal\ GDP_{2004/05} = P_{2004/05} \times Q_{2004/05} \quad (2.9)$$
$$nominal\ GDP_{2004/05} = \$10.50 \times 11 \text{ million} \quad (2.10)$$
$$nominal\ GDP_{2004/05} = \$115.5 \text{ million} \quad (2.11)$$

By comparing (2.8) and (2.11), it is quite evident that nominal GDP has risen by 15.5 per cent from 2003/04 to 2004/05. If we were using GDP as an indicator of national welfare, could we claim that the citizens of this fictitious nation were 15.5 per cent better off at the end of the 2004/05 financial year? No, we could not, because a significant factor underlying the rise in nominal GDP is the 5 per cent rise in prices. Inflation, itself, generates no welfare-related benefit. However, if we were to consider the real GDP for 2004/05 based on 2003/04 prices (i.e., based on a price index of $P_{2003/04}$ = \$10), we would obtain:

$$real\ GDP_{2004/05} = P_{2003/04} \times Q_{2004/05} \quad (2.12)$$
$$real\ GDP_{2004/05} = \$10 \times 11 \text{ million} \quad (2.13)$$
$$real\ GDP_{2004/05} = \$110 \text{ million} \quad (2.14)$$

A comparison of (2.8) and (2.14) reveals that real GDP has increased by 10 per cent – the same percentage rise as the increase in the quantity of goods and services produced from 2003/04 to 2004/05. Thus, if there is any truth in the fact that real GDP is an adequate indicator of a nation's welfare, it is because real GDP is able to reflect the percentage rise in the quantity of goods and services produced from one financial year to the next. For the purposes of this book, real rather than nominal values have been used. This applies to both GDP and the Genuine Progress Indicator (GPI).

One final point of clarification. Most readers will have come across Gross National Product (GNP). GNP is much the same as GDP except that it measures the monetary value of the goods and services annually produced by domestically *owned* rather than domestically located factors of production (i.e., by the natural and human-made capital owned by the citizens of a particular country). Since it is customary to use GDP instead of GNP in relation to national welfare, GDP will generally be referred to in this book. Nonetheless, GNP is discussed in relation to the Japanese GPI in Chapter 7 – a consequence of Japan's historical predilection to use GNP rather than GDP as an indicator of national income.

THE SHORTCOMINGS ASSOCIATED WITH GDP AS A MEASURE OF SUSTAINABLE WELFARE

The best way to embark on an assessment of GDP is to consider firstly whether it serves as an adequate measure of national income. While income is a rather blurry concept, most observers agree that income is best defined in the John Hicks tradition as the maximum amount that can be consumed over a specific period without undermining the capacity to produce and consume the same amount in future periods (Hicks, 1946). The key aspect of this definition is the need to keep income-generating capital intact. Failure to ensure this means essentially two things. Firstly, it means that the ability to sustain the same level of output over time will be compromised. Secondly, it means that the current level of output will overstate 'true' income. Indeed, the overstated portion of income will effectively equal the amount by which income-generating capital has been drawn upon to augment current output.

To understand the Hicksian concept of income, consider the following simple example of a timber plantation. The plantation consists of 1000 cubic metres of timber that regenerates at 5 per cent per annum. So long as the maximum quantity of timber harvested each year does not exceed 50 cubic metres (i.e., 1000 $m^3 \times 0.05$), the plantation will generate a sustainable supply of timber into the future. What, however, if 100 cubic metres of timber is extracted each year? At the end of the first year, 950 cubic metres of timber will remain. That is:

Beginning of first year	1000 m^3 of timber
During the first year	
timber regeneration (1000 $m^3 \times 0.05$)	+ 50 m^3 of timber
timber extracted	– 100 m^3 of timber
End of the first year	950 m^3 of timber

At the end of the second year of harvesting 100 cubic metres of timber, 897.5 cubic metres of timber will remain. That is:

Beginning of second year	950 m^3 of timber
During the second year	
timber regeneration (950 $m^3 \times 0.05$)	+ 47.5 m^3 of timber
timber extracted	– 100 m^3 of timber
End of the second year	897.5 m^3 of timber

It is not too difficult to see that, should this harvesting policy continue, the timber plantation will eventually cease to exist. Given the definition of income suggested by Hicks, would it be justifiable to regard the 100 cubic metres of timber harvested each year as income? The answer is no. Assuming that all the timber harvested is consumed and not used to establish a replacement asset, only 50 cubic metres of the timber harvested in the first year can be classified as income. The other 50 cubic metres constitutes the depletion or drawing down of income-generating capital – namely, of the timber plantation itself. In the second year, only 47.5 cubic metres of the 100 cubic metres can be classified as income, with 52.5 cubic metres equating to capital depletion.

What does this mean for GDP? In order to constitute a first approximation of national income, it is necessary to determine what portion of GDP involves the depletion of income-generating capital. This refers not only to natural capital but also to human-made capital since some portion of GDP must be set aside to replace worn-out and depreciated producer goods such as plant, machinery, and equipment. Consequently, the portion of a nation's output that is required to maintain income-generating capital ought not to be used for current consumption purposes. This portion cannot, therefore, be classed as true income.

In addition to this, there are other elements of a nation's annual output that are used for defensive and rehabilitative purposes that, in turn, assist in sustaining output over time (Leipert, 1986). For example, vehicle accident repairs and some medical procedures take place to restore human beings and their productive instruments to something approximating their previous condition. In doing so, the output generated in both instances is not used directly for consumption purposes – it is produced merely to maintain the productivity of human beings, as labour, and the existing stock of human-made capital.

Examples of output produced for defensive purposes include flood mitigation projects and crime prevention measures. Somewhat differently, however, output generated in these circumstances occurs to prevent future economic activity from impacting deleteriously on the existing stock of natural and human-made capital (i.e., to minimise future rehabilitative expenditures).

Not unlike the depreciation of human-made and human-made capital, the value of all output produced for rehabilitative and defensive purposes cannot be directly consumed without undermining the capacity to sustain future output. Nor, then, can it be classed as true income.

In all, it has been suggested that a better measure of national income can be calculated by subtracting from GDP the value of depreciated human-made capital and depleted natural capital as well as all defensive and rehabilitative expenditures. Thus, Hicksian national income can be calculated by adhering to the following equation (Daly, 1996):

$$Hicksian\ national\ income = GDP - DHK - DNK - DRE \qquad (2.15)$$

where GDP = Gross Domestic Product; DHK = depreciation of human-made capital (producer goods); DNK = depletion of natural capital; and DRE = defensive and rehabilitative expenditures.

Let us assume that we make an adjustment to GDP as per equation (2.15). We will now possess a better measure of national income, but will we possess an appropriate indicator of sustainable welfare? For the following reason, an increasing number of observers believe not. Although Hicksian income measures the quantity of goods and services that can be sustainably consumed, this alone does not encapsulate the full impact of a growing national economy on human welfare. Still overlooked by Hicksian income are the following:

- non-market production such as non-paid household and voluntary work;
- the social costs of economic activity such as the cost of unemployment (observable and hidden) and underemployment; the cost of crime; and the cost of family breakdown;
- the impact of a rising foreign debt, since it reduces a nation's ownership of welfare-yielding assets; and
- the welfare implications of a change in the distribution of income over time.

The last point is an interesting one for the following reason. Imagine that Hicksian national income remained unchanged from one financial year to the next. Imagine, also, that the richest family's share of Hicksian income increased by $100 per week at the exact expense of the poorest family's share. We shall assume that the welfare contribution made by Hicksian national income to all other citizens remained unchanged. What would happen to the welfare of the richest and the poorest families? Presumably the welfare of the richest family would, *ceteris paribus*, increase very little since the extra $100 per week would impact negligibly on its spending patterns. In addition, the marginal benefit of additional consumption for the rich is much smaller than it is for the poor (Robinson, 1962; Easterlin, 1974; Abramowitz, 1979). Conversely, the $100 per week decline in the income of the nation's poorest family would have dire ramifications for its general welfare. Overall, the aggregate welfare of the nation will have fallen but the constancy of Hicksian national income will not reflect this change. As a consequence, there are a number of commentators calling for an adjustment to reflect the welfare-related impact of a changing distribution of income over time.

While the other overlooked aspects listed above are somewhat self-explanatory, three additional factors are not. The first concerns the very nature of what is being produced and subsequently consumed. If Hicksian income is rising, it implies that the quantity of goods and services that can be sustainably consumed is increasing. But surely the nature of the goods being consumed also matters in relation to human welfare? After all, a nation could consume more goods that collectively make a small additional contribution to human welfare or, instead, produce the same quantity of superior goods and services and increase human welfare considerably. Because Hicksian income only captures the quantitative element of production and consumption, it fails to capture any qualitative improvements that might be associated with production excellence.

A qualitative conundrum also besets the GPI. Some experimental work is currently being undertaken to incorporate qualitative factors into the calculation of the GPI. In addition, Clarke and Islam (2004) have integrated normative social choice theory into their GPI studies to account for the different cultural interpretations of sustainable welfare. This latter approach has the potential to permit qualitative adjustments to some of the items that make up the GPI.

In the case of all GPI studies conducted for this book, qualitative adjustments of the type just described have not been employed. Nevertheless, in some case studies, assumptions have been made about the various categories of consumption (e.g., alcoholic beverages, cigarettes, and tobacco products) that lay the foundation for slightly different GPI values. In other case studies, defensive and rehabilitative forms of expenditure have been identified and subtracted.

The second additional overlooked factor is the timing of welfare-related consumption. Quite a significant proportion of consumption expenditure involves the purchase of consumer durables such as cars, televisions, refrigerators, and so on. Consider someone who has just purchased a $2000 television set. Will he or she receive an immediate $2000 boost in welfare in the same way they receive an immediate $2.50 benefit from purchasing and consuming a fresh but perishable sandwich? The answer is, of course, no. If the television has been purchased on the assumption that it will endure for ten years – i.e., will provide the desired transmission service for a decade – the $2000 spent will equal the sum of the discounted value of the annual service enjoyed over the lifetime of the television. Assuming a discount rate of 7 per cent, the person in question will effectively receive an annual consumption benefit equal to $284.76 for each of the ten years.[2] It is clearly incorrect to count the initial $2000 purchase as a consumption-related benefit during the financial year in which the television was purchased. Yet Hicksian income, like GDP, treats the full amount of the initial purchase in this manner. Worse still, it overlooks the consumption-related benefits that the television provides in future years (Lawn, 2003 and 2005).

It has therefore been suggested that all but expenditure on non-durable goods should be subtracted from a measure of welfare in the year in which the expenditure took place and that the annual service provided by existing durable goods should be added. The latter can be achieved by keeping account of the annual value of the stock of consumer durables; by assuming that the stock depreciates or is 'consumed' at a particular rate (e.g., 10 per cent per annum for a stock of consumer durables that, on average, endures for ten years); by assuming that future consumption benefits are discounted at a particular rate (e.g., 7 per cent per annum); by summing the discounted value of $1 received each year for ten years (e.g., the present value of $10 received in $1 amounts over ten years equals $7.02); and dividing the annual value of the stock by $7.02 (note: $284.76 = $2000 ÷ $7.02). The annual figure calculated for all consumer durables existing at the beginning of any financial year equates to the annual service the entire stock yields during that year.

The final overlooked factor relates to investment expenditure – that is, the accumulation of producer goods such as plant, machinery, and equipment. It has already been pointed out that, in order to calculate Hicksian national income, one must subtract from GDP the value of the output required to keep human-made capital intact. However, unlike investment in most forms of natural capital, the level of investment in human-made capital invariably exceeds this requisite amount. That is, net capital investment (NCI) – which equals gross investment in human-made capital minus its depreciation – is usually positive.

Since Hicksian income represents the quantity of producer goods as well as consumer goods that can be sustainably produced over time, it is entirely legitimate to include net capital investment in a more appropriate measure of national income. But this is not the case with sustainable welfare since what is desired is an indicator that reflects the *welfare* experienced during a specific financial year.

If one considers investment more closely, it effectively amounts to deprived or sacrificed consumption that is undertaken to provide the means required to generate a particular level of future consumption. In a sense, then, current consumption and current net capital investment are the antithesis of each other. The first involves a form of conduct that generates welfare in the present; the second involves a deliberative action in the present that is designed to generate future welfare. To count current net capital investment as welfare-enhancing in the present is logically erroneous.

Does this mean that net capital investment will be overlooked in a measure of sustainable welfare? No, because, to a large extent, the benefit of net capital investment will be felt in future years in terms of future consumption-related welfare. It might also be felt in terms of greater resource-use efficiency that could reduce, in the future, the natural capital depletion costs per unit of consumption. So long as the indicator used to measure sustainable welfare during a particular financial year includes expenditure on non-durable consumption goods during that year, the welfare benefits generated by previous investment – that is, by past sacrificed consumption – will be predominantly captured by the indicator. Better still, it will be captured during the period in which the consumption-related welfare is experienced.

Having said this, not all investment expenditure is directed towards the replacement or accumulation of producer goods. Nor is it ultimately reflected in consumption expenditure over subsequent years. For example, a large percentage of publicly-funded investment expenditure (e.g., capital works) involves the construction of roads, bridges, and highways, of schools and hospitals, and of museums, galleries, and libraries. The benefits of this investment spending flow to the general public in a similar way that services flow to the possessors of consumer durables – i.e., benefits flow as publicly-provided infrastructure depreciates through use. The benefits are not experienced during the financial year that the public investment expenditure took place. Yet, once again, Hicksian income: (a) treats the full amount of this form of investment expenditure as if this were the case; and (b) ignores the welfare benefits that publicly-provided infrastructure provides in future years.

CONCLUDING COMMENTS

GDP, which is better measured in real rather than nominal terms, is an inadequate indicator of sustainable welfare. To begin with, it is a poor measure of national income. But even if GDP is adjusted to ascertain a closer approximation of the quantity of goods and services that a nation can sustainably consume over time (i.e., Hicksian income), it fails to encapsulate the full impact of a growing national economy on sustainable welfare. GDP not only ignores non-market production, it also overlooks many social costs, such as the cost of unemployment and family breakdown, and makes no allowance for the impact that a change in the distribution of income can have on aggregate welfare.

The deficiencies of GDP – as well as Hicksian national income – are also evident in the fact that both indicators only reflect the quantitative element of production and consumption, not the qualitative dimension. In addition, the calculation of GDP assumes that all current consumption expenditure is welfare-enhancing in the present when, to the contrary, current expenditure on consumer durables generates welfare benefits in future years. The value of all current expenditure on consumer durables should therefore be dispersed over the period in which consumer durables generate useful service to their possessors. The same erroneous assumption is made with respect to publicly-provided infrastructure and, as such, should be treated in the same manner as consumer durables.

Finally, not unlike expenditure on consumer durables, the computation of GDP and Hicksian income is based on the erroneous assumption that net capital investment constitutes a current welfare benefit. The benefits of net capital investment are, however, experienced in terms of future consumption. Thus, in relation to sustainable welfare, the inclusion of net capital investment in measures of GDP and Hicksian income is an example of double-counting. It should therefore be omitted.

While it can be argued that GDP was never designed to be an indicator of sustainable welfare, it is falsely used in this manner. As a consequence, policy-makers continue to steer national economies with the wrong economic compass. It is high time that policy-makers utilised a more appropriate compass when designing welfare-enhancing policies. We believe the solution lies, in part, with the deployment of the Genuine Progress Indicator.

NOTES

1. This explanation of nominal and real GDP is based on Australian financial years which begin on 1 July and conclude on 30 June the following year. This means that the 2001/02 financial year constitutes the twelve-month period from 1 July 2001 to 30 June, 2002.
2. It should be noted that, because of the tendency for people to discount future values, the benefit actually experienced in each year from the possession and use of a consumer durable differs from the value assigned to each year's enjoyment at the time of its purchase. For example, at a discount rate of 7 per cent, the present value of a $284.76 annual benefit generated by a consumer durable in ten years' time is $144.76. The individual may currently value the $284.76 annual benefit enjoyed in ten years' time at $144.76 but this will not alter the fact that the annual benefit eventually enjoyed in the tenth year will equal $284.76.

REFERENCES

Abramowitz, M. (1979), 'Economic growth and its discontents', in M. Boskin (ed.), *Economics and Human Welfare*, New York: Academic Press, pp. 3–22.

Clarke, M. and Islam, S. (2004), *Economic Growth and Social Welfare: Operationalising Normative Social Choice Theory*, Amsterdam: North-Holland.

Daly, H. (1996), *Beyond Growth: The Economics of Sustainable Development*, Boston, MA: Beacon Press.

Easterlin, R. (1974), 'Does economic growth improve the human lot? Some empirical evidence', in P. David and R. Weber (eds), *Nations and Households in Economic Growth*, New York: Academic Press, pp. 89–125.

Hicks, J. (1946), *Value and Capital*, 2nd edition, London: Clarendon.

Lawn, P. (2003), 'A theoretical foundation to support the Index of Sustainable Economic Welfare (ISEW), Genuine Progress Indicator (GPI), and other related measures', *Ecological Economics*, **44**, 105–118.

Lawn, P. (2005), 'An assessment of the valuation methods used to calculate the Index of Sustainable Economic Welfare (ISEW), Genuine Progress Indicator (GPI), and Sustainable Net Benefit Index (SNBI)', *Environment, Development, and Sustainability*, **7**, 185–208.

Leipert, C. (1986), 'From gross to adjusted national product', in P. Ekins (ed.), *The Living Economy: A New Economics in the Making*, London: Routledge & Kegan Paul, pp. 132–139.

Robinson, J. (1962), *Economic Philosophy*, London: C.A. Watts.

3. What is the Genuine Progress Indicator and how is it typically calculated?

Philip Lawn and Matthew Clarke

WHAT IS THE GENUINE PROGRESS INDICATOR?

The Genuine Progress Indicator (GPI) is a recently established indicator specifically designed to ascertain the impact of a growing economy on sustainable welfare. Usually comprised of around 20 individual benefit and cost items, the GPI integrates the wide-ranging impacts of Gross Domestic Product (GDP) growth into a single monetary-based index. As such, the GPI includes benefits and costs of the social and environmental kind as well as those of the standard economic variety. Whilst the GPI embraces some of the national accounting values used in the computation of GDP, its calculation accounts for a number of benefits and costs that normally escape market valuation.

If one compares the various GPI studies undertaken over the last decade, it is immediately apparent that the list of items used to arrive at the final index value has varied over time, as have some of the valuation methods (see, for instance, Diefenbacher, 1994; Moffat and Wilson, 1994; Rosenberg and Oegema, 1995; Jackson and Stymne, 1996; Jackson et al., 1997; Stockhammer et al., 1997; Guenno and Tiezzi, 1998; Castaneda, 1999; Hamilton, 1999; Lawn and Sanders 1999; Lawn, 2000; Clarke and Islam, 2004). The reasons for these disparities are usually related to the availability of data and the preference researchers have for specific valuation methods.

THE INDEX OF SUSTAINABLE ECONOMIC WELFARE (ISEW)

Some readers will be aware of a similar index to the GPI called the Index of Sustainable Economic Welfare (ISEW). The two indexes essentially differ in name only, although, not unlike the GPI itself, there are variations in the items used and the valuation methods employed in their calculation.

The index was initially labelled the ISEW because the original designers believed it would better reflect the *economic welfare* associated with economic activity and, by including resource depletion and pollution costs, incorporate a *sustainability* element similar to that of Hicksian income (see Daly and Cobb, 1989). Thus, 'ISEW' was chosen as a functional name to describe its statistical purpose.

It is becoming increasingly common for updated calculations of the index to be referred to as the GPI. The reason for the name alteration has nothing to do with changes in the rationale or theoretical foundation supporting the two indexes which, it should be added, are identical in every way (Lawn, 2003). The preference for GPI was primarily motivated by a desire to raise the profile of the index and to increase the public appeal for an alternative welfare indicator to GDP.

THE SUSTAINABLE NET BENEFIT INDEX (SNBI)

Another less-known variation of the GPI and ISEW is the Sustainable Net Benefit Index (SNBI). Once again, there is little disparity between the SNBI methodology and that used to calculate the GPI and ISEW. Where the SNBI does differ is in relation to the explanation given for an alternative index and the presentation of the items used in its calculation (Lawn and Sanders, 1999; Lawn, 2000 and 2003). Rather than having all the items presented in one table, the SNBI involves their dichotomisation into separate 'benefit' and 'cost' accounts.

The SNBI is obtained by subtracting the total of the cost account from the benefit account. The potential advantage of this approach over the GPI and ISEW is that it directly compares the benefits and costs of a growing economy. In so doing, it strengthens its own theoretical case as well as that of the GPI and ISEW.

THE ITEMS TYPICALLY USED TO CONSTRUCT AND CALCULATE THE GPI

Since the aim of the GPI is to provide a more appropriate measure of sustainable welfare, its construction is primarily based on overcoming the shortcomings associated with GDP and Hicksian income that were discussed in Chapter 2.

Table 3.1 lists the items typically used in the construction of the GPI. The rationale for the inclusion of each item will now be given. As will become clear in later chapters, the approach employed by the individual chapter contributors varies from one country to the next. Having said this, the contributors have endeavoured to follow, as best as possible, an approach consistent with the methodology we are about to outline in this chapter. Diversions from our methodology are explained at length in the individual GPI chapters.

Consumption Expenditure (*CON*) (Private and Public)

Although it will soon become evident that the GPI begins with consumption expenditure as its foundation item, the rationale for the items used to calculate the GPI is best explained by focusing again on GDP. Employing the standard national accounting framework, GDP can be calculated by using either the 'expenditure' or 'income' approach. If the expenditure approach is adopted, GDP is denoted by the following:

$$GDP = CON + INV + G + X - M \tag{3.1}$$

where GDP = Gross Domestic Product; CON = private sector consumption expenditure; INV = private sector investment expenditure (i.e., expenditure on human-made capital); G = public sector consumption and investment expenditure; X = exports (foreign expenditure on domestically produced goods); M = imports (domestic expenditure on foreign produced goods).

Since we wish to estimate the welfare that a nation's citizens derive directly from economic activity, we first need to make an adjustment to equation (3.1) on the basis that the welfare benefits of exported goods are enjoyed by foreigners, not by locals, while the welfare benefits of imported goods are enjoyed domestically. That is, we must subtract

Table 3.1 Items typically used to calculate the GPI

Item	Welfare contribution	Item notes
Consumption expenditure (*CON*)	+	*CON* = private sector + public sector consumption expenditure
Defensive and rehabilitative expenditures (*DRE*)	–	*DRE* is usually confined to expenditures on health and education (private and public) but is often extended to the cost of vehicle accidents and insurance services (private consumption); and defence, environmental protection, and public order and security (public consumption)
Expenditure on consumer durables (*ECD*)	–	*ECD* equals the sum of all household expenditure on consumer durables
Service from consumer durables (*SCD*)	+	Equal to the depreciation value of the existing stock of consumer durables
Adjusted consumption		Timing adjustment to consumption benefits • *Adjusted CON = CON – DRE – ECD + SCD*
Distribution Index (*DI*)	+/–	*DI* based on the change in income distribution over the study period (first year of study period has an index value of 100)
Adjusted consumption (weighted) (**)		Adjusted CON weighted by the Distribution Index (*DI*)
Welfare generated by publicly-provided infrastructure (*WPPI*) (**)	+	Welfare assumed to equal the depreciation value of the existing stock of publicly-provided infrastructural capital
Value of non-paid household labour (**)	+	Equal to the number of non-paid household labour hours × assumed wage
Value of volunteer labour (**)	+	Equal to the number of volunteer labour hours × assumed wage
Cost of unemployment and underemployment (**)	–	Calculated by multiplying the number of unemployed people by the estimated cost per unemployed person

Table 3.1 (continued)

Item	Welfare contribution	Item notes
Cost of crime (**)	–	Calculated by multiplying various crime indexes by the estimated cost of each crime category
Cost of family breakdown (**)	–	Calculated by multiplying the approximate number of dysfunctional families by the estimated cost per family breakdown
Change in foreign debt position (**)	+/–	Annual cost (benefit) equals the annual change in net foreign liabilities
Cost of non-renewable resource depletion (*)	–	Equal to the opportunity cost of lower non-renewable resource stocks
Cost of lost agricultural land (*)	–	Calculated to reflect the amount required to compensate future citizens for the cumulative impact of past and present agricultural practices
Cost of timber depletion (*)	–	Equal to the opportunity cost of declining timber stocks brought about by harvesting rates exceeding the rate of timber regeneration and plantation establishment
Cost of air pollution (*)	–	Equal to the estimated annual cost of air pollution
Cost of waste-water pollution (*)	–	Equal to the estimated annual cost of waste-water pollution
Cost of long-term environmental damage (*)	–	Calculated to reflect the amount required to compensate future citizens for the long-term environmental impact of energy consumption
Lost natural capital services (*LNCS*) (**)	–	Sum of (*) items. The *LNCS* sub-total reflects the cost of sacrificing some of the source, sink, and life-support services provided by natural capital
Genuine Progress Indicator (GPI)		Sum of (**) items beginning with Adjusted CON (weighted)

export spending from GDP and retain import spending that is conventionally subtracted from the categories of *CON*, *INV*, and *G*.

To simplify matters, we can also include public sector consumption and investment expenditure in the categories of *CON* and *INV* since the conventional isolation of *G* in the national accounts is undertaken merely to differentiate private and public sector spending. This now leaves us with Stage 1 of the GPI:

$$GPI_{Stage1} = CON\,(private + public) + INV\,(private + public) \quad (3.2)$$

Because, as explained in Chapter 2, current investment expenditure constitutes deprived consumption that is undertaken to generate welfare benefits in the future, we must subtract *INV* (private and public) from equation (3.2). We therefore obtain the following:

$$GPI_{Stage2} = CON\,(private + public) \quad (3.3)$$

Having obtained equation (3.3), it can be clearly seen why consumption expenditure serves as the foundation item of the GPI. Understandably, many people question the use of consumption as the basis for any measure of sustainable welfare. After all, excessive consumption is often blamed for contemporary concerns regarding environmental degradation, social fragmentation, and the inability of people to live purposeful and more satisfying lives (Hamilton, 2003). While we harbour similar concerns about 'consumerism', there is little doubt that welfare benefits are generated from the consumption of goods. Just how much welfare is generated is a point of conjecture not discussed in this chapter. Indeed, apart from the welfare impact of a changing distribution of income, it is generally assumed that the first dollar of consumption expenditure yields the same welfare benefit as the last dollar spent on consumption.

Nevertheless, the GPI does not ignore the welfare costs associated with increased consumption. Presumably higher consumption levels demand greater work effort that can lead to ill-health, relationship damage, and family breakdown. Furthermore, unless there is greater efficiency of resource use, an increased level of consumption results in a higher rate of resource depletion, pollution, and ecosystem destruction. As can be seen from Table 3.1, these costs are captured by other items that make up the GPI. The consumption expenditure item merely captures the welfare benefit of consumption that cannot be ignored or denied. While it is true that an increase in consumption will exert a positive influence on the GPI, it is possible for the GPI to fall if the social and environmental costs of higher consumption increase at a more accelerated rate than consumption expenditure.

We therefore think it is best if consumption is classed as a 'necessary evil'. It is necessary in the sense that one must consume and, in a sense, destroy goods to experience the benefit they yield.[1] But if more consumption can be enjoyed without having to place greater strain on families, social relationships, and the natural environment, the evil side-effects of consumption can be contained. In turn, this will bring about a rise in the GPI. Equivalently, the GPI will also rise if the same level of consumption is enjoyed and the many social and environmental costs that make up the GPI are reduced in magnitude.

Overall, electing to have consumption expenditure as the base item of the GPI does not mean that consumption must increase for the GPI to rise. Nor does it mean that the GPI cannot rise if consumption is falling.

Defensive and Rehabilitative Expenditures (*DRE*)

In Chapter 2, we pointed out that defensive and rehabilitative expenditures should not be considered welfare-enhancing for the reason that they serve to maintain and restore the productive capacity of the economy. Although a clear benefit emerges from such expenditure, it is not felt in the present but in later years by way of future consumption. To include current consumption expenditure along with defensive and rehabilitative spending would amount to double-counting. Since a great deal of consumption expenditure includes spending of a defensive and rehabilitative nature, it is necessary to identify and subtract this form of spending.

In most calculations of the GPI, defensive and rehabilitative expenditures are confined to household spending on health and education, whereby some portion of both is treated as non-welfare-increasing. However, some calculations of the GPI have been extended to include the subtraction of: (a) vehicle accident costs, the imputed value of dwelling rent, and the cost of insurance services (private consumption); and (b) defence spending, expenditure on environmental protection, and the cost of public order and security (public consumption).

The subtraction of defensive and rehabilitative expenditures (*DRE*) yields the following welfare adjustment:

$$GPI_{Stage3} = CON - DRE \tag{3.4}$$

Expenditure on Consumer Durables (*ECD*)

The third item used in the calculation of the GPI relates to the expenditure on consumer durables. Because it is incorrect to count the spending on consumer durables as a consumption-related benefit during the financial year in which the expenditure took place, all such expenditure must be subtracted from the base consumption item. This results in the following adjustment to equation (3.4):

$$GPI_{Stage4} = CON - DRE - ECD \tag{3.5}$$

Service from Consumer Durables (*SCD*)

The fourth item is included because existing consumer durables provide an annual benefit or service as they depreciate through use. To determine the level of service enjoyed, it is often assumed that the stock of consumer durables will, on average, endure for ten years. This implies that the stock depreciates or is 'consumed' at the rate of 10 per cent per annum. The annual service generated by the existing stock of consumer durables is then calculated by multiplying the non-capitalised value of the stock by a 10 per cent depreciation rate.[2]

Adjusted Consumption

The next item listed in Table 3.1 is not an individual benefit or cost item but a sub-total to indicate the pre-weighted welfare contribution of all consumption expenditure. The adjusted consumption value – Stage 5 in the construction of the GPI – is calculated by applying the following basic formula:

$$GPI_{Stage5} = Adjusted\,CON = CON - DRE - ECD + SCD \tag{3.6}$$

Distribution Index (*DI*)

This particular item involves the construction of a Distribution Index (DI). In Chapter 2, we discussed the impact that the distribution of income can have on the aggregate welfare contribution of consumption expenditure. In order to incorporate this welfare impact into the GPI, a Distribution Index is often used to weight the adjusted consumption measure in accordance with changes in the distribution of income over time. The Distribution Index is usually constructed by assigning it a value of 100 for the first year of the study period. Any subsequent rise/fall in the index value signifies a growing/diminishing disparity between the income of the rich and the poor.

Adjusted Consumption (Weighted)

This particular item is calculated by weighting the adjusted consumption measure in line with changes in the Distribution Index over the study period. Given the manner in which the Distribution Index is usually constructed, the weighting of adjusted consumption is invariably made as per the following basic formula:

$$\begin{aligned} GPI_{Stage6} &= GPI_{Stage5}\,(weighted) \\ &= Adjusted\ CON\ (weighted) \\ &= \frac{(CON - DRE - ECD + SCD)}{Distribution\ Index} \times 100 \qquad (3.7) \end{aligned}$$

Welfare from Publicly-Provided Infrastructure (*WPPI*)

This next item is incorporated into the calculation of the GPI because a large percentage of publicly-funded investment expenditure is not directed towards the accumulation of producer goods (e.g., plant, machinery, and equipment). It is instead directed towards the provision of infrastructural capital such as roads, bridges, schools, hospitals, and museums. These examples of infrastructural capital generate a flow of services not unlike the stock of consumer durables – that is, in the years following their initial provision. Hence, like consumer durables, it is erroneous to count current expenditure on publicly-provided infrastructure as though it is enhancing current welfare.

Having said this, it is necessary to estimate the welfare flowing from past expenditure on publicly-provided infrastructure. This level of welfare has been calculated using a variety of different methods. In a more recent study (Lawn and Clarke, 2006), it was assumed that 75 per cent of all government investment spending is devoted to infrastructural capital rather than producer goods. The welfare from publicly-provided infrastructure was then estimated to be equal to the public sector consumption of fixed capital (depreciation of existing capital goods) multiplied by the 75 per cent share of government investment expenditure allocated to the accumulation of infrastructural capital. Irrespective of the method employed to estimate this item, its annual value is added as per equation (3.8) to obtain the following:

$$GPI_{Stage7} = Adjusted\ CON\ (weighted) + WPPI \qquad (3.8)$$

Value of Non-Paid Household Labour

Despite the enormous benefits provided by market-based economic activity, a great deal of welfare-enhancing activity occurs outside the market domain. One such category of non-market activity is non-paid household labour.

To derive the value of non-paid labour, it is first necessary to estimate the number of non-paid household labour hours occurring in a country each year. Secondly, a wage or opportunity cost must be assigned to each non-paid working hour. The former is then multiplied by the latter to obtain the total annual value of non-paid household labour.

Value of Volunteer Labour

The value of volunteer labour is included in the calculation of the GPI for the same reason as non-paid household labour. The process involved in calculating the annual value of volunteer labour is invariably the same as non-paid household labour.

Together, the value of non-paid household and volunteer labour (non-paid labour) are added in the following manner to obtain equation (3.9):

$$GPI_{Stage8} = Adjusted\ CON\ (weighted) + WPPI + non\text{-}paid\ labour \tag{3.9}$$

Cost of Unemployment and Underemployment

Perhaps one of the most significant yet recently tolerated social costs is the cost of unemployment. The modern predilection that national governments have for a low-inflation, low-interest rate economic environment has led to the widespread adoption of a 'fight inflation first' stance to macroeconomic policy. In particular, it has resulted in governments and central banks targeting what is often referred to as the non-accelerating inflation rate of unemployment or NAIRU (Mitchell and Muysken, 2002; Lawn, 2004).

The unfortunate feature of the NAIRU policy is obvious – its success relies on the existence of an unemployed pool of labour. Thus, the macroeconomic health of a nation seemingly depends on the misfortune of a substantial number of 'sacrificed' citizens (Blinder, 1987; Modigliani, 2000; Mitchell and Mosler, 2001).

There is a further downside to the NAIRU stance on macroeconomic policy and the recent attempt in most countries to increase labour market flexibility. Rather than increasing the work choices for people engaged in full-time occupations, it has led to the rapid rise in the number of people employed in part-time and casual work. Furthermore, it has brought about an increase in the proportion of all underemployed workers (Mitchell and Carlson, 2002).

Many attempts have been made to measure the full cost of unemployment and underemployment and the estimates vary considerably. The factors taken into account to determine the cost of 'unemployment' in the broader sense include (Sen, 1997):

- the loss of current output;
- social exclusion and the loss of personal freedom;
- skill deterioration;
- psychological harm;
- ill-health and reduced life expectancy;
- reduced levels of self-motivation;
- an undermining of human relations and family life;

- racial and gender inequality, particularly with respect to income and wealth differentials;
- a loss of social values and responsibility.

We believe that the cost of some of these factors is reflected in the items used to calculate the GPI. To incorporate them into a cost estimate of unemployment and underemployment would amount to double-counting. For example (refer to Table 3.1):

- Reduced output results in fewer goods for consumption purposes. It is therefore evidenced by a relative decline in the base consumption item (*CON*).
- The undermining of human relations and family life is revealed in terms of an increase in the cost of crime and family breakdown.
- A loss of social values and responsibility is also reflected by an increasing cost of crime.
- Rising ill-health brings about an increase in health spending of which some portion is invariably included in GPI calculations as a form of rehabilitative expenditure. It is therefore reasonable to believe that rising ill-health would reduce the proportion of welfare-enhancing consumption expenditure. If so, it would have a negative impact on the adjusted consumption item (GPI_{Stage5}).

The first step required when measuring the cost of unemployment and underemployment is to estimate the annual number of unemployed hours applicable to all labour force participants. In the case of underemployed labour, this amounts to the difference between the desired and actual number of hours worked. The total number of unemployed hours is then multiplied by a pecuniary figure which is designed to reflect the cost per unemployed hour over and above the unemployment-related costs reflected in other items which make up the GPI.

Cost of Crime

The cost of crime reflects the degradational impact that economic activity has on human relations, social institutions, and the self-esteem of some individual citizens. Again, one must be careful not to include crime costs that are reflected in other GPI items. For example, arson and sabotage reduce the productive capacity of a nation's economy which, presumably, is reflected in lower values for consumption expenditure (*CON*) and higher values for defensive expenditure, such as increased fire prevention and security expenditures (*DRE*).

Cost of Family Breakdown

The family unit is a social institution that not only provides individuals with a secure, stable, and organised environment, but one that serves a crucial child-rearing function. In more recent times, the family unit has become a major casualty of the drive towards higher rates of GDP growth. The cost of family breakdown is usually calculated by using the divorce rate as a proxy for family disunity and dysfunctionality.

In all, the cost of unemployment, underemployment, crime, and family breakdown constitute the social costs associated with the operation of a modern, complex, and imperfect modern economy. Failure to subtract social costs would overstate the value or welfare added in production to the incoming resource flow. As such, Stage 9 of the GPI involves the following welfare adjustment to equation (3.9):

$$\begin{aligned} GPI_{Stage9} = & \text{ Adjusted CON (weighted)} \\ & + WPPI \\ & + \text{non-paid labour} \\ & - \text{social costs} \end{aligned} \tag{3.10}$$

Change in Net Foreign Debt

This item is included in the calculation of the GPI because a nation's long-term capacity to sustain the welfare generated by its economic activity depends very much on whether natural capital and human-made capital is domestically or foreign owned. Evidence indicates that many countries with large foreign debts have difficulty maintaining the investment levels needed to keep their stock of human-made capital intact. Furthermore, they are often forced to deplete natural capital stocks to repay debt (George, 1988).

The value for this item is not represented by the total debt position at the end of each financial year but by the change in the net foreign debt position from year to year. As equation (3.11) reveals, the change in net foreign debt can be either positive or negative.

$$GPI_{Stage10} = Adjusted\ CON\ (weighted) + WPPI + non\text{-}paid\ labour - social\ costs +/- change\ in\ net\ foreign\ debt \quad (3.11)$$

Cost of Non-Renewable Resource Depletion

The items so far discussed from Table 3.1 relate to the economic and social benefits and costs of economic activity. This next particular item – the cost of non-renewable resource depletion – relates to the first of the environmental costs used to calculate the GPI.

Non-renewable resources differ from their renewable counterparts in the sense that they cannot be sustainably exploited. Since the calculation of the GPI requires incorporation of the Hicksian sustainability concept (i.e., the maintenance of welfare-generating capital), this poses a potential problem. We believe the problem can be adequately dealt with by deducting the so-called 'user cost' of non-renewable resource depletion, not the total extraction value of non-renewable resources. In many GPI studies, the user cost approach is employed. However, this is not always the case and, indeed, not all the GPI studies undertaken for this book have employed the user cost method.

The user cost is calculated by determining what proportion of depletion profits should be set aside to establish a renewable resource asset capable of generating a sustainable annual flow of income equal to the annual income previously generated by the exhausted resource (El Serafy, 1989; Lawn, 1998 and 2005). To do this, an income and capital (user cost) component of the finite series of earnings generated by a non-renewable resource must be identified. This can be achieved with the use of the following equation:

$$X/R = 1 - \frac{1}{(1+r)^{n+1}} \quad (3.12)$$

where X = true income (resource rent); R = total net receipts (gross receipts less extraction costs); r = discount rate; n = number of periods over which the resource is to be liquidated; $R - X$ = user cost or the amount of total net receipts that must be set aside to establish a replacement asset to ensure a perpetual income stream.

The two key parameters in the determination of the income and capital components are the number of periods over which the resource is to be liquidated (n) and the chosen discount rate (r). The greater the values of these two parameters, the more substantial is the income component and the smaller is the amount that needs to be set aside each period to ensure a perpetual income stream.

The number of periods over which the resource is to be liquidated is relatively easy to estimate and, in the majority of cases, depends on the size of a non-renewable resource deposit as well as expected future resource prices. The major difficulty lies in determining the most appropriate discount rate. Our view is that the chosen discount rate should be equivalent to the real interest rate of the cultivated renewable resource.[3] This happens to be its natural regeneration rate (Lawn, 1998).

Once the user cost component has been estimated, it can be deducted in the calculation of the GPI. And what of the income component? It can be safely used to finance consumption expenditure – if that is what a nation desires – because it will not, by itself, undermine the nation's capacity to sustain the same level of consumption over time.

Cost of Lost Agricultural Land

Unlike many non-renewable resources, there is essentially no substitute for fertile agricultural land. Indeed, agricultural land is not only used to produce a nation's sustenance-based commodities, it is also required to establish renewable resource assets to replace depleted non-renewable resources.

The unique nature of agricultural land demands that a different approach be taken to calculate its loss compared to non-renewable resource assets. In particular, the cost of lost agricultural land for any given year should reflect the amount required to compensate a nation's citizens – in a sense, a compensatory fund – for the cumulative impact of past and present agricultural endeavours.

Again, not unlike the cost of non-renewable resource depletion, a wide variety of methods have been used in past GPI studies to calculate this item. With each of the studies conducted in this book employing a different valuation method, this volume is a clear example of this.

Cost of Timber Depletion

As a renewable resource, timber stocks can be sustainably exploited so long as the rate at which they are harvested does not exceed their ability to regenerate. Timber stocks can also be increased through plantation establishment. However, should timber stocks decline, the impact is not unlike the exhaustion of a non-renewable resource. As such, we believe the cost of timber depletion should be calculated by employing the previously explained 'user cost' method. Once more, the methods used to calculate this item vary widely from study to study. The different valuation methods employed in this book are just a small sample of the various methods that have been used in the past.

Cost of Air and Water Pollution

The costs of air and water pollution are both associated with the loss of the natural environment's waste-assimilative or sink capacity. In simple terms, the environment's sink capacity diminishes each time the quantity and the quality of the waste generated by economic activity exceeds the innate capacity of the natural environment to safely absorb it. It is our considered opinion that a decline in the environment's sink capacity occurs whenever the emission of various forms of pollution imposes discernible environmental costs.

Although pollution is generated in a wide variety of forms, most GPI studies confine pollution costs to air and water pollution. The cost of noise pollution was incorporated into some early GPI and ISEW studies; however, few studies have managed to capture the impact that heavy industry has exacted in terms of soil and urban land contamination.

Cost of Long-Term Environmental Damage

To account in some way for the loss of the natural environment's life-support function, an item is invariably included to reflect the long-term environmental impact of increasing energy consumption. Why energy consumption? Firstly, energy consumption is a major contributing factor to greenhouse gas emissions and the projected change in global climate patterns. Climate change, as the IPCC (2007) has recently reported, is likely to result in a significant loss of the world's biodiversity and, in the case of many countries throughout the Asia-Pacific region, dramatically increase the frequency of droughts and the intensity of other extreme weather events, such as tropical cyclones.

Secondly, eons of evolution have resulted in the biosphere being able to deal adequately with a particular rate of energy throughput (Blum, 1962; Daly, 1979; Capra, 1982; Norgaard, 1988). An increasing rate of human-induced energy consumption means, inevitably, the degradation of natural capital and the subsequent diminution of the life-support services it provides.

Cost of Lost Natural Capital Services (*LNCS*)

The penultimate item involved in the calculation of the GPI is a sub-total indicating the environmental costs of economic activity. Equalling the sum of the items marked by a single asterisk (*) in Table 3.1, or by equation (3.13) below, this item reflects the lost source, sink, and life-support services provided by natural capital.

$$\begin{aligned} LNCS = \ & \textit{cost of non-renewable resource depletion} \\ & + \textit{cost of lost agricultural land} \\ & + \textit{cost of timber depletion} \\ & + \textit{cost of air and water pollution} \\ & + \textit{cost of long-term environmental damage} \end{aligned} \tag{3.13}$$

Genuine Progress Indicator (GPI)

The GPI can finally be calculated by summing (subtracting) the double-asterisked (**) items appearing in Table 3.1. This, in effect, means adhering to the following equation:

$$\begin{aligned} \mathrm{GPI}_{\mathrm{Final}} = \ & \textit{Adjusted CON (weighted)} \\ & + \ \textit{WPPI} \\ & + \ \textit{non-paid labour} \\ & - \textit{social costs} \\ & +/- \ \textit{change in net foreign debt} \\ & - \textit{LNCS} \end{aligned} \tag{3.14}$$

As equation (3.14) shows, the GPI effectively represents the welfare benefits generated by the economic process minus the associated social and environmental costs. The GPI must be positive in order for the economic process to be a worthwhile exercise. A negative GPI is, however, most unlikely. Notwithstanding this, a decline in the GPI, particularly if accompanied by an increase in GDP, would reflect a greater increase in the social and environmental costs of GDP growth than the additional welfare benefits generated. This would render the economic process 'uneconomic' at the margin and raise the question as to whether a nation should shift its focus from GDP growth to natural capital maintenance, value-adding in production, distributional equity, and the development and application of efficiency-increasing rather than throughput-increasing technological progress.

Population

To ascertain the genuine progress of the average person living in a particular country, it is necessary to calculate the GPI on a per capita basis. This requires the nation's annual population to be included in Table 3.1.

Per Capita GPI

The per capita GPI of a particular country is calculated, as per equation (3.15), by dividing the final GPI value by the nation's population.

$$Per\ capita\ GPI = GPI_{Final} \div population \qquad (3.15)$$

CONCLUDING COMMENTS

We have endeavoured to explain the rationale for the GPI and the various items used in its construction. We believe the theory behind the GPI is very sound, although debate continues as to which items should be included in the GPI. Other concerns exist in relation to the valuation methods employed to calculate some of the GPI items. Chapter 4 has therefore been included to outline and discuss these issues in more detail. We do, however, invite the reader to consult Stockhammer et al. (1997), Neumayer (1999), Lawn (2003 and 2006), Daly and Cobb (1989), and Redefining Progress (1995) to make up their own mind as to the applicability of the GPI and the valuation methods employed.

Clearly, valuation issues will have some bearing on the strength of the conclusions drawn in the chapters on individual countries as well as the chapter comparing the GPI results across the Asia-Pacific region (Chapter 12). We, along with the chapter contributors, have highlighted the main caveats and limitations of each study. In doing so, we believe this book is able to provide greater insight into the genuine progress being made across the Asia-Pacific region.

We have also argued in this chapter that a decline in the GPI could be a reflection of 'uneconomic' GDP growth. In these circumstances, we have suggested a realignment of growth-based policies to ensure continued progress within a nation. However, serious problems are likely to eventuate in countries where the decline in the GPI occurs prior to the satisfaction of many citizens' basic needs. A situation of this kind is more probable for a nation with a very large population and a significant number of people living in abject poverty. Given the high per capita consumption levels of many industrialised nations, some form of redistribution from rich to poor countries will be required to ensure both adequate and equitable per capita GPI levels across the globe. Moreover, rich countries will need to reduce their consumption while heavily populated countries will need to devote greater attention to the population issue.

Of all the Asia-Pacific countries covered in this book, China and India fall into the high-risk category. Australia, New Zealand, and Japan, on the other hand, are three Asia-Pacific countries where absolute poverty is largely non-existent and where policy realignment is likely to be less painful. However, the division between relative wealth across the Asia-Pacific region ensures the issues of consumption, inequity, and population and GDP growth emerge repeatedly throughout this book. Indeed, they take centre stage in Chapter 12 when comparisons are made of trend movements in the GPI and what might be required to facilitate genuine progress across the Asia-Pacific region.

NOTES

1. In actual fact, no goods are truly destroyed or consumed. Because of the *law of conservation of matter and energy*, the matter embodied in goods and services cannot be destroyed. What is destroyed, however, is the use value embodied in goods and services that is initially added to matter-energy during the production phase of the economic process. Also destroyed in both the production and

consumption phases of the economic process is the 'usefulness' of matter-energy – a consequence of the *Entropy Law*. This is why there is a constant need to extract virgin resources to fuel the economic process irrespective of the rate of recycling which, in any case, only applies to matter, not energy, and can never be 100 per cent efficient.

2. The non-capitalised value is higher than the capitalised value and is used because the price paid for a durable good – that is, its capitalised value – reflects the *present value* of the annual services that a consumer expects to enjoy from possessing the good from initial purchase until its full depreciation. However, it is necessary to estimate the actual service enjoyed in each year which, for example, in the fifth year following the purchase of a durable good, would be greater than the consumer's present value of the expected fifth year of service at the time the good was purchased.

   To illustrate the point more clearly, consider a durable good that is expected to provide a \$10 annual service over a ten-year period. At a discount rate of 7 per cent, the present value of the annual service at the time of purchase will be \$9.35 for the first year (\$10/1.07), \$8.73 for the second year ($\$10/1.07^2$), and so on, and finally \$5.08 for the tenth year ($\$10/1.07^{10}$). Over the entire ten-year period, the present value of the service enjoyed in each year sums to \$70.24. This is what we would expect the consumer to pay for the durable good. However, the consumer eventually enjoys \$100 worth of service over a ten-year period (\$10 × 10 years). It is the \$10 annual service which should be added when calculating the annual values of the GPI. To obtain this value, the price of the good – its capitalised value – is multiplied by 1.42 (i.e., \$100/70.24) based on the two assumptions that the good endures for ten years and the discount rate is 7 per cent. This yields a non-capitalised value of \$100. This is then divided by 10 (\$100/10 years) to obtain the annual service value of \$10.

3. We believe that the use of the real interest rate of the cultivated renewable resource ensures the user cost estimate is in keeping with the strong sustainability notion of keeping natural capital intact (Lawn, 2007).

REFERENCES

Blinder, A. (1987), *Hard Heads, Soft Hearts*, New York: Addison-Wesley.

Blum, H. (1962), *Times Arrow and Evolution*, 3rd edition, Princeton, NJ: Harper Torchbook.

Capra, F. (1982), *The Turning Point*, London: Fontana.

Castaneda, B. (1999), 'An index of sustainable economic welfare (ISEW) for Chile', *Ecological Economics*, **28**, 231–244.

Clarke, M. and Islam, S. (2004), *Economics Growth and Social Welfare: Operationalising Normative Social Choice Theory*, Amsterdam: North-Holland.

Daly, H. (1979), 'Entropy, growth, and the political economy of scarcity', in V.K. Smith (ed.), *Scarcity and Growth Reconsidered*, Baltimore, MD: John Hopkins University Press, pp. 67–94.

Daly, H. and Cobb, J. (1989), *For the Common Good: Redirecting the Economy Toward Community, the Environment, and a Sustainable Future*, Boston, MA: Beacon Press.

Diefenbacher, H. (1994), 'The index of sustainable economic welfare in Germany', in C. Cobb and J. Cobb (eds), *The Green National Product*, New York: University Press of America, pp. 215–245.

El Serafy, S. (1989), 'The proper calculation of income from depletable natural resources', in Y. Ahmad, S. El Serafy and E. Lutz, E. (eds), *Environmental Accounting for Sustainable Development*, World Bank, Washington, DC: World Bank, pp. 10–18.

George, S. (1988), *A Fate Worse than Debt*, New York: Grove.

Guenno, G. and Tiezzi, S. (1998), 'An Index of Sustainable Economic Welfare for Italy', Working Paper 5/98, Fondazione Eni Enrico Mattei, Milan.

Hamilton, C. (1999), 'The genuine progress indicator: methodological developments and results from Australia', *Ecological Economics*, **30**, 13–28.

Hamilton, C. (2003), *Growth Fetish*, Sydney: Allen & Unwin.

Intergovernmental Panel on Climate Change (IPCC) (2007), *Climate Change 2007: Impacts, Adaptation, and Vulnerability*, Cambridge: Cambridge University Press.

Jackson, T. and Stymne, S. (1996), *Sustainable Economic Welfare in Sweden: A Pilot Index 1950–1992*, Stockholm: Stockholm Environment Institute, The New Economics Foundation.

Jackson, T., Laing, F., MacGillivray, A., Marks, N., Ralls, J. and Styme, S. (1997), *An Index of Sustainable Economic Welfare for the UK, 1950–1996*, University of Surrey Centre for Environmental Strategy, Guildford.

Lawn, P. (1998), 'In defence of the strong sustainability approach to national income accounting', *Environmental Taxation and Accounting*, **3**, 29–47.

Lawn, P. (2000), *Toward Sustainable Development: An Ecological Economics Approach*, Boca Raton: CRC Press.

Lawn, P. (2003), 'A theoretical foundation to support the Index of Sustainable Economic Welfare (ISEW), Genuine Progress Indicator (GPI), and other related measures', *Ecological Economics*, **44**, 105–118.

Lawn, P. (2004), 'Reconciling the policy goals of full employment and ecological sustainability', *International Journal of Environment, Workplace, and Employment*, **1**, 62–81.

Lawn, P. (2005), 'An assessment of the valuation methods used to calculate the Index of Sustainable Economic Welfare (ISEW), Genuine Progress

Indicator (GPI), and Sustainable Net Benefit Index (SNBI)', *Environment, Development, and Sustainability*, 7, 185–208.

Lawn, P. (ed.) (2006), *Sustainable Development Indicators in Ecological Economics*, Cheltenham, UK and Northampton, MA: Edward Elgar.

Lawn, P. (2007), *Frontier Issues in Ecological Economics*, Cheltenham, UK and Northampton, MA: Edward Elgar.

Lawn, P. and Clarke, M. (2006), *Measuring Genuine Progress: An Application of the Genuine Progress Indicator*, NewYork: Nova Science Publishers.

Lawn, P. and Sanders, R. (1999), 'Has Australia surpassed its optimal macroeconomic scale? Finding out with the aid of benefit and cost accounts and a sustainable net benefit index', *Ecological Economics*, **28**, 213–229.

Mitchell, W. and Carlson, E. (2002), 'Labour underutilisation in Australia and inflation', Centre of Full Employment and Equity Working Paper 02–10, September.

Mitchell, W. and Mosler, W. (2001), 'Fiscal policy and the Job Guarantee', Centre of Full Employment and Equity Working Paper 01–09, August.

Mitchell, W. and Muysken, J. (2002), 'The Phillips Curve, the NAIRU, and unemployment asymmetries', Centre of Full Employment and Equity Working Paper 02–05, June.

Modigliani, F. (2000), 'Europe's Economic Problems', Carpe Oeconomiam Papers in Economics, Third Monetary and Finance Lecture, Freiburg, 6 April.

Moffat, I. and Wilson, M. (1994), 'An index of sustainable economic welfare for Scotland, 1980–1991', *International Journal of Sustainable Development and World Ecology*, **1**, 264–291.

Neumayer, E. (1999), 'The ISEW – Not an index of sustainable economic welfare', *Social Indicators Research*, **48**, 77–101.

Norgaard, R. (1988), 'Sustainable development: a co-evolutionary view', *Futures*, **December**, 606–620.

Redefining Progress (1995), 'Gross production vs genuine progress', *Genuine Progress Indicator: Summary of Data and Methodology*, San Francisco, CA: Redefining Progress.

Rosenberg, K. and Oegema, T. (1995), *A Pilot ISEW for The Netherlands 1950–1992*, Amsterdam: Instituut Voor Milieu – En Systeemanalyse.

Sen (1997), 'Inequality, unemployment, and contemporary Europe', *International Labour Review*, **136**, 155–171.

Stockhammer, E., Hochreiter, H., Obermayr, B. and Steiner, K. (1997), 'The index of sustainable economic welfare (ISEW) as an alternative to GDP in measuring economic welfare: the results of the Austrian (revised) ISEW calculation 1955–1992', *Ecological Economics*, **21**, 19–34.

4. In defence of the Genuine Progress Indicator

Philip Lawn and Matthew Clarke

THE WEAKNESSES OF THE GPI

In the chapters to come, the individual assessments of the genuine progress of Asia-Pacific economies will rely almost exclusively on the Genuine Progress Indicator (GPI) results obtained by the various contributors. Naturally, the credibility of these assessments will depend on how accurately the GPI reflects the sustainable welfare of the citizens living in the respective Asia-Pacific nations. In recent times, a number of critics have claimed that the GPI is riddled with too many flaws to enable worthwhile conclusions to be drawn from the results of individual GPI studies. They therefore argue that the index is deprived of any policy-guiding value.

Although considerable effort was taken in Chapter 3 to substantiate the application of the GPI, we believe it is incumbent upon us to pause for a moment and discuss its weaknesses. In order to do so, we will focus on some of the criticisms levelled at the GPI. Whilst there is little doubt that the GPI is an imperfect indicator of sustainable welfare, we aim to show that: (a) some of the criticisms directed towards the GPI are unjustified; and (b) via the establishment of a more informative indicator framework, better data sources, and improved valuation methods, the few existing weaknesses of the GPI can be overcome. This, we believe, would greatly improve the reliability of future GPI studies.

The Lack of an Exhaustive List of Items

The first and most obvious weakness of the GPI is that the list of benefit and cost items used in its calculation is not in any way exhaustive. Following a quick perusal of any list of items used to calculate the GPI (e.g., Table 3.1), most people have little difficulty identifying at least one overlooked welfare factor. Examples typically include the value of leisure time (or the value of lost leisure time), the cost of noise pollution and urbanisation, the irksome nature of certain forms of employment, and the environmental costs of solid-waste pollution, coral reef destruction, and dwindling fish stocks. Whilst some of these items have been spasmodically incorporated into previous GPI studies (e.g., Daly and Cobb, 1989; Lawn and Sanders, 1999; Hamilton, 1999; Clarke and Islam, 2004), the extensive range of benefit and cost items used in most GPI studies still fails to prevent at least one major welfare-related factor from being overlooked or omitted.

In defence of the GPI, no indicator can possibly incorporate all relevant factors. So long as the GPI is able to capture the most important benefits and costs, it is difficult to argue that the GPI suffers more in terms of a lack of comprehensiveness than any other welfare indicator. That the GPI incorporates up to 20 individual benefit and cost items suggests that its coverage of relevant welfare factors is more extensive than equivalent indicators of human welfare (e.g., the Human Development Index). What's more, the omission of many benefit and cost items is often attributable to the lack of suitable data sources required to make reliable monetary estimates of certain items. Thus this first weakness of the GPI could be significantly overcome if an indicator framework was specifically established to procure the data needed to make GPI calculations. The issue of data availability is taken up again later in this chapter.

The Overwhelming Effect of Dominant Items

The second major weakness of the GPI is that small variations in a dominant item (e.g., consumption-related welfare) can overwhelm large variations in a lesser item (e.g., cost of urban waste-water pollution) (Neumayer, 1999). There are two ways to respond to this criticism. In the first instance, we believe that the domination of one item over another simply indicates that it has greater welfare significance. In addition, a dominant item invariably constitutes the aggregation of smaller related items. For example, consumption-related welfare involves a wide variety of goods and services that serve different welfare-related functions. Thus, it might be useful to disclose each consumption category as a separate item. Even so, disaggregation of a dominant item would not alter the final GPI value.

In the case of some GPI studies, consumption expenditure is disaggregated into the various national accounting categories (e.g., food; cigarettes and tobacco; transport services; hotels, cafes, and restaurants; and so on) and adjustments are made to better reflect their welfare contribution (e.g., Lawn and Clarke, 2006). In these instances, each category can be left as a separate benefit item, but they are usually re-aggregated. Indeed, this approach has been used in this book when calculating the GPI for Australia and India. In all, the domination of certain items is an issue more to do with presentation than the existence of dominant items which, in our opinion, do not undermine the integrity and usefulness of the GPI.[1]

The second response concerns the fact that many factors affecting the GPI are reflected in more than one of the GPI items. As explained in Chapter 3, unemployment reduces economic output, dilutes social values, increases the rate of ill-health, and undermines human relations and family life. Hence, rising unemployment is likely to be indirectly reflected by lower than expected consumption levels (CON), a rise in health-related defensive and rehabilitative expenditures, and an increased cost of crime and family breakdown. In addition, since rising rates of crime and family breakdown also reduce the productive capacity of a nation's economy, they too are likely to be reflected by lower levels of consumption.

To avoid double-counting, the *indirect* impacts of unemployment, crime, and family breakdown are, as previously explained, deliberately excluded from the items that are designed merely to capture the associated *direct* costs. What therefore appears to be huge disparities between the values of some GPI items is not a true reflection of the varying intensity of impact that certain factors have on the final GPI value. Hence, the dominance of a particular GPI item does not necessarily imply a corresponding dominant source of impact on the GPI – at least not to the same extent to which it is reflected by the relative differences in the values of each GPI item.

Inadequate Valuation Methods

The validity of the criticisms levelled at the GPI is greatest in relation to its third major weakness – namely, the valuation methods used in its calculation (see Mäler, 1991; Atkinson, 1995; Hamilton, 1994 and 1996; Neumayer, 1999 and 2000). The bulk of the criticism has been directed at the valuation of the following GPI items: consumption-related welfare; the Distribution Index (DI); defensive and rehabilitative expenditures; the cost of non-renewable resource depletion; and, finally, the tendency to deduct the 'cumulative' cost of various environmental damages (e.g., lost agricultural land and long-term environmental damage). To respond to these criticisms, we will now deal with each item individually, starting with consumption-related welfare.

Consumption-related welfare

There are two aspects to consumption-related welfare that have attracted criticism. The first relates to the qualitative dimension of consumption; the second relates to the use of *real* values or constant prices in the valuation of consumption-related welfare. As to the first aspect, it is argued that a consumption-based item cannot capture the qualitative features of the various goods and services consumed. We have already alluded to this problem in Chapter 2 and, in some GPI studies, it is overcome by adjusting some forms of consumption expenditure (e.g., spending on alcoholic beverages, cigarettes, and tobacco) to reflect more accurately their contribution to human welfare. But, certainly, more needs to be done to deal with this issue adequately.

In relation to the second aspect, consumption expenditure is measured in real rather than nominal money values in order to reflect the change in the physical quantity of goods consumed over time. However, for two good reasons, an increase in real consumption expenditure cannot be directly equated with a proportionate increase in welfare. The first is due to the principle of 'diminishing marginal utility' which suggests that as someone augments their consumption of physical goods, the benefits they enjoy increase at a diminishing rate. The second is due to the fact that an increase in the rate at which certain goods are consumed may not increase the benefits they yield. Consider, for example, the lighting of a room by a light bulb. Is more welfare experienced if three light bulbs are worn out or 'consumed' over one year compared to just one light bulb that lasts the full year? No, the total welfare in both cases is the same, yet, in the former instance, more goods have been consumed.

Despite these potential accounting flaws, real consumption expenditure may still prove to be a worthy reference point in the estimation of consumption-related welfare. Why? It is generally recognised that people will pay a higher price for a good embodying superior welfare-yielding qualities. Consequently, a measure of consumption-related welfare ought to be computable through the use of market prices. For instance, the rental value of a car, a house, a TV, or a refrigerator – i.e., the amount paid to rent durable goods for a one-year period – is widely considered to be a proxy measure of the annual services they yield. On this basis, the full market price of a non-durable good should approximate the service it yields during the accounting period in which it was initially purchased and ultimately consumed (Daly, 1991).

Unfortunately, the market prices and rental values of goods vary for reasons other than the change in their welfare-yielding qualities. The price of a good is also affected by: (a) the relative prices of the different forms of resources used in its production; (b) the actual quantity or supply of the good itself; and (c) changes in taxes, the nominal money supply, and the opportunity cost of holding money. Clearly, for market prices to remain a proxy indicator of welfare, it is necessary to eliminate all price-influencing factors other than those related to a good's welfare-yielding qualities. Given that this is a near impossible task, there are two choices available. The first option is to leave prices as they are – that is, to rely on current or nominal prices. The second option is to deflate the nominal annual value of consumption expenditure by an aggregate price index. If the former option is chosen, the nominal value of all consumption expenditure will embody unwanted price influences over and above any welfare-related influences. If the latter option is chosen, one obtains the real value of all consumption expenditure. But, in so doing, one also eliminates the price-influencing effect of a variation in the welfare-yielding qualities of all goods – the very influence that one wants to maintain in order for prices to constitute an approximate measure of welfare.

We believe that the latter option – the one adopted in virtually all GPI studies – is desirable for the following reason. While the principle of diminishing marginal utility suggests that an increase in welfare will be proportionately less than the increase in the quantity of physical goods consumed, the principle is based on the assumption that there is no change in their welfare-yielding qualities. It is reasonable to assume that, through technological progress, the welfare-yielding qualities of most goods will continue to increase for some time to come. If so, this will largely offset the effect of the principle of diminishing marginal utility. To what extent it does so, one cannot ascertain; however, it should be sufficient to ensure that any positive impact that consumption-related welfare has on the GPI is well reflected by an increase in real rather than nominal consumption expenditure.[2]

The Distribution Index (DI)

There has been some considerable criticism directed at the distributional indexes used in the calculation of the GPI. In most cases, the Gini coefficient of income inequality is employed to construct the DI used in GPI studies. It has been suggested that welfare adjustments other than those involving the celebrated Atkinson (1970) index of distributional inequality are indefensibly subjective and ad hoc (e.g., Neumayer, 2000). It is claimed that the Atkinson index is less subjective because it makes explicit the researcher's assumption regarding a society's aversion to income inequality.

We disagree with this criticism. Furthermore, we believe the subjectivity argument applies to the Atkinson index. By starting with an index value of 100 at the beginning of the study period – an approach adopted in most GPI studies – the DI involves no subjective assumption about the desirability of the distribution of income at the beginning of the study period. One merely makes the assumption that an improvement/deterioration in the distribution of income has a positive/negative impact on the overall welfare of a nation's citizens. This is hardly subjective given that the welfare impact of a changing distribution of income has empirical support (Easterlin, 1974; Abramowitz, 1979). Conversely, the Atkinson index requires the researcher to make an explicit choice as to what society's aversion to income inequality is at the beginning of the study period. This seems to be far more open to subjectivity.

We do, nevertheless, recognise the value of the Atkinson index and are in no way critical of those who have employed it when calculating the GPI. Indeed, the Atkinson index has been used in this book in the calculation of the GPI for Japan and Thailand (Chapters 7 and 10). We simply reject the criticism directed towards the use of anything but the Atkinson index as a means of weighting the welfare contribution of consumption expenditure.

Defensive and rehabilitative expenditures

The policy of subtracting defensive and rehabilitative expenditures in the calculation of the GPI has been widely questioned (Mäler, 1991; United Nations Statistical Division, 1993; Hamilton, 1994 and 1996; Neumayer,

1999). It has been suggested that the concept of defensive expenditure is very dubious because it is impossible to draw a line between what does and does not constitute a defensive form of expenditure. For example, as Neumayer (1999, p. 83) argues: 'If health expenditures are defensive expenditures against illness, why should food and drinking expenditures not count as defensive expenditures against hunger and thirst? Are holiday and entertainment expenditures defensive expenditures against boredom? Should they all be subtracted from personal consumption expenditures?' Furthermore, a United Nations review of national accounting has argued that when the concept of defensive expenditure is pushed to its logical conclusion, scarcely any consumption expenditure contributes to an improvement in human welfare.

There is some degree of truth in the above criticism. However, there is a fundamental difference between expenditure over and above the amount deemed necessary to satisfy base-level needs and expenditure people feel increasingly required to make to protect themselves against the unwanted side-effects of economic activity. It is safe to say that the latter are defensive in character and the majority of the former are not. In addition, if all consumption expenditure was purely defensive, a lot less spending would take place since, for example, expenditure on gourmet food at a restaurant would be pointless. Why pay a large sum for high-quality food and waiting service if one can pay a much smaller sum to meet defensive consumption needs?

There is no doubt that the assumptions made in GPI studies regarding defensive and/or rehabilitative forms of expenditure are purely arbitrary. What's more, they can often result in a significant adjustment to consumption expenditure. However, we believe that the assumptions made in most GPI studies are reasonable for the simple reason that, as Neumayer himself suggests, a great deal of consumption expenditure *is* defensive and/or rehabilitative in nature.

The cost of non-renewable resource depletion

The criticism directed at the valuation methods used in calculating the cost of non-renewable resource depletion is twofold. In the first instance, it is argued that the wide variety of techniques used reflects a general lack of methodological consistency on the part of GPI advocates. We, to a considerable extent, agree. Indeed, we believe there is a genuine need to establish a standardised set of items and valuation techniques. Not only would this strengthen the case for the GPI, it would also allow for more meaningful welfare comparisons across various nations and within world regions.

In the second instance, Neumayer (2000) has been particularly critical of the widespread use of the replacement cost approach. Neumayer believes a resource rent approach should be used. Although the resource rent method has been employed in a number of GPI studies, it typically involves a deduction of the *total* cost of non-renewable resource depletion. In many instances, it also involves the assumption of escalating non-renewable resource prices (e.g., Daly and Cobb, 1989). Neumayer argues against the deduction of the total cost of non-renewable resource depletion by claiming that El Serafy's (1989) 'user cost' formula is the correct means of calculating resource rents. The significance of El Serafy's user cost formula is that only a portion of the total cost of resource depletion is deducted – not the total cost as is widely practiced.

We agree entirely with Neumayer regarding the El Serafy user cost formula. Where we depart from Neumayer's argument is his objection to the use of a replacement cost approach. Neumayer dislikes the replacement cost approach because he believes there is no reason why non-renewable resources need to be fully replaced in the present when there are reserves available for many years to come. If there is no current requirement to fully replace non-renewable resources then, according to Neumayer, it is wrong to use a replacement cost approach to calculate the cost of depletion.

We disagree with Neumayer because, in our view, the GPI is designed to incorporate a Hicksian sustainability element within it. As such, the GPI captures the sustainable nature of economic activity, albeit imperfectly, as well as the economic welfare it generates. While the present quantity of resources being extracted from non-renewable resource stocks can be sustained for some time without having to find or establish a renewable resource replacement, this does not mean that it can be sustained indefinitely. And while it may not be necessary to think about a replacement resource for some time, for proper accounting purposes, the actual cost of establishing a renewable resource substitute must be attributed to the point in time when the depletion took place. Indeed, this is the basis behind the El Serafy user cost method.

It might be argued that we are being inconsistent here – after all, we are arguing in favour of the replacement cost approach while also promoting the use of El Serafy's user cost formula. The El Serafy user cost formula is regarded as one of many ways to execute the resource rent approach. However, the beauty of the El Serafy user cost formula is that it can be used to calculate resource rents and replacement costs. It is a resource rent method in that the portion of the proceeds from resource extraction that does not constitute a user cost is a genuine resource rent. It is also a replacement cost method in that the portion of the proceeds that constitutes a user cost is, in fact, the genuine cost of resource asset replacement. Since it is the user cost that ought to be deducted when calculating the GPI, the El Serafy formula serves its purpose as a replacement cost means of estimating the cost of resource depletion. Therefore, it is incorrect to say that the user cost approach is exclusively a resource rent method.

In this book, the El Serafy method has not always been adopted to calculate the cost of non-renewable resource depletion. The reason for this is due, in most cases, to the unavailability of appropriate data. Where an alternative method has been used, the researcher has attempted to justify its use and explain the impact that their chosen method has had on the GPI. We believe that the researchers in this situation have successfully supported the use of an alternative valuation method. As a consequence, we believe the comparisons made in Chapter 12 across the various Asia-Pacific countries have not been compromised.

Assuming the escalation of resource prices over time

It was pointed out above that the cost of non-renewable resource depletion is often calculated on the assumption of escalating resource prices over the study period. This, too, has been criticised given that most commodity prices have historically fallen in real terms (Neumayer, 2000).

Neumayer's observation that most commodity prices have not increased in real terms is entirely correct. So why have many GPI researchers made a conflicting assumption? In view of the expected life of many non-renewable resources and the projected rates of depletion, the price of non-renewable resources should have already begun to rise to reflect their impending absolute scarcity. That they have not simply demonstrates that markets, while very good at signalling relative scarcities (e.g., the scarcity of oil relative to coal), are woefully inadequate at signalling the absolute scarcity of the total quantity of all resources available for current and future production (Howarth and

Norgaard, 1990; Norgaard, 1990; Bishop, 1993; Daly, 1996; Lawn, 2004a).

Should one use the actual market prices of non-renewable resources to assist in the calculation of the GPI if they fail to reflect their increasing absolute scarcity? Many GPI researchers think not. To get an accurate picture of sustainable welfare, it is suggested that the best estimate of rising non-renewable resource prices should be employed when calculating the cost of non-renewable resource depletion. Many GPI studies have involved the use of a 3 per cent escalation factor. In the calculation of the GPI for Australia and India in this book (Chapters 5 and 8), a 2 per cent escalation factor was assumed. In all, an assumed escalation of non-renewable resource prices seems in our mind to be justified.

Cumulative environmental costs

The final contentious valuation issue relates to whether the deduction term for the cost of lost agricultural land, excessive irrigation water use, and long-term environmental damage should, in each case, be a cumulative total. By cumulative we mean that the amount deducted for each year is equal to the annual cost plus the accumulated cost from previous years. Neumayer (2000) believes this practice is flawed since it involves double-counting. As such, Neumayer argues that only the present cost should be deducted.

Neumayer has a very good point here and unless accumulation of the cost can be adequately justified, it should be abandoned. However, we believe accumulation can be justified because, in the case of many environmental costs, the natural assets being degraded are non-substitutable (e.g., the global climate system, stratospheric ozone, fresh water, and fertile agricultural land). As a consequence, the welfare being experienced at a particular point in time is not, for example, reduced by last year's soil erosion, but by the accumulated loss of agricultural land. Hence, the total cost in any given year must reflect the amount required to compensate a nation's citizens in that year for the cumulative impact of past as well as present economic activities.

To ensure consistency, where a particular natural resource can serve as an adequate substitute for another resource (e.g., solar energy for coal and stone for timber), the practice of cost accumulation is not employed. Hence, the costs of timber and non-renewable resource depletion are not accumulated in the same manner as the cost of land degradation and long-term environmental damage. The annual cost of timber and non-renewable resource depletion merely reflect the user cost incurred during the year in which the depletion took place.

There is, nonetheless, a potential dilemma that arises in relation to cost accumulation given the ability of many non-substitutable resources to recover over time. For example, if global CO_2 levels were to be restricted to an appropriate level, one would expect the world's climate system to stabilise (barring normal evolutionary change). Since, in these circumstances, the cost of CO_2 emissions would decline, it would be misleading to deduct *ad infinitum* the same cumulative environmental cost each year. Thus, in the case of the Australian GPI study (Chapter 5), the cumulative costs of lost agricultural land and long-term environmental damage have been weighted downwards by a recovery factor – 1 per cent per annum in the case of lost agricultural land and 2 per cent per annum in the case of long-term environmental damage. To our knowledge, this is the first time such an approach has been applied when costing of the depletion of non-substitutable resources.

The GPI is Not a True Measure of 'Sustainable' Welfare

Although the fundamental aim of the GPI is to measure the sustainable welfare of a nation's citizens, it has been suggested that the GPI fails in terms of the 'sustainability' side of the coin. To understand why, we need to reconsider the Hicksian concept of sustainability outlined in Chapters 2 and 3.

In the specific case of sustainable welfare, the key aspect of Hicks's concept is the need to keep welfare-generating capital intact. As already mentioned, capital comes in essentially two forms: (a) human-made capital, such as producer goods (plant, machinery, and equipment) and durable consumer goods; and (b) natural capital, such as forests, sub-soil assets, fisheries, water resources, and critical ecosystems.

There are, however, two schools of thought as to what form of capital must be kept intact to 'sustain' the welfare of a nation's citizens. The first is commonly referred to as the 'weak' sustainability school. To achieve weak sustainability, it is only deemed necessary to maintain a combined stock of human-made and natural capital. It matters not whether one of the two forms of capital is in decline since it is assumed that both forms of capital are adequate substitutes for each other (Pearce and Turner, 1990; Daly, 1996).

The second school of thought is the 'strong' sustainability school. Advocates of strong sustainability believe that natural capital provides a range of critical sustainability services that human-made capital is unable to fully replicate. They therefore believe that human-made and natural capital are complements not substitutes and, in order to achieve sustainability, the two forms of capital must be individually kept intact – especially natural capital.

We belong to the strong sustainability school for the simple reason that we believe human-made and natural capital are complementary forms of capital. It is undeniably true that advances in the technology embodied in human-made capital can, for some time at least, reduce the resource flow required from natural capital to produce a given physical quantity of physical goods. However, for three related reasons, this does not amount to substitution (Lawn, 1999). Firstly, technological progress only reduces the high entropy waste generated in the transformation of natural capital to human-made capital.[3] It does not allow human-made capital to 'take the place of' natural capital.

Secondly, because of the first and second laws of thermodynamics, there is a limit to how much production waste can be reduced by technological progress. This is because 100 per cent production efficiency is physically impossible; there can never be 100 per cent recycling of matter; and there is no way to recycle energy at all.

Thirdly, a value of one or more for the elasticity of substitution between human-made and natural capital is necessary to demonstrate the adequate long-run substitutability of the former for the latter. It has recently been shown that the value of the elasticity of substitution derived from a production function obeying the first and second laws of thermodynamics is always less one (Lawn, 2004b). Thus, the production of a given quantity of human-made capital requires a minimum resource flow and, therefore, a minimum amount of resource-providing natural capital (Meadows et al., 1972; Pearce et al., 1989; Costanza et al., 1991; Folke et al., 1994; Daly, 1996). It is for these reasons that we believe that natural capital maintenance is required to ensure the ecological sustainability of economic activity.

The problem with the GPI is that it merely counts the cost of the various natural capital services lost in the provision of welfare-yielding goods. While it is vital to obtain a better measure of welfare by subtracting the cost of environmental damage, it is equally important to know if a nation's stock of natural capital has declined to such an extent as to render the welfare it enjoys ecologically unsustainable. The GPI does not provide this information. The GPI should therefore be strictly regarded as more of a 'welfare' indicator than a 'sustainable welfare' indicator. Having said this, the GPI does, as previously mentioned, incorporate a sustainability element insofar as the estimated costs of environmental degradation in this book have been calculated on the premise that natural capital should be kept intact. We consequently believe the GPI provides a good approximation of a nation's sustainable welfare. More particularly, we are adamant that the GPI is a far superior indicator of sustainable welfare than real Gross Domestic Product (GDP) or any other single indicator so far devised.

Given the need to keep natural capital intact to achieve sustainability and the fact that the GPI does not provide evidence of whether this is occurring, we believe the GPI should be supplemented to accurately reveal the sustainable welfare of a nation's citizens. Indeed, we advocate that biophysical assessments of resource stocks and critical ecosystems be undertaken with the subsequent information presented in a natural capital account. Diminution of natural capital over time would indicate that a nation's welfare – whether rising or falling – is becoming increasingly unsustainable. As a back-up to the natural capital account, a comparison between a nation's ever-changing ecological footprint and biocapacity could also be provided (see Wackernagel et al., 1999). As was explained in Chapter 1, the surpassing of the latter by the former indicates the potential unsustainable nature of economic activity.

It should be said that natural capital accounts have not been compiled for the seven case study countries covered in this book. We did, nonetheless, reveal the ecological surplus/deficit of each country in Chapter 1 (Table 1.10). To recall, Table 1.10 indicated that five of the seven case study counties experienced an ecological deficit in 2003. The estimated ecological surplus/deficit of each country should be borne in mind when pondering the GPI results revealed in Chapters 5–11.

The GPI Ignores Transboundary Costs

One of the potential weaknesses of the GPI is that it is ignores many transboundary and international trade issues. There are, of course, two major exceptions – namely, the change in foreign debt item and the cost of long-term environmental damage (since the latter treats the cost of excessive energy consumption and CO_2 emissions from a global perspective). Nevertheless, transboundary resource depletion and environmental degradation are generally overlooked in the calculation of the GPI. For example, a country can enjoy the significant benefits of importing natural resources (i.e., the maintenance of its own natural capital) while the cost is largely borne by the resource-exporting country. The former will have an inflated GPI; the latter a lower GPI. In reality, the healthy GPI of the resource-importing country is simply being artificially supported by the resource exporter, as is the former's long-run capacity to sustain its inflated welfare.

Attempts have been made to deal with transboundary accounting issues in relation to standard national accounting (e.g., Lange, 2003; Proops, 2004). No such adjustments have been made in the GPI studies conducted in this book. In future, they should be, although care will need to be taken given that a resource exporter is undeniably incurring a cost upon itself and it would be erroneous to transfer the entire cost to a resource-importing country.

It should be pointed out that adjustment to the GPI to account for the international trade in resources is discussed by Makino in Chapter 7. Makino argues the case for an open economy GPI with reference to Japan's heavy reliance upon imported natural resources. In the concluding section of the chapter, Makino explains how an adjustment could be made to the GPI of the resource importer and exporter and why, in Japan's case, it is likely to result in a much lower GPI value.

The GPI Fails to Reflect the Potential Future Impact of Present Actions

The final weakness of the GPI relates to its failure to reflect the potential impact of present actions and policies. For example, while the GPI conveys useful information about the current manifestations and immediate effects of past and present activities, it reveals little if anything about the potential impact of current activities. This weakens the policy-guiding value of the GPI.

It might, therefore, be expedient to calculate a second GPI value that incorporates the probable future benefits and costs of current actions (i.e., attributes future benefits and costs to the present calculation of the GPI). This could be achieved by employing forecasting techniques put forward by Asheim (1994 and 1996), Pezzey (1993), and Pezzey and Withagen (1998). Ideally, if a nation introduced policies to move the economy towards a more sustainable, just, and efficient mode of operation, the value of the second GPI value would be higher than the standard GPI to reflect the forecast net benefits. A lower accompanying measure of economic welfare would reflect the failure of present policies. Indeed, if the upcoming chapters reveal that high rates of GDP growth beyond a particular threshold level have a dampening impact on sustainable welfare, the implementation of growth-based policies should result in a lower rather than a higher supplementary GPI value. In addition, the failure to introduce qualitative improvement initiatives ought to be reflected by a gradual widening of the gap between the supplementary GPI and the standard GPI.

THE NEED FOR A MORE INFORMATIVE INDICATOR AND DATA-COLLECTING FRAMEWORK

The assessment of the performance of the various Asia-Pacific economies conducted in this book was made inordinately difficult by the lack of appropriate data sources. It not only forced some of the contributors to confine their analysis to short study periods, it also meant that certain items could not be calculated using the customary valuation methods. In addition to this, data limitations forced all contributors to make heroic valuation assumptions regarding monetary estimates and potential welfare impacts which inevitably resulted in some items being, at best, distant approximations of their correct value. This conceded, all the researchers applied their chosen valuation methods consistently over the study period and were at pains to ensure their estimations of the social and environmental costs erred on the conservative side. Hence, while the total GPI values may not be entirely accurate, we are relatively confident that the trend movement in the GPI for all the Asia-Pacific countries studied in this book is a reliable indication of the changing welfare of the citizens in these countries.

The impact of data limitations on the various GPI studies is obvious – all contributors were forced to make heroic valuation assumptions regarding monetary estimates and welfare impacts that inevitably resulted in some items being, at best, distant approximations of their correct value. This conceded, all the researchers applied their chosen valuation methods consistently over the study period and were at pains to ensure their estimations of the social and environmental costs erred on the conservative side. Hence, while the total GPI values may not be entirely accurate, we are relatively confident that the trend movement in the GPI for all the Asia-Pacific countries studied in this book is a reliable indication of the changing welfare of the citizens in these countries.

Since ecological footprint estimates and/or natural capital accounts have not been provided for each country, we are far less confident that the respective GPIs reflect a level of welfare that is ecologically sustainable. However, we are adamant that the per capita GPI values are better indicators of sustainable welfare than the per capita GDP values of Asia-Pacific countries that have gained such widespread recent attention.

To improve the reliability of future GPI estimates, we believe it would be efficacious to establish indicator frameworks that are specifically designed to accurately measure the values of each component item. An indicator framework of this nature would be doubly valuable because it would: (a) provide researchers and policy-makers with detailed statistical information concerning each item; and (b) advance the capacity of policy-makers to address issues of concern through the formulation of appropriate remedial measures.[4]

On the whole, most economic data exists in a quite detailed form in most countries at the national level. The same cannot be said of social and environmental data which invariably exists in an inconsistent and incongruous form that would appear to reflect the piecemeal approach to policy-making in these two areas.

Much credit, however, should be given to the various national statistical agencies across the Asia-Pacific region. Great improvements have been made in recent years in the collection of social and environmental data. Unfortunately, its compilation is often the product of irregular studies where, to make matters worse, the data-gathering process and the valuation methods employed differ over time. This renders the use of data across time ineffectual. It is also explains why, in most GPI studies, researchers are forced to select a point value estimate of a benefit or cost item and then establish an index to weight the value over the study period.

From the point of view of environmental data, there is an urgent need to establish stock and flow accounts of the various resource types and other natural capital assets at the national level. Regular ecosystem monitoring and annual updates of ecosystem health are also crucial. We find it extraordinary that data of this type does not exist in a comprehensive and user-friendly form.

Also desperately required are regular valuation studies to estimate the different social and environmental benefits and costs of GDP growth. Of course, to be of value, these studies would ideally make use of annually updated data so as to ensure the consistency of valuations across time. We also think it is bewildering that the cost of such things as native vegetation clearance, the loss of old-growth forests, and land degradation is not regularly and scrupulously estimated by relevant government departments. In all, much could and should be done to facilitate more accurate estimates of the GPI and other alternative indicators of sustainability and human welfare.

NOTES

1. If it has one negative aspect, it is the fact that it may render causality between the GPI and its component items more difficult to establish.
2. There are attempts being made to capture the qualitative dimension of goods, in particular, producer goods, through the use of hedonic pricing techniques (Moulton, 2001). Some GPI researchers are currently engaged in experimental work to adjust the prices of certain types of goods (e.g., computers and telecommunication goods) to reflect their rapid qualitative improvement in recent years.
3. To understand what is meant by low and high entropy matter-energy, the importance of the first and second laws of thermodynamics must be revealed. The first law of thermodynamics is the *law of conservation of energy and matter*. It declares that energy and matter can never be created or destroyed. The second law is the *Entropy Law*. It declares that whenever energy is used in physical transformation processes, the amount of usable or 'available' energy always declines. While the first law ensures the maintenance of a given quantity of energy and matter, the Entropy Law determines that which is usable. This is critical since, from a physical viewpoint, it is not the total quantity of matter-energy that is of primary concern, but the amount that exists in a readily available form.

   The best way to illustrate the relevance of these two laws is to provide a simple example. Consider a piece of coal. When it is burned, the matter-energy embodied within the coal is transformed into heat and ash. While the first law ensures the total amount of matter-energy in the heat and ashes equals that previously embodied in the piece of coal, the second law ensures the usable quantity of matter-energy does not. In other words, the dispersed heat and ashes can no longer be used in a way similar to the original piece of coal. To make matters worse, any attempt to reconcentrate the dispersed matter-energy, which requires the input of additional energy, results in more usable energy being expended than that reconcentrated. Hence, all physical transformation processes involve an irrevocable loss of available energy or what is sometimes referred to as a 'net entropy deficit'.

This enables one to understand the use of the term *low entropy* and to distinguish it from *high entropy*. Low entropy refers to a highly ordered physical structure embodying energy and matter in a readily available form, such as a piece of coal. Conversely, high entropy refers to a highly disordered and degraded physical structure embodying energy and matter that is, by itself, in an unusable or unavailable from, such as heat and ash. By definition, the matter-energy used in economic processes can be considered low-entropy resources whereas unusable by-products can be considered high-entropy wastes.

4. Having said this, many of the items are interrelated and thus, from a policy perspective, cannot be dealt with in isolation. Given that a high rate of GDP growth appears to be a major underlying cause of escalating environmental costs, policies to reduce environmental damage will need to focus on 'scale-related' issues, not just improved environmental management.

REFERENCES

Abramowitz, M. (1979), 'Economic growth and its discontents', in M. Boskin (ed.), *Economics and Human Welfare*, New York: Academic Press, pp. 3–22.

Asheim, G. (1994), 'Net national product as an indicator of sustainability', *Scandinavian Journal of Economics*, **96**, 257–265.

Asheim, G. (1996), 'Capital gains and net national product in open economies', *Journal of Public Economics*, **59**, 419–434.

Atkinson, A. (1970), 'On the measurement of inequality', *Journal of Economic Theory*, **2**, 244–263.

Atkinson, G. (1995), 'Measuring sustainable economic welfare: a critique of the UK ISEW', Working Paper GEC 95–08, Centre for Social and Economic Research on the Global Environment, Norwich and London.

Bishop, R. (1993), 'Economic efficiency, sustainability, and biodiversity', *Ambio*, **May**, 69–73.

Clarke, M. and Islam, S. (2004), *Economics Growth and Social Welfare: Operationalising Normative Social Choice Theory*, Amsterdam: North-Holland.

Costanza, R., Daly, H., and Bartholomew, J. (1991), 'Goals, agenda, and policy recommendations for ecological economics', in R. Costanza (ed.), *Ecological Economics: The Science and Management of Sustainability*, New York: Columbia University Press, pp. 1–20.

Daly, H. (1991), *Steady-State Economics: Second Edition with New Essays*, Washington, DC: Island Press.

Daly, H. (1996), *Beyond Growth: The Economics of Sustainable Development*, Boston, MA: Beacon Press.

Daly, H. and Cobb, J. (1989), *For the Common Good: Redirecting the Economy Toward Community, the Environment, and a Sustainable Future*, Boston, MA: Beacon Press.

Easterlin, R. (1974), 'Does economic growth improve the human lot? some empirical evidence', in P. David and R. Weber (eds), *Nations and Households in Economic Growth*, New York: Academic Press, pp. 89–125.

El Serafy, S. (1989), 'The proper calculation of income from depletable natural resources', in Y. Ahmad, S. El Serafy and E. Lutz (eds), *Environmental Accounting for Sustainable Development*, Washington, DC: World Bank, pp. 10–18.

Folke, C., Hammer, M., Costanza, R. and Jansson, A. (1994), 'Investing in natural capital – why, what, and how', in A. Jansson, M. Hammer, C. Folke and R. Costanza (eds), *Investing in Natural Capital*, Washington, DC: Island Press, pp. 1–20.

Hamilton, C. (1999), 'The genuine progress indicator: methodological developments and results from Australia', *Ecological Economics*, **30**, 13–28.

Hamilton, K. (1994), 'Green adjustments to GDP', *Resources Policy*, **20**, 155–168.

Hamilton, K. (1996), 'Pollution and pollution abatement in the national accounts', *Review of Income and Wealth*, **42**, 291–304.

Howarth, R. and Norgaard, R. (1990), 'Intergenerational resource rights, efficiency, and social optimality', *Land Economics*, **66**, 1–11.

Lange, G.-M. (2003), 'Policy applications of environmental accounting', World Bank Environment Department, Environmental Economics Series, Paper No. 88.

Lawn, P. (1999), 'On Georgescu-Roegen's contribution to ecological economics', *Ecological Economics*, **29**, 5–8.

Lawn, P. (2004a), 'How well are resource prices likely to serve as indicators of natural resource scarcity?', *International Journal of Sustainable Development*, **7**, 369–397.

Lawn, P. (2004b), 'How important is natural capital in sustaining real output? Revisiting the natural capital/human-made capital substitutability debate', *International Journal of Global Environmental Issues*, **3**, 418–435.

Lawn, P. and Clarke, M. (2006), *Measuring Genuine Progress: An Application of the Genuine Progress Indicator*, New York: Nova Science Publishers.

Lawn, P. and Sanders, R. (1999), 'Has Australia surpassed its optimal macroeconomic scale? Finding out with the aid of benefit and cost accounts and a sustainable net benefit index', *Ecological Economics*, **28**, 213–229.

Mäler, K. (1991), 'National accounts and environmental resources', *Environmental and Resource Economics*, **1**, 1–15.

Meadows, D.H., Meadows, D.L., Randers, J., and Behrens, W. III. (eds) (1972), *The Limits to Growth*, New York: Universe Books.

Moulton, B. (2001), 'The expanding role of hedonic methods in the official statistics of the United States', Bureau of Economic Analysis Working Paper, June.

Neumayer, E. (1999), 'The ISEW – not an index of sustainable economic welfare', *Social Indicators Research*, **48**, 77–101.

Neumayer, E. (2000), 'On the methodology of the ISEW, GPI, and related measures: some constructive suggestions and some doubt on the threshold hypothesis', *Ecological Economics*, **34**, 347–361.

Norgaard, R. (1990), 'Economic indicators of resource scarcity: a critical essay', *Journal of Environmental Economics and Management*, **19**, 19–25.

Pearce, D., Markandya, A. and Barbier, E. (1989), *Blueprint for a Green Economy*, London: Earthscan.

Pearce, D. and Turner, R. (1990), *Economics of Natural Resources and the Environment*, London: Harvester Wheatsheaf.

Pezzey, J. (1993), 'The optimal sustainable depletion of non-renewable resources', University College Working Paper, London.

Pezzey, J. and Withagen, C. (1998), 'The rise, fall, and sustainability of capital-resource economies', *Scandinavian Journal of Economics*, **100**, 513–527.

Proops, J. (2004), 'The growth and distributional consequences of international trade in natural resources and capital goods: a neo-Austrian analysis', *Ecological Economics*, **48**, 83–91.

United Nations Statistical Division (1993), *Integrated Environmental and Economic Accounting*, Handbook of National Accounting, Series F, No.61, New York: United Nations.

Wackernagel, M., Onisto, L., Bello, P., Callejas Linares, A., Susana Lopez Falfan, S., Mendez Garcia, J., Suarez Guerrero, A.I. and Suarez Guerrero, Ma.G. (1999), 'National natural capital accounting with the ecological footprint concept', *Ecological Economics*, **29**, 375–390.

PART II

Measuring the genuine progress of Asia-Pacific nations

5. Genuine progress in Australia: time to rethink the growth objective

Philip Lawn

INTRODUCTION

This chapter on the genuine progress of Australia is the first of a series of chapters devoted to measuring and presenting the Genuine Progress Indicator (GPI) results of selected countries from the Asia-Pacific region. In each chapter, the contributor begins with a description of the current economic, social, and environmental features of the studied country as well as a brief overview of the nation's historical economic developments. This provides a contrasting image of each country's realisations and potentialities. It also puts into context the state of each nation's genuine progress at the beginning of the chosen study period and the probable factors affecting the direction and rate of genuine progress thereafter.

The GPI results are then revealed along with: (a) a summary of the items used to calculate the GPI given that data availability and the peculiar features of a country can influence the items chosen; and (b) the valuation methods employed in the calculation of some of the GPI items. Each chapter concludes with an identification of the major items impacting on the studied nation's GPI and what is required to advance its genuine progress into the future.

AUSTRALIA'S ECONOMIC DEVELOPMENT: HISTORICAL BACKGROUND AND RECENT DEVELOPMENTS

1788–1945: European Settlement of Australia

In a contemporary sense, economic development was unknown in Australia prior to European settlement in 1788. Indigenous Australians were nomadic hunters and gatherers who, rather than exploit the resource base as a source of wealth, lived in general harmony with the natural environment. European settlement and the process of economic development beyond 1788 did not involve the usual transformation of an existing society. It involved the extermination or submission of indigenous Australians and the installation of Anglicised institutions that reflected the British origin of Australia's European settlement (Sinclair, 1976).

Initially established as a penal colony, Australia's rate of economic development between 1788 and 1820 correlated almost entirely to the periodic despatching of British convicts. Indeed, economic development did not generally begin until the 1830s and 1840s following a more concerted effort to exploit the continent's natural resource endowments (Sinclair, 1976). Until 1850, the major contributing factor in Australia's economic development was the production of wool. Whilst wool production continued to dominate Australia's growth in economic output between 1850 and 1880, the discovery and mining of gold in the 1860s led to a significant increase in Australia's national product as well as a more diverse product mix.

The expanding fortunes of Australia between 1850 and 1880 gave rise to an investment boom that was primarily financed by a massive inflow of foreign capital between 1880 and 1890. By the end of this decade, expected returns on investment declined sharply which, compounded by a long and crippling drought, initiated the withdrawal of foreign capital and an economic depression that endured throughout the 1890s (Boehm, 1971).

As a consequence of technological progress and the diversification of agricultural products, the inflow of foreign capital into Australia returned to pre-depression levels in the early years of the twentieth century. This led to a construction boom, particularly in the private residential sector, as the population of the state capital cities grew rapidly.

Not unlike the late 1880s, investment returns began to decline once more in the late 1920s. With foreign capital again retreating and State and Federal Governments dramatically reducing infrastructural expenditure, Australia succumbed in the 1930s to its most severe economic depression (Copland, 1934; Butlin, 1962). Australia's real Gross Domestic Product (GDP) fell sharply during the early years of the 1930s and did not recover until the latter part of the decade. The official unemployment rate in the early 1930s peaked at over 25 per cent, thus causing considerable hardship amongst Australia's working-class communities (Sinclair, 1976).

1945–1982: The Long Boom Followed By the Stagflation Years

The post-World War II period from 1945 to 1974 is often regarded as Australia's 'long boom'. This era was characterised not only by a strong rate of economic expansion – indeed, per capita real GDP effectively doubled – but also by a dramatic reorientation of Australia's output mix. Facilitated by a combination of the military demands of World War II, American investment, and newly introduced tariffs and import quotas, Australia's manufacturing sector grew rapidly. This increased Australia's self-sufficiency and reduced its heavy reliance upon export revenue from primary products. Moreover, it diminished Australia's dependence on imported manufactured goods (Sinclair, 1976).

Nevertheless, the government policy that cultivated Australia's manufacturing industries in the 1950s and 1960s failed to encourage advances in productivity. Whilst the protection offered to the Australian manufacturing sector shielded it from overseas competition, the cost of Australian manufactured goods rose relative to the goods produced by overseas counterparts (Pincus, 1995). This had two major effects: firstly, it impeded the contribution made by the manufacturing sector towards Australia's economic output (Anderson, 1995); secondly, it led to a decline in overseas investment in Australian manufacturing. Australia's per capita real GDP continued to increase to 1974 but was largely made possible during the late 1960s and early 1970s by a mining boom that was destined to subside.

As the demand for Australian mineral exports declined following the first oil price shock of 1973, Australia, along with many industrialised nations, experienced a period of 'stagflation' between 1974 and 1983 (INDECS, 1992a). Unemployment rose and remained at official rates not seen since the 1930s depression. Inflation was simultaneously fuelled by cost-push pressures and the inability of the Reserve Bank of Australia to control the growth in the nation's money supply (INDECS, 1992b).

1983 to the Present: The Economic Reformist Years

In 1983, a change in the Federal Government gave rise to a number of economic reforms. The Australian dollar was floated on foreign exchange markets, import tariffs were progressively cut, domestic markets were deregulated, the industrial relations system was modified to permit collective bargaining at the enterprise level, and various public assets were privatised. Between 1983 and 1989, productivity increased across the

Australian economy. As a consequence, Australian industry became internationally more competitive (Ryan et al., 2003). Australia's real GDP subsequently rose very steeply which, in turn, gradually reduced the official unemployment rate although not to the same low levels experienced during the post-World War II 'long boom'.

At the same time, Australia developed both an insatiable desire for cheap imported products and a reduced inclination to save. This led to a massive increase in Australia's current account deficit and an accumulated foreign debt equal to 34.5 per cent of real GDP by 1989 (Foster, 1996, Table 1.21).[1] Concerned by the long-term impact of Australia's rising debt, the Australian Federal Government instituted a tight monetary policy to rein in private sector spending. To achieve this, interest rates were increased to cripplingly high levels in the early 1990s. A recession ensued in Australia between 1990 and 1992 that was compounded by a downturn in GDP growth throughout most of the global economy.

Whilst the Labor Government survived the 1993 federal election, it was overwhelmingly ousted in the 1996 election. The incoming Liberal-National coalition Government pushed ahead with more extreme economic reforms, such as a Goods and Services Tax (GST), the further privatisation of public assets, and the continued deregulation of labour markets. Assisted by a commodities boom and a property market that has thrived since the late 1990s, Australia's per capita real GDP has grown strongly over the past decade. Inflation has remained low while the official unemployment rate has fallen to its lowest level since the early 1970s.

Summary

Nearly two centuries of economic development has enabled Australia to enjoy one of the highest per capita levels of real GDP in the world. The Australian economy is both technologically advanced and accompanied by a strong, albeit recently diluted, welfare safety net. Australians are generally well educated and highly skilled (although skills shortages have emerged in recent times in certain industry sectors), which is largely the product of a high-quality and broadly accessible education system. The same can also be said of the Australian health system.

Australia currently enjoys a relatively low official rate of unemployment compared to most industrialised nations and has a rapidly expanding service sector that presently contributes 71 per cent of its real GDP (World Bank, 2006). Whilst Australia remains heavily dependent upon revenue from agricultural and mineral exports, the export of manufactured products has grown considerably in recent times. Notwithstanding this, Australia continues to experience current account deficits despite increasingly favourable terms-of-trade between 2004 and 2007.

From a socio-political perspective, Australia is a cosmopolitan society with a generally high degree of tolerance towards non-European races and different creeds and religions. Unfortunately, Australia continues to have a poor record of treatment of its indigenous population, many of which have an average life expectancy 20 to 30 years lower than other Australians. Australia is a politically stable country with strong liberal-democratic institutions and low levels of corruption.[2]

Although Australia enjoys a very low population density, it possesses poor soils and chronic water shortages. Indeed, the great majority of the Australian continent is unable to support any intensive form of agriculture. It is a nation extremely vulnerable to drought and various forms of land degradation, and is heavily reliant at present upon fossil fuels to meet its energy needs, although many believe this need not be the case (Saddler et al., 2004). As Chapter 1 revealed (Tables 1.7, 1.9, and 1.10), Australia has a very high ecological footprint and, on a per capita basis, is guilty of having one of the world's highest rates of CO_2 emissions and energy consumption.

Despite severe resource constraints, Australia is a country favourably positioned to lay the foundations for a just, efficient, and ecologically sustainable society necessary to facilitate a high rate of genuine progress into the future. Exactly how well Australia has capitalised on its favourable circumstances is, of course, debatable and the subject of the remainder of this chapter.

AUSTRALIA'S GENUINE PROGRESS INDICATOR, 1967–2006

The following section describes, in some detail, the approach used to calculate the GPI for Australia over the period 1967–2006.[3] Being a 40-year study period, Australia's genuine progress can be examined over an extended duration that includes the latter part of the post-World War II boom, the stagflation years of the 1970s, the economic reform measures of the 1980s, and the rapid growth period since the mid-1990s. Importantly, this allows conclusions to be drawn on any association between genuine progress and the different rates of GDP growth experienced during

Australia's four most recent economic development phases. As we shall see, there is not only an apparent association between Australia's GDP growth rate and its rate of genuine progress, but the nature of the relationship appears to have altered during the study period. This has significant policy implications for Australia.

The Calculation of the GPI for Australia

In many ways, the methodology used to calculate Australia's GPI is similar to the standard approach outlined in Chapter 3. However, a number of items have been added and a more comprehensive estimation of defensive and rehabilitative expenditures has been adopted. Whilst a full list of the items and the valuation methods used in their calculation is provided in Table 5.1, the following discussion is confined to variations on the standard GPI methodology.

Defensive and rehabilitative expenditures

One of the more notable differences associated with the approach adopted in this study is the treatment of *defensive and rehabilitative expenditures*. As explained in Chapter 3, adjustments are usually confined to household spending on health and education. In some instances, defensive and rehabilitative expenditures are extended to include such things as vehicle accident costs and the cost of insurance services. In this particular study on Australia, a range of further adjustments have been made. These include adjustments to expenditure on food (25 per cent deemed defensive), on dwelling rents (25 per cent deemed defensive), on electricity, gas, and other fuel (25 per cent deemed defensive), on health (50 per cent deemed defensive and/or rehabilitative), on transport services and the operation of vehicles (25 per cent deemed defensive), on communications (25 per cent deemed defensive), on education services (25 per cent deemed defensive), on hotels, cafes, and restaurants (12.5 per cent deemed defensive), and on insurance and other financial services (50 per cent deemed defensive).

Because of the interventionist role of governments and their widespread provision of public goods, it was assumed that 25 per cent of all government-based consumption expenditure was of a defensive and/or rehabilitative nature. Overall, the amount deducted each year as a defensive and rehabilitative form of expenditure averaged around 20 per cent of total consumption expenditure (private plus public sector).

Table 5.1 Items and valuation methods used to calculate the GPI for Australia, 1967–2006

Item	Welfare contribution	Method of valuation
Item *a*: Welfare contribution of consumption expenditure (*CON*)	+	*CON* = private sector *plus* public sector consumption expenditure *less* all spending on cigarettes and tobacco *less* 0.25 × spending on alcoholic beverages
Item *b*: Defensive and rehabilitatve expenditures (*DRE*)	–	*DRE* involves the subtraction of the following: • 0.25 × spending on food (defensive) • 0.25 × spending on rent and dwelling services (defensive) • 0.25 × spending on electricity, gas and other fuel (defensive) • 0.5 × consumption spending on health (defensive and/or rehabilitative) • 0.25 × spending on the operation of vehicles (defensive) • 0.25 × spending on transport services (defensive) • 0.25 × spending on communications (defensive) • 0.25 × consumption spending on education (defensive) • 0.125 × spending on hotels, cafes and restaurants (defensive) • 0.5 × spending on insurance and other financial services (defensive) • 0.25 × consumption spending by general government (defensive and/or rehabilitative)
Item *c*: Expenditure on consumer durables (*ECD*)	–	*ECD* equals the sum of all household expenditure on consumer durables
Item *d*: Service from consumer durables (*SCD*)	+	Equals the net present depreciation value of the existing stock of consumer durables (assumed that stock endures for ten years; discount rate of 7%) • *SCD* = 0.142 × value of consumer durables
Item *e*: Adjusted consumption	+	Timing adjustment to consumption benefits • *Adjusted CON* = *CON* – *DRE* – *ECD* + *SCD*
Item *f*: Distribution Index (*DI*)	+/–	*DI* based on the change in income distribution over the study period as measured by the Gini coefficient (first year of study period has an index value of 100)

Table 5.1 (continued)

Item	Welfare contribution	Method of valuation
Item *g*: Adjusted consumption (weighted) (**)	+	Adjusted CON weighted by the Distribution Index • *Adjusted CON* ÷ *DI* × 100
Item *h*: Infrastructural services (**)	+	Welfare from infrastructural capital assumed to equal the depreciation value of the existing stock of non-dwelling capital assets provided by the private sector, publicly-owned corporations, and general government
Item *i*: Value of non-paid household labour (**)	+	Non-paid household labour is valued using the net opportunity cost method • Equal to the number of non-paid household labour hours × assumed wage at 2004–05 prices
Item *j*: Value of volunteer labour (**)	+	Volunteer labour is valued using the net opportunity cost method • Equal to the number of volunteer labour hours × assumed wage at 2004–05 prices
Item *k*: Cost of unemployment and underemployment (**)	–	Calculated by multiplying the CU8 number of unemployed and underemployed people by the estimated cost per unemployed person (CofFEE, 2007)
Item *l*: Cost of crime (**)	–	Calculated by multiplying various crime indexes by the estimated cost of each crime category
Item *m*: Cost of family breakdown (**)	–	Calculated by multiplying the approximate number of dysfunctional families (based on divorce numbers) by the estimated cost per family breakdown
Item *n*: Cost of overwork (**)	–	Cost of average number of work hours in excess of 37.5 hours per week undertaken by full-time workers × value of overworked hour
Item *o*: Direct disamenity cost of air pollution (**)	–	Cost reflects reduced aesthetic aspect of and immediate irritation caused by air pollution (as opposed to its long-term health effects) • Equal to 0.2 × total air pollution cost based on sulphur dioxide and nitrogen oxide emissions

Table 5.1 (continued)

Item	Welfare contribution	Method of valuation
Item *p*: Change in net foreign debt position (**)	+/–	Annual cost (benefit) equal to the average change in net foreign liabilities over previous five-year period
Item *q*: Cost of non-renewable resource depletion (*)	–	Calculated by using the El Serafy (1989) 'user cost' formula to determine the amount to set aside to sustain a flow of income equal to that generated by the exhausted resource • Equal to value of non-renewable resource extraction × 0.44
Item *r*: Cost of lost agricultural land (*)	–	Calculated to reflect the amount required to compensate citizens for the cumulative impact of past and present agricultural practices • Equal to estimated annual cost of land degradation weighted by the area of land annually used for agricultural purposes. Annual cost is accumulated to satisfy the strong sustainability condition that: (a) human-made capital is not a substitute for natural capital; and (b) agricultural land has no natural capital replacement
Item *s*: Cost of excessive irrigation water use (*)	–	Calculated to reflect the amount required to compensate citizens for the cumulative impact of excessive irrigation water use • Equal to $90.97 million per megalitre of excess water use × (total annual diversions *less* 7500 megalitres). Annual cost is accumulated to satisfy the strong sustainability condition that: (a) human-made capital is not a substitute for natural capital; and (b) water has no natural capital replacement
Item *t*: Cost of timber depletion (*)	–	Calculated to reflect the opportunity cost of lower timber stocks brought about by harvesting rates exceeding the rate of timber regeneration and plantation establishment • Equal to value of timber depletion × 0.44
Item *u*: Cost of fisheries depletion (*)	–	Calculated to reflect the opportunity cost of lower fisheries stocks brought about by harvesting rates exceeding the rate of fisheries regeneration and aquacultural establishment • Equal to value of fisheries depletion × 0.44

Table 5.1 (continued)

Item	Welfare contribution	Method of valuation
Item *v*: Cost of air pollution (lost natural capital service) (*)	–	Calculated to reflect lost air pollution sink capacity • Equal to 0.8 × total air pollution cost based on SO_X and NO_X emissions
Item *w*: Cost of urban waste-water pollution (*)	–	Calculated to reflect the estimated annual cost of waste-water pollution • Equal to waste-water pollution cost per urban Australian × number of urban Australians
Item *x*: Cost of solid waste pollution (*)	–	Calculated to reflect the solid waste pollution control costs weighted by a solid waste pollution index
Item *y*: Cost of lost wetlands, mangroves and saltmarshes (*)	–	Equal to cumulative cost of lost wetlands, mangroves and saltmarshes • lost wetlands valued at $1000 per hectare at 2004–05 prices • lost mangroves valued at $20 000 per hectare at 2004–05 prices • lost saltmarshes valued at $2000 per hectare at 2004–05 prices
Item *z*: Cost of long-term environmental damage (*)	–	Calculated to reflect the amount required to compensate citizens for the long-term environmental impact of energy consumption
Item *aa*: Lost natural capital services (*LNCS*)	–	Sum of (*) items. The *LNCS* sub-total reflects the cost of the sacrificed source, sink, and life-support services provided by natural capital
Item *bb*: Ecosystem Health Index (*EHI*)	+/–	*EHI* based on the change in remnant vegetation over the study period (first year of study period has an index value of 100)
Item *cc*: Lost natural capital services (weighted) (**)	–	LNCS weighted by the Ecosystem Health Index • *LNCS* ÷ *EHI* × 100
Item *dd*: Genuine Progress Indicator (GPI)	+	Sum of (**) items beginning with Adjusted CON (weighted)
Item *ee*: Population		Population of Australia
Item *ff*: Per capita GPI	+	GPI ÷ population

Infrastructural services

Another variation on a common GPI item is the inclusion of a benefit item referred to as *infrastructural services*. In many cases, the GPI includes a benefit item to account for the services generated by publicly-provided infrastructure (e.g., Daly and Cobb, 1989; Redefining Progress, 1995; Hamilton, 1999). Unfortunately, this item overlooks the infrastructural services also provided by the private sector and publicly-owned corporations. Not only do both these sectors invest heavily in such infrastructure as roads, highways, bridges, schools, and hospitals, but their relative contribution has dramatically increased as more and more public assets have been privatised in recent decades. The inclusion of infrastructural services is therefore designed to overcome this past deficiency.

The cost of overwork and the direct disamenity cost of air pollution

Two additional economic and social cost items have been included in this GPI study. The first is the *cost of overwork*.[4] The average number of hours overworked per week by Australian full-time workers has increased from 1.5 hours in the early 1980s to around 4.5 hours by the mid-2000s.[5] This is having a significant impact on the amount of leisure time enjoyed by Australians as well as the quality time spent with family and friends.

The second additional social cost included in this GPI study is the *direct disamenity cost of air pollution*. Whilst air pollution is essentially an environmental cost that reflects a diminution of the sink function provided by natural capital, it also has direct aesthetic implications and constitutes an immediate health irritant to people with respiratory ailments (as opposed to its long-term health effects). For this reason, it was assumed that the disamenity cost of air pollution constituted 20 per cent of the total cost of air pollution. Accordingly, the remaining 80 per cent of the total cost of air pollution was deemed to be an environmental cost.

Cost of excessive water use

Australia is the driest inhabited continent on Earth. Not surprisingly, Australia is beset with water shortages that, as a consequence of climate change, appear to be increasing in frequency and intensity. For example, rainfall in the south-west of the state of Western Australia has declined by 25–30 per cent since the mid-1970s, while the south-east of the continent is currently suffering its longest drought since European settlement.

Due in part to rainfall deficiencies and mismanagement, the water of the Murray-Darling Basin – a basin that comprises many of Australia's major rivers and drains one-seventh of the Australian continent – is seriously overallocated. The urgency of the situation has prompted the Federal Government to introduce a management plan to assume control over water allocation rights within the Murray-Darling Basin.[6] In light of this, the *cost of excessive irrigation water use* has been included to cater for an environmental dilemma in many ways unique to Australia.

Cost of fisheries depletion

The lack of data on fish stocks often results in the *cost of fisheries depletion* being overlooked in most GPI studies. Sufficient data exists in Australia's case to warrant inclusion of this item. Although the magnitude of this cost is relatively small and does not have a dramatic impact on the trend movement of Australia's GPI, its inclusion serves to highlight the rapid depletion of Australia's fish stocks arising from unsustainable harvesting practices.

Cost of solid waste pollution and lost wetlands

Two further environmental costs have been included in the calculation of the GPI for Australia. The first relates to a growing problem caused by Australia's enormous generation of solid waste. Despite an increase in the rate of waste recycling in Australia, the per capita quantity of solid waste making its way to landfill sites continues to rise.[7] This leads to the growing contamination of soil and groundwater aquifers. Hence, the *cost of solid waste pollution* has been included as a further example of the diminution of the sink function provided by natural capital.

The next additional environmental cost deals with another commonly overlooked factor in many GPI studies. A considerable percentage of the land reclaimed in Australia for agricultural, industrial, and residential purposes involves the draining of wetlands or the clearing of mangroves and saltmarshes. Land use changes of this nature are invariably undertaken in the false belief that wetlands constitute unproductive swamps or 'wastelands'. To the contrary, wetlands and estuaries are amongst the most productive of all ecosystems and provide a range of valuable source, sink, and life-support services (Common and Stagl, 2005).[8] Given this fact, plus Australia's poor record of wetland and mangrove conservation, the *cost of lost wetlands, mangroves, and saltmarshes* has been included in the calculation of Australia's GPI.

Ecosystem Health Index

Finally, in the case of almost every GPI study undertaken, the individual environmental cost items are merely subtracted from the running total to calculate the aggregate value of the GPI. In this study, the environmental costs are initially summed to obtain what can be classed as the cost of lost natural capital services (LNCS). This sub-total reflects the source, sink and, to some extent, life-support services provided by natural capital that are sacrificed in the process of converting natural capital to human-made capital.

The LNCS sub-total has been weighted by an *Ecosystem Health Index* (EHI) on the basis that the impacts of many resource-extractive and pollutive activities are not confined to the damage inflicted on the natural environment's source and sink functions. Damage also extends to ecosystem degradation. A good example is strip mining – a resource-extraction practice requiring the initial removal of terrestrial fauna and flora. Another is agriculture – again, an activity first requiring the clearance of native vegetation.

With this in mind, the EHI is constructed on the premise that remnant vegetation loss constitutes the 'greatest threat to biodiversity' and, therefore, to ecosystem functioning (Biodiversity Unit, 1995). A base index value of 100 is assigned to the first year of the study period (i.e., 1967 = 100) and is adjusted in line with the annual changes in the area of relatively undisturbed land. As the area of relatively undisturbed land declines/increases over the study period, the EHI correspondingly falls/rises. Hence, a fall in the EHI signifies a worsening state of ecosystem health that, in turn, leads to an upward weighting of the cost of lost natural capital services.

Results of the Australian GPI Study[9]

Individual GPI items

The results of the GPI study on Australia are summarised in Table 5.2 (valued at June 2005 prices).[10] Column *A* represents the annual welfare contribution collectively made by durable and non-durable consumption goods weighted by the Distribution Index (DI). As such, this column summarises the welfare impact of Items *a–f* in Table 5.1. Column *A* indicates that Australia's weighted consumption increased from $139.1

Table 5.2 Genuine Progress Indicator (GPI) and real GDP for Australia, 1967–2006

Year	Weighted CON_{ADJ} ($)	Infrastr. services ($)	Non-paid labour ($)	Social costs ($)	Weighted LNCS ($)	GPI ($)	GDP ($)	Australian population (000s)	Per capita GPI ($)	Per capita GDP ($)	Per capita GPI 1967 = 100	Per capita GDP 1967 = 100
	A	*B*	*C*	*D*	*E*	*F*	*G*	*H*	*I*	*J*	*K*	*L*
1967	139 174	14 536	266 226	-19 005	-65 463	335 469	245 464	11 799	28 432	20 804	100.0	100.0
1968	149 276	15 590	268 465	-18 961	-67 338	347 031	258 101	12 009	28 898	21 492	101.6	103.3
1969	158 038	16 378	271 565	-20 523	-69 193	356 264	276 259	12 263	29 052	22 528	102.2	108.3
1970	169 440	18 324	274 384	-21 455	-71 696	368 997	296 031	12 507	29 503	23 669	103.8	113.8
1971	178 938	19 072	283 603	-23 639	-73 840	384 134	307 920	13 067	29 397	23 565	103.4	113.3
1972	188 850	20 722	286 080	-23 769	-75 606	396 277	320 073	13 304	29 786	24 058	104.8	115.6
1973	199 942	21 555	287 773	-21 107	-77 271	410 892	328 598	13 505	30 425	24 332	107.0	117.0
1974	212 670	21 979	289 756	-20 505	-79 496	424 404	341 871	13 723	30 926	24 912	108.8	119.7
1975	213 687	22 652	290 743	-25 791	-81 613	419 677	345 961	13 893	30 208	24 902	106.2	119.7
1976	212 093	22 452	291 112	-27 316	-83 135	415 206	355 317	14 033	29 588	25 320	104.1	121.7
1977	210 907	21 838	291 828	-33 037	-85 196	406 341	367 620	14 192	28 632	25 903	100.7	124.5
1978	207 509	21 729	292 670	-38 828	-86 881	396 198	370 917	14 359	27 592	25 832	97.0	124.2
1979	204 060	20 992	293 293	-41 561	-89 154	387 631	386 460	14 516	26 704	26 623	93.9	128.0
1980	207 417	21 556	294 304	-47 009	-91 873	384 396	398 578	14 695	26 158	27 123	92.0	130.4
1981	213 136	20 396	296 191	-48 287	-94 042	387 394	412 068	14 923	25 960	27 613	91.3	132.7
1982	218 264	20 232	298 635	-52 603	-96 106	388 421	425 137	15 184	25 581	27 999	90.0	134.6
1983	222 446	23 401	300 092	-59 099	-98 161	388 680	415 056	15 394	25 249	26 962	88.8	129.6
1984	227 220	23 910	301 059	-59 391	-99 555	393 243	434 458	15 579	25 242	27 887	88.8	134.0
1985	238 925	23 146	302 424	-60 108	-103 233	401 154	457 594	15 788	25 409	28 984	89.4	139.3
1986	242 367	23 831	304 127	-66 045	-105 138	399 142	477 932	16 018	24 918	29 837	87.6	143.4

Table 5.2 (continued)

Year	Weighted CON_{ADJ} ($)	Infrastr. services ($)	Non-paid labour ($)	Social costs ($)	Weighted LNCS ($)	GPI ($)	GDP ($)	Australian population (000s)	Per capita GPI ($)	Per capita GDP ($)	Per capita GPI 1967 = 100	Per capita GDP 1967 = 100
	A	*B*	*C*	*D*	*E*	*F*	*G*	*H*	*I*	*J*	*K*	*L*
1987	236 102	25 557	306 050	-72 927	-106 182	388 600	489 481	16 264	23 893	30 096	84.0	144.7
1988	249 702	26 317	308 319	-69 457	-108 153	406 727	514 739	16 532	24 602	31 136	86.5	149.7
1989	253 858	26 649	310 771	-72 980	-108 997	409 302	533 794	16 814	24 342	31 746	85.6	152.6
1990	260 841	28 292	312 630	-70 872	-112 919	417 971	554 819	17 065	24 493	32 512	86.1	156.3
1991	264 014	33 199	313 909	-74 765	-115 857	420 500	551 261	17 284	24 329	31 894	85.6	153.3
1992	267 822	35 612	315 016	-77 015	-117 344	424 091	551 722	17 495	24 241	31 537	85.3	151.6
1993	270 462	33 344	316 002	-81 360	-119 451	418 998	571 887	17 667	23 716	32 370	83.4	155.6
1994	274 859	31 468	317 209	-74 436	-121 298	427 802	595 360	17 855	23 960	33 345	84.3	160.3
1995	285 507	28 025	318 857	-71 598	-124 160	436 631	622 057	18 072	24 161	34 421	85.0	165.5
1996	296 088	28 494	320 814	-70 013	-127 647	447 736	647 659	18 311	24 452	35 370	86.0	170.0
1997	306 889	28 912	322 660	-75 682	-129 802	452 977	673 099	18 518	24 462	36 349	86.0	174.7
1998	312 046	29 522	322 942	-75 196	-132 153	457 162	703 258	18 711	24 432	37 585	85.9	180.7
1999	325 999	31 668	323 970	-77 931	-134 406	469 301	739 629	18 926	24 797	39 080	87.2	187.9
2000	338 626	32 286	325 172	-75 834	-137 960	482 291	769 045	19 153	25 180	40 152	88.6	193.0
2001	349 285	36 634	326 838	-76 807	-143 280	492 671	784 017	19 413	25 378	40 386	89.3	194.1
2002	360 576	35 187	327 983	-73 219	-145 378	505 148	813 542	19 641	25 719	41 421	90.5	199.1
2003	374 655	32 579	329 160	-89 440	-146 367	500 588	839 187	19 873	25 190	42 228	88.6	203.0
2004	393 790	31 787	330 123	-86 293	-145 877	523 529	873 197	20 092	26 057	43 461	91.6	208.9
2005	411 407	32 285	331 493	-94 257	-153 363	527 564	896 568	20 340	25 938	44 080	91.2	211.9
2006	425 649	35 075	333 086	-94 030	-163 564	536 215	921 747	20 605	26 023	44 733	91.5	215.0

Note: All monetary values are in millions of 2004–05 dollars except where indicated.

billion in 1967 to $425.6 billion in 2006. This constitutes a rise of 205.8 per cent over the study period or an average rate of increase equivalent to 2.9 per cent per annum. Only in the years 1976–79 and in 1987 did the value of this item decline. On a per capita basis, weighted consumption rose by 75.1 per cent from $11 795 to $20 658 per Australian, which is equivalent to an average rate of increase of 1.4 per cent per annum.

Interestingly, the welfare contribution of weighted consumption was equivalent to just 52.3 per cent of the welfare contribution made by non-paid labour in 1967 (column *C*) but was 27.8 per cent higher than non-paid labour by the end of the study period. This not only reflects technological advances in household appliances – thereby reducing the time spent performing household chores – but also, more particularly, the increasing participation rate of women in the Australian labour force and a transference of many household tasks into the market domain (e.g., child care).

Another major economic benefit, the service provided by infrastructural capital, is revealed in column *B* of Table 5.2 (Item *h* in Table 5.1). Whilst infrastructural capital is an essential feature of a well-functioning economy, column *B* indicates that its contribution to Australia's welfare was considerably less than the contribution made by durable and non-durable consumption goods. At $14.5 billion in 1967, the services provided by infrastructural capital constituted just 10.4 per cent of the welfare contribution made by consumption goods. Whilst the services provided by infrastructural capital increased to $35.1 billion by 2006, its welfare contribution had fallen to a mere 8.2 per cent of the contribution generated by consumption goods.

Column *C* in Table 5.2 reveals what is essentially both an economic and social benefit – namely, the value of non-paid labour (Items *i* and *j* in Table 5.1). Throughout the entire study period, non-paid labour constituted a major component of the aggregate GPI value. However, despite increasing from $266.2 billion in 1967 to $333.1 billion in 2006, the value of non-paid labour fell on a per capita basis from $22 563 to $16 165 per Australian. Some of the reasons for this decline were outlined above. There are, nonetheless, deeper underlying reasons for the per capita fall in non-paid labour that are symptomatic of other welfare-declining factors. These will be discussed in the policy section of the chapter.

The social costs associated with the growing Australian economy are presented in column *D* of Table 5.2. The annual values in this column are equal to the aggregation of Items *k–p* in Table 5.1. Although the change in foreign debt need not be a negative value, Item *p* was included in the social cost category because its value was negative in all but one year. Australia's social costs increased dramatically over the study period from $19 billion in 1967 to $94 billion in 2006. This represents a 394.8 per cent increase or an average rise of 4.2 per cent per annum. From a per capita perspective, social costs grew from $1611 to $4563 per Australian over the study period which constitutes a 183.3 per cent increase or an average rise of 2.7 per cent per annum.

Some of Australia's more significant social cost items were:

- the cost of unemployment and underemployment (Item *k*), which increased from $1.4 billion in 1967 to $15.2 billion in 2006, although it peaked at $19.9 billion in 1993;
- the cost of crime (Item *l*), which increased from $4.4 billion in 1967 to $13.2 billion in 2006, although it peaked at $18.2 billion in 2001;
- the cost of overwork (Item *n*), which increased from $7.5 billion in 1967 to $21.7 billion in 2006;
- the change in net foreign debt (Item *p*), which began at –$3.8 billion in 1967, fell to negligible levels in the mid-1970s, but generally rose thereafter to be –$37.2 billion by 2006.

The most significant cost resulting from the growth of the Australian economy was the weighted value of lost natural capital services – in effect, the cost of natural capital depletion (Column *E* in Table 5.2). Beginning at $65.5 billion in 1967, the weighted value of lost natural capital services increased every year, except in 2004, to finish at $163.6 billion in 2006. Overall, the value in column *E* grew by 149.9 per cent over the study period or by an average rate of 2.4 per cent per annum. On a per capita basis, the weighted value of Australia's lost natural capital services increased from $5548 to $7938 per Australian between 1967 and 2006.

Contributing most to the large rise in Australia's lost natural capital services were the costs of non-renewable resource depletion (Item *q*), land degradation (Item *r*), excessive irrigation water use (Item *s*), long-term environmental damage (Item *z*), and, to a lesser extent, the cost of air pollution (Item *v*). The Ecosystem Health Index (EHI) used to weight the sum total of lost natural capital services fell considerably from 100 to 90.5 over the study period. When compared to 1967, native vegetation clearance contributed a further 10 per cent to the combined cost of Australia's natural capital depletion in 2006.

Australia's GPI versus GDP

The annual values of Australia's GPI are revealed in Column *F* of Table 5.2 and equal the sum of the values contained in columns *A* to *E*. Overall, Australia's GPI increased from $335.5 billion in 1967 to $536.2 billion in 2006. This amounts to a 59.8 per cent rise over the study period or an average rate of increase of 1.2 per cent per annum. However, it should be noted that the value of Australia's GPI was virtually the same in both 1974 and 1992 ($424.4 billion and $424.1 billion respectively). It also fluctuated considerably during this 18-year period. Conversely, Australia's real GDP (column *G* in Table 5.2) increased every year except in 1983 and 1991 and, moreover, grew at a much higher average rate of 3.5 per cent per annum.

Of particular significance is the observation that Australia's GPI was considerably higher than its real GDP in 1967 ($335.5 billion compared to $245.5 billion) but massively lower in 2006 ($536.2 billion compared to $921.7 billion). Australia's real GDP overtook the GPI in 1980 after which the disparity between the two indicators grew in every year apart from 1983, 1991, and 1992.

In many ways, per capita values are more relevant than aggregate values since they convey enhanced information about the genuine progress of the average citizen. With this in mind, the per capita values of Australia's GPI and GDP are revealed in Columns *I* and *J* of Table 5.2. They are also diagrammatically presented in Figure 5.1. In order to provide a clearer picture of the relative changes between Australia's per capita GPI and GDP, both indicators are provided in indexed form in Columns *K* and *L* of Table 5.2. They are also presented in Figure 5.2.

The most disturbing feature about Australia's per capita GPI is that it is lower in 2006 ($26 023 per Australian) than in 1967 ($28 432 per Australian). Worse still, Australia's per capita GPI peaked at $30 926 per Australian in 1974. Thus, while the average Australian experienced an 8.8 per cent increase in sustainable welfare between 1967 in 1974, sustainable welfare fell by 30.4 per cent to $23 716 per Australian in 1993, before rising by 9.7 per cent between 1993 and 2006. In all, Australia's per capita GPI was 8.5 per cent lower in 2006 than in 1967.

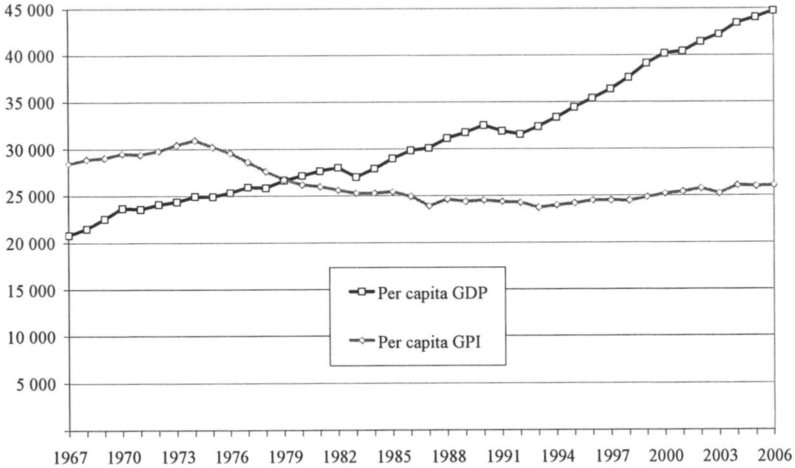

Note: Valued at 2004/2005 prices.

Figure 5.1 Per capita GPI versus per capita GDP: Australia, 1967–2006

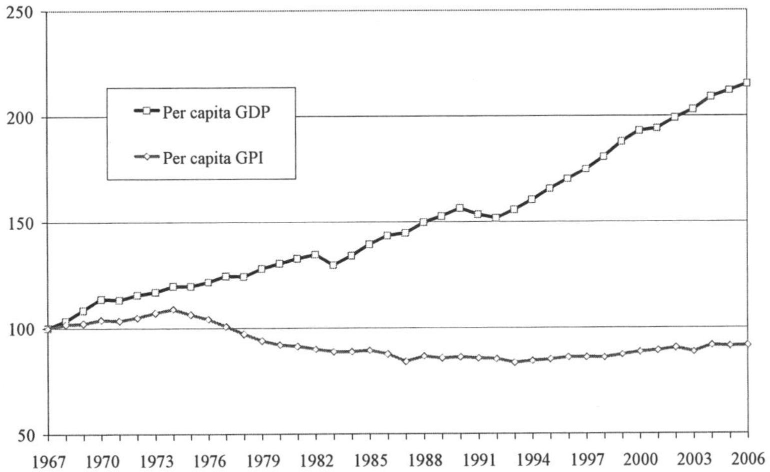

Note: 1967 = 100.

Figure 5.2 Index values of per capita GPI and per capita GDP: Australia, 1967–2006

Australia's per capita GDP, on the other hand, rose in almost every year between 1967 and 2006 and finished 115 per cent higher by the end of the study period ($20 804 per Australian in 1967 compared to $44 733 per Australian in 2006). By 2006, Australia's per capita GDP was $18 710 per Australian more than its per capita GPI.

Given the enormous and growing disparity between the per capita values of Australia's GPI and GDP, it is clear that per capita GDP greatly overstated the genuine progress made by Australia over the study period. Indeed, Australia's per capita GPI suggests that little if any genuine progress was forged over the past 20 years which, as Figure 5.1 illustrates, followed a period of decline in sustainable welfare between the mid-1970s and mid-1980s. In addition, there appears to have been a change in the relationship between Australia's per capita GPI and GDP. Early in the study period (1967–74), the relationship was strictly a positive one – that is, Australia's per capita GPI rose and fell in unison with fluctuations in per capita GDP. Beyond 1974, the relationship was predominantly a negative one suggesting that Australia's 'threshold' level of per capita GDP may have been reached in the mid-1970s.

The comparison between Australia's per capita GPI and GDP poses a number of important questions. They are:

- Would Australia's per capita GPI have been higher if its real GDP had grown at a substantially lower rate but been qualitatively better, in terms of both its content and the means by which it was generated? That is, could a smaller but qualitatively superior rate of economic output have yielded greater welfare benefits and reduced the social and environmental costs of Australia's economic activity?
- Should a high rate of growth of real GDP continue to be the prime objective of Australian economic policy, can Australian policy-makers be certain that the economic benefits of growth will increase in the future, as they have in the past, when it is clear that the social and environmental costs of growth are on the rise and show no sign of abating?

The final question may prove to be as important as the previous two insofar as a continuing high-growth policy could eventually result in a dramatic fall in Australia's per capita GPI. If so, Australia will urgently need to make the transition to a lower rate of growth and discover ways to increase sustainable welfare without the need for higher rates of economic output.

Dominant Influences on Australia's GPI

To assist in answering the above questions, this section involves a close examination of the factors that have had the greatest impact on Australia's GPI over the study period. Examination of the underlying influences provides policy guidance in the sense that an understanding of how and why particular items have affected Australia's GPI brings to attention the action required to augment the positive influences and minimise the negative factors.

Figure 5.3 graphically presents Australia's per capita GPI as well as the per capita values of the major benefit and cost categories in Table 5.2. Figure 5.3 clearly shows that two of the major benefit categories – weighted consumption and non-paid labour – had a much greater influence over Australia's per capita GPI than infrastructural services.

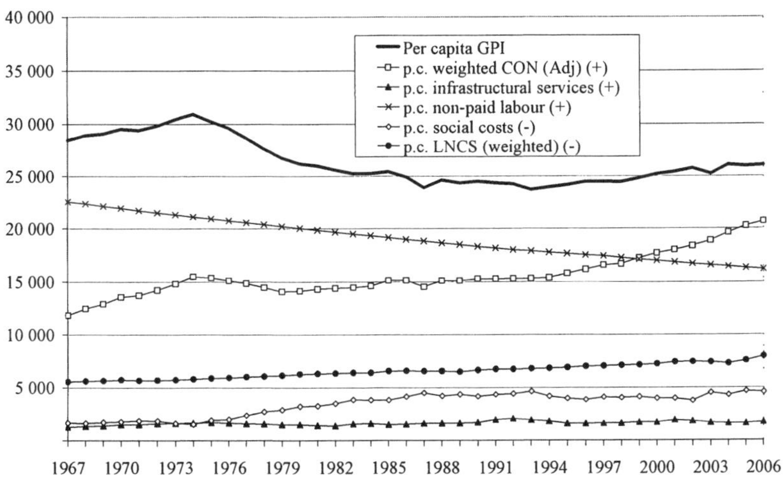

Note: Valued at 2004/2005 prices.

Figure 5.3 Per capita GPI and its major component categories: Australia, 1967–2006

Whilst the gradual diminution in the per capita value of non-paid labour played a considerable role in the general decline in Australia's per capita GPI, as mentioned earlier, this fall largely reflected the transference of many non-paid household services into the market domain. One would therefore have expected corresponding upward pressure on the weighted consumption item in the form of increased household expenditure on takeaway food, child care, household cleaning services, and so on. This certainly eventuated; however, per capita weighted consumption did not always rise. Indeed, for a lengthy spell during the study period (mid-1970s to mid-1990s), per capita weighted consumption remained quite steady – a reflection over this 20-year period of a weak rise in total consumption expenditure and a deterioration in the distribution of income.

This aside, per capita weighted consumption had a significant impact on the trend movement of Australia's per capita GPI. From 1967 to 1974, per capita weighted consumption rose sharply at a time when Australia's per capita GPI rapidly increased. The decline in per capita weighted consumption between 1974 and 1979 corresponded with the steepest fall in Australia's per capita GPI, while the meagre general increase in per capita weighted consumption between 1979 and 1993 occurred at a time when Australia's per capita GPI also fell, albeit at a much reduced rate.

Between 1994 and 2006, per capita weighted consumption again rose sharply but, interestingly, its positive influence on the rise in Australia's per capita GPI was not nearly as strong as it was during the 1967–74 period. This, it seems, was due to the more rapid increase in social and environmental costs that accompanied the larger Australian economy of the 1994–2006 period. In other words, the physical scale of the Australian economy required to generate the consumption-related benefits enjoyed by Australians between 1994 and 2006 came at a considerably higher social and environmental cost than in the 1967–74 period.

Turning, now, to the social and environmental cost categories, the impact of social costs on Australia's per capita GPI was mixed. For example, until 1974, per capita social costs were relatively inconsequential and therefore had little impact on Australia's per capita GPI. However, between 1974 and 1987, per capita social costs steadily increased. In fact, the rise in per capita social costs during this period played a more influential role in the decline of Australia's per capita GPI than per capita environmental costs – the result of a ballooning foreign debt and the rising costs of crime and unemployment.

In the second half of the study period (1987–2006), per capita social costs varied considerably. They consequently played a key part in the fluctuating fortunes of Australia's per capita GPI over the latter part of the study period. This was due to a number of factors. Firstly, the cost of unemployment rose sharply in the early 1990s but declined towards the end of the study period. Secondly, the cost of underemployment began to loom large from the mid-1990s onwards. Thirdly, the cost of crime increased between 1987 and 2001 but fell in the last five years of the study period. Fourthly, the cost of overwork increased between 1987 and 1993, fell significantly between 1993 and 1996, and rose dramatically after 2002. Finally, the growth of Australia's foreign debt slowed between 1987 and 1998 but escalated rapidly towards the end of the study period.

From an environmental perspective, the steady rise in the per capita weighted value of lost natural capital services was an instrumental factor in the general downward movement of Australia's per capita GPI between 1974 and 1993. However, environmental costs had little to do with the year-to-year fluctuations of Australia's per capita GPI except, perhaps, in the last three years of the study period when Australia experienced one of its rare declines in the per capita weighted value of lost natural capital services only to be followed by the two highest annual increases in this major cost category.

Returning to the earlier questions, it is difficult to estimate what Australia's per capita GPI might have been had Australia produced a lower but qualitatively superior rate of economic output. There is little doubt, however, that Australia's environmental costs would have been substantially lower, as too might have been Australia's foreign debt because better rather than more production reduces the need to import high value-added goods. Furthermore, it increases the potential export revenue earned from wealthy nations hungry for high-tech goods and services.

Exactly in what direction other social costs may have moved over the study period is, again, difficult to ascertain. Presumably the cost of overwork would have been much lower, along with the cost of crime and family breakdown, since having to work fewer hours reduces the strain on families and lessens the incidence of psychological disorders. Having said this, the cost of unemployment and underemployment might have been higher which, as mentioned in earlier chapters, can lead to a rise in social costs. Should a low rate of growth or eventual transition to a steady-state economy be necessary to lower environmental costs or, more dramatically, to ensure ecological sustainability, the challenge clearly exists for policy-makers to devise ways to maintain healthy employment levels without the need for high rates of GDP growth. In Australia and elsewhere, there appears to be minimal if any evidence of employment levels being maintained in all but the presence of growing economic output. Worse still, very little research has been conducted on this issue. It is therefore a challenge to academicians as well as policy-makers to overcome this potential environment–employment dilemma (Lawn, 2004).

Much the same can be said in relation to the distribution of income and its probable impact on Australia's per capita GPI. There is a very strong possibility that the aggregate welfare contribution of consumption would have been substantially higher over the middle and latter parts of the study period had the distribution of Australia's income become more rather than less equitable, or at least if Australia's income distribution had not deteriorated after the mid-1970s.

There will, of course, be some observers who will point out that attempts to equalise the distribution of income over time eventually dilutes the incentive structure built into a market economy which, in turn, reduces productivity. They might therefore argue that had Australia focused its attention primarily on redistributing income from the rich to the poor, the associated decline in productivity would have brought about a reduction in economic benefits reflected by significantly lower levels of consumption expenditure. There is no doubt that the marginal benefit of an increasingly equal share of income is eventually outweighed by the marginal cost.[11] However, the improvement in the distribution of income between 1967 and 1974 coincided, not with a decline in consumption, but with a 41.2 per cent increase in raw consumption expenditure. This, in itself, does not indicate with certainty what the productivity implications would have been had Australia adopted a more austere redistribution policy throughout the entire study period. Nevertheless, it is fairly safe to assume that maintaining the relative distribution of income as it was in 1974 would not have undesirably impacted on Australia's productivity. Indeed, there might well have been further room for additional redistribution gains. Above all, and given the burgeoning social and environmental costs of a growing Australian economy as depicted by Figure 5.3, a policy focus on distributional equity would probably have done a great deal more to boost Australia's per capita GPI beyond the mid-1970s than the standard approach to poverty alleviation – namely, a high growth rate of real GDP.

Finally, in answer to the last question, there is certainly no guarantee that the marginal benefits of a growing Australian economy will continue to outweigh the marginal costs and that Australia's per capita GPI will continue to rise at the minuscule rate that it has since 1993. Indeed, given the rapid rate at which Australia's social and environmental costs have continued to escalate, there is a strong likelihood that Australia's per capita GPI will again start declining if Australian policy-makers persist with a high-growth objective. It would therefore seem apparent that Australia should initially move to a lower rate of growth and eventually make the full transition to a steady-state economy.

By steady-state economy I do not mean a dull, static, and stultifying economy. I mean an economy that, while effectively non-growing in a physical sense, is in dynamic equilibrium with the ecosystem that supports it, which means, first and foremost, it is designed to be ecologically sustainable. Furthermore, as intimated in Chapter 1, it is an economy that qualitatively improves in terms of: (a) the goods existing within the economy (thereby increasing the service each good yields); (b) the means by which all goods are produced and maintained (thereby reducing the environmental impact per unit of economic activity as well as the cost of overwork, unemployment, crime, and family breakdown); (c) the distribution of income and wealth (thereby increasing the aggregate welfare contribution of consumption); and (d) the purpose for which the entire stock of goods is intended.

Irrespective of how quickly the growth rate in real GDP should be slowed, advancing Australia's GPI will undoubtedly require a greater policy focus on value-adding in production, greater resource use efficiency, distributional equity, and natural capital maintenance.[12] But it will be natural capital maintenance, more than any other factor, which will govern the necessary deceleration rate of Australia's real GDP.

Critics will be quick to stress that Australia's per capita GPI declined at its greatest rate during the stagflation years of 1974–83 when per capita GDP rose at an average rate of just 0.9 per cent per annum. They would therefore argue that a return to a low-growth regime might just as easily condemn Australians to a dramatic decline in sustainable welfare. There is, however, a fundamental difference between zero growth in a stagflation environment and a steady-state economy exhibiting clear signs of qualitative improvement. The former, it has to be said, is effectively a euphemism for a failed growth economy and is in no way a portent to what can be expected in the presence of a successfully functioning steady-state economy.[13]

POLICY IMPLICATIONS

The need for Australia to rethink its obsession with a high growth rate and to make the eventual transition to a steady-state economy has considerable policy implications. To begin with, Australian policy-makers must ensure the rate of material and energy throughput – that is, the input of resources and the output of pollution and waste – remains within the regenerative and waste-assimilative capacities of Australia's renewable natural capital. Not only is this a sustainability requirement (i.e., it prevents the diminution of renewable natural capital), it is also necessary if Australia is to overturn the rising cost of land degradation, excessive water use, fisheries depletion, long-term environmental damage, and air and solid waste pollution.

Policies to Maintain Natural Capital and Lower Environmental Costs

In order to impose quantitative restrictions on the rate of material and energy throughput, Australian policy-makers are best advised to introduce a system of tradeable resource use permits.[14] Unlike Pigouvian taxes, which cannot guarantee a sustainable rate of throughput (see Daly, 1991 and 1992; Lawn, 2007), a system of tradeable resource use permits explicitly limits the quantity of resources exploited and used over a specific time period. This is achieved by limiting the number of permits periodically auctioned off by a relevant government authority. With the power to regulate the incoming resource flow, the government authority is able to select the number of permits it makes available for sale to ensure that the rate of throughput is consistent with the regenerative and waste-assimilative capacities of the existing stock of renewable natural capital. As an added bonus, the premium paid by resource buyers for resource use permits acts as a throughput tax to facilitate the efficient allocation of the incoming resource flow, thereby encouraging greater production efficiency, more durable goods, and higher rates of materials recycling. So as to maximise the effectiveness of the system, a specific arrangement would exist for each renewable resource type and for different geographical and jurisdictional locations within Australia.

Whilst a system of tradeable resource use permits is able to regulate the quantity of waste generated by the economic process – a consequence of the first law of thermodynamics – it cannot influence the qualitative nature of the wastes generated.[15] For this reason, Australian policy-makers need to introduce pollution taxes or, better still, consider introducing assurance bonds to discourage the generation of particular forms of pollution (Costanza and Perrings, 1990). With assurance bonds, a polluting firm pays a bond equal to the cost of the worst-case pollution scenario. Should the owners of a bond-paying firm demonstrate that the pollution they have subsequently generated has had no deleterious impact on the natural environment, they receive the bond back in full plus any interest accrued over the period in which the bond has been held by a government authority. If the pollution has an undesirable impact on the natural environment, the bond is confiscated either in full (where pollution damage equals the worst-case scenario) or in part (where pollution damage is something less than the worst-case scenario). If the worst-case scenario is unacceptably risky (i.e., it involves highly toxic substances), the generation of the substances in question may require prohibition or generation under strictly controlled conditions. Together with the premiums paid for resource use permits, confiscated bond money should be used for redistribution purposes and environmental rehabilitation projects.

In view of the 9.5 per cent decline in Australia's Ecosystem Health Index (EHI) over the study period, Australian policy-makers need to halt the clearance of native vegetation. In addition, future exploitation of Australia's natural capital should be confined to areas already significantly modified by past human activities. This, in turn, facilitates the preservation, restoration, and rehabilitation of critical ecosystems. Unfortunately, while in some states of Australia vegetation clearance is strictly controlled, in other states it is not. A sensible policy response requires the establishment of co-ordinated clearance controls at the national level where, importantly, the Federal Government is better positioned to compensate affected land owners than State Governments. Compensation is necessary both for equity reasons and to encourage land owners to conserve and manage protected vegetation.

Australia must also introduce policies to encourage the cultivation of renewable resources to offset the inevitable depletion of non-renewable resources. Whilst Australia relies heavily upon the proceeds from non-renewable resource depletion to finance its expenditure on household goods and its accumulation of human-made capital (producer goods), the lack of any broad-scale augmentation of its renewable resource stocks indicates that Australia is failing to utilise some of its depletion profits to keep its total stock of natural capital intact. The El Serafy formula outlined in Chapter 3 (equation 3.12), which was used in this study to calculate the cost of Australia's non-renewable resource depletion, should be operationalised by compelling resource liquidators to establish a 'capital replacement' account in the same way that it is necessary for most business managers to establish a superannuation fund for employees (Lawn, 1998). This could be done through appropriate changes in Australia's accounting legislation.

Policies to Lower Social Costs

In terms of social costs, there is an urgent need for Australia to introduce policies that minimise the cost of overwork, crime, and family breakdown. Current incentives and disincentives – caused largely by market distortions such as the failure to publicly remunerate non-paid household work – are restricting the options available to Australians and forcing them to make choices that are not always in their welfare interests. For example, many Australians have been forced to spend more time in paid forms of employment which has led to a marked increase in the expenditure on child care, house cleaning and gardening services, and unhealthy forms of fast food (Pocock, 2004). Australian policy-makers should therefore consider introducing a negative income tax. A negative income tax involves both a universal payment to each citizen (separate to any other form of welfare payment – e.g., pension) and taxation at the margin on all sources of income. Ideally, the so-called demogrant would reflect the average person's non-paid contribution to the aggregate welfare of Australia. This would overcome the current labour market distortion as well as induce a real labour supply withdrawal that, in turn, would reduce the level of real GDP required to achieve full employment (Lawn, 2005).

Similar criticism can also be levelled at recent modifications to Australia's industrial relations system. Despite increasing the flexibility of labour markets in some respects, they appear to have undermined a number of basic conditions of employment critical to the welfare of workers and the family unit (Denniss, 2003).[16] Given that labour market flexibility is a vital component in any attempt to increase labour productivity, existing flexibility should not be indiscriminately sacrificed. However, there is an urgent need for Australian policy-makers to refine the current industrial relations system so it promotes genuine labour market flexibility without undermining the minimum awards and conditions of employment that Australians have fought long and hard to obtain.

More also needs to be done by Australian policy-makers to reduce unemployment and, in particular, the growing incidence of underemployment. The continuing acceptance of high unemployment rates is not only morally unjustified, it is also unnecessary (Wray, 1998; Mitchell and Watts, 2002; Tcherneva, 2006). As previously mentioned, this will require policies to eliminate unemployment and underemployment without the perceived need to increase economic output. One possibility is the introduction of a so-called Job Guarantee – a demand-side policy whereby the central government acts as a buffer stock employer to absorb all unemployed labour displaced by the private sector (Mitchell and Watts, 1997).

Although, on the surface, it appears as though a Job Guarantee would increase real GDP, this would not be the case if it was combined with a negative income tax and a system of tradeable resource use permits as outlined above. As mentioned, the negative income tax would induce a real labour supply withdrawal whilst tradeable resource use permits would limit economic output to an ecologically sustainable level. Initially, some people could be pushed out of private sector employment into a Job Guarantee occupation but, eventually, given the faster rate of resource-saving technological progress that a system of tradeable resource use permits is likely to induce, private sector employment ought to rise to pre-Job Guarantee levels, if not increase overall.

Finally, Australian policy-makers need to overturn the growing imbalance between rich and poor. The public remuneration of non-paid work and a greater commitment to full employment through a Job Guarantee would assist enormously in this regard. In addition, some of the revenue raised from the sale of resource use permits, pollution taxes, and confiscated assurance bonds can also be used for redistribution purposes.

Policies to Facilitate Production Excellence

As for the need to improve the quality of Australia's production, the Australian taxation system is not particularly helpful. It discourages value-adding in production by excessively taxing income, wages, and profit. To make matters worse, it encourages investment in unproductive 'rent-seeking' endeavours.[17] This is a disconcerting trend compounded by a lack of tax incentives to facilitate the development of resource-saving and pollution-reducing technologies. Clearly, the Australian taxation system requires modification to ensure appropriate incentives and disincentives are in place to promote beneficial forms of economic activity, to bring about a more equitable distribution of income and wealth, and to overcome the current market distortion caused by the non-remuneration of household and volunteer work.

If Australian policy-makers were to combine a reduction in taxes on income, wages, and profit with a system of tradeable resource permits and assurance bonds they would essentially be instituting what is now popularly termed *ecological tax reform* (Lawn, 2007). And, since confiscated assurance bonds and permit premiums could, in part, finance the tax cuts needed to encourage production excellence, ecological tax reform can offer a tax revenue-neutral means of achieving sustainable development in Australia.

It goes beyond saying that production excellence depends critically on the quality of a nation's workforce. Australia, like any nation, must continue to invest heavily in education and training to maintain a workforce capable of producing the high-quality goods of today as well as the superior goods of tomorrow. But it must also ensure that its infrastructural capital, particularly the infrastructural assets provided by governments, is maintained at adequate levels and is of appropriate quality. Unfortunately, the fall in the relative welfare contribution of Australia's infrastructural capital suggests there is a growing propensity for Australia to consume excessively at the expense of urgently needed infrastructural investment. Of course, it might instead reflect the accumulation of a more productive and efficient stock of infrastructural capital. Evidence has recently emerged indicating that infrastructural 'bottlenecks' have impeded Australia's productivity growth in recent years (Brown, 2005). It is therefore likely that the former position is the correct one. Assuming this to be the case, governments at all levels need to place greater emphasis on future infrastructural investment.

CONCLUDING REMARKS

Although well placed to lay the foundation for a just, efficient, and ecologically sustainable society, it would appear that Australia has failed to make any significant genuine progress since the mid-1970s. Australia has continued to adopt a high-growth-rate policy as reflected by a doubling of its per capita real GDP between 1967 and 2006. Despite considerable increases in the economic benefits of this growth, the social and environmental costs have escalated to such an extent that, should a high rate of GDP growth remain the prime objective of Australian economic policy, a rise in the sustainable welfare of the average Australian cannot be guaranteed into the future.

Australian policy-makers should therefore begin the transition to a lower rate of growth to enable Australia to make the smooth transition to a steady-state economy. Within the low-growth context, policies must be redirected towards value-adding in production, greater resource use efficiency, natural capital maintenance, and a more just distribution of income and wealth. A number of policies have been put forward in this chapter to make such a transition and to bring about a rise in Australia's per capita GPI. Perhaps the most significant of all is the concept of ecological tax reform, since it offers the best hope for Australia in terms of resolving the three critical macro goals of ecological sustainability, distribution equity, and allocative efficiency – the latter particularly important if Australia is to experience qualitative improvement and reduced environmental stress per unit of economic activity.

To be ultimately successful, ecological tax reform will require Australian policy-makers to introduce something akin to assurance bonds and a system of tradeable resource use permits. At the very least, they will need to introduce a policy mechanism designed to quantitatively restrict the rate of material and energy throughput. Given the political hurdles that are likely to emerge in this regard, Australian policy-makers may have to be content with the initial levying of depletion and pollution taxes – a deficient sustainability instrument – to prepare the Australian economy, and its citizens, for the eventual imposition of much harsher throughput constraints.

NOTES

1. The ratio of external debt to GDP continued to increase to 41.5 per cent by 1993 (Foster, 1996, Table 1.21).
2. Australia's Corruption Perception Index in 2005 was 8.8, where a maximum score of 10 implies zero corruption. This compares favourably with other low-corruption countries such as Sweden (9.2), Canada (8.4), the USA (7.6), and Japan (7.3) (Transparency International, 2005).
3. The choice of years was largely dictated by the availability of data, most of which appears in a comprehensive form beyond the financial year of 1966/67.
4. The cost of overwork has been included in some past GPI studies (e.g., Redefining Progress, 1995).
5. This is based on 37.5 hours being a standard working week. Overwork therefore constitutes the difference between the average number of hours worked by full-time workers and 37.5 hours.
6. Constitutionally, the plan must be approved by the relevant states of New South Wales, Victoria, Queensland, and South Australia. To date, approval has not been given.
7. As at 2006, close to one tonne of solid waste per year per Australian ends up at a landfill site. This amounts to around 3 kilograms per day or 20 kilograms per week.
8. Swamps and marshes have a net primary productivity per unit area of 800–3500 tonnes per square kilometre (average of 2000 tonnes), while estuaries have a net primary productivity of 2000–3500 tonnes per square kilometre (average of 2500 tonnes) (Jackson and Jackson, 2000). This compares with cultivated land (average 650 tonnes).
9. The results of this study differ to GPI results calculated in the past on Australia in Lawn (2000) and Lawn and Clarke (2006). The 2000 study includes different items and some alternative valuation methods, the latter due largely to the availability of superior data. The 2006 study compared the Australian state of Victoria to the rest of Australia and thus required the use of comparable data sets. This impacted on the items chosen to calculate the GPI and, again, the valuation methods employed. In addition, the Victoria versus rest of Australia study spanned the shorter time period of 1986–2003.
10. The years appearing in Table 5.2 are financial years. In Australia, a financial year begins on 1 July and concludes on 30 June. Hence, the first year of the study period, 1967, refers to the financial year ending on 30 June 1967.
11. It also often requires the introduction of unjust forms of redistribution.
12. Based on the strong sustainability stance (see Chapter 4).
13. Daly has likened the difference between a growth economy and a steady-state economy to the difference between an aeroplane and a helicopter. To perform successfully (in the conventional sense), the growth economy must expand at a certain rate just like an aeroplane must travel at a certain speed to fly. If a growth economy ceases to expand at the necessary rate it malfunctions. Similarly, an aeroplane that fails to move forward at the necessary speed falls from the sky. But a steady-state economy need not grow at all to perform

successfully (i.e., to facilitate a rise in the GPI) in the same way that a helicopter need not move forward to fly or, indeed, to fly higher.

14. More detail on how a tradeable resource use permit system would operate can be found in Lawn (2007), Chapter 11.
15. Because of the first law of thermodynamics, the quantity of matter-energy embodied in the resources entering the economy must inevitably equal the quantity of matter-energy embodied in the waste products exiting the economy. Hence, the quantity of waste returning to the natural environment can be controlled simply by regulating the quantity of resources initially entering the economy. There is, therefore, no need to introduce a system of tradeable pollution permits to limit pollution levels. Having said this, tradeable resource use permits cannot influence the qualitative nature of the wastes generated.
16. While it is true that the introduction of Australian Workplace Agreements – effectively a contractual agreement made between employers and individual employees – appears to have resulted in higher take-home pay for workers, it has been at the expense of overtime penalty rates, sick-leave entitlements, and annual leave entitlements. Many might argue that this is the result of a choice made by Australian workers. Others argue that it is the consequence of an imbalance of power in favour of employers as evidenced by the paradox of surveys indicating a strong preference amongst working Australians for fewer working hours yet, strangely, very few Australian Workplace Agreements involving less pay as a trade-off for a shorter working week and more extensive non-pay-related awards.
17. Rent-seeking is defined in a number of ways. In this context, it involves the investment of financial capital into assets that yield the owner economic or scarcity rents, which are effectively profits earned from the increasing scarcity of the assets owned and not because of any improvements made to the assets.

REFERENCES

Anderson, K. (1995), 'Australia's changing trade pattern and growth performance', in R. Pomfret (ed.), *Australia's Trade Policies*, Melbourne: Oxford University Press.

Biodiversity Unit (1995), 'Native vegetation clearance, habitat loss, and biodiversity decline: an overview of recent native vegetation clearance in Australia and its implications for biodiversity', Department of Environment, Sports, and Territories, Biodiversity Series Paper No. 6, AGPS, Canberra.

Boehm, E. (1971), *Twentieth Century Economic Development in Australia*, Melbourne: Longman.

Brown, R. (2005), 'Reserve Bank buys into infrastructure debate', *Local Government Focus*, http://loc-gov-focus.aus.net/editions/2005/march/resbank.html.

Butlin, N. (1962), *Australian Domestic Product, Investment, and Foreign Borrowing 1861–1938/39*, Cambridge: Cambridge University Press.
Centre of Full Employment and Equity (CofFEE) (2007), 'CofFEE labour market indicators', http://e1.newcastle.edu.au/coffee.
Common, M. and Stagl, S. (2005), *Ecological Economics: An Introduction*, Cambridge: Cambridge University Press.
Copland, D. (1934), *Australia in the World Crisis 1929–32*, Cambridge: Cambridge University Press.
Costanza, R. and Perrings, C. (1990), 'A flexible assurance bonding system for improved environmental management', *Ecological Economics*, **2**, 57–76.
Daly, H. (1991), *Steady-State Economics: Second Edition with New Essays*, Washington, DC: Island Press.
Daly, H. (1992), 'Allocation, distribution, and scale: towards an economics that is efficient, just, and sustainable', *Ecological Economics*, **6**, 185–193.
Daly, H. and Cobb, J. (1989), *For the Common Good: Redirecting the Economy Toward Community, the Environment, and a Sustainable Future*, Boston, MA: Beacon Press.
Denniss, R. (2003), 'Annual leave in Australia: an analysis of entitlements, usage, and preferences', Australia Institute Discussion Paper Number 56, July, Canberra: Australia Institute.
El Serafy, S. (1989), 'The proper calculation of income from depletable natural resources', in Y. Ahmad, S. El Serafy and E. Lutz (eds), *Environmental Accounting for Sustainable Development*, Washington, DC: World Bank, pp. 10–18.
Foster, R. (1996), 'Australian economic statistics: 1949/50 to 1994/95', Reserve Bank of Australia Occasional Paper No. 8, Sydney: RBA.
Hamilton, C. (1999), 'The genuine progress indicator: methodological developments and results from Australia', *Ecological Economics*, **30**, 13–28.
INDECS (1992a), 'Inflation', *State of Play*, Sydney: Allen & Unwin.
INDECS (1992b), 'Money and Credit', *State of Play*, Sydney: Allen & Unwin.
Jackson, A. and Jackson, J. (2000), *Environmental Science: The Natural Environment and Human Impact*, 2nd edition, Harlow: Longman.
Lawn, P. (1998), 'In defence of the strong sustainability approach to national income accounting', *Environmental Taxation and Accounting*, **3**, 29–47.
Lawn, P. (2000), *Toward Sustainable Development: An Ecological Economics Approach*, Boca Raton: CRC Press.
Lawn, P. (2004), 'Environment, workplace, and employment: an introduction', *International Journal of Environment, Workplace, and Employment*, **1**, 4–39.

Lawn, P. (2005), 'Full employment and ecological sustainability: comparing the NAIRU, Basic Income, and Job Guarantee approaches, *International Journal of Environment, Workplace, and Employment*, **1**, 336–353.

Lawn, P. (2007), *Frontier Issues in Ecological Economics*, Cheltenham, UK and Northampton, MA, USA: Edward Elgar.

Lawn, P. and Clarke, M. (2006), *Measuring Genuine Progress: An Application of the Genuine Progress Indicator*, New York: Nova Science Publishers.

Mitchell, W. and Watts, M. (1997), 'The path to full employment', *Australian Economic Review*, **30**, 436–444.

Mitchell, W. and Watts, M. (2002), 'Restoring full employment: the Job Guarantee', in E. Carlson and W. Mitchell (eds), *The Urgency of Full Employment*, Sydney: University of New South Wales Press, pp. 95–114.

Pincus, J. (1995), 'Evolution and political economy of Australian trade policies', in R. Pomfret (ed.), *Australia's Trade Policies*, Melbourne: Oxford University Press.

Pocock, B. (2004), 'Work and family futures: how young Australians plan to work and care', Australia Institute Discussion Paper Number 69, August, Canberra: Australia Institute.

Redefining Progress (1995), 'Gross production vs genuine progress', *Genuine Progress Indicator: Summary of Data and Methodology*, San Francisco, CA: Redefining Progress.

Ryan, N., Parker, R. and Brown, K. (2003), *Government, Business, and Society*, Sydney: Prentice Hall.

Saddler, H., Diesendorf, M. and Denniss, R. (2004), *A Clean Energy Future for Australia*, Sydney: Clean Energy Future Group.

Sinclair, W. (1976), *The Process of Economic Development in Australia*, Sydney: Longman Cheshire.

Tcherneva, P. (2006), 'Universal assurances in the public interest: evaluating the economic viability of basic income and job guarantees', *International Journal of Environment, Workplace, and Employment*, **2**, 69–88.

Transparency International (2005), *2005 Corruption Perception Index*, Berlin: Transparency International.

World Bank (2006), *2006 World Development Indicators*, Washington, DC: World Bank.

Wray, R. (1998), *Understanding Modern Money: The Key to Full Employment and Price Stability*, Cheltenham, UK and Lyme, USA: Edward Elgar.

6. Calculating the New Zealand Genuine Progress Indicator

Vicky Forgie, Garry McDonald, Yanjiao Zhang, Murray Patterson, and Derrylea Hardy

INTRODUCTION

Unlike most of the Genuine Progress Indicator (GPI) studies that have been produced to date, this particular GPI study of New Zealand has been funded by a national government.[1] The current New Zealand Government has a commitment to sustainability and, in the words of the Prime Minister, 'in the years to come, the pride we take in our quest for sustainability and carbon neutrality will define our nation, just as our quest for a nuclear free world has over the past twenty three years' (Clark, 2007). The building of the New Zealand GPI has come about as the result of pursuits to find better and more meaningful ways to express the balance required between social, economic, environmental, and cultural elements on the sustainability journey.

Historical Background of New Zealand's Development

New Zealand is a small land mass situated in the southern Pacific Ocean. It is 27 million hectares in size – about the same as the British Isles or Japan. The nation is long and thin with a backbone of high mountainous country. The three largest islands are more than 1600 km long but only 450 km wide at the widest point (Ministry for the Environment, 1997). Approximately one-third of the country, mostly of high elevation, is conservation estate.

Isolation has been a feature of both the biological and economic development of New Zealand. The country was one of the last sizable land masses to be inhabited by humans. The absence of large native mammals (the only endemic mammals are two species of small bats) and people has resulted in a unique biodiversity that has evolved slowly over a long period of time. It is also extremely sensitive to change (Department of Conservation and Ministry for the Environment, 1997).

With a population of just over 4 million, the population density is low by international standards. Settlement by humans has only taken place over the last 800–1000 years but, in this relatively short time period, people have made a notable impact on the unique biodiversity. The first people to do this were the indigenous Maori who introduced new species, such as the kiore (rat) and hunted to extinction large endemic bird species. Trips back to previous settlements were undertaken to introduce exotic plants, such as the kumera.

The arrival of European settlers in the early 1800s heralded the start of major economic and environmental change. Native forests were cleared for agriculture, which became, and continues to be, the mainstay of the New Zealand economy. Economic progress and infrastructural development was led by the government. Public bodies were empowered to use resources to provide services for the population, such as water supply, roads, sewage disposal, and electricity (Wheen, 2002). Agricultural interests, regarded as critical to the nation's economy, were protected and encouraged by legislation.

From a social perspective, isolation allowed New Zealand to set its own norms and values. Many of the European immigrants were keen to leave behind the class systems and social structures of their home countries and exploit the opportunity to own their own land. This provided an impetus for progressive social systems. New Zealand was the first country to give women the vote. Welfare provisions for the general population were first introduced with the Social Security Act 1938, which provided universal superannuation, medical, hospital, and maternity benefits (King, 2003).

Economic, Social, and Environmental Characteristics of New Zealand 1970–2005

In the 1950s and 1960s, New Zealand's per capita Gross Domestic Product (GDP) was one of the highest in the world. The agriculturally-based economy produced goods efficiently and yielded good returns from what were secure markets for butter, meat, and wool in Britain. Loss of access to the British market after Britain joined the European

Economic Community in 1973 reduced the capacity to earn overseas exchange.

During the 1970s and early 1980s, government policies were principally aimed at shielding New Zealanders from the impacts of this change. Monetary policy was directed at maintaining high employment levels and self-sufficiency in energy production, and to control inflation. To achieve these outcomes, the government relied on the protection of domestic industry and extensive overseas borrowing. This policy became untenable with the government eventually having financial difficulty meeting loan repayments and interest costs.

The need for a new policy direction brought about major economic reforms, which were undertaken from 1984 onwards. In the words of the New Zealand Treasury:

> The reforms included the floating of the exchange rate; abolition of controls on capital movements; the ending of industry assistance; the removal of price controls; deregulation across a number of sectors of the economy; corporatisation and privatisation of state-owned assets; and labour market legislation aimed at facilitating more flexible patterns of wage bargaining (The Treasury, 2007, p. 11).

The government was forced to withdraw from many areas of the economy, and the open free market subjected New Zealand industry to competitive pressures and world prices. After a readjustment period in the late 1980s, New Zealand's GDP performance improved significantly during the 1990s.

The New Zealand economy is small by international standards (GDP in 2005 was $148.9 billion) and the openness of the economy subjects the country to significant fluctuations in the exchange rate. A high value for the New Zealand dollar has the effect of reducing the demand for exports while promoting imports at the expense of domestic production. Although the present government has a large budget surplus, the country as a whole possesses a growing current account deficit.

In the 1970s and early 1980s, New Zealand experienced little change in levels of employment, underemployment, and overwork; private defensive expenditure on health and education; and personal consumption. This was principally due to the highly regulated nature of the New Zealand economy which, among other things, featured subsidies to control price and wage fluctuations, state housing and mortgage subsidies for low-income people, and an unemployment rate of 4 per cent or less (Ajwani et al., 2003).

The economic reforms introduced in 1984, which opened the New Zealand economy to the global market, had very drastic social impacts. Impacts of the social dimension included 'a substantially flattened tax system, fully targeted income support, a regressive consumption tax (GST), market rentals for housing, privatised major utilities, user charges for health, education, and other government services, and a restructured labour market designed to facilitate "flexibility"' (Mowbray 2001, cited in Ajwani et al., 2003, p. 50). Further, social welfare cuts in 1990 reduced the mean equivalent disposable income of households receiving welfare benefit payments (Ajwani et al., 2003).

These reforms spiralled New Zealand society into periods of sometimes quite severe change, especially in terms of employment patterns which, accordingly, had flow-on effects. One significant and far-reaching result was the substantial widening of income inequalities and, because socio-economic factors, including income, are known to be a major determinant of health, widened health inequalities. These disparities remain to this day. The impact was therefore felt by many New Zealanders, but not equally. The reforms were beneficial for the people who experienced great increases in personal wealth, incomes, and consumption. But for others (e.g., people who faced unemployment or underemployment coupled with a reduction in comparative real income), the impact was severe.

The move to the free market economy in the late 1980s was accompanied by a restructuring of New Zealand's environmental laws that were aimed at minimising the cost of environmental consents to business, while at the same time setting environmental bottom lines. Environmental law in New Zealand has always facilitated resource development to promote GDP growth (Wheen, 2002). Legislation has enabled access to minerals, fossil fuels, and water. Large-scale transformations of the New Zealand environment have been undertaken by the government for infrastructure construction (e.g. ports, transport networks, and electricity generation) and to bring land into agricultural use (farming and forestry). Major public works have been undertaken to provide employment, social stability, and to stimulate the economy.

The restructured legislation – the Resource Management Act (RMA) 1991 – combined more than 50 statutes and most laws pertaining to the management of air, land, and water (the exceptions related to Crown-owned minerals and fisheries) into the one Act. The purpose of the Act is 'to promote the sustainable management of natural and physical resources'. The legislation to achieve this was 'effects-based and enabling'. 'The focus of the new legislation is seen to be on controlling externalities arising from economic activities rather than the control of the activities themselves (i.e., regulating resource allocation)' (Grundy, 2000, p. 70). The RMA therefore continues to support resource development to promote GDP growth with the constraint that the associated resource use must be sustainable and meet predetermined environmental bottom lines. The Act adopts the 'weak sustainability' ideology with a need to safeguard life-supporting ecosystem services but no requirement to keep intact the stock of natural capital. As stated in Part II, Section 5 of the Act:

> (2) In this Act, *sustainable management* means managing the use, development, and protection of natural and physical resources in a way, or at a rate, which enables people and communities to provide for their social, economic, and cultural wellbeing and for their health and safety while:
> a) Sustaining the potential of natural and physical resources (excluding minerals) to meet the reasonably foreseeable needs of future generations; and
> b) Safeguarding the life-supporting capacity of air, water, soil, and ecosystems; and
> c) Avoiding, remedying, or mitigating any adverse effects of activities on the environment.

The RMA has not prevented environmental degradation from the growth of the New Zealand economy fuelled by an increasing population with higher material demands. Environmental pressure from agriculture, transport, tourism, and energy production and consumption is increasing (Organisation for Economic Co-operation and Development, 2007). New Zealanders pride themselves on their 'clean, green' and '100 per cent pure' environment but misconceptions about the state of the environment are numerous. Current environmental trends are poor, with high energy use, high waste outputs, and degraded water commonplace.

Despite these trends, New Zealanders regard the environment and the outdoor lifestyle as important aspects of their national character:

> In a 2004 study that sought to gauge public concern about growth and innovation, respondents ranked economic growth 10th out of the 12 aspects of New Zealand that were important to them – quality of life, education, and the

> environment were the top three. Further questioning showed there was concern that economic growth should not come at the cost of environmental degradation or lifestyle (Growth and Innovation Advisory Board cited in Pratt and Lowndes, 2005, p. 127).

For successive New Zealand governments, as in other countries, growth in GDP has been the driving force of policy. GDP was never intended as a measure of welfare but has been adopted for this purpose in the absence of more fitting measures. An indicator with a broader perspective is needed if sustainability is an important societal goal.

THE CALCULATION OF THE NEW ZEALAND GPI

For the New Zealand GPI, 13 different social and economic categories and ten different environmental categories were included. The items, whether their welfare impact is positive or negative, and the methods of valuation are listed in Table 6.1.

Social and Economic Categories

The major contributions of the socio-economic categories of the GPI are similar to those incorporated in the GPIs of other nations (see Chapter 3).

Environmental Categories

To calculate the actual dollar value of the change in natural capital stocks, it has been necessary to incorporate elements and use methodologies that are unique to New Zealand. To ensure a consistent treatment of environmental change over time, the following general principles have been adhered to:

1. If expenditure is for production purposes, an adjustment is not made to the GPI (e.g., tuberculosis vector control). Long-term loss of productivity from the loss of an asset (such as soil loss due to the length of time soil takes to replace itself) is considered an environmental cost. A negative adjustment is made accordingly. Short-term losses, such as the loss of output from soil compaction or 'pugging' that can be rectified with appropriate management techniques (over a 20-year period), are assumed to have had a direct

Table 6.1 Items and valuation methods used to calculate the New Zealand GPI, 1970–2005

Item	Welfare impact	Method of valuation
Personal consumption	+	Annualised time-series of private final consumption expenditure obtained from Statistics New Zealand (SNZ). Includes all household outlays on consumer goods and services along with expenditure on non-capital items by private non-profit organisations serving households.
Weighted personal consumption	+	Adjusts personal consumption for income inequality using an Income Distribution Index (IDI) based on Gini coefficients. The year with the smallest recorded inequality (1973) was set as the base year with an index of 100. Derived by dividing personal consumption by the IDI, and then multiplying by 100.
Public consumption (non-defensive)	+	A time series of input–output tables was used to establish the non-defensive proportion of public consumption expenditure by category.
Value of household and community work	+	Calculated as non-leisure time spent on household and community work. Disaggregated by time spent on household and community work in 1999 by age–sex cohort. Adjusted through time for known changes in age–sex cohort demographics. Time use estimates converted to dollars using median wage rate for housekeepers.
Cost of unemployment	–	Indirectly values the involuntary leisure time that unemployment brings. Calculated as total unemployed hours per week multiplied by a cost per hour and then annualised. The cost per hour is calculated as the minimum wage rate per hour less the unemployment benefit divided by 40 hours. Allowances are made for both full- and part-time employment.
Cost of underemployment	–	Indirectly values the involuntary leisure time that underemployment brings. Calculated as total part-time employees looking for work multiplied by the average hours wanted to work per week (23.8 hours) and, in turn, multiplied by the average hourly wage rate. Results are then annualised.
Cost of overwork	–	Calculated as the loss of leisure time. Hours overworked per week (difference between average hours worked and the lowest hours worked in any given year) multiplied by total employment and the average wage rate. Results are annualised.

Table 6.1 (continued)

Item	Welfare impact	Method of valuation
Cost of private defensive expenditure on health and education	–	Calculated as the private defensive expenditure on health and education taken directly from SNZ time–series data. Defensive proportion for health assumed to be 70% in the 1970s, 75% in the 1980s, and 80% from 1990 onwards. Defensive expenditure for education was 10% over time. Adjusted for price changes using the Consumer Price Index.
Services of public capital	–	The services rendered by government-owned capital stocks. Allowances are made for non-defensive (50%) and non-market services (80%). Estimated as the depreciation of capital stocks (adjusted for non-defensive and non-market services) plus the opportunity cost of government investment funds elsewhere in order to gain interest.
Cost of commuting to work	–	Incorporates both the direct (i.e. vehicle purchases, maintenance, bus and train fares etc.) and time costs of commuting to work. Direct costs are calculated for both private and public components of commuting to work. Time costs are estimated as total employment multiplied by hours spent on commuting, multiplied by a cost per hour.
Cost of crime	–	Private sector property loss, property damage and associated administration costs borne by insurance companies. Calculated as total offences multiplied by cost per offence. Requires scaling of recorded offences to derive an estimate of 'actual' offences; this is performed using 'multipliers' provided by the New Zealand Police.
Net capital growth/decline	+/–	Calculated as the difference between two consecutive years' net capital stock. An adjustment is also made for changes in the growth rate of the labour force.
Net foreign borrowing	+/–	Calculated as difference between foreign borrowing and lending as recorded by SNZ on New Zealand's International Investment Position. Indexed to GDP prior to 1992 due to data paucity.
Loss and damage to terrestrial ecosystems	–	The main component of costs is damage caused by invasive pests, which has been identified as the single greatest threat to biodiversity on land, surpassing even habitat (Department of Conservation and Ministry for the Environment, 1998). To calculate loss and damage to terrestrial ecosystems, pest-related annual expenditure by central government is used. Biodiversity loss from milling is valued on the basis of sawn timber extracted.

Table 6.1 (continued)

Item	Welfare impact	Method of valuation
Loss of wetlands	–	Calculated by estimating the number of hectares of wetlands drained and their biodiversity value.
Loss of soils	–	Soil loss in New Zealand is mainly from erosion. There is a high natural background erosion rate as a result of geologically young landforms, tectonism, a steep topography and a maritime climate. Unsuitable agricultural activity accelerates erosion and has long-term effects. It is estimated erosion scars take 100 years to reach 80% of their former productivity (Parfitt, 2005). Erosion results in lost productivity and damage that requires defensive expenditure by other sectors of the economy to correct. The tonnes of soil lost annually have been estimated and a value put on this using a 1998 costing. Only erosion as a result of agricultural activity has a negative environmental impact for the GPI. Hectares of agricultural land lost to urban expansion have been valued on the basis of biodiversity loss and production loss.
Loss of air quality	–	Calculated by weighing the loss of life years and reduced activity days for 2004 by an air pollution index.
Solid waste contamination	–	Equal to the tonnes of waste going to landfills multiplied by the 'full accounting cost' of disposal has been included as a proxy for contaminated sites in New Zealand.
Cost of climate change	–	This category is similar to that referred to in other studies as the 'cost of long-term environmental damage' and covers all greenhouse gas emissions from the country, not just energy related. New Zealand generates just under half (49.4% in 2004) of its greenhouse gas emissions from agriculture, which is production related. Climate change costs have been calculated from estimates of greenhouse gas emissions multiplied by the European Union (NZ$ equivalent) December 2005 value of a carbon credit.

Table 6.1 (continued)

Item	Welfare impact	Method of valuation
Loss of water quality	–	Pollution of New Zealand's freshwater resources is a major environmental concern (Ministry for the Environment, 1997; Parliamentary Commissioner for the Environment, 2005). The method arrived at for valuing water quality is the cost of riparian planting lowland river margins and planned restoration work on eutrophic lakes. This valuation method is different from that used for water quality in other nation's GPIs, but is consistent with the 'Clean Streams Accord' approach used in New Zealand to prevent further loss of water quality.
Cost of ozone depletion	–	New Zealand does not produce or consume high volumes of ozone-depleting substances, but its people are more exposed to the impact of ozone depletion than most other countries. For this reason, instead of using volumes of CFCs produced or consumed, the loss of life years from death from melanoma cancer has been used for valuation purposes.
Loss of non-renewables resources	–	Calculated by using the Stockhammer 'value added' for non-renewable mining and quarrying (this ANZSIC category also includes oil and gas). To reflect scarcity, oil and gas have also been valued at the generation cost of replacement energy.
Noise pollution	–	The increase in the use of vehicles and the associated noise has been used to approximate the loss of amenity from the continual exposure to noise in the environment. This has been calculated from vehicle kilometres travelled and a 1995 study by the Ministry of Transport of environmental externalities associated with motor vehicle use.

impact on GDP and are therefore already taken into account. To be incorporated in the GPI calculations, environmental damage must therefore be long-term, not short-term.

2. An adjustment is not for the preventative expenditure undertaken to reduce environmental damage since this constitutes a normal production practice where the environmental externalities become a cost borne by the producer. If involuntary expenditure to rectify environmental damage is required (such as work to improve water quality in eutrophic lakes), an adjustment to GPI is needed. Such expenditure includes defensive expenditure, damage costs, restoration costs, and health costs. To put a monetary value on non-marketed environmental goods and ecosystem services for the GPI, potential defensive costs have at times been used.
3. For the environmental categories, only the damage that has occurred since 1970 has been included in the calculations. This means that any cumulative change over time (such as loss of soil from erosion, or wetland loss) have only accumulated with a start point of 1970. This approach differs from other GPI studies (e.g., Cobb et al., 1995; Anielski and Rowe, 1999; Hamilton and Denniss, 2000), but can be likened to the Kyoto Protocol system of 'drawing a line in the sand' and working forward from that point in time.
4. New Zealand's natural capital assets only need to be maintained in terms of their total volume (physical stock not in value terms) rather than on a per person basis. The stock of natural capital therefore need not increase over time with population growth. This treatment is different to human-made capital where adjustments to GPI imply that the quantity of capital per worker remains constant (Lawn, 2003).

THE NEW ZEALAND GPI RESULTS

The New Zealand GDP, at constant 2004/05 dollars, increased from $57 674 million in 1970 to $148 912 million in 2005, a rise of 158.2 per cent. Conversely, while the GPI began in 1970 at a similar value of $58 835 million, it only rose as high as $91 495 million by 2005. This was a rise of just 55.5 per cent over the study period.

As is shown in Figure 6.1, prior to the major structural reforms of the economy that commenced in 1984, the GPI mirrored the growth in GDP. During this period, the GPI was on average 2 per cent higher than GDP. A crossover occurred around 1983 when, from that point onwards, the GPI for New Zealand lagged behind its GDP.

From the perspective of the individual citizen, New Zealand's per capita GPI began the study period at $20 553. It increased gradually to a peak of $25 169 by 1981 but declined to $15 456 by 1993. It recovered to reach $22 715 by 2005; however, this was considerably less than the per capita GDP value of $36 970 for the same year. Apart from being lower than the 1981 peak value, the per capita GPI in 2005 was just 10.5 per cent higher than its 1970 value, whereas GDP was 83.5 per cent higher.

For purposes of analysis, the New Zealand GPI can be divided into three distinct time periods: pre-reform up to 1984; during the reform process, from 1984 to 1994; and post reform, the ten years from 1995 to 2005. To assist in this analysis, a data by component table is presented in Table 6.2.

As mentioned earlier, during the pre-reform period, the New Zealand economy was highly regulated by the Central Government, with heavy-handed macroeconomic policies prevailing. With the exception of traditional colonial ties with Britain, New Zealand was not part of the wider global economy. This soon changed following the economic jolt of losing access to secure export markets once Britain joined the European Economic Community in 1973 which was compounded not long after by the first Organization of Petroleum Exporting Countries (OPEC) oil price shock.

The government reaction to the resulting balance of trade deficit was to increase agricultural production (despite limited overseas markets) and invest in 'think big' projects to assist New Zealand in becoming more energy self-sufficient. Both policies had the impact of boosting employment – thus maintaining a full employment economy – yet also increasing inflation as the economy was protected from outside competition. During this period, security of employment was high, social welfare systems comprehensive, and relative wage rates protected by powerful unions. New Zealanders worked a 40-hour week and weekends, a time when businesses were closed, were devoted to sporting and family activities. The exceptions were essential services (where

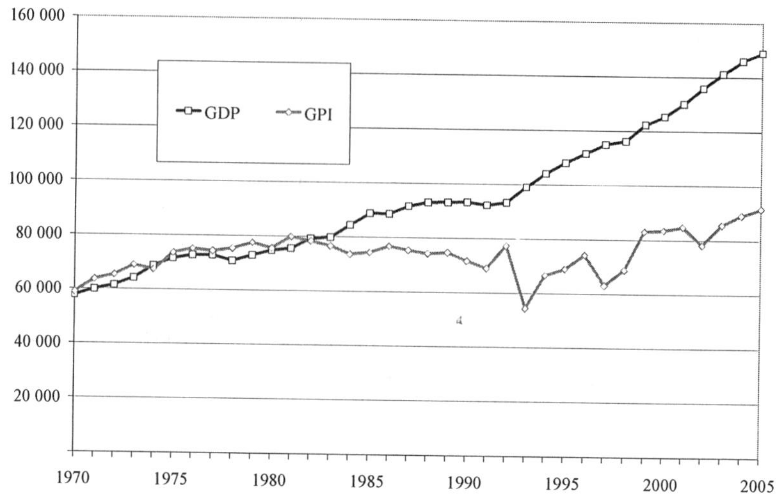

Note: Valued in millions of New Zealand dollars at 2005 prices.

Figure 6.1 Genuine Progress Indicator (GPI) and GDP: New Zealand, 1970–2005

people were paid high overtime rates) and the corner shop and local garage.

In the 1970s, water quality in rivers adjacent to urban areas and major industries was poor. Rivers were the receptacle for untreated sewage, chemical waste, and animal fats from built-up urban areas, freezing works, woollen mills, pulp and paper mills, and other industrial sources. Government subsidies to boost agricultural production (cheap fertiliser and supplementary minimum prices) brought marginal land into farming. The environmental impact of the conversion of wetlands and steep hill country, much of which was covered in native bush, is still being felt today.

The reform period from approximately 1984 to 1994 was a time of severe restructuring aimed at making the New Zealand economy more flexible and efficient, albeit at the time of a worldwide economic recession. On average, the GPI accounted for 77 per cent of GDP during this period. The financial sector was transformed from being the most to the least regulated of all the OECD countries (Kelsey, 1999). The

Table 6.2 The New Zealand GPI for 1970–2005: data by component

Year *	Personal cons. Expend.	Dist. Index (DI)	Personal cons. adjusted by DI	Public cons. exp. (non-def.)	Household and community work	Services from public capital
	(2005$mil)	(1973 = 100)	(2005$mil)	(2005$mil)	(2005$mil)	(2005$mil)
1970	40 280	101	40 021	3 341	16 136	4 724
1971	41 769	102	41 050	3 652	19 108	5 185
1972	42 911	103	41 719	3 658	19 080	5 802
1973	45 546	100	45 546	3 842	19 422	5 792
1974	47 908	107	44 695	4 066	20 229	6 088
1975	48 699	107	45 703	4 715	22 722	7 274
1976	48 168	109	44 178	4 966	22 715	8 132
1977	47 759	112	42 830	4 718	22 727	8 097
1978	46 555	110	42 476	5 111	21 843	8 430
1979	47 353	107	44 234	5 680	23 753	9 085
1980	47 786	116	41 275	5 755	24 190	9 378
1981	48 273	112	42 936	6 265	25 698	9 613
1982	49 057	113	43 447	6 673	26 662	9 807
1983	48 640	113	42 863	6 520	24 155	9 506
1984	50 400	111	45 453	6 603	23 628	9 938
1985	52 794	116	45 385	6 756	23 295	10 176
1986	54 142	118	45 894	7 074	24 106	10 123
1987	55 885	120	46 690	7 148	23 458	9 944
1988	56 143	121	46 576	7 056	23 062	9 635
1989	57 824	120	48 361	7 075	23 205	8 743
1990	58 197	125	46 518	7 368	23 085	8 236
1991	58 037	131	44 292	7 438	23 731	7 950
1992	56 891	128	44 415	7 404	24 240	7 591
1993	57 392	129	44 611	7 485	24 295	7 471
1994	59 216	127	46 703	7 593	24 542	7 317
1995	62 391	128	48 662	7 660	24 801	7 400
1996	64 354	132	48 796	8 064	24 999	7 395
1997	67 063	135	49 845	8 195	25 252	7 334
1998	69 194	129	53 502	8 853	26 157	7 459
1999	71 843	131	54 770	8 802	26 575	7 807
2000	74 491	133	55 992	9 305	27 758	8 132
2001	75 283	135	55 792	9 109	27 244	8 216
2002	77 153	135	57 158	9 491	27 000	8 548
2003	80 077	135	59 303	9 618	28 927	8 942
2004	84 005	135	62 189	9 938	29 554	9 134
2005	87 641	136	64 506	10 539	29 395	9 555

Table 6.2 (continued)

Year *	Net capital growth	Change in net foreign debt (+/-)	Cost of unemploy-ment	Cost of under-empl.	Cost of overwork	Private def. exp. on health & educ.
	(2005$mil)	(2005$mil)	(2005$mil)	(2005$mil)	(2005$mil)	(2005$mil)
1970	4 427	-1 480	- 50	- 98	- 464	-1 035
1971	5 019	-1 730	- 54	- 111	- 498	-1 074
1972	5 571	-1 229	- 79	- 114	- 506	-1 103
1973	6 184	-2 187	- 91	- 121	- 535	-1 171
1974	6 344	-3 710	- 77	- 135	- 611	-1 231
1975	6 825	-2 241	- 81	- 138	- 658	-1 252
1976	8 319	- 968	- 91	- 128	- 612	-1 238
1977	9 333	- 44	- 73	- 124	- 594	-1 228
1978	9 363	1 610	- 49	- 122	- 576	-1 197
1979	9 718	-1 697	- 66	- 124	- 589	-1 217
1980	10 516	-1 499	- 80	- 120	- 604	-1 307
1981	10 818	- 648	- 152	- 112	- 610	-1 320
1982	11 203	-2 993	- 192	- 121	- 640	-1 342
1983	11 568	- 410	- 287	- 120	- 645	-1 330
1984	11 199	-4 291	- 406	- 117	- 682	-1 378
1985	11 675	-2 390	- 337	- 117	- 717	-1 444
1986	12 079	- 611	- 325	- 121	- 716	-1 481
1987	12 402	-1 774	- 389	- 133	-1 394	-1 528
1988	12 053	-1 162	- 359	- 161	-1 122	-1 473
1989	11 841	-1 186	- 380	- 226	- 538	-1 533
1990	11 815	- 99	- 498	- 234	- 916	-1 573
1991	11 849	- 96	- 825	- 367	0	-1 637
1992	12 081	9 014	- 881	- 502	- 99	-1 816
1993	12 141	-13 264	- 958	- 544	- 439	-1 908
1994	12 187	-2 954	- 774	- 515	-1 162	-1 879
1995	12 622	-3 023	- 513	- 489	-1 780	-1 903
1996	13 232	2 390	- 462	- 433	-1 511	-1 876
1997	13 622	-9 163	- 665	- 457	- 876	-2 060
1998	13 923	-10 186	- 657	- 538	- 809	-2 125
1999	14 163	3 106	- 694	- 607	-1 030	-2 206
2000	14 481	930	- 604	- 603	-1 456	-2 288
2001	14 862	2 490	- 574	- 505	-1 132	-2 312
2002	15 155	-6 491	- 555	- 509	- 537	-2 369
2003	15 330	-4 273	- 543	- 456	-1 008	-2 459
2004	16 123	-6 239	- 551	- 443	- 698	-2 580
2005	16 934	-7 634	- 483	- 439	- 727	-2 692

Table 6.2 (continued)

Year *	Cost of commuting	Cost of crime	Loss of water quality	Cost of climate change	Loss of air quality	Loss of wetlands
	(2005$mil)	(2005$mil)	(2005$mil)	(2005$mil)	(2005$mil)	(2005$mil)
1970	-1 470	- 881	-1 144	-1 525	- 333	- 156
1971	-1 550	- 948	-1 066	-1 473	- 336	- 315
1972	-1 552	-1 003	-1 117	-1 518	- 340	- 474
1973	-1 572	-1 024	-1 094	-1 493	- 345	- 635
1974	-1 718	-1 106	-1 103	-1 503	- 350	- 798
1975	-2 093	-1 203	-1 092	-1 518	- 354	- 962
1976	-1 976	-1 251	-1 087	-1 510	- 356	-1 126
1977	-1 817	-1 308	-1 092	-1 546	- 354	-1 292
1978	-1 769	-1 387	-1 090	-1 512	- 352	-1 459
1979	-1 713	-1 457	-1 088	-1 457	- 349	-1 627
1980	-1 717	-1 944	-1 131	-1 503	- 347	-1 795
1981	-1 757	-1 993	-1 133	-1 512	- 346	-1 963
1982	-1 778	-2 100	-1 132	-1 553	- 347	-2 132
1983	-1 891	-2 278	-1 123	-1 571	- 349	-2 301
1984	-1 968	-2 355	-1 133	-1 608	- 349	-2 469
1985	-1 917	-2 513	-1 131	-1 613	- 349	-2 637
1986	-1 989	-2 552	-1 150	-1 718	- 347	-2 805
1987	-1 915	-2 499	-1 109	-1 667	- 347	-2 972
1988	-1 901	-2 563	-1 111	-1 689	- 346	-3 138
1989	-2 096	-2 609	-1 072	-1 693	- 345	-3 303
1990	-2 228	-3 240	-1 063	-1 700	- 346	-3 466
1991	-2 196	-3 530	-1 067	-1 777	- 357	-3 627
1992	-2 145	-3 674	-1 078	-1 921	- 358	-3 786
1993	-2 182	-3 657	-1 118	-1 964	- 359	-3 943
1994	-2 182	-3 539	-1 148	-1 996	- 361	-4 097
1995	-2 479	-3 677	-1 178	-1 973	- 364	-4 247
1996	-2 664	-3 777	-1 190	-2 020	- 367	-4 393
1997	-2 874	-3 744	-1 194	-2 044	- 368	-4 535
1998	-2 918	-3 651	-1 210	-1 913	- 369	-4 673
1999	-3 300	-3 464	-1 232	-1 955	- 368	-4 807
2000	-3 366	-3 784	-1 276	-1 991	- 367	-4 935
2001	-3 275	-3 758	-1 312	-2 098	- 367	-5 058
2002	-3 626	-3 864	-1 361	-2 087	- 369	-5 175
2003	-3 841	-3 960	-1 380	-2 108	- 372	-5 286
2004	-3 891	-3 774	-1 397	-2 003	- 374	-5 392
2005	-4 337	-3 507	-1 433	-2 003	- 374	-5 500

Table 6.2 (continued)

Year *	Loss of non-renewables	Solid waste contamin-ation	Cost of ozone depletion	Loss and damage to native forest	Cost of soil degradation	Cost of noise pollution
	(2005$mil)	(2005$mil)	(2005$mil)	(2005$mil)	(2005$mil)	(2005$mil)
1970	- 497	- 225	- 31	- 226	- 102	- 97
1971	- 584	- 228	- 34	- 221	- 204	- 105
1972	- 635	- 233	- 48	- 212	- 308	- 115
1973	- 675	- 237	- 48	- 204	- 414	- 127
1974	- 732	- 243	- 22	- 207	- 520	- 138
1975	- 875	- 247	- 94	- 205	- 626	- 147
1976	-1 486	- 250	- 151	- 211	- 733	- 157
1977	-2 424	- 251	- 124	- 204	- 839	- 163
1978	-2 516	- 251	- 75	- 174	- 946	- 171
1979	-1 941	- 250	- 104	- 160	-1 053	- 192
1980	-1 687	- 251	- 102	- 156	-1 161	- 191
1981	-2 097	- 252	- 105	- 158	-1 269	- 196
1982	-3 118	- 254	- 127	- 159	-1 377	- 210
1983	-3 562	- 269	- 120	- 159	-1 484	- 217
1984	-4 000	- 283	- 174	- 161	-1 590	- 233
1985	-5 292	- 298	- 143	- 169	-1 695	- 236
1986	-6 109	- 313	- 132	- 172	-1 801	- 246
1987	-5 833	- 328	- 136	- 172	-1 905	- 259
1988	-6 327	- 343	- 144	- 137	-2 009	- 270
1989	-6 689	- 357	- 125	- 145	-2 113	- 283
1990	-6 908	- 372	- 166	- 154	-2 215	- 294
1991	-7 393	- 384	- 171	- 164	-2 389	- 300
1992	-7 675	- 388	- 143	- 174	-2 494	- 305
1993	-7 656	- 393	- 157	- 157	-2 603	- 318
1994	-7 403	- 398	- 143	- 173	-2 709	- 338
1995	-6 675	- 398	- 159	- 181	-2 814	- 352
1996	-8 008	- 395	- 159	- 188	-2 918	- 362
1997	-9 005	- 392	- 151	- 213	-3 017	- 378
1998	-7 773	- 390	- 212	- 257	-3 117	- 387
1999	-8 079	- 387	- 191	- 250	-3 219	- 399
2000	-7 948	- 384	- 205	- 265	-3 316	- 404
2001	-7 992	- 381	- 185	- 281	-3 409	- 427
2002	-7 473	- 378	- 185	- 297	-3 541	- 441
2003	-5 903	- 375	- 210	- 315	-3 669	- 461
2004	-5 366	- 379	- 212	- 333	-3 793	- 475
2005	-4 958	- 382	- 217	- 352	-3 912	- 483

Table 6.2 (continued)

Year *	GPI	GDP	NZ pop.	GPI per capita	GDP per capita	GPI as % of GDP
	(2005$mil)	(2005$mil)	(000s)	(2005$)	(2005$)	(%)
1970	58 835	57 674	2 863	20 553	20 147	102%
1971	63 485	59 816	2 914	21 785	20 527	106%
1972	65 240	61 339	2 966	21 992	20 677	106%
1973	68 815	64 048	3 020	22 788	21 209	107%
1974	67 219	68 643	3 074	21 866	22 329	98%
1975	73 450	71 419	3 129	23 471	22 822	103%
1976	74 978	72 618	3 132	23 938	23 185	103%
1977	74 231	72 672	3 135	23 679	23 181	102%
1978	75 187	70 677	3 138	23 962	22 525	106%
1979	77 387	72 780	3 141	24 642	23 174	106%
1980	75 519	74 637	3 143	24 026	23 745	101%
1981	79 708	75 439	3 167	25 169	23 821	106%
1982	78 217	79 147	3 191	24 514	24 805	99%
1983	76 497	79 654	3 215	23 795	24 778	96%
1984	73 623	84 250	3 239	22 730	26 011	87%
1985	74 286	88 656	3 263	22 764	27 168	84%
1986	76 687	88 462	3 285	23 344	26 928	87%
1987	75 283	91 374	3 307	22 764	27 629	82%
1988	74 127	92 809	3 329	22 265	27 877	80%
1989	74 531	92 972	3 352	22 238	27 740	80%
1990	71 552	93 091	3 374	21 207	27 591	77%
1991	68 981	92 072	3 421	20 161	26 910	75%
1992	77 307	93 113	3 470	22 281	26 837	83%
1993	54 381	98 917	3 518	15 456	28 114	55%
1994	66 572	104 072	3 568	18 658	29 168	64%
1995	68 940	108 128	3 618	19 053	29 884	64%
1996	74 151	111 581	3 642	20 361	30 639	66%
1997	63 110	114 908	3 665	17 218	31 349	55%
1998	68 709	116 229	3 689	18 624	31 505	59%
1999	83 036	122 264	3 713	22 362	32 927	68%
2000	83 407	125 293	3 737	22 317	33 525	67%
2001	84 649	130 029	3 794	22 313	34 275	65%
2002	78 092	135 840	3 851	20 279	35 274	57%
2003	85 498	141 091	3 909	21 872	36 093	61%
2004	89 039	145 927	3 968	22 439	36 775	61%
2005	91 495	148 912	4 028	22 715	36 970	61%

Note: * Fiscal year from 1 April to 31 March.

resulting influx of capital fuelled share-market and property speculation. In the words of Kelsey (1999, p. 149):

> This speculative spree gutted the productive base of the country, ruining many solid businesses that had fallen prey to raiders. Other companies were burdened with debt. Some closed. Many were sold cheap, mainly to offshore buyers because there was no local capital. Investors were left with worthless shares, and often big debts. Unemployment spiralled.

This period also saw an increase in non-renewable resource consumption with oil and gas fields developed as part of the 'think big' strategy to increase output. Greenhouse gas emissions increased dramatically following the deregulation of the transport sector. Less freight was carried by rail while cheap second-hand car imports increased the number of vehicles on the roads. These factors, plus the reduced role of the government in the economy, a lack of markets for exports, a decrease in the returns to capital, and the sharp increase in unemployment, impacted negatively on the welfare of New Zealanders. It is thus reflected by the decline in the GPI during this period and even more so by the sharp fall in the New Zealand's per capita GPI.

Post-reform (i.e., after 1994), GDP and the GPI diverged further, with the GPI experiencing a lower average growth rate (respectively rising at 3.3 and 2.8 per cent per annum). There is little doubt that, following the reform period, the New Zealand economy began to recover in terms of the growth in GDP. As a consequence of the structural reforms, financial assets were reallocated into industries with greater competitive advantage. This, in turn, has provided New Zealand with a more liberalised and competitive economy from a global perspective. As such, it has been accompanied by increases in GDP growth, employment, and business confidence. However, the growing economy is putting additional pressure on the environment, especially in terms of increased levels of greenhouse gas emissions and poorer water quality, the latter of which is being driven by intensified agriculture. Tourism is also having an environmental impact with over 2 million tourists a year repeatedly visiting the same locations renowned for their natural beauty.

As at 31 March 2005, the GPI accounted for 61.5 per cent of GDP. As shown in Figure 6.2, the largest positive components of the GPI are personal consumption (56.9 per cent), the value of household and community work (19.1 per cent), and net capital growth (11 per cent).[2] The most significant negative components of the GPI are income

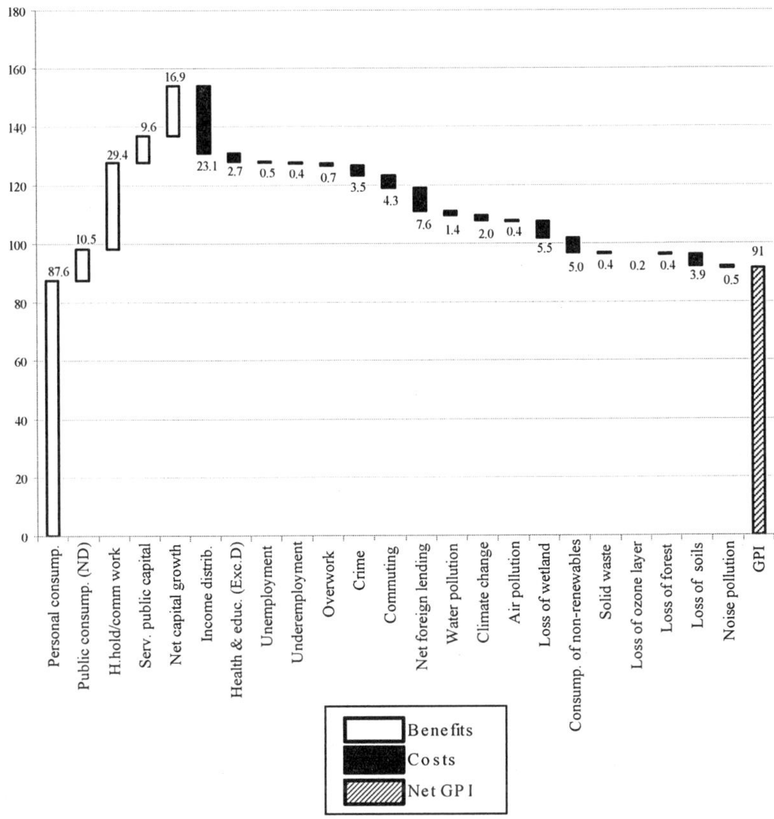

Figure 6.2 Component contributions to the New Zealand GPI for the 2005 financial year (NZ$$_{2005}$ billion)

inequality (37 per cent), net foreign borrowing (12.2 per cent), loss of wetlands (8.8 per cent) and the depletion of non-renewable resources (8 per cent).[3]

INSIGHTS INTO THE NEW ZEALAND GPI RESULTS

Because New Zealand is a small country with relatively advanced economic and social accounting systems, attempts have been made to value the inputs into the GPI using the most rigorous methods available. However, many attempts to do this have proved futile given that New Zealand is information rich but system poor. As a result, available data, especially for the environmental categories, was either difficult to compare over time or was not in an appropriate form to use for GPI calculations. Traditionally, the emphasis has been on economic and social data systems with few requirements for environmental accounting. This reflects the adage that 'we only manage what we measure', and accordingly, the New Zealand economy has been the focus of political and hence statistical processes.

The social and economic data for the GPI has been calculated using existing data series largely obtained from Statistics New Zealand. Measurement over time has required the combining of different data series and the construction of indices. Where an index has been used, the starting point has not always been 1970. For example, for the Income Distribution Index (IDI) the year with the smallest recorded inequality (1973) was set as the base year with an index of 100.

The construction of a GPI for any country is very dependent on the underlying assumptions made within the methodological framework of the index – and New Zealand is no exception. This is especially pertinent for the environmental categories as, for example, an assumption regarding whether or not to accumulate, and the start point for accumulation, can have a significant impact on the final GPI. For the New Zealand GPI, soil loss and wetland loss have been accumulated from 1970 onwards. The rationale for this is that utility from personal consumption is measured for a given year. Since the starting point for the GPI is 1970, we are therefore observing changes from this point onwards. Losses from flows of natural capital assets need to be compared over the same period of time. While other studies (Cobb et al., 1995; Hamilton and Denniss, 2000) have accumulated losses since pre-settlement, this was not done for New Zealand. There would of course be some point in time when the marginal social costs of lost ecosystem services were greater than the marginal social benefits derived from any replacement activity, but the actual point of crossover is not known other than that it is believed to be pre-1970.

Long-term environmental damage has been calculated based on annual emissions of greenhouse gases. Pricing is based on the trading price for a tonne of carbon dioxide emissions which, in theory, should reflect the marginal social cost of emitting a tonne of carbon dioxide into the atmosphere. Therefore, emissions have not been accumulated.

When estimating the depletion costs for non-renewable resources, a combination of approaches have been used. Neumayer (2003) has proposed that there is no need to preserve natural assets as an input into the production process since the market place will find appropriate substitutes once resources become sufficiently scarce. This economic theory does not hold for the life-support services provided by ecosystems (which are not substitutable). Hence they need to be treated differently. Acceptance of this argument centres on the stance taken in the weak versus strong sustainability debate (see Chapter 4). For the New Zealand GPI, it has been accepted that technology has set the present and past value of non-renewables and therefore they are substitutable. The value-added contribution (as per Stockhammer et al., 1997) has been used to cost the depletion of non-renewable natural assets. The El Serafy method (El Serafy, 1989), which leads to lower estimates than the Stockhammer approach of the true depreciation of natural capital (Neumayer, 2003, p. 164) was not used due to uncertainty with regards to the size of present stocks, future uses, and what would be the most appropriate discount rate to apply. Such uncertainty requires assumptions to be made about each of the 40-plus minerals mined in New Zealand. Given, for example, the unknowns associated with the future use of coal, which is a plentiful resource but may be left unused due to impacts on climate change, it seemed prudent to avoid making such assumptions.

While it has been argued that natural assets as an input into the production process are substitutable, apart from their life-support services, a different view is sometimes voiced with respect to oil and natural gas reserves (Anielski and Rowe, 1999; Hamilton and Denniss, 2000). Non-renewable energy-producing resources need to be treated differently because technology runs on energy. Because oil and gas are the main sources of cheap energy, their depletion is a significant cost to future generations. Past and present exploitation of oil and gas has allowed people on modest incomes to enjoy a resource-intensive lifestyle, but this is not sustainable indefinitely and will clearly have an impact on future generations once supplies are exhausted. For this reason, when valuing non-renewable natural capital, an additional amount has been added to reflect the scarcity value of natural gas and crude oil extracted in New Zealand. For each petajoule of energy consumed from natural gas and crude oil, the 2005 replacement cost for a petajoule of renewable wind energy is added.

The GPI boundaries are generally regarded as 'nation' boundaries. Unlike the Ecological Footprint (Wackernagel and Rees, 1996), the importation of natural capital and the subsequent resource depletion in other nations is not included in the GPI calculations of the resource-consuming country. However, often the impact of a nation's behaviour seriously impacts on the welfare of people elsewhere. For example, the hole in the ozone layer leads to higher numbers of deaths from melanoma in fair-skinned people in New Zealand. Valuation on the basis of the production of chlorofluorocarbons (CFCs) as per the USA (see Cobb et al., 1995), the consumption of CFCs as per Sweden (see Jackson and Stymne, 1996), and the emission of other ozone-depleting substances does not reflect this impact. For this reason, the valuation of this item has been based on the years of life lost from melanoma cancer. The approach used for ozone depletion introduces the issue of how responsible a country is for the impacts it has on another nation's welfare. Increases in greenhouse gases in the atmosphere are also predicted to have similar welfare transfers. It is expected that countries in Africa already susceptible to severe droughts will have even drier climatic conditions as a result of climate change. This issue of transboundary accounting problems is taken up in greater detail in Chapter 7.

At this moment in time, methodologically sound ways for valuing changes in water quality are still being researched. Several different approaches were trialled for the New Zealand GPI and subsequently abandoned due to insufficient data or logic flaws. While there is data that indicates water quality, especially in lakes and lowland rivers, is declining (Vant and Smith, 2004; Gibbard et al., 2006; NIWA, 2006), quantifying the annual extent of the decline and placing a dollar value on this is very problematic.

CONCLUSION

While the GPI may lack preciseness of measurement, it is a more accurate indicator of welfare than GDP because it does not arbitrarily place a zero value on social and ecological capital, which are essential for the welfare of any society (Cobb et al., 1995). The New Zealand GPI builds on past efforts at improving measures of national welfare as well as providing assessments appropriate for New Zealand. The absence of data is an obstacle to rigorous GPI calculations but it must be remembered that the System of National Accounts, from which the GDP is extracted, has been developed over a 50-year plus period. This has provided ample time for conventional national accounting systems to be improved. This aside, the systems for collecting national accounting data are not completely comprehensive and a number of adjustments have to be made. As such, it is not possible to estimate the accuracy of GDP because it is a statistic calculated by 'combining a complex mix of data from many sources, many of which require adjustment to put them into a national accounts database and which are further adjusted to improve coherence, often using non-scientific methods' (Lequiller and Blades, 2006, p. 36).

National accounting data are approximations, but are accepted because the information is of value to business and policy-makers. The GPI should not be critiqued on the basis of the quality of data used in its calculation since this is an area that can be dramatically improved. Instead, the GPI needs to be evaluated on the basis of whether or not it can be developed into a tool that can better aid decision-making. A good example of this is the greenhouse gas inventory required by the United Nations Framework Convention on Climate Change. The speed with which the framework was established demonstrates that it is possible to devise international standards to measure environmental resources.

An advantage of building a national GPI is that it highlights what measures need to be incorporated to reflect the welfare of a nation. It acknowledges the importance of non-economic contributions to welfare and looks at the best ways to best incorporate such contributions into a meaningful measure. A disadvantage of the current GPI methodology is the lack of standardised systems and the implications this has for international comparability. The researcher has to decide which items will be incorporated into the methodology of the index and which valuation methods are best to employ. Both decisions are usually made on the basis of data availability.

Bleys (2007) advances the concept of a Simplified Index of Sustainable Economic Welfare (SISEW) which involves the omission of items with low quantitative significance while encouraging the monitoring of sustainable economic welfare using fewer data items which can be readily estimated using more robust valuation methods. Development of an internationally accepted index would allow the GPI to be reported alongside GDP statistics to reflect the impact that GDP growth or decline is having on social and ecological capital. This has not yet emerged and remains an elusive goal 18 years after the need for alternative measures was first mooted by Daly and Cobb (1989).

NOTES

1. The New Zealand Government kindly made the research funding available for this study through the Foundation for Research, Science and Technology (Contract MAUX0306).
2. For the year ended 31 March 2005, the total value of all benefits was NZ$154 billion.
3. For the year ended 31 March 2005, the total value of all costs was NZ$62.5 billion.

REFERENCES

Ajwani, S., Blakely, T., Robson, B., Bonne, M., and Tobias, M. (2003), *Decades of Disparity: Ethnic Mortality Trends in New Zealand 1980–1999*, Wellington: Ministry of Health.

Anielski, M. and Rowe, J. (1999), *The Genuine Progress Indicator 1998 Update*, San Francisco, CA: Redefining Progress, www.rprogress.org.

Bleys, B. (2007), 'A simplified Index of Sustainable Economic Welfare for the Netherlands, 1971–2004', Working Paper, Vrije Universiteit Brussel.

Clark, H. (2007), 'Prime Minister's statement to parliament', www.beehive.govt.nz/ViewDocument.aspx?DocumentID=28357, 1 April.

Cobb, C., Halstead, T. and Rowe, J. (1995), *The Genuine Progress Indicator: Summary of Data and Methodology*, San Francisco, CA: Redefining Progress.

Daly, H.E. and Cobb, J. (1989), *For the Common Good*, Boston, MA: Beacon Press.

Department of Conservation and Ministry for the Environment (1997), *New Zealand Biodiversity Strategy: An Outline Strategy for Public Consultation*, Wellington: Department of Conservation & Ministry for the Environment, http://www.biodiversity.govt.nz/picture/doing/nzbs/index.html.

Department of Conservation and Ministry for the Environment (1998), 'Restoring the dawn chorus', Wellington.

El Serafy, S. (1989), 'The proper calculation of income from depletable natural resources', in Y. Ahmad, S. El Serafy and E. Lutz (eds), *Environmental Accounting for Sustainable Development*, Washington, DC: World Bank, pp. 10–18.

Gibbard, R., Roygard, J., Ausseil, O. and Fung, L. (2006), 'Water quality trends in the Manawatu-Wanganui region 1989–2004', Horizons Regional Council.

Grundy, K. (2000), 'Purpose and principles: interpreting Section 5 of the Resource Management Act', in P. Memon and H. Perkins (eds), *Environmental Management and Planning in New Zealand*, Palmerston North: Dunmore Press, pp. 64–73.

Hamilton, C. and Denniss, R. (2000), 'Tracking well-being in Australia: the Genuine Progress Indicator', Paper Number 35, Canberra: The Australia Institute.

Jackson, T. and Stymne, S. (1996), *Sustainable Economic Welfare in Sweden: A Pilot Index 1950–1992*, Stockholm: Stockholm Environment Institute, The New Economics Foundation.

Kelsey, J. (1999), *Reclaiming the Future: New Zealand and the Global Economy*, Wellington: Bridget Williams Books.

King, M. (2003), *The Penguin History of New Zealand*, Auckland: Penguin Books.

Lawn, P. (2003), 'A theoretical foundation to support the Index of Sustainable Economic Welfare (ISEW), Genuine Progress Indicator (GPI), and other related measures', *Ecological Economics*, **44**, 105–118.

Lequiller, F. and Blades, D. (2006), *Understanding National Accounts*, Paris: Economica.

Ministry for the Environment (1997), *The State of New Zealand's Environment 1997*, Wellington: Ministry for the Environment.

National Institute of Water and Atmospheric Research (NIWA) (2006), 'National river water quality network national monthly median data 1989–2004', 8 March.

Neumayer, E. (2003), *Weak Versus Strong Sustainability*, 2nd edition, Cheltenham, UK and Northamption, MA, USA: Edward Elgar.

Organisation for Economic Co-operation and Development (OECD) (2007), *OECD Environmental Performance Review of New Zealand*, Paris: Organisation for Economic Co-operation and Development.

Parfitt, R. (2005), 'The 100-year Manawatu flood event – one year on: a soils perspective', *Soil Horizons*, **11**, 2.

Parliamentary Commissioner for the Environment (2005), *Growing for Good: Intensive Farming, Sustainability and New Zealand's Environment*, 2nd edition, Wellington.

Pratt, M. and Lowndes, T. (2005), 'Regional economic development and sustainability', J. Rowe (ed.), *Economic Development in New Zealand*, Aldershot: Ashgate, pp. 127–148.

Stockhammer, E. and Hochreiter, H., Obermayr, B. and Steiner, K. (1997), 'The index of sustainable economic welfare (ISEW) as an alternative to GDP in measuring economic welfare: the results of the Australian (revised) ISEW calculation 1955–1992', *Ecological Economics*, **21**, 19–34.

The Treasury (2007), *New Zealand Economic and Financial Overview 2007*, http://www.treasury.govt.nz/economy/overview/2007/nzefo-07.pdf.

Vant, B. and Smith, P. (2004), 'Trends in river water quality in the waikato region, 1997–2002', *Environment Waikato Technical Report 2004/02*, Hamilton, http://www.ew.govt.nz/publications/technicalreports/documents/TR04-02.pdf.

Wackernagel, M. and Rees, W. (1996), *Our Ecological Footprint: Reducing Human Impact on the Earth*, Philadelphia, PA: New Society Publishers.

Wheen, N. (2002), 'A history of New Zealand environmental law', in E. Pawson and T. Brooking (eds), *Environmental Histories of New Zealand*, Oxford: Oxford University Press, pp. 261–274.

7. Genuine progress in Japan and the need for an open economy GPI

Matsuyo Makino

INTRODUCTION

The Post-War Development of the Japanese Economy

In 1956, the White Paper on the Economy declared that the post-World War II recovery was complete. The White Paper ushered in the start of Japan's phenomenal Gross Domestic Product (GDP) growth performance over the next two decades. In 1960, Prime Minister Hayato Ikeda announced the famous 'income-doubling plan' which aimed at attaining an annual growth rate of 7.2 per cent or a doubling of GDP in the following ten years. Although the growth target appeared unachievable, it somehow pulled together a national consensus to accomplish the goal. The desired doubling of real GNP from ¥13 600 billion to ¥26 000 billion was attained much sooner than expected, indeed, by 1967, with the actual growth of GNP during the plan's ten-year span averaging 11 per cent per annum. Heavy industrialisation and the exportation of manufactured goods formed the engine of Japan's GDP growth.

Exports grew even more rapidly at 18.4 per cent per annum during the 1960s. From the early 1950s to the mid-1970s, manufactured exports continued to account for more than 80 per cent of the total exports. This share peaked at 95 per cent in the 1970s. On the other hand, raw materials accounted for 60 per cent of Japan's total imports (80 per cent if food is included), while the imports of machinery and manufactured goods constituted less than 20 per cent of the import total. Meanwhile, as a reflection of the change in Japan's domestic industrial structure, the core manufactured exports shifted from textiles in the 1950s to steel in the 1960s, and to machinery and transport equipment in the 1970s.

During the high-growth era, Japan became more dependent than ever on primary material and energy imports. Nevertheless, Japan was able to move forward along a road of economic development by increasing the value-added content of its exports and by securing a cheaper and more stable supply of raw materials and energy from abroad.

Average household consumption increased fourfold with a marked decline in the Engel coefficient.[1] The lifestyle of the average citizen was rapidly Westernised and, by 1975, more than 80 per cent of the total households owned a telephone, while 50 per cent owned a dining set and a private car. Dieting habits also changed remarkably from rice and the traditional Japanese diet to an increased intake of bread and food with a high animal protein component.

Rapid GDP growth, however, was not without cost. In fact, sharp criticism against a growth-focused policy had already surfaced during the second half of the 1960s in response to severe cases of industrial pollution, urban problems, double-digit inflation, large-scale labour disputes, and other social conflicts and insecurity. Japan witnessed serious environmental disasters between the mid-1960s and mid-1970s, among which appeared the 'four great pollution lawsuits' or court cases involving the claim for compensation for victims of Minamata disease in Kumamoto, Itai-itai (ouch-ouch) disease in Toyama, the second Minamata disease in Niigata, and Yokkaichi asthma. Controversy over GDP growth became intense and thus began a quest for an alternative economic and social policy. In response, a New National Welfare Development Committee was established within the Economic Council in 1971. The Committee developed and published a welfare measure called New National Welfare (NNW) in 1973 (Economic Council, 1973).

The 1973 world oil crisis and its aftermath severely shook Japan's trade-dependent economy. The year 1974 saw the beginning of the worst post-war recession in Japan with the first year of negative growth (−1.8 per cent) in three decades. The economy eventually recovered, but growth slowed from the previous 10 per cent level to an average of 3.6 per cent per annum during the period 1974–79, and 4.4 per cent per annum during the decade of the 1980s.

Despite the lower growth rate, Japan's industrial competitiveness was maintained by innovative and cost-saving production technology and increased energy efficiency in manufacturing. However, the second oil crisis in 1979 forced Japan to shift from heavy industry to more technology- and information-intensive industries, such as semiconductors and computers. The continued success in manufactured exports cast aside any serious doubt about Japan's high trade dependence.

In 1985, the Plaza Accord led to the appreciation of the yen (¥) which forced the Japanese Government to create financial measures to enhance domestic demand. This eventually brought about the 'bubble' economy between 1987 and 1990 which subsequently burst at the end of 1990. The post-bubble recession continued through the second half of the 1990s and the early 2000s. Growth in real GNP during the period 1993–2003 remained low at an average rate of 1.19 per cent per annum.

In 2001, Prime Minister Junichiro Koizumi implemented a policy package of structural reform. Under the slogan of 'no growth without reform', various measures were introduced, such as the privatization of many public assets (notably of the Japan Postal Service), deregulation, and the tightening of the government budget on social security. During the five years of Koizumi's term, which ended in 2006, the downward growth spiral of real GNP slowly turned upwards with the Japanese economy resuming a higher positive growth rate.

The return to a more robust growth rate of Japan's GNP cannot, however, necessarily be attributed to the structural reforms introduced by Koizumi. Indeed, it might simply have been the result of Japanese companies having sufficient time to adjust to the new conditions of the post-bubble Japanese economy as well as to a new-look global economy. Furthermore, the meagre recent success of the Japanese economy appears to have been enjoyed by a limited segment of the economy (e.g., the automobile industry and other industry sectors serving the demands of a rapidly growing China). Evidence suggests there has been little improvement in the economic conditions of the majority of Japanese people. Nevertheless, at this moment in the Japanese society and history, the prevailing voice continues to call for 'growth again' and 'reform without retreat'.

The New National Welfare (NNW) and Attempts to Measure the GPI

The New National Welfare (NNW) published in 1973 (Economic Council, 1973) was an indicator similar in principle to the Measure of Economic Welfare (MEW) proposed by Nordhaus and Tobin in 1972. The distinct contribution of the NNW was that, for the first time, it explicitly included environmental costs in a measure of welfare – namely, air and water pollution, and industrial and household wastes.

Following the lead of Nordhaus and Tobin (1972), the NNW excluded investment expenditure on the grounds that investment goods constitute 'intermediate goods'. That is, investment goods do not provide direct and immediate welfare benefits, but indirect benefits in the form of future consumer goods. Given that consumption expenditure is included in the NNW as a positive item, investment expenditure is therefore captured by the NNW in later years (see also Chapters 2 and 3 of this book).

The NNW made two further advances. Firstly, the NNW emphasised the distinction between the stock of capital and the flow of service emanating from it (also the cost of lost service); and secondly, the NNW explicitly accounted for the benefits generated by existing consumer durables and publicly-provided social overhead capital (Economic Council, 1973; Kanamori et al., 1977; Uno, 1989, pp. 308–309). In total, the NNW consisted of the following nine items:

1. Government consumption, excluding defensive expenditures[2]
2. Personal consumption, excluding consumer durables and defensive or non welfare-enhancing expenditures[3]
3. Services from publicly-provided social overhead capital[4]
4. Services from consumer durables
5. Benefits from leisure
6. Extra-market activities, such as household labour
7. Defensive expenditure on environmental protection or maintenance
8. Environmental pollution
9. Cost of urbanization (costs of commuting and traffic accidents).

The estimation of the NNW for Japan initially covered the years of 1955, 1960, 1965, and 1970. It was updated to include 1975 by Kanamori et al. (1977), and further extended to cover 1980 and 1985 by Uno (1989). They found that, during these years, the NNW increased consistently and that the level of Japan's NNW was higher than its GNP in 1955 and 1960. Beyond 1960, the growth rate of the NNW was lower than it was for GNP, except for 1970–75, during which time the world oil crisis took place (1973), thereby enabling the NNW growth to outweigh the sluggish GNP growth.

After the seminal work of Daly and Cobb (1994), there were several attempts to estimate the Index of Sustainable Economic Welfare (ISEW) or Genuine Progress Indicator (GPI) in the USA, Europe, and Australia.

It was as late as 2003 when several researchers, including the present author, formed a GPI group to review past GPI country studies and estimate the GPI for Japan for the period 1955–2000. The research was conducted in 2002 and 2003 with the aid of an environmental research grant from the Sumitomo Foundation. The results of this study were first published in 2003 (GPI Version 1). The methodology was improved and a revised version of Japan's GPI (GPI Version 2) was estimated and presented at the 2003 Conference of the Canadian Society of Ecological Economics (Makino et al., 2003).[5] Another GPI study of Japan was conducted independently by Toshikazu Mito, who computed the Japanese GPI for the period 1985–2002 (Mito, 2003).

THE METHODOLOGY USED FOR THE JAPANESE GPI

The earlier Japanese GPI estimated by the GPI research group in 2003 (GPI Version 1 and Version 2) drew on the methodologies of the GPI and ISEW used previously on other countries, as well as the NNW computed in Japan in 1973. Of late, some stimulating debates have taken place over the methodology of the GPI, notably by Neumayer (2000) and Lawn (2003). Learning from these efforts, the present study employs the Atkinson index to adjust personal consumption for income inequality. It also involves the adoption of a more cautious approach to the treatment of defensive expenditures and the computation of services from the capital stock.

Income Inequality

The Atkinson index is one of the few inequality measures that explicitly incorporates normative judgments about the impact of the distribution of income on social welfare (Atkinson, 1970). Based on the assumption of decreasing marginal utility (benefit) of income or consumption, the index is defined by:

$$I = 1 - \left[\sum_i \left(\frac{y_i}{\bar{y}} \right)^{1-\varepsilon} f(y_i) \right]^{\frac{1}{1-\varepsilon}} = 1 - \frac{y_E}{\bar{y}} \qquad (7.1)$$

where y_i is the proportion of total income earned by the ith income group, $\bar{y}$ is the average income, and f_i is the proportion of the total population in the ith income group.

The equally distributed equivalent level of income to the mean of the actual distribution is given by:[6]

$$y_E = \left[\sum_i (y_i)^{1-\varepsilon} f(y_i) \right]^{\frac{1}{1-\varepsilon}} \tag{7.2}$$

The critical variable is ε which is a measure of the degree of inequality aversion of society or the relative sensitivity of society to welfare transfers at different income levels. It reflects a society's preference for equality (or aversion to inequality).[7] The value of the parameter ε has been estimated in various studies of consumer behaviour and of taxation. In this study, a value of $\varepsilon = 1.59$ was adopted, which was estimated for Japan using an econometric study on progressive taxation with an equal sacrifice principle (Young, 1990). The value of 1.59 is considerably higher than the 0.8 used for an ISEW study of the UK by Jackson et al. (1997).

The Atkinson index measures the proportion of the present total income that would be required to achieve the same level of social welfare that presently exists if a nation's income was equally distributed amongst its population. That is, a value of 0.3 indicates that a nation could, if its income was equally distributed amongst the population, attain the same level of social welfare with only (1 – 0.3) or 70 per cent of its present total income. Alternatively, the gain from redistribution to achieve complete income equality would be equivalent to raising total income by 30 per cent.

In the GPI studies of the USA and many other countries, the Gini coefficient is generally used to adjust personal consumption for income inequality. Usually the first year of the study period is set at an index value of 100, and the remaining years are indexed relative to this base year in accordance with an improvement/deterioration in the distribution of income. Undertaken this way, it has been argued by some observers that it is more difficult to directly compare the weighted value of personal consumption with actual personal consumption in the same year. Correspondingly, it is also difficult to directly compare the absolute level of the resulting GPI with the absolute level of GDP or GNP. Only relative changes in each indicator are meaningfully comparable.

With the Atkinson index, weighted personal consumption is ultimately derived according to the following formula:

$$C_{GPI} = \overline{C}(1-I) \cong W = E(U)\left(\frac{y_E}{\overline{y}}\right) \quad (7.3)$$

It is now assumed that the welfare of a society directly stems from its average level of consumption with some adjustments and correction for society's intolerance of inequality. It is further assumed that an individual's satisfaction from consumption is the same as the consumption level itself.

Public Consumption and Capital

In many past GPI studies, many forms of public consumption have been excluded from the computation of the GPI on the grounds that they are defensive in nature. An exception is the element of public consumption that is regarded as a form of investment in 'service capital' that provides public service without charge. Since the GPI does not include investment, only the service generated from public capital of this sort is considered. The GPI studies of the USA by Daly and Cobb (1994) and Redefining Progress (1995 and 1999) only included the services generated by highways and roads for the reason that services of other types of public capital involve the charging of fees. Included in this Japanese GPI study are the imputed values of services from other forms of public infrastructure – namely, public schools, museums, and libraries. Because data on asset values of public health facilities was unavailable, the services they provide were not computed.[8]

Public spending on education and health is also important for the welfare of a nation since it generates significant spillover benefits. Even if public spending on education and health is regarded as defensive, as is the case in many GPI studies, the spending can still be considered a form of investment in human capital since it generates benefits in terms of the additional services provided by healthy and educated human resources (so far not considered in the GPI accounting). Included in the GPI in this particular study, therefore, was public spending on national schools, hospitals, education, culture, and social security. Excluded were all other items considered as non-welfare-enhancing.

Natural Resource Depletion

The United Nations Handbook and Manual on the System of Integrated Environmental and Economic Accounting (SEEA) (United Nations, 1993 and 2000) classifies environmental expenditures and the cost related to the loss of environmental capacity into the following:

1. the restoration cost to reach a sustainable target;
2. the cost to restore depletion and degradation from past activities;
3. the cost to restore depletion and degradation from current activities;
4. actual environmental expenditures to avoid or prevent future environmental degradation.

In practice, the SEEA only attempts to measure categories 2–4, thereby excluding the first environmental cost category. To account for depletion of 'economic' natural capital, the SEEA recommends computation of categories 2 and 3 using 'the accounting methods to include the permanent loss of the income-generation capacity [of depleted natural capital] and of other amenities derived from their use.' (parentheses added)

As explained in Chapter 3, El Serafy (1989) has developed a method to address the difficult task of deriving the appropriate accounting method to compute the cost of non-renewable resource depletion. The El Serafy user cost method was used in the original ISEW study of the USA; however, Lawn and Clarke (2006) have further extended its application to the overexploitation of renewable resources. Following Lawn and Clarke, this Japanese GPI study has employed the user cost method to compute the cost of the sacrificed source function of non-renewable mineral resources and renewable timber stocks.

Defensive Expenditures

Standard GPI accounting practices involve the subtraction of 'defensive expenditures' from consumption. Sometimes the concept of defensive expenditures is criticised on the basis that what should count as defensive is rather arbitrary. In accounting for environmental degradation (pollution), the SEEA recommends the estimation of the cost to compensate for the degradation emanating from current economic activities and actual environmental expenditures for avoidance or prevention of future degradation.

The compensation cost for depletion and degradation from current activities can be captured in terms of maintenance costing. Maintenance costs are those that would have been incurred had operators avoided the emission of residuals and other degrading impacts of current economic activities. Since these are hypothetical costs, the market values of the negative impacts need to be imputed.

Actual environmental expenditures, on the other hand, are expenditures that have in fact been undertaken to prevent or reduce pollution (e.g., investment in recycling and developing substitutes) or to reduce the net depletion of renewable resources (e.g., planting trees, restocking rivers with fish, and plugging leaks in water distribution systems). Since investment should not be included in the calculation of the GPI, only consumption-related expenditures of these types (e.g., air purifiers and water filters) should be subtracted.

In this study, two types of environmental costs were considered. The first were actual environmental expenditures for avoidance or prevention of environmental degradation (i.e., defensive expenditure, narrowly defined). The second were imputed costs to compensate for actual degradation from current activities following any preventive efforts made. The distinction between these different cost categories is a useful approach, not only in terms of environmental costs, but also when calculating many economic and social costs. In principle, these costs must at least include defensive and maintenance expenditures. Earlier examples of such costing appeared in the NNW in 1973. The NNW did not compute the cost of crime because, in the early 1970s, actual expenditure on justice and police could only be regarded as sufficient to prevent deterioration of public safety. On the other hand, the same did not apply to environmental degradation for which preventive measures could not avoid actual deterioration. In this case, the NNW included both the expenditure on prevention of pollution and the imputed maintenance cost of actually emitted pollution. This approach was used in this study, whenever possible, to compute economic, social, and environmental costs.

Time Use and the Cost of Work

In valuing costs and benefits of leisure and work, most GPI country studies include the loss of leisure and the cost of underemployment. This methodology does not consistently account for the value of time use. For example, while the presence of unemployment and underemployment effectively constitutes unwilling leisure, the loss of leisure does not always reflect the unwilling loss of time (e.g., overwork). Hence, there is a possibility of double-counting.

The treatment of leisure and work in this study follows the approach adopted in an Australian GPI study by Hamilton (1999). Hamilton's study classified time engaged in various activities into two broad categories: (a) *voluntary activities*, which includes paid work (except for the involuntary component), housework and parenting, volunteer work, and other leisure activities; and (b) *involuntary activities* consisting of involuntary leisure (unemployment), involuntary work, and the involuntary loss of leisure, such as the time spent commuting. While the former category of activities contributes to welfare, the latter diminishes it.

Workers and potential workers are therefore classified into full-time employees (who may be overworked), fully unemployed and underemployed part-time employees (who are willing to work longer hours), and those outside the labour force. Because the opportunity cost of work is foregone leisure and the opportunity cost of leisure is foregone wages from work, the benefit of paid work can be regarded as offsetting the cost of engaging in it. The value of paid work is reflected in personal consumption while the value of housework, parenting, and voluntary work is imputed elsewhere in the GPI. Thus, the Japanese GPI does not include the loss of leisure, but includes the costs of unemployment, underemployment, and overwork.

Investment and Services From the Capital Stock

GPI accounting, which aims to measure all relevant welfare-equivalent items, excludes investment because the addition to capital stock should not be regarded as something that contributes to current welfare. As Lawn (2003, p. 106) has pointed out, the sustainable economic welfare implied in the GPI/ISEW is 'the welfare a nation enjoys at a *particular point in time* given the impact of past and present activities'. Yet, it has been customary in GPI studies to include two items related to investment – namely, 'net foreign borrowing/lending' and 'net capital growth'.

Net foreign borrowing/lending is the net addition to the financial assets/liabilities of a nation. As such, it is related to net investment. It is true that the economic sustainability of a nation is affected by net foreign borrowing to the extent that it must rely on foreign funding to finance its current consumption. However, the extent to which foreign debt affects current consumption is not related to the amount of net foreign borrowing itself but to the 'debt services' for the year – in other words, the scheduled repayment for the year of part of the principal (total accumulated liabilities), interest payments, and other payments in the form of dividends.

Evidence shows that debt services are often large enough to adversely affect heavily indebted developing countries (e.g., debt services constitute more than 30 per cent of their GDP). This, in turn, decreases the nation's *current consumption* of basic necessities, such as education and health. Since debt services are already accounted for in consumption or investment in national accounts and reflected in current consumption, this item, I believe, should not be included in the GPI accounting. In the present study, net foreign lending was calculated for expository purposes in order to emphasise the characteristics of Japanese economy. The GPI was computed with and without this item included.

Net capital growth, in the context of the GPI, is not the net addition to capital stock in the usual sense, but is defined as changes in the stock of capital above the amount required to keep the quantity of producer goods (human-made capital) per worker intact. Inclusion of this item has been justified in the past on the basis that sustainable economic welfare requires both human-made and natural capital to be non-decreasing and that, in terms of human-made capital, the quantity of producer goods per worker must not fall.

However, it is still unclear whether this requirement should involve the inclusion of net capital growth, as defined. It would therefore appear necessary to properly define 'GPI investment'. So far, there has not been much discussion on capital and investment in past GPI studies. While GPI accounting makes careful adjustments to consumption in relation to consumer durables and social overhead capital, it makes no corresponding adjustments for investment in producer goods. Also, there is no consideration of a broader concept of capital that might include human capital and social capital.

At this moment, the GPI is best thought of as a measure of current welfare but not a direct measure of sustainability. Even so, its concern with sustainability is reflected indirectly, but powerfully, in the welfare gain or loss from the change in the service of the capital stock. For this reason, it was decided that this item would not be included in the Japanese GPI.

COMPONENTS OF JAPAN'S GPI

The Genuine Progress Indicator (GPI) for Japan is calculated for the period 1970–2003. The calendar year is used as a basis for all calculations. All values of the components of the GPI as well as the GPI itself are converted to 2000 constant prices using relevant deflators.

Consumption-Related Welfare

Two different measures are calculated to represent the welfare contribution of consumption expenditure. The first involves the sum of personal and public consumption as they appear in the national accounts (*CON(1)* = *PCON(1)* + *GCON(1)*). The second involves the exclusion of defensive and/or undesirable expenditures from personal and public consumption (*CON(2)* = *PCON(2)* + *GCON(2)*).

Unadjusted consumption *CON(1)* and adjusted consumption *CON(2)* are revealed as columns *b* and *c* in Table 7.1. As Table 7.1 shows, *CON(1)* increased rapidly and steadily during the study period, except after 1996, when the growth in GNP stagnated in response to the recent economic slowdown and recession in Japan. *CON(2)* exhibits similar trends, but the growth rate was much slower and was in fact negative in the last few years of the study period. The difference between *CON(1)* and *CON(2)* widened over time.

Expenditure on Consumer Durables (ECD), Service from Consumer Durables (SCD) and Welfare from Publicly-Provided Service Capital (WPPSC)

GPI accounting usually involves two kinds of adjustment to consumption. The first one deals with the services generated from both the existing stock of consumer durables (*SCD*) and from publicly-

Table 7.1 Genuine Progress Indicator (GPI) for Japan, 1970–2003

Year	CON(1)	CON(2)	ECD	SCD	Durables-calibrated CON(1)	Durables-calibrated CON(2)	Distrib. Index
a	*b*	*c*	*d*	*e*	*f*	*g*	*h*
1970	136 382	102 217	2 235	2 823	136 970	102 805	0.632
1971	145 378	108 273	2 456	2 743	145 665	108 559	0.675
1972	160 734	120 093	3 019	2 798	160 514	119 872	0.737
1973	174 940	130 942	3 654	2 896	174 182	130 184	0.733
1974	174 334	129 165	3 212	2 500	173 622	128 453	0.730
1975	183 151	133 713	3 493	2 837	182 495	133 057	0.713
1976	187 988	138 029	3 873	3 172	187 287	137 328	0.732
1977	194 277	142 426	4 305	3 579	193 551	141 700	0.726
1978	204 358	150 790	4 754	4 012	203 616	150 048	0.746
1979	216 748	160 426	5 456	4 495	215 788	159 466	0.718
1980	218 991	148 393	5 223	4 672	218 440	147 842	0.744
1981	222 767	149 910	5 316	4 943	222 394	149 537	0.740
1982	231 775	155 579	5 868	5 357	231 264	155 068	0.719
1983	240 288	160 790	6 405	5 831	239 714	160 217	0.715
1984	247 127	165 615	6 908	6 229	246 448	164 935	0.712
1985	255 769	170 960	7 368	6 734	255 135	170 325	0.709
1986	264 833	176 297	8 476	7 028	263 385	174 849	0.705
1987	277 359	184 338	10 008	7 974	275 325	182 303	0.694
1988	290 472	192 529	12 336	9 290	287 425	189 482	0.676
1989	303 624	201 137	14 197	10 721	300 148	197 661	0.673
1990	316 136	209 018	16 484	12 529	312 181	205 063	0.678
1991	324 327	213 571	17 307	13 478	320 498	209 743	0.655
1992	333 300	219 139	17 042	14 700	330 958	216 797	0.662
1993	337 922	221 562	17 189	15 620	336 352	219 993	0.677
1994	347 014	225 805	17 692	16 595	345 917	224 709	0.641
1995	354 957	230 095	19 148	16 010	351 819	226 957	0.669
1996	364 021	233 475	21 383	17 714	360 352	229 805	0.638
1997	364 424	232 191	21 330	17 928	361 023	228 790	0.635
1998	363 160	232 145	21 228	18 337	360 269	229 254	0.653
1999	364 893	234 413	20 952	18 644	362 585	232 105	0.635
2000	369 769	231 342	22 556	19 392	366 605	228 177	0.634
2001	375 010	229 134	26 436	20 422	368 996	223 120	0.642
2002	378 178	229 529	26 682	21 352	372 848	224 199	0.625
2003	377 838	227 170	28 369	22 876	372 345	221 677	0.642

Table 7.1 (continued)

Year	Weighted CON(1)	Weighted CON(2)	WPPSC	Unpaid h/hold labour	Volunteer labour	Net foreign lending	Cost of unemp. & underemp.
a	*i*	*j*	*k*	*l*	*m*	*n*	*o*
1970	86 560	64 969	952	44 545	924	1 844	- 85
1971	98 389	73 326	1 106	48 457	1 066	4 925	- 246
1972	118 242	88 304	1 278	54 220	1 261	4 661	- 165
1973	127 630	95 391	1 452	59 794	1 466	- 68	- 228
1974	126 683	93 726	1 654	62 581	1 613	-2 279	- 506
1975	130 193	94 924	1 833	67 310	1 819	- 320	-1 005
1976	137 141	100 558	1 988	69 540	1 968	1 596	- 967
1977	140 581	102 920	2 205	71 735	2 121	3 945	-1 066
1978	151 885	111 926	2 479	74 792	2 306	4 619	-1 038
1979	154 888	114 461	2 741	76 352	2 451	-2 541	- 982
1980	162 466	109 958	3 069	76 208	2 543	-3 152	-1 092
1981	164 667	110 722	2 789	77 881	2 699	1 348	-1 204
1982	166 244	111 471	3 037	79 635	2 861	2 049	-1 618
1983	171 504	114 627	3 286	82 105	3 055	5 631	-1 655
1984	175 483	117 442	3 521	84 195	3 241	9 231	-1 638
1985	180 801	120 701	3 735	86 243	3 431	12 474	-1 779
1986	185 752	123 312	3 969	89 566	3 679	15 081	-2 093
1987	191 187	126 592	4 262	93 171	3 947	13 325	-2 056
1988	194 326	128 107	4 524	95 524	4 171	10 762	-1 979
1989	201 961	133 000	4 811	99 255	4 463	8 122	-1 906
1990	211 703	139 061	5 074	101 579	4 699	5 263	-1 945
1991	210 025	137 446	5 310	104 579	4 974	8 878	-2 076
1992	219 010	143 464	4 924	107 156	5 237	13 619	-2 684
1993	227 546	148 828	4 122	110 843	5 562	13 960	-2 709
1994	221 753	144 052	4 414	114 165	5 879	12 632	-2 954
1995	235 248	151 757	3 412	117 566	6 208	9 828	-3 204
1996	229 725	146 501	3 376	119 460	6 466	6 632	-3 635
1997	229 101	145 188	3 523	121 576	6 741	10 630	-4 671
1998	235 177	149 653	3 669	121 682	6 907	13 463	-4 831
1999	230 377	147 473	3 811	121 128	7 037	10 979	-4 958
2000	232 387	144 639	3 944	122 776	7 295	11 881	-5 375
2001	236 790	143 179	4 008	124 646	7 572	10 793	-5 990
2002	233 050	140 137	4 066	126 126	7 831	14 517	-6 127
2003	238 939	142 253	4 091	126 783	8 041	16 407	-5 180

Table 7.1 (continued)

Year	Cost of overwork	Cost of crime	Cost of family b/down	Non-ren. resource depletion	Lost farmland	Timber depletion	Lost wetlands
a	*p*	*q*	*r*	*s*	*t*	*u*	*v*
1970	-5 528	-272	- 506	- 297	- 948	197	-240
1971	-2 940	-281	- 532	- 284	-1 127	292	-244
1972	-4 013	-298	- 577	- 259	-1 317	188	-249
1973	0	-305	- 601	- 269	-1 435	165	-253
1974	-7 518	-280	- 609	- 353	-1 539	114	-257
1975	-11 150	-279	- 638	- 360	-1 680	134	-260
1976	-11 553	-278	- 645	- 407	-1 797	183	-264
1977	-12 555	-278	- 664	- 422	-1 866	162	-267
1978	-13 029	-274	- 668	- 426	-1 935	149	-270
1979	-11 587	-275	- 687	- 444	-2 000	91	-274
1980	-11 211	-270	- 694	- 498	-2 042	1 557	-277
1981	-12 556	-276	- 710	- 494	-2 104	2 187	-280
1982	-13 810	-280	- 741	- 502	-2 157	2 705	-284
1983	-13 961	-284	- 858	- 500	-2 206	1 702	-287
1984	-12 060	-290	- 844	- 468	-2 255	1 477	-290
1985	-12 893	-294	- 801	- 467	-2 310	1 675	-293
1986	-14 070	-297	- 845	- 425	-2 379	1 459	-297
1987	-14 216	-304	- 793	- 357	-2 438	1 294	-300
1988	-14 651	-310	- 763	- 321	-2 513	840	-303
1989	-15 750	-307	- 738	- 316	-2 637	886	-306
1990	-16 541	-306	- 717	- 298	-2 755	828	-309
1991	-17 331	-306	- 735	- 304	-2 882	890	-313
1992	-19 186	-312	- 776	- 290	-3 010	896	-316
1993	-21 842	-318	- 787	- 268	-3 144	1 002	-319
1994	-22 224	-327	- 809	- 258	-3 278	970	-322
1995	-23 423	-335	- 826	- 243	-3 425	955	-326
1996	-20 513	-343	- 857	- 248	-3 568	859	-329
1997	-19 597	-352	- 915	- 221	-3 716	813	-332
1998	-20 866	-364	-1 121	- 199	-3 859	811	-335
1999	-25 567	-372	-1 129	- 191	-3 987	801	-339
2000	-26 099	-406	-1 134	- 177	-4 104	- 500	-342
2001	-26 178	-426	-1 159	- 161	-4 222	598	-345
2002	-26 916	-446	-1 179	- 137	-4 327	743	-348
2003	-25 098	-462	-1 210	- 137	-4 412	765	-352

Table 7.1 (continued)

Year	Cost of air pollution	Cost of water pollution	L-T environ. damage	LNCS	GPI (1)	GPI = GPI (2)	Un-weighted GPI
a	*w*	*x*	*y*	*s* to *y*	*z*	*aa*	*ab*
1970	-4 608	-23 563	- 834	-30 293	98 140	76 549	114 385
1971	-4 219	-24 737	- 890	-31 210	118 733	93 670	119 738
1972	-3 829	-25 912	-1 027	-32 404	142 206	112 267	134 786
1973	-3 440	-27 086	-1 251	-33 569	155 571	123 331	149 209
1974	-3 051	-28 260	-1 314	-34 660	146 679	113 721	139 684
1975	-2 662	-29 435	-1 348	-35 610	152 153	116 884	146 420
1976	-2 487	-31 108	-1 498	-37 377	161 411	124 829	152 993
1977	-2 311	-32 781	-1 601	-39 086	166 937	129 277	159 476
1978	-2 136	-34 453	-1 681	-40 754	180 319	140 360	169 960
1979	-1 961	-36 126	-1 821	-42 535	177 825	137 398	173 971
1980	-1 786	-37 799	-1 897	-42 743	185 124	132 616	162 192
1981	-1 705	-33 811	-1 919	-38 127	196 511	142 565	174 351
1982	-1 623	-29 823	-1 938	-33 622	203 756	148 982	186 727
1983	-1 542	-25 835	-2 092	-30 760	218 063	161 186	202 000
1984	-1 461	-21 847	-2 217	-27 060	233 779	175 738	219 435
1985	-1 380	-17 859	-2 298	-22 932	247 984	187 884	234 594
1986	-1 353	-16 961	-2 324	-22 279	258 463	196 023	245 007
1987	-1 327	-16 064	-2 527	-21 718	266 806	202 211	255 707
1988	-1 300	-15 167	-2 791	-21 555	270 049	203 830	263 305
1989	-1 273	-14 269	-3 000	-20 916	278 996	210 035	273 088
1990	-1 247	-13 372	-3 233	-20 386	288 423	215 781	280 445
1991	-1 267	-12 447	-3 425	-19 748	293 570	220 991	292 200
1992	-1 187	-11 523	-3 596	-19 025	307 963	232 417	304 873
1993	-1 106	-10 599	-3 655	-18 088	318 290	239 571	310 046
1994	-1 148	-9 674	-4 032	-17 743	314 787	237 085	317 241
1995	-1 089	-8 750	-4 192	-17 070	327 404	243 914	318 724
1996	-1 058	-7 825	-4 390	-16 560	323 750	240 527	323 576
1997	-1 026	-6 901	-4 528	-15 911	330 124	246 211	329 671
1998	- 995	-5 976	-4 500	-15 054	338 664	253 139	332 692
1999	- 963	-5 052	-4 794	-14 524	326 781	243 877	328 533
2000	- 931	-4 127	-4 990	-15 172	330 097	242 349	325 965
2001	-1 032	-3 203	-5 371	-13 737	336 318	242 708	322 768
2002	-1 001	-2 278	-5 692	-13 040	337 883	244 970	329 168
2003	- 969	-1 354	-5 918	-12 377	349 935	253 249	332 806

Table 7.1 (continued)

Year	GDP	Population (000s)	Per capita GPI (1)	Per capita GPI (2)	Per capita GDP
a	*ac*	*ad*	*ae*	*af*	*ag*
1970	186 792	104 665	938	731	1 785
1971	194 525	106 100	1 119	883	1 833
1972	210 908	107 595	1 322	1 043	1 960
1973	227 915	109 104	1 426	1 130	2 089
1974	225 413	110 573	1 327	1 028	2 039
1975	232 142	111 940	1 359	1 044	2 074
1976	241 614	113 094	1 427	1 104	2 136
1977	252 254	114 165	1 462	1 132	2 210
1978	265 401	115 190	1 565	1 219	2 304
1979	279 954	116 155	1 531	1 183	2 410
1980	303 494	117 060	1 581	1 133	2 593
1981	311 195	117 902	1 667	1 209	2 639
1982	317 916	118 728	1 716	1 255	2 678
1983	322 844	119 536	1 824	1 348	2 701
1984	334 435	120 305	1 943	1 461	2 780
1985	353 036	121 049	2 049	1 552	2 916
1986	366 642	121 660	2 124	1 611	3 014
1987	379 510	122 239	2 183	1 654	3 105
1988	405 107	122 745	2 200	1 661	3 300
1989	426 922	123 205	2 264	1 705	3 465
1990	447 792	123 611	2 333	1 746	3 623
1991	463 661	124 101	2 366	1 781	3 736
1992	468 575	124 567	2 472	1 866	3 762
1993	467 493	124 938	2 548	1 918	3 742
1994	470 706	125 265	2 513	1 893	3 758
1995	480 118	125 570	2 607	1 942	3 824
1996	497 060	125 859	2 572	1 911	3 949
1997	505 764	126 157	2 617	1 952	4 009
1998	500 093	126 472	2 678	2 002	3 954
1999	499 728	126 667	2 580	1 925	3 945
2000	511 462	126 926	2 601	1 909	4 030
2001	512 510	127 291	2 642	1 907	4 026
2002	511 188	127 435	2 651	1 922	4 011
2003	517 674	127 619	2 742	1 984	4 056

Note: Valued in billions of yen, 2000 prices; per capita values valued in thousands of yen, 2000 prices.

provided service capital (*WPPSC*). The current national accounting system, which is used to calculate GDP and GNP, implicitly classifies personal expenditure on consumer durables (*ECD*) and government investment in social overhead capital as a form of 'consumption' insofar as it assumes that they both contribute directly to the welfare experienced in the year in which the expenditures have taken place. In GPI accounting, it is the service from the increased stock of publicly-provided service capital and consumer durables (assets owned by households) that contribute to current welfare. The GPI accounting reclassifies these expenditures as investment, and imputes the value of the services from the existing stock of consumer durables and publicly-provided social overhead capital.

As mentioned, the calculation of the GPI for the USA only considers highways and streets when calculating the service generated by publicly-provided capital. Included in this study of Japan is the service from other forms of publicly-provided infrastructure provided free of charge or at a low price.

The imputed value of service from consumer durables (column *e*) is added to, and the actual expenditure on consumer durables (column *d*) is subtracted from, personal consumption *PCON(1)* and *PCON(2)* in order to construct values for *Durables-calibrated CON(1)* (column *f*) and *Durables-calibrated CON(2)* (column *g*). These items and the welfare from publicly-provided service capital (column *k*) appear in Table 7.1. The table reveals that *ECD* and *SCD* increased drastically during the bubble period (1982–92) and, despite some fluctuations, continued to increase thereafter. Mass consumption of electrical products and automobiles was a distinct feature of the period, but *ECD* increased at a slower rate during the same period.

Table 7.1 also shows that the welfare generated by publicly-provided service capital (*WPPSC*) (column *k*) increased gradually until 1992, declined between 1992 and 1996, but hovered between ¥3811 billion and ¥4091 billion from 1999 to 2003.

Distribution-Weighted Consumption

The next adjustment to consumption follows the standard GPI procedure of weighting *Durables-calibrated CON(1)* (column *f*) and *Durables-calibrated CON(2)* (column *g*) by an appropriate distribution index. Although the Atkinson index was chosen as the appropriate measure of inequality, a Gini coefficient was also computed for the study period.

The degree of income inequality was generally low in the 1960s and 1970s with the Gini coefficient ranging between 0.33 and 0.36 and Atkinson index between 0.25 and 0.29. The high growth rate accompanied by the relatively low level of inequality during the 1970s has often been described as the period of 'redistribution with growth' or 'shared growth' in the development literature (World Bank, 1993). However, inequality increased rapidly in the 1980s and 1990s. The Gini coefficient rose from 0.33 in 1972 to 0.40 in 2002, while the Atkinson index increased from 0.26 to 0.38 during the same period.

The Distribution Index (column *h*) as measured by (1 – Atkinson index) was used as a weighting factor to adjust consumption for income inequality and to thus arrive at *Weighted CON(1)* (column *i*) and *Weighted CON(2)* (column *j*) in Table 7.1. While total consumption expenditure (adjusted for defensive expenditures) (column *c*) rose rapidly throughout the 1980s and continued to increase in the first half of the 1990s, the distribution-weighted consumption expenditure (column *j*) stagnated in the early 1990s and has since declined. The gap between the two measures widened in the 1980s and 1990s but has stabilised in more recent years.

Value of Unpaid Work

Unpaid household work such as housekeeping, parenting, and caretaking has always made a significant contribution to social welfare. In recognition of this importance, several attempts have been made in Japan, including one by the Economic Planning Agency,[9] to estimate the value of unpaid work. Studies reveal that the number of volunteer work hours per person has not increased since the 1970s. Hours of both unpaid household and volunteer work increased between 2000 and 2005, but whether this shows any significant move away from the previous pattern is yet to be confirmed. Male participation in household work has been remarkably low, while the level of engagement in volunteer work shows no such gender difference.

As can be seen in Table 7.1, unpaid household labour (column *l*) was the second largest positive component of Japan's GPI. It ranged from ¥44 545 billion in 1970 to ¥126 783 billion in 2003. This constitutes an average annual increase of 3–4 per cent which is a rise almost as rapid as that of total consumption expenditure. The value of volunteer labour (column *m*) was ¥924 in 1970. It increased steadily, but at a much higher rate than unpaid household labour, to eventually reach ¥8040 billion in 2003.

Net Foreign Lending/Borrowing

Unlike other GPI country studies, where the foreign debt item invariably appears as 'net foreign borrowing', it better reflects 'net foreign lending' (column *n*) in the Japanese case. Except for the few years after the first and second oil crisis (1973 and 1979), the annual values of this item were positive, predominantly ranging between ¥5000 billion and ¥15 000 billion per year (Table 7.1). Although there were many fluctuations in this item between 1970 and 2003, it is clear that Japan's stock of overseas assets increased substantially over the study period.

Social Costs of Unwilling Time Use (Unemployment, Underemployment, and Overwork)

Unwilling time use (unemployment, underemployment, and overwork), as well as crime and family breakdown represent the negative social consequences of economic activity. Due to the high growth in GNP fostered by Keynesian-based economics, Japan enjoyed many years of full employment in the 1960s and early 1970s. Unemployment only emerged following the 1973 oil crisis. Unemployment rates were still as low as 0–1 per cent throughout the rest of the 1970s and 1980s, but rose to the 4 per cent level after the burst of the bubble economy in the late 1980s and early 1990s. According to the latest *Labour Force Survey* (Statistics Bureau), the unemployment rate reached 4.1 per cent in 1998, and further rose to 5 per cent in 2001 and 5.4 per cent in 2002. It declined slightly to 5.3 per cent in 2003. The average number of unemployed people in 2003 was 3.5 million – a decrease of 90 000 from 2002.

Perhaps more serious than the problem of unemployment is underemployment and the increase in the labour force engaged in non-regular employment (e.g., dispatched work). Underemployment in the form of part-time work emerged in the mid-1970s when the female labour participation rate started to rise. Since then, engagement in part-time labour has been typical among female workers. Despite the enactment of the Equal Employment Opportunities Law (1985), the majority of working women continue to work in part-time or non-regular jobs, while the gap in earnings and working conditions between female professionals and the remaining female workforce has further widened. The famous M-shaped pattern of typical female labour – namely, quitting jobs for marriage or parenting and returning to the labour market later in their life – still applies as late as 2002. More recently, unemployment has become prevalent among middle-aged males and the young, while underemployment among Japanese youth has also been increasing.

Another serious labour problem in Japan is the excessive and often hidden degree of overwork among regular full-time workers. Official labour statistics show that scheduled working hours and overtime have been declining steadily since the late 1980s. However, this does not reflect the real situation in that: (a) the share of workers working less than 35 hours per week increased rapidly, masking the increase in working hours among full-time workers; and (b) the officially reported working hours do not reflect 'true' working hours.

Statistical figures for labour hours vary according to two labour surveys on the average hours of work per month: one based on data from the *Monthly Labour Survey* (Ministry of Health, Labour and Welfare); the other based on data derived from the *Labour Force Survey* (Statistics Bureau). According to a report from the Japan Productivity Center for Socio-Economic Development, the former survey is conducted every month at business establishments with the reported figures indicating company-paid labour hours. The latter survey is based on direct responses of individual workers to a questionnaire reflecting self-declared, more realistic, labour hours. On average, the difference between the two surveys is at least ten working hours, and more than 15 working hours since 1998. Moreover, the business establishment survey shows no indication of declining working hours in the years 1997–2003. The difference in working hours between the two survey data can be considered a proxy for the unreported and unpaid portion of overtime work.

The combined cost of unemployment and underemployment (Table 7.1, column *o*) started to rise in 1973 from what was, at the time, a negligible value. It did not increase greatly during the 1970s and 1980s, but noticeably accelerated in the 1990s and early 2000s. It was estimated at ¥5.180 billion in 2003. On the other hand, the cost of overwork (column *p*) dramatically increased after the burst of the bubble economy in the early 1990s. It then declined during the severe recession around

1998, before rising again and stabilising in the 2000s. In 2003, the estimated cost of overwork reached a high of ¥25 098 billion.

Social Costs of Crime and Family Breakdown

According to the National Police Agency (*Criminal Statistics*, annual issues), the number of designated crime cases and offence rates during the post-World War II period were lowest in the early to mid-1970s. This was at a time when the original NNW study of Japan was published. Since then, designated crime cases and offence rates have risen significantly.

The cost of crime (Table 7.1, column *q*) was assigned according to the classification of crimes by the National Police Agency. Table 7.1 indicates that the estimated cost of crime was not very high throughout the 1970–2003 period. However, it generally increased over the study period, except for the years between 1973 and 1979, beginning at ¥272 billion in 1970 and rising to ¥462 billion in 2003.

The cost of divorce and suicide was used to represent the cost of family breakdown (Table 7.1, column *r*). The number of divorces increased from 95 937 in 1970 to 178 786 in 1984. The divorce rate decreased somewhat to 157 608 in 1990 before rising again thereafter. Overall, the divorce rate exhibited an increasing trend over the study period where, in 2003, it reached a high of 289 836. This was effectively three times the number in 1970. On the other hand, the number of suicides experienced two peak periods. The first peak period was 1983–86, while the second peak period occurred after 1997.

The estimated cost of divorce between 1970 and 2003 increased from ¥192 billion in 1970 to ¥568 billion in 2003. By 2003, the estimated cost of suicide was ¥642 billion. Table 7.1 reveals that the combined cost of divorce and suicide – i.e., the cost of family breakdown (column *r*) – increased from ¥506 billion in 1970 to ¥1210 billion in 2003.

Cost of Sacrificed Source Services of Natural Capital: Non-Renewable Resource Depletion, Lost Farmland, and Timber Depletion

Natural capital contributes to human welfare in many ways. Typically, it is a provider of natural resource inputs into production (source services) and environmental services of waste absorption (sink services), and assumes ecological functions, such as habitat and flood and climate control. Natural capital also supplies other non-economic amenities, such as health and aesthetic values.

Mineral resources are representative economic assets that provide necessary inputs to the production process. However, the cost of using those resources is not properly reflected in the total net receipts from resource extraction (net of extraction cost). Sustainable welfare and consumption requires this so-called 'user cost' or 'depletion factor' to be set aside as a form of capital investment (which is not in the current national income accounting). Since the aim of the GPI is to measure *current* sustainable welfare, and thus excludes current net investment, the user cost of economic assets must be subtracted from current consumption. It must, therefore, also be subtracted when calculating the GPI.

As previously mentioned, the El Serafy approach to compute the user cost of the non-renewable mineral resources was employed in the calculation of the GPI for Japan. Included in this calculation for Japan were the following non-renewable mineral resources: metallic and non-metallic ores, coal, crude petroleum, and natural gas.

The estimated cost of non-renewable resource depletion for Japan was low (Table 7.1, column *s*), ranging from ¥297 billion in 1970 to ¥137 billion in 2003. Despite the low cost of non-renewable resource depletion, it is not true that mineral resources are scarce in Japan. Coal mining, for example, was at one time a core industry and played a key role in the post-war reconstruction of the Japanese economy. The production of coal decreased dramatically in the late 1960s and early 1970s, and declined to nearly zero in 2002. This was the result of a government policy to switch Japan's energy sources from domestically produced coal to cheaper imported petroleum. Since the oil crisis of 1973, there was a less discernible shift away from imported oil to nuclear power as a source of electricity. However, the uranium used in nuclear plants was, again, totally imported from abroad. Thus, the cost of the depletion of *domestic* non-renewable resources has been low simply because of Japan's heavy dependence on imported non-renewable resources.

Farmland is important not only for the provision of essential agricultural products, but also in terms of other valuable ecosystem functions. Urbanisation removes the productive capacity of farmland by decreasing farm areas. In this study of Japan, the loss of farmland was computed by accounting for the cost of lost farm products and the cost of lost sink and ecological services.[10] Taking the area of farmland in 1961 as a base year (the year in which the area of farmland peaked in the post-World War II period), the annual cost of lost farm products was computed in terms of the lost services from the source function of farmland. The estimated cost of lost farm products increased from ¥548 billion in 1970 to ¥2552 billion in 2003. The environmental cost from lost farmland was not included here but incorporated into the GPI as a sacrificed ecosystem service. This is discussed in the next sub-section.

The stock of timber in Japan increased every year between 1970 and 2003. It was therefore necessary to compute the benefits from, rather than the cost of, the services generated by additional timber stocks (Table 7.1, column *u*). The data on timber stocks for each five–year period between 1970 and 2000 were taken from National Forestry plan. Annual prices of the three major varieties of trees were derived from the *Report on Demand and Supply of Timber* (MAFF). The benefits from increased timber stocks were valued at ¥197 billion in 1970. This increased to ¥765 billion by 2003, although it peaked as high as ¥2705 billion in 1982.

Cost of Lost Sink and Ecological Functions of Farmland and Wetlands

The Ministry of Agriculture, Forestry, and Fisheries (MAFF) recently adopted the 'multi-functionality of agriculture' as a key concept for the future development of primary industries and rural communities. The National Agricultural Research Center (NARC, 1998) identified eight functions of farmland:

- flood prevention
- water cultivation
- prevention of land erosion
- prevention of mudslides
- absorption of organic wastes
- air purification
- climate stabilisation
- recreation and relaxation.

The NARC estimated the value of the multi-functionality of Japanese agriculture at ¥6879 billion per year. This amounts to a value of ¥1.377

million per hectare per year (at 2000 prices). In this study, the multi-functionality of agriculture was regarded as a form of non-paid benefits generated by the sink and ecological functions of farmland.

Taking the farm area in 1961 again as a base year, the annual costs of lost sink and ecological services during the study period were estimated at ¥400 billion and ¥1860 billion respectively in 2003. Combined with the cost of the lost source function (lost farm products), the total cost of lost farmland (Table 7.1, column *t*) was ¥948 billion in 1970. This cost rose to ¥4412 billion by 2003, which equates to a 365.5 per cent increase over the study period.

Both wetlands (marsh) and tidelands are included in the computation of the cost of lost wetlands (column *v*) used in this GPI study of Japan. The cost of lost wetlands was incorporated into the study given the important role wetlands play in terms of water purification, flood control, and the provision of wildlife habitat. The method used to calculate this item was based on the approach used by Costanza et al. (1997). The estimated cost of lost wetlands was ¥240 billion in 1970, which increased to ¥352 billion in 2003 (Table 7.1).

The GPI calculated for the USA contains an item on the loss of primary forests which emphasises the ability of forests to maintain biological diversity, to provide habitat for sensitive species, and to deliver other important ecological functions. The 2003 report for Japanese GPI also computed the cost of lost primary forest; however, the computation involved the use of data based on area rather than stock. It was also based on a rather crude assumption on the unit cost of lost forest.

The annual loss of old-growth forests increased in the 1950s and 1960s, and peaked in the second half of 1960s. However, it decreased substantially thereafter as the importation of timber and forest products increased. Since better information has not become available, and the total cost, if it could be calculated, would be small, the computation of the cost of lost primary forest was omitted from the present study.

Cost of Air and Water Pollution: Sacrificed Sink Function of Natural Capital

As stated in the introduction, environmental degradation was acute in Japan between the mid-1960s and early-1970s. The keen awareness of this by the NNW Committee and the fact that environmental degradation was largely an opportunity cost of the high growth rate of GNP became the impetus for including pollution in the estimation of Japan's NNW. The report on New National Welfare (NNW) focused on the pollution related to industrial activities (Economic Council, 1973).

According to the United Nations Handbook and Manual on Systems of Integrated Environmental and Economic Accounting (United Nations, 1993 and 2000), the cost of pollution, which is described as 'defensive expenditure', consists of the actual expenditure incurred to eliminate or prevent pollution plus the imputed cost of discharged pollutants. Actual expenditure includes: (a) household expenditure on pollution abatement, such as outlays for water purifiers and bottled water; (b) government investment in social overhead capital, such as sewage disposal plants; and (c) investment by companies in water treatment facilities and equipment. Due to the difficulty in finding appropriate data, the abatement expenditure by households was not included. Furthermore, because the latter two categories of expenditure are forms of investment, they too have been excluded from the GPI calculation.

The cost of air pollution (Table 7.1, column *w*) was computed by using SO_x (sulphur oxide) and NO_x (nitrogen oxide) emissions as indicators of air pollution. The cost was estimated by multiplying the quantity of the emitted air pollutant by the relevant marginal cost. As for the cost of water pollution (Table 7.1, column *x*), indexes of biological oxygen demand (BOD) and chemical oxygen demand (COD) were closely considered. Other types of water pollution, such as phosphate (P), nitrogen (N), and heavy metals, although important, were left for future studies. The estimation method used to calculate the cost of water pollution was similar to that used for air pollution.

Table 7.1 illustrates the change in the cost of air and water pollution. The estimated cost of air pollution was ¥4608 billion in 1970. However, it steadily decreased thereafter and was just ¥969 billion in 2003. The estimated cost of water pollution was ¥23 563 billion in 1970 but increased to ¥37 799 billion in 1980. It then drastically decreased to be as low as ¥1354 billion in 2003.

Cost of Long-Term Environmental Damage

Most GPI studies include the cost of long-term environmental damage (Table 7.1, column *y*) which typically involves the cost of ozone depletion and climate change. This item is different in nature from other items in the GPI in that it deals with a global environmental cost. Many have questioned the inclusion of the cost of global environmental damage given that GPI accounting is largely confined to the loss of environmental source and sink functions in the domestic context.

In the computation of the Japanese GPI, the cost of long-term environmental damage was estimated in terms of Japan's share of internalising the loss of global public goods – which, in this case, is the sink function of the atmosphere. Although previous Japanese GPI studies included both the cost of ozone depletion and global climate change, the present GPI takes only climate change into account. The computation of the cost of ozone depletion in the previous GPI study was not based on entirely accurate data on the production and sales of chlorofluorocarbons (CFCs) in Japan. Nor was it possible to prepare improved data in time for the present study.[11]

To estimate the cost of Japan's contribution towards climate change, cumulative CO_2 emissions were multiplied by the marginal social cost (MSC) of emissions in each year. Japan's cumulative CO_2 emissions were computed using emissions data dating back to the year 1900. The data on Japan's CO_2 emissions were derived from official energy statistics.

A variety of estimates of the marginal social cost of carbon emissions were made by the Intergovernmental Panel on Climate Change in the 1990s (IPCC, 1996 and 2001). For the purpose of Japan's GPI, the MSC in 1990 was assumed to be US$20 per tonne in 1990 prices or ¥3070 per tonne in 2000 prices (Cline, 1992 and 1995).[12] It was then assumed that the MSC of a tonne of CO_2 emissions increased every year beyond 1990. This assumption was made given that the MSC per tonne of emitted CO_2 can be considered a positive function of the accumulated stock of carbon in the atmosphere. As such, the MSC in any year beyond 1990 was assumed to be proportional to the change in cumulative CO_2 emissions from 1990 to the year in question (i.e., MSC in 1995 = ¥3070 × 1995 cumulative CO_2 emissions/1990 cumulative CO_2 emissions).

Cumulative CO_2 emissions in Japan increased from 2715 million tonnes of carbon units in 1970 to 7344 million tonnes of carbon units in 2003. Column *y* in Table 7.1 reveals that the cost of long-term environmental damage for Japan was ¥834 billion in 1970. The cost steadily increased to reach ¥5918 billion in 2003.

THE GPI OF JAPAN: RESULTS AND DISCUSSION

Long-Run Trends of Per Capita GDP and Per Capita GPI

Japan's GPI was derived from the aggregation of the components described in the previous section. The GPI is based on consumption expenditure adjusted for defensive and/or undesirable expenditures – that is, *Durables-calibrated CON(2)* (column *g*). For this reason, the GPI referred to throughout this section, unless stated otherwise, is GPI(2) or column *aa* in Table 7.1. GPI(1), which is provided for illustrative purposes, is a GPI based on *Durables-calibrated CON(1)* (column *f*). It is revealed in Table 7.1 as column *z*. Japan's GPI(1), GPI(2), and GDP also appear in Table 7.1 in per capita terms – namely, per capita GPI(1) (column *ae*), per capita GPI(2) (column *af*), and per capita GDP (column *ag*).

Figure 7.1 exhibits the trend of Japan's per capita GPI and per capita GDP over the study period, 1970–2003. During this period, per capita GPI increased from ¥0.731 million per person to ¥1.984 million per person, while per capita GDP rose from ¥1.785 million per person to ¥4.056 million per person. As Figure 7.1 shows, the pattern of growth of the two indicators did not differ much; however, per capita GPI grew at a much slower rate than per capita GDP. In particular, while per capita GPI showed little or no growth tendency between 1973 and 1980 and the remainder of the study period after 1993, per capita GDP continued to grow over the entire study period, including the recession period after 1990, albeit at a very much reduced rate. There were two brief periods – the early 1970s and the early 1980s – when per capita GPI grew faster than per capita GDP. Notwithstanding this, the disparity between the two measures generally widened over the study period.

Positive Components of the GPI

Figure 7.2 illustrates the relative contribution of the positive components of Japan's GPI. *Weighted CON(2)*, weighted by income inequality (column *j*), is the base item of the GPI computation. In 1970, it accounted for 57 per cent of the total positive components (85 per cent of the GPI value). This share declined to 47.7 per cent (56 per cent of the GPI value) by 2003.

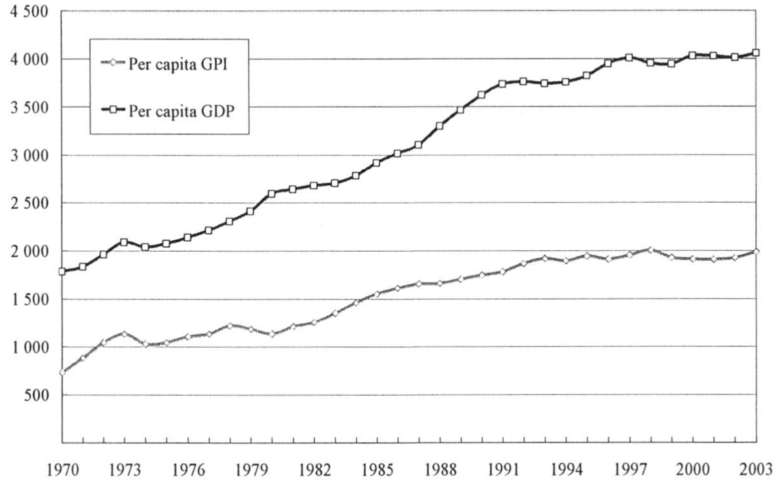

Note: Valued in thousands of yen at 2000 prices.

Figure 7.1 Per capita GPI and per capita GDP: Japan, 1970–2003

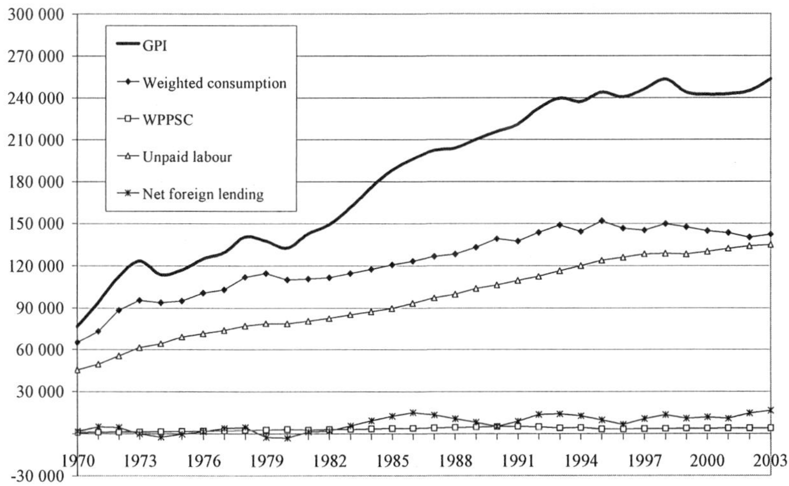

Note: Valued in billions of yen at 2000 prices.

Figure 7.2 Positive components of Japan's GPI, 1970–2003

Together, the values of household and volunteer labour (columns *l* and *m*) were the second largest component of Japan's GPI, contributing 40–45 per cent of the GPI value over the study period. While the share of the value of household labour decreased slightly from 66.2 per cent in 1970 to 46.4 per cent in 1993, it rose to 50 per cent in 2003. On the other hand, the share of volunteer labour was minimal throughout, even though it increased very gradually from 1.4 per cent in 1970 to 3.2 per cent in 2003.

While net foreign borrowing has been a major negative component of the GPI for many countries (e.g., the USA, Australia, New Zealand, and India), net foreign lending (column *n*) was consistently an important positive component of Japan's GPI. The amount of net foreign lending increased over the study period and its share of the total positive component of the GPI rose from 2.4 per cent in 1970 to 6.5 per cent in 2003.

The Effects of Adjustments to Consumption: Non Welfare-Enhancing Expenditure and Income Inequality

Both the subtraction of non-welfare-enhancing consumption and the weighting by a Distribution Index (column *h*) had strong effects on the magnitude of the GPI. For example, the subtraction of non-welfare-enhancing consumption decreased the value of the GPI – that is, GPI(1) versus GPI(2) – by an average of 24.6 per cent each year over the study period. In addition, the weighting of consumption expenditure in accordance with changes in the distribution of income further decreased the GPI by an average of 22.1 per cent per year.

Negative Components of the GPI

The relative impacts of the negative components of Japan's GPI are revealed in Figure 7.3. The combined cost of air and water pollution (columns *w* and *x*) was the largest negative factor between 1970 and 1987. In 1970, these costs collectively constituted 81 per cent of the negative components of Japan's GPI. This fell to 60 per cent by 1983, after which it declined very rapidly to be just 4.9 per cent by 2003.

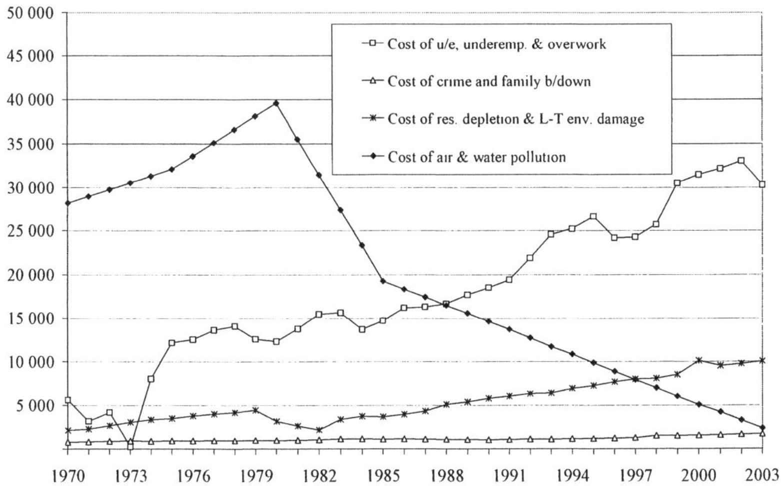

Note: Valued in billions of yen at 2000 prices.

Figure 7.3 *Negative components of Japan's GPI, 1970–2003*

The decline in the contribution made by air and water pollution towards the cost of economic activity was due to a number of factors. These include energy savings at the industry level (particularly following the 1973 oil crisis), the shift from an industrial to a service-based economy, a rise in environmental awareness, and the introduction of stricter environmental standards.

The cost of unemployment, underemployment, and overwork (columns *o* and *p*) became the largest factor to suppress the GPI after 1987. Whilst unemployment and underemployment were almost non-existent in the 1950s, the total cost of unemployment, underemployment and overwork increased modestly into the 1960s and 1970s and substantially after the mid-1970s. By 2003, it constituted 67 per cent of the negative components of Japan's GPI. Furthermore, the cost of overwork accounted for more than 80 per cent of total labour-related costs.

The cost of long-term environmental damage (column *y*) gradually increased during the study period, reaching 13 per cent of the total negative components by 2003. The share could have been much higher except for the fact that the estimation of this item was conservatively based on a low marginal social cost of US$20 per tonne of CO_2.

The cost of natural resource depletion remained very low, although its share of the total negative components of Japan's GPI reached 11 per cent by 2003. As stated in the previous section, this is not so much an indication of Japan's resource-saving efforts but largely due to Japan's heavy dependence on the importation of cheap foreign natural resources.

CONCLUSION

Most GPI studies reveal a widening gap between a nation's GDP and GPI, with the latter often beginning to stagnate or decrease by the early 1980s. This chapter reveals that the time-series pattern of the Japanese GPI is similar to that of other countries. The GPI of Japan increased very little during the time of the bubble economy (1984–91) and was largely stagnant in the decade following the 1973 oil crisis (1973–83). The GPI of Japan then decreased slightly after 1991. Increasing inequality in the 1980s and 1990s contributed considerably to Japan's depressed GPI.

On the positive side, apart from the contribution of the aggregate (adjusted) consumption and unpaid work (household labour and volunteer labour), net foreign lending was the third-largest positive component of the GPI. On the negative side, the contribution of environmental degradation and natural capital depletion was not as substantial as one might have expected, particularly towards the end of the study period. This was due essentially to Japan's relative success at reducing its domestic or local pollution which was once notoriously bad during the 1960s and the early 1970s. The depletion of natural resources, particularly non-renewable resources, was kept to a minimum during the study period.

Whilst Japan relied initially on its own coal deposits to power its post-war industrialisation process, it has been able to switch successfully from domestic coal to oil imports to meet its energy needs. But Japan remains resource poor and is likely to remain heavily dependent on imported natural resources into the future.

The importance of net foreign lending on Japan's GPI and the subsequent accumulation of external financial assets underscores the key role played by the rise in manufactured exports towards Japan's genuine progress. Both more than offset the negative impact on Japan's GPI of rising resource imports. As for social costs, the cost associated with unwilling time use (i.e., the cost of unemployment, underemployment, and overwork) has been substantial. Indeed, so much so, it constituted the largest impact of all the costs on Japan's GPI. More should therefore be done to balance labour demand and labour supply in order to simultaneously reduce unemployment and the growing trend towards overwork among Japan's full-time workers.

Towards an Open Economy GPI

The Japanese GPI highlights an important issue that needs to be investigated further. It relates to the impacts that international trade and trans-boundary resource depletion and environmental degradation have on GPI accounting. Japan is unique in the sense that its high import spending on natural resources (or natural resource-intensive goods) is financed by extensive exports of manufactured products and services. However, as Daly and Cobb (1994) have pointed out, 'A single country may substitute man-made for natural capital (the flow of natural resources and services) from other countries that have retained their natural capital to a greater degree. In other words, the demands of complementarity can be evaded at the national level, but only if they are respected at the international level.' Japan is exactly the case in question.

In a world where natural resources are becoming increasingly scarce, one could imagine a situation where a country with an ever-increasing reliance on foreign imports of food, energy, and other natural resources would not be sustainable in the long-run. Apart from cultural and moral issues, there is a legitimate reason to expect future changes in the terms of trade eventually to reflect the rise in relative resource scarcity. Examples which are likely to affect Japan include the rapid rise in the price of corn, which is used in the production of ethanol (a substitute for petroleum), and unclaimed resource rents (user cost) that might eventually increase the cost of natural resource imports.

In the past, GPI accounting has attempted to measure sustainable economic welfare in a purely national context. Major exceptions to this include the incorporation of net foreign borrowing/lending and long-term environmental damage. In the treatment of long-term environmental damage, the cost of CO_2 emissions is viewed from a global perspective by assigning the entire cost to the emitting country. On the other hand, the cost of natural resource depletion is viewed only from a national perspective. In particular, where natural resources are traded, the cost of the depletion of both non-renewable and renewable natural resources, including the future change in prices, is borne entirely by the extracting (exporting) country but not by the consuming (importing) country. Knowing this, it would be extremely unwise if the extracting (exporting) country did not shift this cost to the consuming country by adding the user cost to the export price.

With this in mind, future GPI accounting exercises might be improved by: (a) having the resource-extracting country bear the cost of depleted resources allocated for domestic use; and (b) having all resource-importing countries bear the resource rent (user cost) associated with the international trade in resources. The United Nations Handbook of National Accounting on Integrated Environmental and Economic Accounting (SEEA) (United Nations, 1993) touches upon this and other transboundary problems in the following passage:

> Exports include not only cross-boundary product flows to foreign economies (as in SNA) but also flows representing the uses of, and the effects on, the natural environment of other countries by the domestic economy. Flows from the rest of the world to the domestic economy include only imports of products, which are recorded as a sub-item of total uses. (United Nations, 1993, p. 77, Paragraph 211).

The Japanese version of the SEEA has attempted to compute the influence of Japanese oil imports from the rest of the world on the depletion cost of non-renewable resources using the El Serafy user cost method. In 1995, Japan's user cost of oil imports was estimated at ¥513.7 billion or US$5.47 billion (in 1995 prices and exchange rates). The user cost is also likely to be substantial for a range of manufacturing metals that Japan also imports in large quantities (e.g., iron ore). Were these user costs to be included in the estimation of Japan's GPI for 1995, it would undoubtedly reduce its aggregate value quite significantly.

Clearly we should all learn from this practice and construct an open economy version of the GPI for future accounting purposes. In addressing this issue, the current confinement in GPI calculations to the cost of ozone depletion and climate change should also be extended to incorporate other important global public goods, such as biodiversity and ocean fish stocks.

NOTES

1. The Engel coefficient reflects the proportion of income spent on food. A rise in the coefficient indicates that a greater proportion of total income is devoted to food expenditure; a fall in the coefficient denotes the opposite.
2. Defensive expenditures included government expenditure on such things as justice, the police, and public administration.
3. Private defensive expenditures included the cost of travel to work (partially deducted), self-employment costs, and spending for social obligations.
4. Excluded from this calculation were non-welfare-enhancing services, services with charges, or services from defensive government investment (e.g., waste treatment facilities).
5. Yoshihiko Wada, Katsura Nakano, and other members of the Japanese GPI research group made valuable contributions to the earlier versions of the Japanese GPI. We thank the Sumitomo Foundation for its generous support for the research.
6. The Atkinson Index represented by equations (7.1) and (7.2) is for $\varepsilon \neq 1$. A different formula is used for $\varepsilon = 1$.
7. The value of the parameter ε ranges from zero, which means that society is indifferent about the distribution of income, to infinity, which means that society is concerned only with the position of the lowest income group. As ε rises, society attaches more weight to income transfers at the lower end of the distribution and less weight to transfers at the top. Typically used values of ε include 0.5 and 2.
8. In principle, services from public capital charging fees should also be included provided that the imputed values of the services outweigh the fees, but this is beyond current capacity.
9. The Economic Research Institute of the Economic Planning Agency (presently Economic and Social Research Institute (ESRI), Cabinet Office) published two reports in 1997 and 1998 on the valuation of non-paid household work and social activities (ESRI, 1998).
10. The computation of the cost for lost farmland and lost wetlands can be attributed to Yoshihiko Wada.
11. Since quite complete sets of data on the emission, production, and sales of CFC-related materials at world and regional levels are available through the AFEAS (Alternative Fluorocarbons Environmental Acceptability Study), the inclusion of the cost of ozone depletion, which has remained substantial even after the production and sales of influencing materials were regulated, should be taken into consideration in future GPI studies.
12. The assumptions in Cline's estimation are: (a) the period of damage is up to 2276; (b) there is a 2.5°C increase in global temperatures; (c) the damage is 1.4 per cent to 2.5 per cent of GDP in developed countries and 1.8 per cent to 4 per cent in developing countries; and (d) the social rate of time preference (discount rate) is 1.5 per cent.

REFERENCES

Atkinson, A. (1970), 'On the measurement of inequality', *Journal of Economic Theory*, **2**, 244–263.

Cline, W. (1992), *The Economics of Global Warming*, Washington, DC: Institute for International Economics.

Cline, W. (1995), *Pricing Carbon Dioxide Pollution*, Victoria, BC: Ministry of Transportation and Highways.

Costanza, R., d'Arge, R., de Groot, R., Farber, S., Grasso, M., Hannon, B., Limburg, K., Naeem, S., O'Neill, R., Parvelo, J., Raskin, R., Sutton, P. and van den Belt, M. (1997), 'The value of the world's ecosystem services and natural capital', *Nature*, **15 May**, 253–260.

Daly, H. and J. Cobb, Jr. (1994), *For the Common Good: Redirecting the Economy Toward Community, the Environment, and a Sustainable Future*, 2nd edition, Boston, MA: Beacon Press.

Economic and Social Research Institute, Cabinet Office (ESRI) (1998), 'Social Infrastructure in Japan', Tokyo: ESRI.

Economic Council (1973), *New Indicator of Welfare NNW*, Tokyo: Ministry of Finance Printing Bureau.

El Serafy, S. (1989), 'The proper calculation of income from depletable natural resources', in Y. Ahmad, S. El Serafy and E. Lutz (eds), *Environmental Accounting for Sustainable Development*, Washington, DC: World Bank, pp. 10–18.

Hamilton, C. (1999), 'The Genuine Progress Indicator methodological developments and results from Australia', *Ecological Economics*, **30**, 13–28.

Intergovernmental Panel of Climate Change (IPCC) (1996), *Climate Change 1995: Economic and Social Dimensions of Climate Change*, Cambridge: Cambridge University Press.

Intergovernmental Panel of Climate Change (IPCC) (2001), *Climate Change 2001: Impacts, Adaptation and Vulnerability*, Geneva: World Meteorological Organisation.

Jackson, T. and Stymne, S. (1996), *Sustainable Economic Welfare in Sweden: A Pilot Index 1950–1992*, Stockholm: Stockholm Environment Institute, The New Economics Foundation.

Jackson, T., Laing, F. and MacGillivray, A. (1997), 'An Index of Sustainable Economic Welfare for the UK, 1950–1996', University of Surrey Centre for Environmental Strategy, Guildford.

Kanamori, H., Takase, Y. and Uno, K. (1977), 'Japanese economic growth and economic welfare', Center Paper No. 31, Japan Economic Research Center.

Lawn, P. (2003), 'A theoretical foundation to support the Index of Sustainable Economic Welfare (ISEW), Genuine Progress Indicator (GPI), and other related indexes', *Ecological Economics*, **44**, 105–118.

Lawn, P. and Clarke, M. (2006), *Measuring Genuine Progress: An Application of the Genuine Progress Indicator*, New York: Nova Science Publishers.

Makino, M., Nakano, K. and Wada, Y. (2003), 'Genuine Progress Indicator (GPI) for Japan: a long term estimation 1955–2000', paper presented at 2003 Biannual Conference of Canadian Society of Ecological Economics (CANSEE).

Mito, T. (2003), Toward a new indicator to show genuine welfare: investigation of the Genuine Progress Indicator through a case study of Japan, Masters research paper presented to University of Waterloo, Ontario, Canada.

National Agricultural Research Center (NARC) (1998), 'Estimation of multi-functionality of agriculture and rural area using replacement cost approach', *Nogyo sogo kenkyu*, **52(4)** (in Japanese).

Neumayer, E. (2000), 'On the methodology of the ISEW, GPI, and related measures: Some constructive suggestions and some doubt on the threshold hypothesis', *Ecological Economics*, **34**, 347–361.

Nordhaus, W. and Tobin, J. (1972), 'Is growth obsolete?', *Economic Growth*, New York: National Bureau of Economic Research.

Redefining Progress (1995), *The Genuine Progress Indicator, Summary of Data and Methodology*, Oakland, CA: Redefining Progress.

Redefining Progress (1999), *The Genuine Progress Indicator: 1998 Update*, Oakland, CA: Redefining Progress.

United Nations (1993), *Integrated Environmental and Economic Accounting*, New York: UN.

United Nations (2000), *Integrated Environmental and Economic Accounting: An Operational Manual*, New York: UN.

Uno, K. (1989), 'Economic Growth and Environmental Change in Japan: Net National Welfare and Beyond', in F. Archibugi and P. Nijkamp (eds), *Economy and Ecology: Towards Sustainable Development*, Dordrecht, Kluwer, chapter 17.

World Bank (1993), *The East Asian Miracle*, London: Oxford University Press.

Young, H. Peyton (1990), 'Progressive taxation and equal sacrifice', *American Economic Review*, **80(1)**, 253–266.

SOURCES OF STATISTICAL DATA

Agency of National Resources and Energy, *Statistical Survey of Estimated Mining Amount*, published every five years.

Bank of Japan, *Long-Term Time Series Data*, http://www.boj.or.jp/en/type/stat/dlong/index.htm.

Economic and Social Research Institute (ESRI), Cabinet Office, *Annual Report on National Accounts*.

Economic and Social Research Institute (ESRI), Cabinet Office, *On New Integrated Environmental and Economic Accounting*, http://www.esri.cao.go.jp/jp/sna/sateraito/041012/kankyou.html.

Economic Planning Agency (1955, 1970), *National Wealth Survey*.

Ministry of Agriculture, Forestry and Fisheries (MAFF), *Statistical Yearbook of Ministry of Agriculture*, annual issues.

Ministry of Agriculture, Forestry and Fisheries (MAFF), *Report on Demand and Supply of Timber*, annual issues.

Ministry of Economy, Trade and Industry (METI), *Trend of Mining Industry in Japan*, published every five years.

Ministry of Health, Labour and Welfare (MHLW), *Basic Survey on Wage Structure*, annual issues.

Ministry of Health, Labour and Welfare (MHLW), *Vital Statistics*, annual issues.

Ministry of Health, Labour and Welfare (MHLW), *Basic Survey on Wage Structure*, annual issues.

Ministry of Health, Labour and Welfare (MHLW), *Monthly Labour Survey Handbook*, annual issues.

Ministry of Health, Labor and Welfare (MHLW), *Comprehensive Survey of Living Conditions*, large-scale surveys: every three years since 1986; small-scale surveys in interim.

Ministry of Justice, *White Paper on Crime*, annual issues.

National Police Agency, *Criminal Statistics*, annual issues.

National Police Agency, *Crimes in Japan*, annual issues.

Statistics Bureau, Ministry of Internal Affairs and Communications, *Japan Statistical Yearbook*, annual issues, http://www.stat.go.jp/english/ or http://www.jstat.or.jp/english/index.html.

Statistics Bureau, Ministry of Internal Affairs and Communications, *Survey on Time Use and Leisure Activities*, published every five years since 1976.

Statistics Bureau, Ministry of Internal Affairs and Communications, *Annual Report on the Labour Force Survey*.

8. Genuine progress in India: some further growth needed in the immediate future but population stabilisation needed immediately

Philip Lawn

INTRODUCTION

The Genuine Progress Indicator (GPI) studies revealed so far in this book involve countries which have long been industrialised. The remaining studies involve countries which, until recently, have relied heavily upon primary industries as the major source of national income and employment. Indeed, in Thailand and Vietnam (Chapters 10 and 11), the agricultural, forestry, and fisheries industries continue to be national economic mainstays. On the other hand, the economies of India and China (this chapter and Chapter 9) have become increasingly reliant upon the role played by manufacturing and the services sector although primary forms of production remain the principal source of income for people living outside the major urban centres.

It should be noted from the outset that the GPI study of India conducted in this chapter is limited to the period spanning 1987 to 2003. The restricted length of the study period can be attributed almost entirely to the lack of suitable data, particularly in relation to many of the social and environmental items that make up the GPI. While this precludes any comparison between the low- and high-growth phases of India's contemporary economic development, it does not rule out an assessment of the genuine progress impact of India's recent growth spurt. An assessment of India's recent economic development performance is undertaken at the conclusion of the chapter where a number of policy implications for India's future economic development are briefly outlined and discussed.

INDIA'S ECONOMIC DEVELOPMENT: HISTORICAL BACKGROUND AND RECENT DEVELOPMENTS

Pre-British Colonial Rule

Within what is recognised today as India, the first permanent and largely urban form of settlement can be attributed to the Indus Valley civilisation.[1] Thriving between the years 2800 and 1800 BC, the Indus Valley civilisation established an advanced economic system based on agriculture, animal husbandry, and the use of tools manufactured from bronze, copper, and tin. Sophisticated urban planning was a prominent feature of this ancient civilisation as was its strong trade links with other similarly organised societies (Chopra et al., 1974, Vol. I).

For reasons not yet fully understood, the Indus Valley civilisation rapidly declined to be all but non-existent by 1700 BC. Over the next 2000 years, the Indo-Aryans from central Asia developed a Brahmanic civilisation from which Hinduism gradually evolved (Chopra et al., 1974, Vol. I). It is also believed that the Indo-Aryan migrants established the Indian caste system that still exists today, albeit in a more diluted form.[2] The Brahmanic civilisation slowly spread eastwards from Punjab as it sought to exploit the fertile alluvial plains of the Ganges Valley. By 800 BC, the Brahmanic civilisation had established itself in Bihar, Jharkhand, and Bengal (Das, 2006). In the process, the large and influential Magadha Kingdom emerged.

Following the defeat of the Macedonian invasion by Chandragupta in 327–325 BC, the Mauryan Empire was established (Edwardes, 1961). By the third century BC, the Mauryan Empire had encompassed all of modern India except the far south. During this period, southern India was distinctly more prosperous than the north, due in part to the flourishing overseas trade that was established between the Tamil-speaking states of Pandya and Chola and the Roman Empire (Das, 2006).

The Mauryan Empire eventually succumbed to disorder and the destabilising effects of various foreign invasions such that, by 185 BC, it had completely collapsed. Over subsequent centuries, political authority alternated between dominant centralised empires and more dispersed forms of control. During the Gupta Dynasty (AD 350–550), political power was rebuilt from within the Ganges Valley and expanded to encompass Punjab in the west, Bengal in the east, Kashmir in the north, and the Deccan in the south (Das, 2006). This was a period of Indian history made distinctive by sea-based trade with China and South-East Asian countries and land-based trade with Central Asia (Khanna, 2005).

Between the eighth and thirteenth centuries, a number of independent kingdoms grew in strength. However, it was the successful Turkish invasion of 1206 that led, initially, to the establishment of a sultanate in Delhi and, ultimately, to the beginning of a long period of Islamic political dominance (Chopra et al., 1974, Vol. II).

Early in the sixteenth century, the Mongol chief, Babur, defeated the last of the Delhi sultans at Panipat. This gave rise to the Mughal Empire that lasted from 1526 to 1707. The early Mughal emperors were acutely concerned about the economic prosperity of the general population. Commerce and trade thrived during this period as did the development of art and culture (Das, 2006). This aside, Islam was unable to supplant Hinduism as the dominant religion of India.

1757–1947: British Colonial Rule

In the eighteenth century, the political environment of India changed dramatically following a series of dynastic struggles, an Afghan invasion, and continuous revolts by various Hindu kingdoms. With the Mughal Empire exposed and vulnerable, the British East India Company (established in 1600) became embroiled in a bitter feud with the French as both nations sought to harness their strengthening military power to increase trade and usurp Indian wealth. The eventual British triumph over the French coincided with a military challenge from the Mughal Nawab of Bengal. Led by Robert Clive, the British forces secured a decisive victory at the Battle of Plassey in 1757 (Chopra et al., 1974, Vol. III; Metcalf and Metcalf, 2006). Through the agency of the East India Company, Britain gained control of the state finances of Bengal and later extended its territorial power through the Treaty of Paris in 1763 (Dutt, 1956). British colonial rule in India was now formally established.

By 1818, Britain controlled almost all of India and, in the process, had negated the influence of its most powerful Indian enemies. The India Office of the British Government – which directed the activities of the East India Company – governed the large cities and wealthy areas of India leaving the remainder to be governed by princely Indian rulers, albeit under the effective control of selected British residents of India (Das, 2006).

Despite the creation of a modern legal system and a well-developed assemblage of railway and telegraph networks, the British-established infrastructure was largely designed to serve British interests. The infrastructural network ideally positioned Britain to exploit India as both a cheap source of natural resources and a captive goods market (Metcalf and Metcalf, 2006). Indeed, whilst India continued to be a substantial exporter of silk and cotton textiles, it began to suffer at the hands of Britain's growing domestic production might in cloth – a product of the newly emerging Industrial Revolution (Dutt, 1956; Chopra et al., 1974, Vol. III).

By the middle of the nineteenth century, the authority of the East India Company was threatened by social unrest and the growing discontent amongst Muslim noblemen over the high rates of taxation imposed by the British Governor-General of India. This led ultimately to the first battle for independence in 1857 (Metcalf and Metcalf, 2006). The so-called 'Indian Mutiny' was brutally suppressed and, in response, a range of reforms were introduced to prevent reoccurrence of a similar uprising.

Not entirely demoralised, the Indian National Congress was formed in 1884 to campaign for greater Indian participation in public affairs and administration (Metcalf and Metcalf, 2006). Indian nationalism received a boost following the British decision in 1905 to partition Bengal province between Hindu and Muslim regions. The decision provoked a major nationalist reaction and increased the influence of more militant nationalist movements. In response, the Morley-Minto reforms were introduced in 1909 to extend Indian participation in government. Separate electorates were also formed to accommodate India's different religious communities (Metcalf and Metcalf, 2006).

Following a period of civil disobedience in the early decades of the twentieth century, the British Government, in 1935, introduced a limited form of elected responsible government at the provincial level. The Indian National Congress agreed to participate but withdrew its support in 1939 in protest at the British decision to declare India as an active combatant of World War II (Metcalf and Metcalf, 2006). Shortly after, in August 1942, Gandhi launched a Quit India movement in an attempt to force the British to withdraw entirely from India. Mass disobedience followed but was contained by the British administration. However, the end of World War II triggered a major upsurge in nationalist sentiment. The British Government of the time began preparations for a British withdrawal of India and inevitable Indian independence. On 15 August

1947, Indian became an independent nation and Jawaharlal Nehru became India's first Prime Minister.

By the end of British colonial rule, India inherited a largely unindustrialised, agrarian economy that was amongst the poorest in the world. Industrial development had long been stagnant or in decline. Worse still, its agricultural sector was frequently unable to feed its rapidly growing population. In the minds of many, British rule did little but exploit India's natural resources and simultaneously squander its vast economic potential. As a means of illustration, India's per capita Gross Domestic Product (GDP) was higher than the USA's in 1600 but, under early British rule, had declined to 42 per cent of the USA's per capita GDP by 1820.[3] Around the time of Indian independence in 1947, India's per capita GDP had fallen to just 6 per cent of that in the USA (Maddison, 2002).

Post-1947 Independence to 1979

In view of the dire economic circumstances in India at the time of independence, it was generally agreed that policy measures were required to grow the Indian economy and increase the incomes and consumption levels of the most disadvantaged groups of Indian society. In 1950, an eight-member planning commission was established to implement a series of five-year plans (Misra, 1986; Roy and Tisdell, 1992). The aim of the commission was to guide India's economic development process in a manner that would benefit all Indian citizens, not simply a select few. Whilst the objective of the Indian Government was to ensure large segments of industry, finance, and trade remained in the hands of the private sector, it sought to adopt a heavy-handed bureacractic approach to economic development with the unreserved right to nationalise industries if such action was deemed in the national interest (Das, 2006).[4]

Given the susceptibility of India to famine, the first five-year plan (1951–56) accorded top priority to the agricultural sector. A number of irrigation schemes were initiated as were many electricity generation projects. The second five-year plan (1956–61) was specifically designed to rapidly increase the rate of industrialisation, increase real GDP by 25 per cent, and reduce growing inequalities in income and wealth. Despite a considerable improvement in rate of growth of India's real GDP in the 1950s, the performance of the Indian economy did not meet the expectations of India's political leaders. In fact, the growth of India's real GDP continued to lag behind the growth rates of many Asian nations (Das, 2006).

Industrialisation remained the central focus of the third five-year plan (1961–66) with large sums of financial capital invested in transport and communications. The third plan also aimed to rapidly develop and exploit India's vast mineral wealth. As the 1960s progressed, one of the main constraints to economic development was India's expanding trade deficit. The Indian Government also began to experience budget deficit difficulties which, given the weakness of the Indian economy, prevented it from borrowing heavily from abroad. To finance the infrastructural spending consistent with the third five-year plan the Indian Government undertook policies that dramatically increased the Indian money supply. This ultimately led to high rates of inflation which further undermined attempts to strengthen the Indian economy. Economic difficulties were compounded by a series of droughts and sporadic outbreaks of war with neighbouring Pakistan (Metcalf and Metcalf, 2006).

Until the mid-1960s, foreign aid into India had been responsible for underpinning the value of the Indian rupee. With the Indian economy continuing to weaken, future contributions of foreign aid were rendered conditional upon the liberalisation of India's import restrictions. Backed into a corner, the Indian Government was forced to liberalise the economy, loosen its grip on the economic development process, and devalue the rupee (Das, 2006; Metcalf and Metcalf, 2006).

The deteriorating situation in India saw the implementation of the fourth five-year plan delayed until 1969 (1969–74). Furthermore, the Indian Government was forced to refocus its attention on policies to control a series of disastrous fluctuations in agricultural output and to promote a more just distribution of income and wealth. In view of the crisis faced, agriculture and electricity generation and transmission received a substantial increase in government funding. The 'back to basics' approach of the Indian Government was reinforced in 1971 when Indira Gandhi won the national election based on an explicit campaign to 'abolish poverty'.

Unfortunately, attempts to alleviate impoverishment were hampered by yet another outbreak of war with Pakistan ignited by India's interventionist support of the secessionist forces in East Pakistan (Metcalf and Metcalf, 2006). Despite the implementation of a fifth five-year plan (1974–79), mass civil disobedience arose following the 1974 opposition to Congress and, in 1975, Prime Minister Gandhi responded by imposing a state of emergency, suspending various civil liberties, and postponing the 1976 elections.

When elections were finally held in March 1977, Gandhi's Indian National Congress surrendered more than half of its seats to the Janata Party. In view of the political turmoil in India, the fifth five-year plan was suspended in 1978. Under the new Prime Ministership of Morarji Desai, the Janata Party formed the first non-Congress government since Indian independence. However, increasing factionalism and a lack of coherent policies saw Desai resign as Prime Minister in July 1979 (Metcalf and Metcalf, 2006).

In all, the first five development plans implemented between 1951 and 1979 were largely unsuccessful. Although the main aim of each plan was to boost India's real GDP substantially, it only managed to grow at an average rate of 3.1 per cent per year. On a per capita basis, this amounted to an average annual rate of increase of one per cent – clearly a disappointing result for a country so heavily impoverished at the time of independence (IMF, 2000).

1979 to the Present

Implementation of the sixth five-year plan (1980–85) began with India embroiled in political upheaval and mired in an economic recession. Although poverty alleviation remained the central objective of the sixth plan, a much greater emphasis was placed on reinforcing the infrastructure of the agricultural and industrial sectors. It was believed that this could boost export revenue and encourage higher levels of foreign investment which, in turn, would increase the incomes of all Indian citizens (Das, 2004).

The seventh five-year plan (1985–90) continued in much the same vein as the sixth plan. Incorporated into the seventh plan was a target GDP growth rate of 5.2 per cent per annum. With industrial and agricultural output increasing in value by 8 per cent and 4 per cent per annum respectively, the target growth rate in real GDP was exceeded. India was experiencing its highest post-independence rate of growth.

However, by the end of 1990–early 1991, the emerging global recession begun to take its toll on the Indian economy. In 1991, India's per capita GDP declined (Brahmbhatt et al., 1996). In addition, the nation was faced with an emerging debt crisis (Government of India, 2002). The Indian Prime Minister responded by instituting an economic liberalisation and structural adjustment policy as the centrepiece of

India's eighth five-year plan (1992–97). The plan specifically aimed to stimulate the private sector in order to liberate government resources to invest more heavily in basic infrastructural assets. Also included in the eighth five-year plan were taxation and foreign exchange reforms, tariff cuts, and the easing of import restrictions. The eighth plan proved to be very successful in terms of boosting India's real GDP. Indeed, apart from achieving an average annual GDP growth rate of 6 per cent, the eighth plan subdued inflation, substantially increased India's export revenue, and reduced poverty levels (Das, 2006; Metcalf and Metcalf, 2006).

Despite a change in government in 1996, the pace of economic reform continued into the ninth five-year plan (1997–2002) which, for the first time, focused on the privatisation of public assets. With foreign investment levels remaining high, India's real GDP continued to grow at an average annual rate of 5.4 per cent – a considerable feat in view of the widespread impact of the 1997–98 Asian financial crisis (Ahluwalia, 2002). The high growth rate was due, in part, to India's emergence as an attractive location for transnational corporations to develop and exploit the technologies associated with the new information age.

Notwithstanding the high growth rate experienced during the ninth development plan, the Indian Government unveiled the tenth five-year plan (2002–07) with the aim of achieving an average growth rate in real GDP of 8 per cent per annum. This, it was hoped, would reduce the poverty rate in India by 5 per cent by 2007 and assist in reducing it by a further 15 per cent by 2012. A number of environmental objectives were also incorporated into the tenth development plan – namely, an increase in forest cover equivalent to 25 per cent of the nation's land area (up from 20.5 per cent as it stood in 1996); sustained supplies of potable water for all Indian citizens; and the restoration of all seriously polluted rivers by 2007. Although, as the tenth development plan comes to an end, the GDP growth target appears to be on track, it is doubtful whether India will meet its planned environmental objectives.

Summary

India has experienced a long and protracted process of economic development. Having enjoyed around a quarter of the world's income for many centuries (Maddison, 2004), India's share of world income declined rapidly following the establishment of British colonial rule in

1757. Indeed, by 1978, India's national income had fallen to just 3.4 per cent of global GDP (Maddison, 1998).

A massive turnaround in the economic performance of India over the past 15 years (1991–2006) has seen India's real GDP increase by 158 per cent and per capita real GDP increase by 97 per cent. This corresponds to an average rate of increase of 6.5 per cent and 4.6 per cent respectively. It is not surprising, therefore, that absolute poverty levels have fallen dramatically in recent times while average life expectancy has risen sharply. In addition, a growing middle class has emerged, particularly in the major urban centres.

This aside, India has a massive population (estimated at 1.14 billion in 2007) that continues to grow unabated. For all its recent success, the great majority of Indian citizens live a life of extreme poverty due largely to India's sheer population numbers, gross deficiencies in its public welfare system, and the enormous and continuing disparities in income, wealth, and opportunity. Whilst a great number of Indians are well educated, many are not, and it thus remains the challenge of governments to increase the accessibility of education to all its citizens.

In India's favour is the relative political stability it now enjoys. However, massive bureaucratic hurdles continue to plague the Indian economy. This greatly constrains India's ability to procure the efficiency advances it requires to boost productivity, raise wages, and reduce environmental stress. Furthermore, there is growing evidence that infrastructural bottlenecks are beginning to emerge, particularly in the areas of energy and transport, as the Indian economy overtakes the capacity of the private and public sector collectively to provide the infrastructure needed to support India's future economic development (Luthra et al., 2005). At the same time, India is likely to come under growing pressure to improve its environmental performance, both from a wealthier and more discerning Indian population and from other nations increasingly concerned about the potentially disastrous impact of rising CO_2 emissions and ecosystem takeover and destruction. Clearly, the challenge that India confronts to achieve a lasting and sustainable rate of genuine progress rivals whatever might be faced elsewhere in the world, let alone by nations within the Asia-Pacific region.

INDIA'S GENUINE PROGRESS INDICATOR, 1987–2003

In this particular section of the chapter, the approach used to calculate the GPI for India is briefly described. Also revealed are the GPI results for the period 1987–2003 and the items impacting most on the trend change in India's GPI. In view of the truncated nature of the study period, this study of India merely encompasses the latter stages of the seventh five-year plan, the entire eighth and ninth five-year plans, and the very beginning of the tenth development plan. It also encompasses a period in which India has enjoyed relative political stability and its highest rates of growth in real GDP. With this in mind, the section concludes with a terse assessment of the impact that India's recent growth spurt has had on its rate of genuine progress and projections for India's future.

The Calculation of the GPI for India

Not unlike the GPI studies so far conducted in this book, the methodology used to calculate India's GPI closely follows the approach outlined in Chapter 3. However, because of data shortages, a number of items have been excluded or simplified. This aside, the method employed to estimate India's defensive and rehabilitative expenditures is similar to the method adopted in the Australian GPI study (Chapter 5). It involves, therefore, a more comprehensive treatment of defensive and rehabilitative expenditures than what is generally the case in standard GPI studies.

To assist in explaining the modified approach used to calculate India's GPI, Table 8.1 provides a full list of the items used and the valuation methods employed in their calculation. For the sake of brevity, the remainder of this discussion is limited to variations on the standard GPI methodology or, in some cases, the unique approaches adopted to calculate some of the items that make up the Indian GPI.

Defensive and rehabilitative expenditures

As just mentioned, the method used in Chapter 5 to calculate *defensive and rehabilitative expenditures* has largely been employed in this GPI study of India. Where this study differs is that no deduction has been made in relation to education services or household spending on

Table 8.1 Items and valuation methods used to calculate the GPI for India, 1987–2003

Item	Welfare contribution	Method of valuation
Item *a*: Welfare contribution of consumption expenditure (*CON*)	+	*CON* = private sector *plus* public sector consumption expenditure *less* all spending on cigarettes and tobacco *less* 0.25 × spending on alcoholic beverages
Item *b*: Defensive and rehabilitatve expenditures (*DRE*)	–	*DRE* involves the subtraction of the following: • 0.25 × spending on food (defensive) • 0.25 × spending on rent and water services (defensive) • 0.25 × spending on fuel and power (defensive) • 0.5 × consumption spending on health (defensive and/or rehabilitative) • 0.25 × spending on the operation of vehicles (defensive) • 0.25 × spending on transport services (defensive) • 0.25 × spending on communications (defensive) • 0.125 × spending on hotels and restaurants (defensive) • 0.25 × consumption spending by general government (defensive and/or rehabilitative)
Item *c*: Expenditure on consumer durables (*ECD*)	–	*ECD* equals the sum of all household expenditure on consumer durables
Item *d*: Service from consumer durables (*SCD*)	+	Equal to the net present depreciation value of the existing stock of consumer durables (assumed that stock endures for 7 years; discount rate of 7%) • *SCD* = 0.186 × value of consumer durables
Item *e*: Adjusted consumption	+	Timing adjustment to consumption benefits • *Adjusted CON = CON – DRE – ECD + SCD*
Item *f*: Distribution Index (*DI*)	+/–	*DI* based on the change in income distribution over the study period as measured by the Gini coefficient (first year of study period has an index value of 100)
Item *g*: Adjusted consumption (weighted) (**)	+	Adjusted CON weighted by the Distribution Index • *Adjusted CON* ÷ *DI* × 100

Table 8.1 (continued)

Item	Welfare contribution	Method of valuation
Item *h*: Welfare from publicly-provided infrastructure (*WPPI*) (**)	+	Welfare assumed to equal the depreciation value of the existing stock of publicly-provided infrastructural capital
Item *i*: Value of non-paid labour (**)	+	Non-paid labour is valued using the net opportunity cost method • Equal to the number of non-paid labour hours × assumed wage valued at 1993 prices (rupees)
Item *j*: Cost of unemployment (**)	–	Calculated by multiplying the total number of unemployed people by average work hours which is multiplied by the estimated cost per unemployed hour (ILO, various)
Item *k*: Cost of crime (**)	–	Calculated by multiplying crime indexes (based on violent and property crime) by the estimated cost of both crime categories
Item *l*: Change in foreign debt position (**)	+/–	Annual cost (benefit) is equal to the change in net foreign liabilities from one financial year to the next
Item *m*: Cost of non-renewable resource depletion (*)	–	Calculated by using the El Serafy (1989) 'user cost' formula to determine the amount to set aside to sustain a flow of income equal to that generated by the exhausted resource • Equal to value of non-renewable resource extraction × 0.89
Item *n*: Cost of lost agricultural land (*)	–	Calculated to reflect the amount required to compensate citizens for the cumulative impact of past and present agricultural practices • Annual cost equal to 1% of the value of agricultural output. The annual cost is accumulated to satisfy the strong sustainability condition that: (a) human-made capital is not a substitute for natural capital; and (b) agricultural land has no natural capital replacement
Item *o*: Cost of timber depletion (*)	–	Calculated to reflect the opportunity cost of lower timber stocks brought about by harvesting rates exceeding the rate of timber regeneration and plantation establishment • Equal to value of timber depletion × 0.89

Table 8.1 (continued)

Item	Welfare contribution	Method of valuation
Item *p*: Cost of air pollution (*)	–	Calculated to reflect lost air pollution sink capacity • Real output factor × pollution abatement technology factor (assumed that there is a 2% annual rate of progress). Real output factor equal to 0.025 × real GDP
Item *q*: Cost of urban waste-water pollution (*)	–	Calculated to reflect the estimated annual cost of waste-water pollution • Real output factor × pollution abatement technology factor (assumed that there is a 2% annual rate of progress) × water withdrawals factor. Real output factor equal to 0.025 × real GDP
Item *r*: Cost of long-term environmental damage (*)	–	Calculated to reflect the amount required to compensate citizens for the long-term environmental impact of energy consumption
Item *s*: Lost natural capital services (*LNCS*) (**)	–	Sum of (*) items. The *LNCS* sub-total reflects the cost of the sacrificed source, sink, and life-support services provided by natural capital
Item *t*: Genuine Progress Indicator (GPI)	+	Sum of (**) items beginning with Adjusted CON (weighted)
Item *u*: Population		Population of India
Item *v*: Per capita GPI	+	GPI ÷ population

insurance and other financial services. A slightly modified approach was adopted owing to the subsumption of these forms of spending by other consumption categories.[5] All other estimates of defensive and rehabilitative forms of expenditure were treated identically to the Australian study.

The value of unpaid labour

In the case of most GPI studies, the *value of unpaid labour* includes volunteer labour as well as non-paid household labour. The value of volunteer labour was excluded from this Indian GPI study on the basis that the data on volunteer labour was either insufficiently comprehensive or inconsistent across time. Only non-paid household labour was taken into consideration.

Although volunteer labour is of significant welfare importance in most nations – and perhaps of greater importance in poorer nations – the value of non-paid household labour is invariably the larger of the two forms of unpaid labour. The omission of volunteer labour is therefore unlikely to impact adversely on the magnitude of the GPI or its trend change over time.

Cost of unemployment and underemployment

Many GPI studies include not only the cost of unemployment but also the cost of underemployment. In this GPI study of India, the cost of underemployment was ignored. Again, data limitations dictated the nature of the approach adopted.

Cost of family breakdown

The cost of family breakdown is a common item included in the GPI to account for the detrimental impact of economic activity on the family unit. Typically, the cost of family breakdown is measured using the divorce rate as a proxy for family disharmony. In the case of India, divorces are not always officially recorded. Moreover, since divorce is often frowned upon in Indian society, the divorce rate cannot adequately function as a proxy indicator of family breakdown in the same way that it can in Western societies and cultures. Given there were no other means of determining the impact of economic activity on the family unit, the cost of family breakdown was overlooked in this GPI study of India.

Results of the Indian GPI Study

Individual GPI items

The results of the GPI study on India are summarised in Table 8.2 (valued at 1993 prices). Column *A* reveals the annual welfare contribution made by durable and non-durable consumption goods weighted by the Distribution Index (DI). Summarising the welfare impact of Items *a–f* in Table 8.1, column *A* shows that India's weighted consumption, which increased every year over the study period, rose from 4180.2 billion rupees in 1987 to 7905.2 billion rupees in 2003. This equates to a rise of 89.1 per cent or an average rate of increase equivalent to 4.1 per cent per annum. On a per capita basis, weighted consumption rose by 38.8 per cent from 5332 rupees to 7402 rupees per Indian or at an average rate of 2.1 per cent per annum.

The service provided by infrastructural capital is revealed in column *B* of Table 8.2 (Item *h*). Not unlike other GPI studies, column *B* indicates that the contribution made by infrastructural capital to India's well-being was considerably less than the contribution made by durable and non-durable consumption goods. Indeed, at 377.2 billion rupees in 1987, the services provided by infrastructural capital equated to a mere 9 per cent of the welfare contribution made by consumption goods. Between 1987 and 1991, the relative welfare contribution of infrastructural capital remained largely unchanged – a reflection of the infrastructural investment undertaken during the seventh five-year plan of 1985–90. However, the service provided by infrastructural capital fell spectacularly in both absolute and relative terms in 1992 as a consequence of the deep recession and associated debt crisis experienced by India at this point in time.

Fortunately, infrastructural services recovered dramatically between 1992 and 1994 following the implementation of the eighth five-year plan but declined again in response to the privatisation policy inherent in the ninth development plan. By 2003, the welfare contribution of infrastructural capital had increased to 418 billion rupees but, in relative terms, had fallen to just 5.3 per cent of the contribution generated by consumption goods.

Column *C* in Table 8.2 reveals the value of India's unpaid labour (Item *i*). As is typically the case, unpaid labour constituted a major component of the aggregate GPI value. It also increased throughout the study period, rising from an initial value of 3229 billion rupees in 1987 to 3935.5

Table 8.2 Genuine Progress Indicator (GPI) and real GDP for India, 1987–2003

Year	Weighted CON_{ADJ} (R)	WPPI (R)	Unpaid labour (R)	Social costs (R)	LNCS (R)	GPI (R)	Real GDP (R)	Indian Pop. (millions)	GPI p.c. (single R)	GDP p.c. (single R)	GPI p.c. 1987 = 100	GDP p.c. 1987 = 100
	A	*B*	*C*	*D*	*E*	*F*	*G*	*H*	*I*	*J*	*K*	*L*
1987	4 180.2	377.2	3 229.0	- 874.2	-1 981.3	4 930.9	6 233.7	784	6 289.4	7 951.2	100.0	100.0
1988	4 357.0	371.1	3 271.5	- 815.5	-2 073.4	5 110.8	6 848.3	801	6 380.5	8 549.7	101.4	107.5
1989	4 501.5	342.6	3 313.2	-1 094.0	-2 149.6	4 913.7	7 289.5	818	6 007.0	8 911.4	95.5	112.1
1990	4 628.0	336.0	3 353.9	- 768.7	-2 235.2	5 313.9	7 713.0	835	6 364.0	9 237.1	101.2	116.2
1991	4 648.5	394.0	3 393.7	-1 232.1	-2 267.9	4 936.2	7 782.9	852	5 793.6	9 134.8	92.1	114.9
1992	4 715.2	337.4	3 432.6	- 635.2	-2 352.7	5 497.3	8 193.2	869	6 326.0	9 428.3	100.6	118.6
1993	4 947.8	372.9	3 478.4	- 975.5	-2 425.4	5 398.2	8 592.2	888	6 079.1	9 675.9	96.7	121.7
1994	5 094.4	452.0	3 515.5	- 572.2	-2 527.7	5 961.9	9 233.5	905	6 587.8	10 202.8	104.7	128.3
1995	5 388.2	344.3	3 555.5	- 461.4	-2 627.2	6 199.5	9 939.5	923	6 716.7	10 768.6	106.8	135.4
1996	5 728.7	348.8	3 598.4	- 448.0	-2 735.0	6 493.0	10 674.4	942	6 892.7	11 331.7	109.6	142.5
1997	5 968.0	358.4	3 636.6	- 758.6	-2 834.1	6 370.4	11 152.5	960	6 635.8	11 617.2	105.5	146.1
1998	6 387.7	392.8	3 673.9	- 797.1	-2 899.7	6 757.6	11 820.2	978	6 909.6	12 086.1	109.9	152.0
1999	6 828.5	386.5	3 710.3	- 686.4	-3 005.1	7 233.8	12 662.8	996	7 262.9	12 713.7	115.5	159.9
2000	6 949.5	386.2	3 775.1	- 851.5	-3 081.8	7 177.4	13 162.0	1 015	7 071.3	12 967.5	112.4	163.1
2001	7 305.7	387.7	3 830.3	- 641.0	-3 182.0	7 700.7	13 837.1	1 033	7 454.7	13 395.0	118.5	168.5
2002	7 427.0	377.0	3 885.0	- 855.5	-3 292.2	7 541.3	14 406.3	1 051	7 175.4	13 707.3	114.1	172.4
2003	7 905.2	418.0	3 935.5	- 660.4	-3 402.7	8 195.6	15 646.2	1 068	7 673.8	14 650.0	122.0	184.2

Note: All values are in billions of 1993 rupees except where indicated.

billion rupees in 2003. Conversely, the per capita value of unpaid labour fell between 1987 and 2003 from 4119 rupees to 3685 rupees per Indian. The forces behind the per capita fall in unpaid labour are similar to those encountered in other nations, albeit to a lesser extent. This is because paid employment remains inaccessible to many Indian women whilst the great majority of household tasks have yet to permeate their way into the market domain.

Column *C* in Table 8.2 reveals the value of India's unpaid labour (Item *i*). As is typically the case, unpaid labour constituted a major component of the aggregate GPI value. It also increased throughout the study period, rising from an initial value of 3229 billion rupees in 1987 to 3935.5 billion rupees in 2003. Conversely, the per capita value of unpaid labour fell between 1987 and 2003 from 4119 rupees to 3685 rupees per Indian. The forces behind the per capita fall in unpaid labour are similar to those encountered in other nations, albeit to a lesser extent. This is because paid employment remains inaccessible to many Indian women whilst the great majority of household tasks have yet to permeate their way into the market domain.

Accompanying the economic and social benefits of a growing Indian economy were the inevitable social costs, the total of which are revealed in column *D* of Table 8.2. The column equals the aggregated value of Items *j*–*l* in Table 8.1. India's social costs fluctuated over the study period, beginning at 874.2 billion rupees in 1987, reaching a peak of 1232.1 billion rupees in 1991, falling to a low of 448 billion rupees in 1996, before rising once more to 660.4 billion rupees by 2003.

The variation in social costs can be largely attributed to the inclusion of India's changing foreign debt in the social cost category (Item *l*). This approach was also adopted in the Australian GPI study, essentially because Australia's foreign debt rose in every year but one over the study period. The same did not occur for India where, to be precise, India's foreign debt increased in only ten of the 17 years between and including 1987 and 2003. For the sake of convenience and in view of the enormous social impact that India's foreign debt has inflicted from time to time upon its citizens, it was decided that the change in foreign debt would be treated as a social cost item.

Of the other two social cost items – namely, the cost of unemployment (Item *j*) and the cost of crime (Item *k*) – the former increased quite steadily over the study period from 358.2 billion rupees in 1987 to 476.3 billion rupees in 2003 (33 per cent increase). On the other hand, the cost of crime fell between 1987 and 1994 (251.6 billion rupees to 172.3

billion rupees) before rising again to 252.1 billion rupees by 2003 (46.3 per cent increase between 1994 and 2003).

More significant than the social costs arising from a growing Indian economy was the value of India's lost natural capital services (column *E* in Table 8.2). Beginning at 1981.3 billion rupees in 1987, lost natural capital services ballooned to 3402.7 billion rupees by 2003. This constitutes a 71.7 per cent rise over the study period or an average rate of increase of 3.2 per cent per annum. On a per capita basis, the cost of India's lost natural capital services increased from 2527 rupees to 3186 rupees per Indian, which is equivalent to an average annual rise of 1.4 per cent per annum.

The factors contributing most to the large rise in India's environmental costs were the cost of non-renewable resource depletion (Item *m*), land degradation (Item *n*), air and urban waste-water pollution (Items *p* and *q*), and the cost of long-term environmental damage (Item *r*). Given that a range of environmental costs were overlooked due to the lack of appropriate data, and no Ecosystem Health Index (EHI) was used to weight the sum total of lost natural capital services, the cost of India's natural capital depletion can be regarded as conservative. In reality, it is likely to have been much higher than that indicated by column *E* in Table 8.2.

India's GPI versus GDP

The annual values of India's GPI are revealed in column *F* of Table 8.2 and equal the sum of the values contained in columns *A* to *E*. As can be seen from Table 8.2, India's GPI increased from 4930.9 billion rupees in 1987 to 8195.6 billion rupees in 2003. This constitutes a 66.2 per cent rise between 1987 and 2003 or an average rate of increase of 3 per cent per annum. Despite the rise, India's GPI declined in six of the 17 years during the study period. The most significant fall occurred in 1991 which, together with the 1989 decline, resulted in India's GPI being only marginally higher in 1991 than in 1987. Notwithstanding small decreases in 1993, 1997, 2000, and 2002, India's GPI effectively rose between 1991 and 2003.

Also of note when comparing columns *F* and *G* is the growing disparity between India's GPI and real GDP. In 1987, India's real GDP was just 1302.8 billion rupees higher than its GPI. By 2003, the gap between the two indicators had grown to 7450.6 billion rupees.

In order to ascertain the sustainable well-being of the average Indian, columns *I* and *J* in Table 8.2 reveal the per capita values of India's GPI and real GDP. They are also diagrammatically presented in Figure 8.1. Columns *I* and *J* indicate that India's per capita GPI increased in ten of the 17 years over the study period.

Overall, India's per capita GPI grew from 6289.4 rupees per Indian in 1987 to 7673.8 rupees per Indian by 2003. Conversely, India's per capita GDP increased in every year but 1991. Moreover, as the index values in columns *K* and *L* highlight, India's per capita GDP finished 84.2 per cent higher by the end of the study period whereas India's per capita GPI increased by a more modest 22 per cent. India's per capita GDP and GPI respectively grew at average rates of 3.9 per cent and 1.2 per cent per annum. The relative difference in the rate of change of both indicators is graphically illustrated in Figure 8.2.

Given that India's per capita GDP increased more rapidly than its per capita GPI and was 6976.2 rupees per Indian higher in 2003, one can conclude that the per capita GDP substantially overstated the rate of genuine progress made by India over the study period. However, there is little doubt that progress was made, particularly after 1993 when India's per capita GPI was slightly lower than its 1987 value (6289.4 rupees per Indian in 1987 compared to 6079.1 rupees per Indian in 1993). Between 1993 and 2003, India's per capita GPI grew at an average rate of 2.4 per cent per annum.

The comparison between India's per capita GPI and GDP poses a number of immediate questions. They are:

- In light of the estimated rise in India's population, can any future growth in India's real GDP be expected to translate into the moderate rate of genuine progress experienced between 1993 and 2003?
- Would India's per capita GPI have been much higher if India's output was qualitatively better, its rate of population growth much lower, and if the Indian Government had been more resolute in its efforts to provide basic goods and services for the poor?
- If the answer to the previous question is yes, is it not time for India to immediately undertake measures to stabilise its population, increase resource use efficiency, limit natural capital depletion, and ensure its growth in economic output reaches its most impoverished citizens?

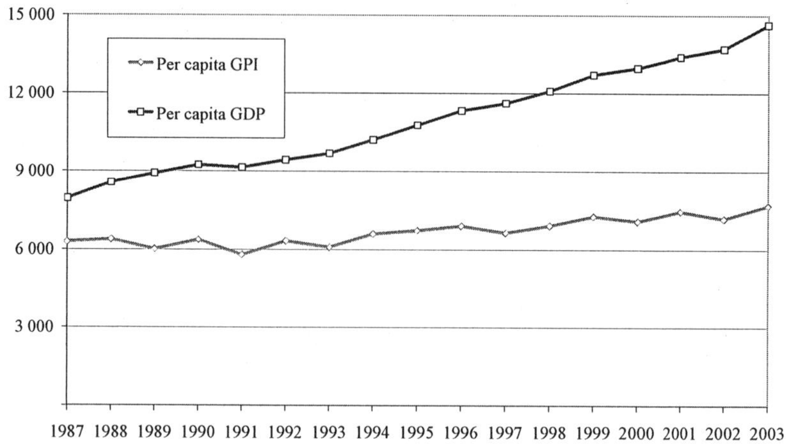

Note: Rupees per capita valued at 2003 prices.

Figure 8.1 Per capita GPI versus per capita GDP: India, 1987–2003

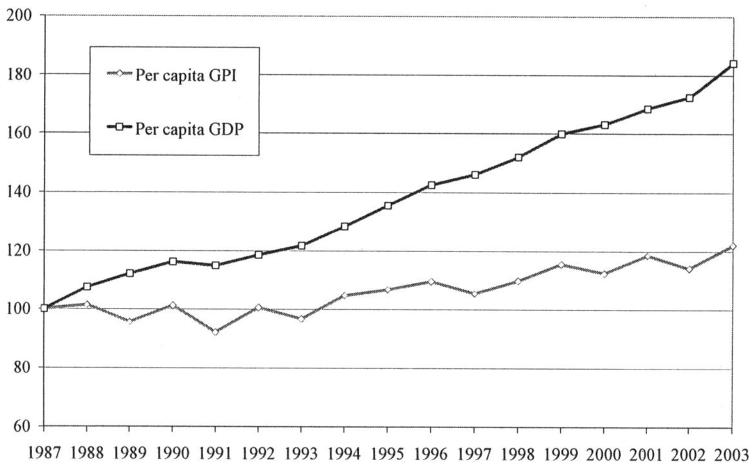

Note: 1987 = 100.

Figure 8.2 Index values of per capita GPI and per capita GDP: India, 1987–2003

- Finally, given the rapid rise in India's social and environmental costs (the former since the mid-1990s), is it possible that, at some stage in the near future, it will be desirable for India to make the transition towards a lower rate of growth?

Answers to these questions are best found by closely examining the factors which have had the greatest impact on India's GPI over the study period. In addition, the examination process can bring forth a range of policy measures aimed at facilitating a rise in the factors impacting positively on India's per capita GPI and/or limiting the impact of any negative factors. These measures should, in turn, lay the foundations for an economic development path that can lead to a lasting and sustainable rate of genuine progress in India.

Dominant Influences on India's GPI

Figure 8.3 reveals India's per capita GPI along with the per capita values of the major benefit and cost categories from Table 8.2. Of the three major benefit categories, publicly-provided infrastructure made by far the lowest contribution towards India's per capita GPI. Moreover, since the annual variations in the per capita value of this item were negligible, it had little impact on the trend movement of India's per capita GPI over the study period. This aside, the decline between 1994 and 2003 in the per capita contribution of publicly-provided infrastructure must be a cause for concern, not only because modest annual rises beyond 1994 would have increased India's per capita GPI by around 3–4 per cent by the end of the study period, but because it provides real evidence of a potential infrastructural constraint on India's future economic development.

The gradual decline in the per capita value of unpaid labour had virtually no impact on the annual fluctuations of India's per capita GPI. It did, nevertheless, play some part in narrowing the difference between India's per capita weighted consumption and per capita GPI. What does this suggest? It suggests two possibilities. Firstly, while an increasing proportion of unpaid household tasks infiltrated the market domain over the study period, this was not reflected by an increase in per capita weighted consumption. Clearly, this can only be true for the period up to the mid-1990s since per capita weighted consumption rose sharply in the

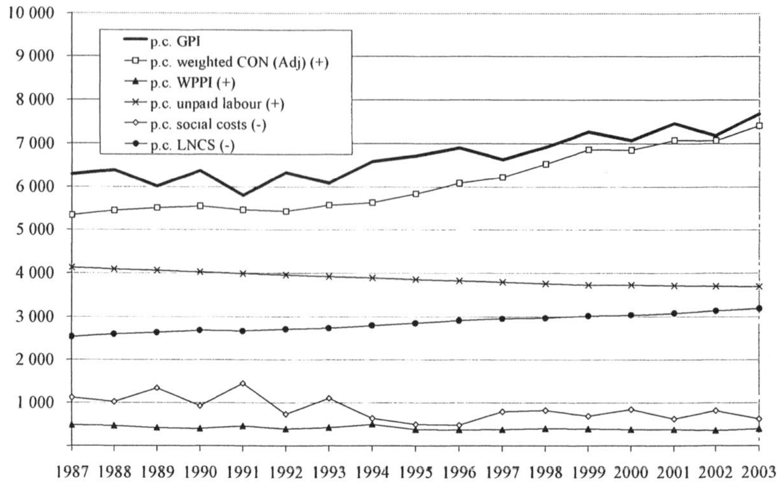

Note: Rupees per capita valued at 2003 prices.

Figure 8.3 Per capita GPI and its major component categories: India, 1987–2003

last ten years of the study period. Secondly, beyond the mid-1990s, the positive impact of the dramatic rise in India's per capita weighted consumption was dampened by the increase in per capita social and environmental costs. Looking at the per capita values for the two major cost categories, this would appear to have been the case, albeit to a much lesser extent with respect to India's per capita social costs. For instance, per capita social costs rose between 1996 and 2003 from 476 to 618 rupees per Indian, while per capita environmental costs increased from 2903 to 3108 rupees per Indian over the same period.

Notwithstanding the negating influence of India's social and environmental costs, per capita weighted consumption considerably affected the overall trend of India's per capita GPI. For example, between 1987 and 1993, when India's per capita weighted consumption failed to increase, India's per capita GPI made no general advancement. Beyond 1993, both per capita weighted consumption and the per capita GPI grew steadily, except in 1997. That having been said, the impact of India's per capita weighted consumption on the annual fluctuations of its per capita GPI was confined to the period after 1997. In the ten years prior to 1997, per capita weighted consumption and the per capita GPI moved in opposite directions on four occasions. Yet, in each of the six years beyond 1997, per capita weighted consumption and the per capita GPI moved in the same direction, including the years of 2000 and 2002 when both fell marginally.

It would be a mistake, however, to believe that the stronger positive influence of India's per capita weighted consumption on its per capita GPI after the mid-1990s was due to the declining influence of India's per capita social and environmental costs since, as already highlighted, both major cost categories increased over the latter part of the study period. But there is little doubt that the overwhelming beneficial impact of per capita weighted consumption was a fundamental factor behind India's moderate rate of progress after 1993. It should not therefore be regarded as anything other than a positive recent development in India. However, it remains to be seen for how long this positive influence will continue in view of the probable future escalation of India's per capita social and environmental costs. It is certainly something that will need to be closely monitored over coming decades.

Turning specifically to the social and environmental cost categories, the impact of India's social costs on its per capita GPI is particularly interesting. Because the social cost category includes the change in foreign debt which, between 1987 and 1994, fluctuated wildly and at times was very substantial, there was initially a very close association between per capita social costs and the per capita GPI. Indeed, both moved very strongly in opposite directions in each year during this seven-year period.

From 1994 to 1996, India's cost of crime and foreign debt declined – the latter quite significantly. Thus, during the mid-1990s, India's per capita social costs had very little impact on its per capita GPI. Beyond 1996, India's per capita social costs again rose following the increase in foreign debt and resurgence in the cost of crime. As a consequence, the pre-1994 dampening effect of India's social costs on the per capita GPI returned. Moreover, the annual variations in per capita social costs over the final four years of the study period (1999–2003) had a definite albeit minor influence on the fluctuating fortunes of India's per capita GPI.

As for India's environmental costs, it has already been stressed that the steady rise in the per capita weighted value of lost natural capital services constrained the overall rise in India's per capita GPI, particularly after 1993. But the rise in environmental costs played no part whatsoever in the year-to-year fluctuations of India's per capita GPI.

If we now consider the questions listed earlier in this section, it is highly likely, in view of the current plight of many Indians, that increases in India's real GDP over the next decade or two will deliver further genuine progress in India. But the rate of progress is unlikely to occur at anything like the recent and projected rates of growth in India's real GDP. Worse still, there is no guarantee, even in the foreseeable future, that India's per capita GPI will grow at the average annual rate of 2.4 per cent experienced between 1993 and 2003.

Given the continuing unequal distribution of income in India and its rapid rate of population growth, India's per capita GPI would almost certainly have been much higher had India managed to stabilise its population, produced better rather than many more goods, and if it had distributed the spoils of its growth in economic output more evenly across the nation. The negating influence of India's rising environmental costs also suggests that India would have been better served by a greater commitment to increased resource use efficiency, especially in relation to energy use and pollution control, and policy measures to reduce the depletion of its natural capital. This would not only have boosted its per capita GPI, it would also have greatly increased India's capacity to sustain the progress it has recently made, particularly in view of its recent high rates of non-renewable resource depletion, land degradation, air pollution, and ecosystem destruction.

To the final question, I believe India will have no choice but to make the transition towards a lower rate of GDP growth, probably within the next two to three decades. Assuming this is achieved, India will then need to seriously consider making the full transition to a steady-state economy by around 2050, although the timing will depend largely upon how well India can rein in its population growth.[6] Should it take longer to stabilise its population, more growth will be needed to meet the needs of a larger number of Indian citizens. Since this would delay the consummation of a steady-state economy, it would unavoidably come at the expense of a lower per capita GPI. It would also bequeath future Indians a socio-ecological system considerably less resilient to external shocks and more vulnerable to ecological collapse and social disharmony.

POLICY IMPLICATIONS

Population Stabilisation

The final point of the previous section highlights a key area requiring immediate attention if India is to enjoy a lasting and sustainable rate of genuine progress. It is, of course, population stabilisation. Irrespective of the country in question, population stabilisation is invariably a controversial issue. Complicating matters is the fact that implementing the means to its achievement is never a straightforward exercise. But the cost of failing to deal with population growth – in effect, the reduced economic and social freedom arising from an excessive population – must, for reasons already given, eventually outweigh the cost arising from reduced reproductive freedom.

Despite the implementation of a number of population stabilisation programmes since independence, there is an urgent need for India to upgrade its delivery of contraception and family planning programmes. At present, there are gross inadequacies in India's existing health infrastructure which continues to result in the unmet need for contraception services. Health care centres are also overburdened and in many cases suffer from a chronic shortage of equipment and qualified personnel (National Commission on Population, 2000).

There are many reasons why the delivery of contraception and family planning programmes has not reached the desired level. One of the more critical factors is funding. According to the Indian Department of Family Welfare, only 50 per cent of budgetary outlays designated for population stabilisation are directly allocated to stabilisation activities, including the procurement of equipment and supplies (National Commission on Population, 2000). Although it is common for government outlays to be absorbed by the bureaucratic process, there is a clear need to improve expenditure efficiency. This aside, it would appear that insufficient money is being devoted to population stabilisation policies in India. This raises the issue of whether the Indian Government has the fiscal capacity to finance the full range of programmes that India so desperately requires. If it does not, it is incumbent upon the international community – in particular, wealthy nations – to assist in the financing of these measures. After all, excessive population in an increasingly affluent India will have significant global environmental consequences.

Apart from increasing the welfare contribution of consumption expenditure, a more equitable distribution of income would also help to reduce India's population growth. Evidence suggests that a just distribution of adequate levels of income can go a long way towards lowering a nation's fertility rate, the major force behind population growth in overpopulated countries (Kuznets, 1974; Peterson, 1975; Pakrasi and Halder, 1981; Todaro, 1994; Daly, 1996). There is little doubt that the increase in India's per capita GDP has played a key role in reducing India's total fertility rate from 6 in 1951 to 3.1 in 2005.[7] However, fertility rates remain high amongst India's very poor. Thus, a more equitable distribution of income would greatly assist in reducing India's total fertility rate to something approaching the desired target rates for 2010 and beyond.[8]

Distributional Equity

The previous point brings us to the policies required to achieve distributional equity. One of the more the obvious equity solutions is a better funded and more extensive welfare system. It would be unfair, at this point in time, to expect India to install a welfare system similar to those operating in wealthy nations (i.e., one that delivers a substantial minimum income for all). This aside, a revamped welfare system should, at the very least, guarantee each and every Indian citizen access to essential goods and services.[9] This could be achieved by providing basic foodstuffs and public housing for all Indians in dire need.

At present, India employs a Public Distribution System (PDS) to supply various foodstuffs to the poor. Unfortunately, only 25 per cent of all subsidised food reaches the people targeted by the PDS (Shah, 2004). The PDS should therefore be reformed or, better still, be replaced by a system of food stamps.[10] According to Panagariya (2002) a well designed system of food stamps would not only increase the quantity of food reaching India's needy, it would also alleviate the cost of collection, storage, and distribution of essential foodstuffs, as well as reduce the corruption that currently plagues the PDS.[11]

Provided that the Indian Government can stabilise the nation's population growth and enhance its natural and productive capital, it should be well positioned in 20 to 30 years' time to provide more elaborate welfare services. This would reduce absolute poverty levels substantially and provide India with an increasingly robust safety net to improve the distribution of income and wealth.

As important as welfare assistance is, it deals largely with the symptoms and not the underlying causes of gross income disparities. Nothing does more to liberate the poor from debilitating levels of poverty than the opportunity to participate in economic life. To achieve this, there must be universal access to adequate education and health services. This is likely to come at a significant cost to the Indian Government which, again, might require international assistance. Fortunately, 'enabling' policies of this type substantially lessen the future reliance of the poor on government handouts. This can reduce the financial burden that a welfare system imposes on governments as well as quickly obviate the need for external financial assistance.

Another important area affecting the distribution of income is a nation's system of industrial relations – that is, the relationship between labour and owners of capital. In general, countries with industrial relations systems that permit free labour unions and protect workers' rights and conditions of employment enjoy a more equitable distribution of income. Unlike many developing countries, India does have a strong history of industrial relations. However, there are a number of factors which have resulted in a recent increase in the asymmetry of power in favour of employer groups.

Firstly, only 3 per cent of the total Indian workforce are members of a relevant trade union (Sodhi and Plowman, 2001). Secondly, the declining financial base of the union movement and its lack of critical mass have significantly reduced its capacity to support its members. Thirdly, the Indian Government has become less sympathetic to the demands of the trade union movement since instituting a raft of economic liberalisation policies in the 1990s (Sodhi and Plowman, 2001).

Given the important role that a nation's industrial relations system can play in promoting distributional equity, there is an urgent need to remedy the current system in order to strike an appropriate balance of power between workers and employers. But in establishing an industrial relations system that better protects workers' rights and conditions of employment, reformists must ensure the system promotes flexible and co-operative workplace arrangements to facilitate advances in labour productivity.

Finally, it was mentioned earlier in the chapter that India has a caste system first introduced many centuries ago by Indo-Aryan immigrants. Despite the introduction of constitutional reforms to weaken the caste system, caste discrimination remains a prominent feature in many parts of the private sector and in rural regions of India. By impeding the rate and extent of social and economic mobility within society, caste discrimination continues to underlie much of the deep-rooted disparities in income and wealth that presently exist in India. There is, therefore, a need for the Indian Government to introduce new reforms to dismantle the caste system further and, in the meantime, to dilute its deleterious impact on occupational opportunity and earning capacity.

Import Replacement Rather Than Export Growth

In view of the significant impact of foreign debt on India's per capita GPI, India should adopt an import-replacement policy. This is a somewhat polemical policy recommendation, largely because the standard approach to international trade is oriented towards export growth. Controversy aside, it cannot be denied that a one million rupee reduction in import spending would have the same beneficial impact on India's balance of trade as a one million rupee increase in export earnings. Hence, in terms of India's Current Account, there is nothing specifically disadvantageous about an import-replacement policy. But there are a number of advantageous aspects worth considering.

To begin with, an import-replacement policy is not, as some believe, 'anti-trade'. Nor does it require the imposition of tariffs and quotas to protect inefficient and underperforming industries. Import replacement occurs when a country reduces its need to import, which it can do by increasing production efficiency so that locally produced goods become comparatively less costly than imported goods. Because an import-replacement policy leaves a country producing a greater range of goods, it increases its self-sufficiency while also reducing its exposure to volatile global market forces.[12]

Secondly, overspecialisation in the quest for higher export income – that is, producing a greater quantity of a reduced range of goods – renders a country more reliant on exports as a source of income that, in turn, renders it 'less free not to trade'. Given the impact that foreign debt has had on the Indian Government's capacity to deliver services and maintain infrastructural spending, a reduced vulnerability to global market forces would be particularly beneficial to India as a whole. But it would clearly be of greatest benefit to the Indian citizens most susceptible to the suffering caused by a deterioration in India's terms of trade – namely, the very poor.

Finally, since the majority of goods produced in India must subsequently be consumed domestically, the focus of attention would shift to the purchasing power of Indian citizens. This would immediately direct the concern of Indian policy-makers to domestic employment levels, a sufficient minimum wage, and the overall distribution of income within India. Whilst it is possible that India's elite would earn less export revenue and thus have less money to purchase imported luxury goods, they are likely to respond by intensifying investment of their surplus at home, thereby generating further benefits for India.

Resource Use Efficiency and Value-Adding in Production

Given India's need for further GDP growth, increased efficiency is absolutely necessary to reduce the rate of resource use per unit of economic activity, to curb India's growing rate of pollution and greenhouse gas emissions, and to slow down the rise in India's cost of lost natural capital services. Greater efficiency also entails the production of better quality goods (i.e., increasing the use value added to new goods in production), augmenting labour productivity in order to boost real wages, and increasing a nation's international competitiveness without relying on low wages and weak environmental standards as a means of obtaining a competitive advantage. The latter, of course, is necessary to successfully achieve the import-replacement policy recommended above.

What can be done to increase the efficiency of resource use in India and the resource allocation process generally? Firstly, depletion and pollution taxes should be used, where practicable, to discourage wasteful resource use and excessive pollution. I say 'practicable' because, in India's circumstances, depletion and pollution taxes could prove particularly damaging to existing industries and future industrial development. That is not to say that Indian industry should be free to wantonly deplete and pollute. Rather, it may be more efficacious to offer tax rebates or subsidies to reward firms that develop and uptake resource-saving technologies. Either way, it is critical that the Indian Central and State Governments introduce appropriate incentives and disincentives to induce less resource-intensive industrial practices.

Where depletion and pollution taxes are employed, the revenue raised should be used, in part, for environmental rehabilitation purposes and to finance the development and uptake of resource-saving technology and renewable energy. To India's credit, it is one of only a small number of countries with a government ministry exclusively devoted to the development of non-conventional energy sources. It also has in place one of the most extensive programmes to promote the use of solar energy. All the same, the substitution towards renewable energy would be greatly enhanced by well-targeted taxes and/or subsidies.

In order to encourage value-adding in production, the Indian Government should reduce taxes on income, wages, and profit relative to the taxes on capital gains. This would discourage speculative forms of investment yet encourage investment in productive business ventures. Such a shift in the tax base would also be boosted by a decrease in the value-added tax (VAT) rate, since a VAT penalises the production of better-quality goods that, in general, command higher market prices. Tax deductions should, nevertheless, apply on expenditures incurred to improve capital assets. In this way, the Indian Government would capture the capital gains emanating from scarcity rents but reward gains from capital maintenance and improvements.

Last but not least, India urgently needs to remove bureaucratic impediments, reduce corruption levels, and increase the ease of operating a business in the Indian economy. In the latter case, India is ranked 134th in the world – a product not simply of bureaucratic hurdles, but of the inability of private and public sector investment in infrastructure to keep pace with growing infrastructural demands (World Bank, 2006). In terms of bureaucratic inefficiencies, India suffers from the post-independence adoption of a heavy-handed bureaucratic approach to economic development. Despite the economic liberalisation policies of the 1990s, there are still vast opportunities to deregulate some of the economic activities undertaken solely by the public sector. In most instances, efficiency-increasing forms of deregulation will require exposure of public sector activities to external competitive forces, although this need not always demand the privatisation of public assets.[13]

Natural Capital Maintenance

As outlined in Chapter 4, this book is largely based on the strong sustainability school of thought – namely, that sustainability requires natural capital maintenance given the inability of human-made capital to replicate the full range of critical services that natural capital provides. Exactly how much and what types of natural capital are needed is a moot point. However, in view of the enormous quantity of natural capital already sacrificed or severely degraded throughout India, the Asia-

Pacific region, and the world generally, many observers believe we can ill-afford to further deplete the aggregate stock of natural capital, in particular, the stock of critical ecosystems (Ehrlich, 1993).

In Table 1.10, it was revealed that India has an ecological deficit of –0.4 hectares per person. An ecological deficit effectively amounts to the liquidation of natural capital stocks. Whilst the mitigation of an ecological deficit is technically possible by augmenting a nation's biocapacity through improved environmental and resource management, the process is subject to severe biophysical limits (Norgaard, 1984). In addition, India's ecological deficit is likely to deteriorate in the light of projected rises in India's population and per capita resource consumption.

Clearly, the immediate aim of Indian policy-makers must be to minimise further diminution of India's natural capital. In the more immediate future, the quantity and quality of India's natural capital stocks must be preserved. This can be facilitated via the depletion and pollution taxes and subsidies already outlined as well as the recommended population stabilisation measures. Eventually, Indian policy-makers will need to introduce a system of tradeable permits to manage the use of renewable resources similar to the system recommended in Chapter 5 for Australia.[14] Permits are required given that taxes and subsidies could not guarantee that the rate of throughput in India would be restricted to the regenerative and waste-assimilative capacities of India's renewable natural capital (Daly, 1992; Lawn, 2007).[15] A permit system can overcome this dilemma by explicitly limiting the quantity of renewable resources to the ecologically sustainable rate, or any rate deemed appropriate at the time.

There are two additional benefits of a permit system. Firstly, it incorporates the benefits of depletion taxes in the sense that the premium paid by resource buyers to acquire permits serves as a throughout tax. This would facilitate the efficient allocation of India's renewable resource flow as well as induce the development and uptake of resource-saving technologies. Secondly, by regulating the number of permits periodically sold to resource buyers, the system would enable the Indian Government to initiate the transition to a lower rate of real GDP growth and, at an appropriate time, the full transition to a steady-state economy.

In the case of non-renewable resources, India needs to cultivate additional renewable resource stocks to offset the rapid and growing depletion of the former resource category. As it is, India's annual cost of non-renewable resource depletion increased by 164.7 per cent between

1987 and 2003 or at an average rate of 6.3 per cent per annum. There was no similar rate of expansion in India's renewable resource stocks, once again confirming the overall diminution of India's aggregate stock of natural capital. Similar to the recommendation offered in Chapter 5, Indian policy-makers should operationalise the El Serafy treatment of non-renewable resource profits (equation 3.12) by compelling resource liquidators to establish 'capital replacement' accounts. Through alterations in accounting legislation, the set-aside portion of the profits contained in these accounts would be used to establish suitable replacement assets (e.g., timber plantations) and/or to increase the productivity of existing renewable resources.

As for agricultural land – effectively a non-renewable resource in view of its low rate of regeneration – tax relief, subsidies, and small grants should be offered to Indian farmers to introduce soil conservation measures and encourage the use of less destructive agricultural practices. In countries such as India, a significant proportion of all land degradation is closely linked to poverty (Daly, 1996, Chapter 8). Since much of India's poverty occurs in rural areas, the policies recommended to alleviate absolute poverty and improve the distribution of India's income would also play a key role in reducing the cost of lost agricultural land.

Finally, protected areas constitute just 5.1 per cent of India's total land area (Table 1.7). This is much lower than the Asian average of 9.9 per cent and lower again than the world average of 11.4 per cent. Notwithstanding the increasing pressures arising from the rise in India's human population, Indian authorities must do more to increase the rate of ecosystem preservation and restoration, in particular, the area devoted to national and conservation parks.

CONCLUDING REMARKS

Despite enormous recent advances in India, the GPI results revealed in this chapter indicate that India's rate of genuine progress has not matched the rise in its per capita GDP. There is one simple explanation for this. While India's economic benefits have increased substantially, as reflected by the rapid rise in the per capita welfare contribution of consumption expenditure, so too have India's social and environmental costs – the latter being the result of an escalation in the cost of non-renewable resource depletion, land degradation, air pollution, and ecosystem destruction.

There is no denying the fact that India requires further growth of its real GDP to alleviate persistent high levels of absolute poverty, especially given the projected rises in India's population. However, it will need to be growth that is characterised by improved production (better-quality goods), a more equitable distribution of income, increased resource use efficiency, and the minimisation of the rate of natural capital depletion. It will also need to be accompanied by effective policies to rapidly stabilise India's population. Even if a 'better' form of growth can be achieved, the rate of increase in India's genuine progress is unlikely to match the recent and projected rises in India's real GDP. Nevertheless, it should at least prevent India's per capita GPI from declining in the immediate future.

Looking beyond the next 10 to 20 years is an entirely different matter altogether. India, like all countries, will need to make the transition to a lower rate of GDP growth. Eventually, however, India will need to think seriously about making the full transition to a steady-state economy. It will need to do this if only because a failure to do so will result in any additional benefits generated from production excellence, increased efficiency, and distributional equity being overwhelmed by the rising costs of an economic system that, inevitably and disastrously, would grow beyond its maximum sustainable scale.

A raft of policy measures has been recommended to enable India to make the smooth transition to a low rate of growth and eventually to a steady-state economy. All have been prescribed with the intention of increasing India's per capita GPI well into the distant future. Recommendations aside, the Indian Government faces a monumental task in trying to deliver a lasting and sustainable rate of genuine progress for its citizens. But it can be achieved, even though it is likely to require external assistance from the world's richest countries. For that matter, the world's richest countries have a clear responsibility to provide financial and moral support for India since they should never lose sight of how fortunate they are to have already enjoyed the spoils from past growth.

NOTES

1. The Indus Valley civilisation existed between 3300 and 1700 BC.
2. The Indian caste system is a traditional system of social stratification where various social classes are defined in terms of a number of endogamous, hereditary groups generally referred to as *jatis* or castes. The jatis are often further classified into one of four *varnas* or classes. A *varna* essentially defines an individual's social standing and occupation. Moreover, within a *jati*, there exists exogamous groups known as *gotras* – a term used for the lineage of a person.

   Although largely identified with Hinduism, the Indian caste system is also observed by followers of other religions. Caste-based discrimination has been formally outlawed by reforms to the Indian Constitution which have helped to weaken the caste system, particularly in large urban areas and in the civic domain. Nevertheless, caste discrimination remains a prominent feature of the private sector whilst caste customs are still strongly adhered to in rural regions. Consequently, social mobility within Indian society continues to be considerably restricted and, in the minds of many, goes a long way towards explaining the deep-rooted disparities in income and wealth.
3. Measured in 1990 international dollars.
4. Das (2006) refers to the excessive degree of government planning and the seemingly unwarranted regulations and controls imposed on the private sector as *dirigisme* – a French term used to describe an economy where the government effectively controls the allocation of resources.
5. It could not be determined which consumption category these various forms of spending were subsumed under. Presumably, household spending on education, insurance, and other financial services was included in the miscellaneous goods and services category. Given the imprecision involved, no deductions were made.
6. The concept of a steady-state economy has been discussed in Chapters 1 and 5. To reiterate, a steady-state economy involves a national economy that does not physically grow but qualitatively improves in terms of the content of the physical goods within the economy, the means by which they are produced and maintained, and the purpose for which they are intended.
7. The total fertility rate (TFR) corresponds to the average number of children born to a woman during her lifetime. The TFR data was sourced from the World Resources Institute database (WRI, http://earthtrends.wri.org).
8. The 2.1 target rate for the year 2010 now appears out of reach.
9. Whilst the 1950 Constitution of India contains provisions to secure the right to work, the right to education, and the right to public assistance in cases of unemployment, old age, sickness, and disablement (e.g., Article 41), they have served as little more than guidelines to direct India's welfare policy. The failure of the Indian Government to establish a comprehensive welfare system stems largely from the proviso in Article 41 that the state's responsibility is subject to the *limits of its economic capacity and development* (Aspalter, 2003).

10. For details on how a well-designed food stamp system might operate in India, see Shah (2004).
11. Panagariya (2002) outlines three key reasons why food stamps are superior to the current PDS system in transferring income to the poor in India.
12. Self-sufficiency was vehemently promoted as a desirable national goal in the United Nations Report on the World Summit on Sustainable Development that was held in Johannesburg (United Nations, 2002).
13. Exposure to competition through deregulation is often confused with privatisation. Some observers believe that deregulation is only effective if accompanied by the selling of publicly-owned assets subjected to competitive market forces. This is not necessarily the case. Indeed, having the government involved in some way enables it to discipline the market in the sense that it can keep prices to the normal economic profit level and/or maintain equity in the system.
14. More detail on how a tradeable resource use permit system would operate can be found in Lawn (2007), Chapter 11.
15. All the same, permits can only control the quantity of pollution (first law of thermodynamics) but not its quality (second law of thermodynamics). For this reason, pollution taxes would still need to be used. In the case of highly toxic substances, there would need to be very strict controls on the production, storage, use, and disposal of them. In some cases, substances would simply have to be prohibited altogether.

REFERENCES

Ahluwalia, I. (2002), 'Economic reforms in India since 1991: has gradualism worked?', *Journal of Economic Perspectives*, **16**, 67–88.

Aspalter, C. (2003), 'The welfare state system in India', in C. Aspalter (ed.), *The Welfare State in Emerging-Market Economies*, Hong Kong: Casa Verde Publishing, Chapter 7.

Brahmbhatt, M., Srinivasan, T. and Murrell, K. (1996), 'India in the global economy', Washington DC: World Bank Policy Research Working Paper No. 1681.

Chopra, P., Puri, B. and Das, M. (1974), *A Social, Cultural and Economic History of India*, Volumes I–III, Delhi: MacMillan.

Daly, H. (1992), 'Allocation, distribution, and scale: towards an economics that is efficient, just, and sustainable', *Ecological Economics*, **6**, 185–193.

Daly, H. (1996), *Beyond Growth: The Economics of Sustainable Development*, Boston, MA: Beacon Press.

Das, D. (2004), *Financial Globalization and the Emerging Market Economies*, London: Routledge.

Das, D. (2006), *China and India: A Tale of Two Economies*, Abingdon: Routledge.

Dutt, R. (1956), *The Economic History of India*, London: Routledge & Kegan Paul.

Edwardes, M. (1961), *A History of India: From the Earliest Times to the Present Day*, London: Thames & Hudson.

Ehrlich, P. (1993), 'Biodiversity and ecosystem function: need we know more?', in E.-D. Schulze and H. Mooney (eds), *Biodiversity and Ecosystem Function*, Berlin: Springer-Verlag, pp. VII–XI.

Government of India (2002), *Economic Survey 2002*, New Delhi: Ministry of Finance.

International Labour Office (ILO) (various), *International Labour Office Yearbook of Labour Statistics*, Geneva: ILO.

International Monetary Fund (IMF) (2000), *World Economic Outlook*, May, Washington, DC: IMF.

Khanna, V.S. (2005), 'The economic history of the corporate form in ancient India', University of Michigan Paper.

Kuznets, S. (1974), 'Fertility differentials between less developed and developed regions: components and implications', Discussion Paper No. 217, New Haven, CT: Yale University Economic Growth Centre.

Lawn, P. (2007), *Frontier Issues in Ecological Economics*, Cheltenham, UK and Northampton, MA, USA: Edward Elgar.

Luthra, S., Mangaleswaran, R. and Padhi, A. (2005), 'When to make India a manufacturing base?', *McKinsey Quarterly*, **September**, 19–28.

Maddison, A. (1998), *Chinese Economic Performance in the Long Run*, Paris: OECD Development Centre.

Maddison, A. (2002), 'Growth and interaction in the world economy: the West and the rest AD 1000–2000', in B. de Macado, C. Jorge and C. Oman (eds), *Development is Back*, Paris: OECD Development Centre.

Maddison, A. (2004), *The World Economy: Historical Statistics*, Paris: OECD.

Metcalf, B. and Metcalf, T. (2006), *A Concise History of Moden India*, 2nd edition, Cambridge: Cambridge University Press.

Misra, B. (1986), *Government and Bureaucracy in India 1947–1976*, Delhi: Oxford University Press.

National Commission on Population (2000), *National Population Policy 2000*, New Delhi: Government of India.

Norgaard, R. (1984), 'Coevolutionary development potential', *Land Economics*, **60**, 160–173.

Pakrasi, K. and Halder, A. (1981), 'Fertility in contemporary Calcutta: a biosocial profile', *Genus*, **37(3/4)** , 201–219.

Panagariya, A. (2002), 'Stamping in nutrition', *Economic Times*, 24 April.

Peterson, W. (1975), *Population*, New York: Macmillan & Co.

Roy, K. and Tisdell, C. (1992), 'Planned development: strategies, instruments, and processes and the place of environment in Indian planning', in K. Roy, C. Tisdell and R. Sen (eds), *Economic Development and Environment: A Case Study of India*, Calcutta: Oxford University Press, pp. 17–41.

Shah, P. (2004), *Food Stamps: A Model for India*, New Delhi: Centre for Civil Society.

Sodhi, J. and Plowman, D. (2001), *Economic Change and Industrial Relations: India and Australia*, Nedlands: Scholastic Press Australia.

Todaro, M. (1994), *Economic Development*, 5th edition, New York: Longman.

United Nations (2002), 'Report of the world summit on sustainable development', Final report on the World Summit on Sustainable Development held in Johannesburg, 26 August–4 September.

World Bank (2006), 'Doing business: explore economies', www.doingbusiness.org/ExploreEconomies/?economyid=89.

World Resources Institute (WRI), 'Population, health and human well-being – demographics: total fertility rate', http://earthtrends.wri.org.

9. From GDP to GPI: quantifying thirty-five years of development in China

Zongguo Wen, Yan Yang, and Philip Lawn

INTRODUCTION

Features of the Chinese Economy

China's rapid economic development over the past 35 years is clearly indicated by the extraordinary growth in its Gross Domestic Product (GDP) (see Figure 9.1). Despite being a largely agrarian society in the mid-1960s, China has transformed itself into an industrial giant and now possesses the world's second-largest economy as measured by real GDP on a purchasing power parity (PPP) basis. More importantly, per capita GDP, which normalises GDP against population growth, has also grown at a staggering rate. Indeed, per capita GDP increased twelve-fold from 1163 to 13 944 yuan per person between 1970 and 2005. This constitutes an average growth rate of 8.6 per cent per annum and shows no signs of flagging.

Even so, China is still regarded as a lower middle-income country with the incomes of over 130 million Chinese citizens below the international poverty line.[1] It will therefore be necessary for the growth in China's real GDP to continue for some time to improve living standards further. As we shall see, the extent to which any genuine progress is likely to be made in the future will depend on the nature of the growth that takes place in China over the coming years and the distribution of the new gains amongst its population.

In effect, the new manufacturing hub of the world economy, China has become a prime location for transnational corporations to manufacture products to be later exported across the world. For example, more than 50 per cent of the world's cameras, 30 per cent of its air conditioners and

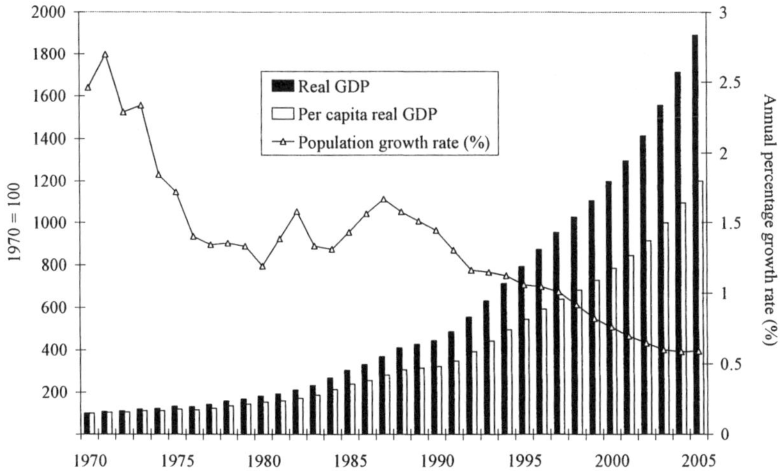

Figure 9.1 *Index of real GDP, per capita GDP, and population growth rate: China, 1970–2005*

televisions, 25 per cent of its washing machines, and almost 20 per cent of its refrigerators are presently manufactured in China (Wen, 2005). With the product list and range continuing to grow, increasing pressure is now being exerted on the natural environment in the form of pollution and resource depletion. As a consequence, the Chinese Government is being forced to meet new policy challenges in the area of environmental protection and sustainable development.

The growth of Chinese manufacturing since the mid-1980s has prompted Jiang (2003) to conclude that China has begun a 'metaphase' of industrialisation. This is supported by Figure 9.2, which shows that the output of China's primary industries continued to fall as a percentage of total output between 1978 and 2005. The contribution of China's secondary industries also declined slightly between 1978 and 1990 (41.3 per cent contribution in 1990), but has changed very little since. Future output expectations project that this contribution is unlikely to fall in the future.

The biggest change in the Chinese economy was the growth in the contribution made by China's tertiary industries. Over the 1978–2005 period, the tertiary sector grew by two-thirds to constitute around 40 per cent of China's total economic output in 2005. Despite the rising urbanisation of the Chinese population since the mid-1980s, it has been

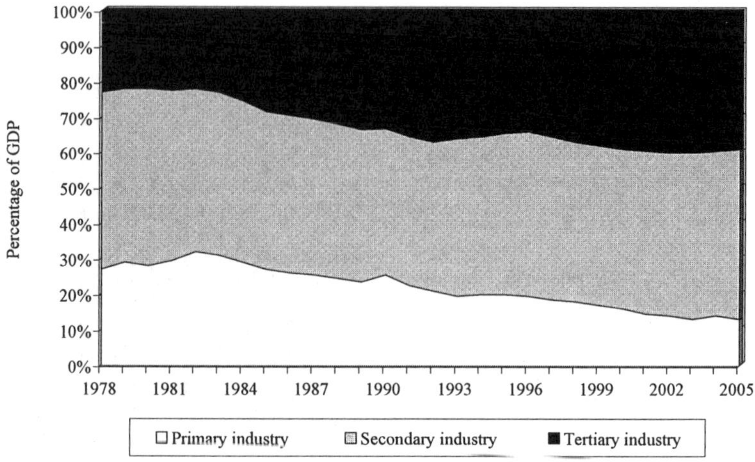

Figure 9.2 Industry sectors as a proportion of real GDP: China, 1978–2005

suggested that further development of the tertiary sector will be limited by China's relatively low rate of urbanisation when compared to most industrialised nations (Li, 2002).

The Natural Environment and Resource Stocks of China

History reveals that economic development usually brings with it severe cases of industrial pollution. China is no exception. Recent expansion of the Chinese economy has led to serious resource and environmental problems that, in view of the need for further growth in real GDP, will continue for some time to come.

In addition, China suffers from chronic shortages of particular resource types with per capita levels of specific resources well below average global levels. For example, in 2005, China's per capita water resource stocks amounted to 2145 cubic metres per citizen. This is one-quarter of the world mean value of 8549 cubic metres (World Resources Institute, 2005). As such, China has been classified as one of 13 countries suffering from a perilously high scarcity of water resources. To make matters worse, water resource use in China is very inefficient. In 2002, total water usage was 539.7 billion cubic metres of which 61.4 per cent was used for agricultural irrigation (Ministry of Water Resources, 2003). With irrigation efficiency at just 43 per cent in 2001 and 45 per cent in 2004, a significant quantity of water is clearly going to waste (Ministry of Water Resources, 2004).

In China's favour is its per capita possession of coal, petroleum, and natural gas reserves which currently stands at 55.7 per cent, 11.1 per cent and 4.4 per cent of the world mean value respectively. However, the consumption rate of natural resources is excessively high and steadily rising. For example, while China's real GDP comprises 13.5 per cent of the world's real GDP, its energy consumption of chief products is 40 per cent higher than that of foreign countries in 2002 (Wen, 2005). Furthermore, in 2004, China's energy consumption intensity (i.e., energy used per unit of real GDP) was 8.4 tonnes of oil equivalent per US$10 000 of real GDP, which corresponds to 3.36 times the world average, four times that of the USA, and eight times that of Japan, England, Germany, and France (Wen, 2005).

The resource-intensive nature of China's economic activity is now having major implications in terms of the quantity of pollution generated and its effect on both the health of the Chinese population and the productivity of the Chinese economy. A recent World Bank report estimates that the combined cost of air and water pollution in 2003 equated to as much as 5.78 per cent of China's GDP (World Bank, 2007). The cost of air pollution alone was equal to 3.8 per cent of GDP, which is only slightly lower than the contribution made towards China's GDP by its entire export of textile goods and clothing.

One of the main contributing factors to the rise in global greenhouse gas emissions is the consumption of coal. Used mainly for electricity generation, world coal consumption grew by 5 per cent in 2005, effectively double the annual growth rate experienced in the mid-1990s. China, as the world's largest coal consumer, increased its domestic consumption of coal by 11 per cent in 2005. Furthermore, China's coal consumption for the year comprised a staggering 80 per cent of the worldwide increase in coal demand. Not surprisingly, China is a major greenhouse gas emitter and a country which is likely to come under increasing international pressure to control its emission levels.

Apart from coal, the depletion of non-renewable resources in general remains very high in China and has increased markedly over the past five years. In addition, the degradation of agricultural land has also risen dramatically. This is of particular concern given that, in 2006, per capita agricultural land was 4245 square metres in China, while the world average value was 82.4 per cent higher at 7741 square metres (World Bank, 2006).[2] It has therefore been projected that both land degradation and the outright loss of agricultural land through industrialisation will undermine China's food production capacity which, in turn, will impact negatively on China's national wealth (Wen, 2005).

As for China's timber stocks, the harvesting of timber for export and domestic consumption remains very high. At the beginning of the study period (1970–75), log increment (forest growth) either exceeded or matched the harvesting of timber, thereby ensuring no net losses of timber stocks. Beyond 1975, however, the rate of timber harvest gradually exceeded the natural rate of forest increment, thus depleting timber stocks in China. The disparity between the harvest and increment grew to a peak of 63 million cubic metres in 1996. Fortunately, the volume of timber harvest has declined since the mid-1990s. Thanks also to reforestation, the gap between consumption and replenishment has narrowed significantly. At current trends, timber stocks could eventually be stabilised in the very near future.

Chinese Society

Population growth brings increasing stress on scarce resources and China's ongoing struggle to stabilise its population is well documented. Although the national fertility rate has dramatically declined, the inertia associated with population growth dynamics will lead to a rapid increase in absolute population numbers for many decades to come.

Another social issue facing China is the problem of uneven regional development. Western China, which covers 70.1 per cent of the country's total landmass, is still extensively impoverished. Shortages of resources, poor efficiency of resource utilisation, and inadequate management continue to impede the region's development. In addition, problems concerning economic development and its impact on the environment are very pronounced.

Given the uneven nature of economic development in China, it should come at no surprise that income inequality has steadily increased. For this study, a Distribution Index (DI) was derived by normalising the Gini coefficient to a base year of 1970 (i.e., 1970 = 100). The DI increased from 100 in 1970 to 191.5 in 2005. This indicates a 91.5 per cent deterioration in the distribution of income in China over the study period. Research by Li et al. (2003) suggests that the Gini coefficient is probably smaller than its actual value because the statistical data fails to capture confidential sources of income. The DI used for this study can therefore be considered a conservative estimate.

Summary

This introductory section paints a picture of a country which, in little more than 35 years, has been transformed from an agrarian economy to a manufacturing giant. Given the geographical scale of China and the size of its human population, this can only be considered an extraordinary phenomenon. Between 1970 and 2005, China experienced a twelvefold increase in per capita GDP which has undoubtedly improved the material standard of living of many of its people.

However, the gains from this staggering rate of growth have not been equitably distributed, both within regions (as indicated by the rise in China's Gini coefficient) and across regions (due to the uneven pattern of regional development). Furthermore, China's economic transformation has come at great cost to the natural environment. Already subject to severe resource constraints, the rapid rise in China's real GDP has further diminished its resource stocks to the point where China relies very heavily on the importation of key resources. Pollution is also a major downside of China's economic transformation, with the health of many Chinese citizens, particularly those in large urban areas, dramatically affected. Defensive and rehabilitative expenditures are already mounting in response to the side-effects of rising pollution; however, they are likely to increase many times over should the growth in pollution emissions continue unabated.

With all this in mind, the logical question that arises is this: To what extent has China experienced genuine progress over the 1970–2005 period? It is hoped that the Genuine Progress Indicator (GPI) results presented in this chapter will offer some useful answers to this question. Whilst we recognise that our results will not provide definitive solutions, we are confident that they will force policy-makers to reassess the nature of the growth taking place in China. In doing so, we hope that they will arouse policy-makers to consider alternative means to a lasting and prosperous future for each and every Chinese citizen.

THE GPI METHODOLOGY EMPLOYED FOR CHINA

Table 9.1 summarises the GPI items used for this study on China. Once again, the methodological framework employed is very similar to that outlined in Chapter 3. However, there are a number of slight variations. These will reveal themselves as we now outline the valuation approaches used to estimate each GPI component used in this study.

Table 9.1 Summary of GPI items used in the Chinese study

GPI items	Welfare contribution
Consumption expenditure	Positive
Expenditure on consumer durables	Negative
Service from consumer durables	Positive
Distribution Index	Positive/negative
Welfare from publicly-provided infrastructure	Positive
Value of non-paid household labour	Positive
Value of volunteer labour	Positive
Cost of unemployment	Negative
Cost of crime	Negative
Cost of family breakdown	Negative
Change in foreign debt position	Positive/negative
Cost of non-renewable resources depletion	Negative
Cost of lost agricultural land	Negative
Cost of excessive irrigation water use	Negative
Cost of timber depletion	Negative
Cost of urban waste-water pollution	Negative
Cost of air pollution	Negative
Cost of long-term environmental damage	Negative

Consumption Expenditure

As the base item of the GPI, the values pertaining to consumption expenditure were sourced directly from the published *China Statistical Yearbook* (NBSC, various).

Expenditure on Consumer Durables (ECD) and Service from Consumer Durables (SCD)

Expenditure on consumer durables (ECD) was derived from the data on household consumption expenditure. Whilst the per capita expenditure on consumer durables by China's urban population can be drawn directly from the *China Statistical Yearbook*, which can then be used to calculate the total urban expenditure on consumer durables, the same information does not exist for China's rural population. The per capita expenditure on consumer durables by China's rural population was estimated by: (a) assuming the proportion of total per capita expenditure on consumer durables was the same for urban and rural citizens; and (b) multiplying the per capita urban expenditure on consumer durables by the ratio of rural to urban per capita household expenditure on 'household facilities, articles, and services' (NBSC, various).

Total expenditure of consumer durables was calculated using the following two equations:

$$ECD = \left(E_U \times P_U\right) + \left(E_R \times P_R\right) \tag{9.1}$$

where E_U = per capita expenditure on consumer durables by urban residents; P_U = China's urban population; E_R = per capita expenditure on consumer durables by rural residents; and P_R = China's rural population. In addition:

$$E_R = E_U \times \frac{F_R}{F_U} \tag{9.2}$$

where F_U = per capita urban expenditure on household facilities, articles, and services; and F_R = per capita rural expenditure on household facilities, articles, and services.

As for the service yielded by the stock of consumer durables, it was assumed that the average serviceable lifetime of a consumer durable is ten years (i.e., consumer durables depreciate at the rate of 10 per cent per annum). The service value (SCD) was assumed to equal the depreciation value which was calculated as:

$$SCD_t = \frac{1}{10} \sum_{k=t-9}^{t} ECD_K \tag{9.3}$$

Distribution Index (DI)

The DI was calculated by normalising the Gini coefficient in reference to 1970, the first year of the study period. The following was therefore used to calculate the annual value for the DI:

$$DI_t = \frac{G_t}{G_{1970}} \times 100 \tag{9.4}$$

where G = Gini coefficient which has been derived by Wen and Chen (forthcoming) from data on individual income from the *China Statistical Yearbook* (NBSC, various).

Welfare from Publicly-Provided Infrastructure (WPPI)

Since the existing stock of public infrastructural assets (e.g., roads, hospitals, schools, universities, and ports) provides welfare benefits through its use over time, WPPI was calculated by assuming that it equals the depreciation rate of all fixed assets multiplied by the ratio of public infrastructure depreciation to fixed assets depreciation. That is:

$$WPPI = W_{fi} \times R_W \tag{9.5}$$

where $WPPI$ = welfare from publicly-provided infrastructure; W_{fi} = the depreciation of fixed assets; and R_W = the ratio of public infrastructure to the depreciation of fixed assets. In order to estimate the annual values using equation (9.5), two further aspects were assumed. Firstly, it was assumed that the depreciation of fixed assets was a particular percentage of Gross National Income (GNI).[3] Hence:

$$W_{fi} = P_{fi} \times GNI \tag{9.6}$$

where P_{fi} = the depreciation of fixed assets calculated as a percentage of China's GNI (depreciation percentage drawn directly from a survey conducted by the China Statistical Bureau and the World Bank (Hamilton, 2005)).

Secondly, it was assumed that the ratio of public infrastructure depreciation to fixed assets depreciation (R_W) was equal to the ratio of government investment in public infrastructure to total investment in fixed assets (R_i). In other words, $R_W = R_i$ such that:

$$R_i = \frac{\sum_{i=4} I_i}{I_t} \tag{9.7}$$

where I_t = the total investment in fixed assets (NBSC, various); and I_i = infrastructural investment, which was estimated by summing investments in:

- transport, storage, postal, and telecommunications services;
- public services;
- health care, sport, and social welfare;
- culture and the arts, education, radio, film and television.

The data on each investment component was sourced from the *China Statistical Yearbook* (NBSC, various).

Value of Non-Paid Household Labour

In 1999, a survey was conducted which concluded that the average number of non-paid household labour hours was 2.35 hours per day per household (Lu and Peng, 1999). For the remaining years of the study period, it was assumed that technological improvements embodied in household appliances reduced the number of household labour hours at the rate of 0.5 per cent per annum (Lu and Peng, 1999; Wen, 2005). Hence, the 2.35 hours was adjusted upwards by 0.5 per cent per annum when working back to 1970 from 1999 and downwards by 0.5 per cent per annum when working forwards from 1999 to 2005.[4]

The daily number of non-paid household labour hours was then multiplied by 365 days and by the changing number of Chinese households over the study period. This generated the total number of non-paid household labour hours per year which was subsequently multiplied by the average hourly wage for resident services at 2005 prices (8.30 yuan per hour).

Value of Volunteer Labour

Volunteer labour, which can take the form of caring for the elderly or performing a community service, is an invaluable welfare-generating activity. Unfortunately, like non-paid household labour, volunteer labour is omitted when calculating GDP. In general, volunteer labour is valued by estimating what it would cost to hire people to carry out equivalent tasks. In this study, a base value for volunteer work was calculated by estimating the contribution from non-paid community service work required by law (e.g., tree planting on Arbor Day).

We have assumed that 70 per cent of all employees in China engage in 'volunteer work', as determined by law, and that this was undertaken twice a year – on Arbor Day and Lei Feng Learning Day. Given these assumptions, the base value of volunteer labour was calculated in the following manner:

$$V = 0.7 \times 2 \times W_S \times N_W \tag{9.8}$$

where V = the value of volunteer labour; W_S = the average wage of staff/workers engaged in community services (yuan per day); and N_W = the number of staff/workers at year end.

It was then assumed that the total value of volunteer labour was ten times the base value. This assumption is predicated on recent evidence which indicates that there are now 75 000 community volunteer organisations in China with over 16 million members (www.worldvolunteerweb.org).

Cost of Unemployment

Unemployment is a social cost in the sense that it can lead to frustration, low self-esteem, suicide, violent crime, mental illness (if unemployment is prolonged), alcoholism, and other forms of substance abuse (Anielski and Rowe, 1999). The number of unemployed people in China generally increased over the study period. In 1978, for example, 5.3 million people were unemployed. By 2005, the number of unemployed people had ballooned to 8.4 million.

For this study, the cost of unemployment was assumed to equal the economic value that would have been generated had the number of unemployed people been fully employed, less central government welfare expenditure. The cost of unemployment (U) was therefore calculated with the use of the following equation:

$$U = \left[\Sigma\left(W_{MINi} \times P_{Ui}\right) \times 12 / 10\,000\right] - E_{MIN} \qquad (9.9)$$

where U = the cost of unemployment; W_{MINi} = the minimum security wage (yuan per month); P_{Ui} = the number of people in urban areas registered as unemployed in each province (10 000 persons); and E_{MINi} = welfare expenditure by the central government to secure minimum living conditions for the unemployed.

The minimum security wage for each province is determined by the Chinese provincial governments and varies considerably across the nation. In 2005, it was 580 yuan per month in Beijing but only 450 yuan in Liaoning province. Central government welfare expenditure was drawn from the *China Statistical Yearbook* (NBSC, various) and amounted to 19.1 billion yuan in 2005.

Cost of Crime

Because crime diminishes social welfare and indirectly hinders the development process, it is considered an important social cost that should not be overlooked in the calculation of sustainable welfare. In the case of this GPI study, the cost of crime was based on insurance premiums paid to property insurance companies and expenditure on both the legal system and law enforcement. All data was sourced from the *China Insurance Yearbook* or the *China Statistical Yearbook* (NBSC, various).

Cost of Family Breakdown

The breakdown of the family unit imposes significant costs to individuals and society at large. These costs invariably emerge in the form of legal fees, medical expenses, and psychological disorders, of which the latter particularly applies to affected children (Anielski and Rowe, 1999; Xu and Ye, 2001). Perversely, the costs associated with the breakdown of the family unit are included in the calculation of a nation's real GDP. This can give the uninitiated the false impression that a nation's welfare is increasing when, quite obviously, the opposite is occurring.

The cost of family breakdown was calculated in this GPI study by a four-step process. In the first instance, the number of divorces was multiplied by the average divorce litigation cost, which was assumed to be 50 yuan per couple. Secondly, the number of affected children was multiplied by an estimated cost of the indirect impact of divorce upon them. Based on a study conducted by (Xu and Ye, 2001), it was assumed that one child was affected in 86 per cent of all divorce cases. In the remaining 14 per cent of cases, it was assumed that no child was involved.

The third step involved adding the two costs (step one and two) to arrive at the total direct cost of family breakdown. Finally, the indirect cost of family breakdown – namely, the property assignment charge arising from divorce proceedings – was added to the direct cost to yield the full cost of family breakdown. Overall, the cost of family breakdown was calculated as:

$$FB = \left[\left(N_D \times C_{DL} + N_C \times C_{IMP}\right) / 10\,000\right] + C_{PA} \tag{9.10}$$

where FB = cost of family breakdown; N_D = number of divorces (10 000 couples), which was 340 998 in 1980 and 1 785 000 in 2005; C_{DL} = average divorce litigation cost; N_C = number of affected children (10 000 persons); C_{IMP} = cost of impact of divorce on an affected child (yuan per affected child), which was 4597 yuan in 1992; and C_{PA} = property assignment charge arising from divorce proceedings.[5]

Also of note is that:

$$N_C = 0.86 \times N_D \tag{9.11}$$

and

$$C_{PA} = 0.01 \times S_D \times \frac{N_d}{N_t} \tag{9.12}$$

where S_D = savings deposit at the year end; N_t = total number households; and 0.01 = supposed charge for property assignment as a percentage of savings deposit.

Change in Net Foreign Debt Position

As explained in Chapter 3, the sustainability of a nation's welfare is subject not only to the quantity of available productive capital, but also to the extent to which the nation must borrow from abroad to finance its current consumption expenditure (i.e., implying that it has insufficient domestic capital to support its current consumption). This item is negative if, for a particular year, a nation's net foreign debt increases or, equivalently, if its net foreign assets decline. Should a nation's net foreign debt decrease or its net foreign assets rise, this item is positive.

The data required to calculate this item was sourced directly from the *China Statistical Yearbook* (NBSC, various) and multiplied by the exchange rate variation between the US dollar and the Chinese yuan. Since dramatic exchange rate variations can accentuate the impact of net foreign debt on a nation's sustainable welfare, a five-year moving average was calculated to smooth out extreme year-to-year fluctuations.

Cost of Non-Renewable Resource Depletion

The cost of non-renewable resource depletion in China accounted for the extraction of 14 different resources – namely, four types of non-renewable energy resources (crude oil, natural gas, hard coal, and lignite), and ten varieties of minerals (bauxite, copper, gold, iron, lead, nickel, phosphate, silver, tin, and zinc). The cost of depletion in each case was calculated using the El Serafy (1989) user cost formula outlined in Chapter 3 (equation 3.12). In order to employ the El Serafy formula, it was assumed that the average mine life of the various resources was 50 years (i.e., $n = 50$) and the regeneration rate of the replacement assets was 1 per cent per annum (i.e., $r = 1$ per cent). This implies that the set-aside component from non-renewable resource extraction constitutes 40 per cent of the net receipts obtained. On the basis that market prices undervalue the absolute scarcity of non-renewable resources by one-half, the user cost percentage was doubled to 80 per cent.

The per tonne value obtained from each non-renewable resource type was assumed to equal the difference in its international market price and the average cost of its extraction (i.e., average production cost). This value was subsequently multiplied by the production volume to obtain the total net receipts from each of the non-renewable resources accounted for in the study. That is:

$$R = \left(P_{INT} - AC\right) \times Q_{NR} \tag{9.13}$$

where R = net receipts from non-renewable resource depletion; P_{INT} = international market price (per tonne); AC = average production cost (per tonne); and Q_{NR} = production volume (tonnes). Overall, the total depletion of each non-renewable resource (NR) was determined with the use of the following equations:

$$NR = \left[2 \times \left(1 - \frac{1}{(1.01)^{51}}\right)\right] \times \left[\left(P_{INT} - AC\right) \times Q_{NR}\right] \tag{9.14}$$

or

$$NR = 0.8 \times \left[\left(P_{INT} - AC\right) \times Q'_{NR}\right] \tag{9.15}$$

Cost of Lost Agricultural Land (Land Degradation)

The cost of lost agricultural land includes the decline in agricultural productivity, the opportunity cost of rehabilitative expenditures incurred to restore damaged farmland, and the loss of ecological services (Liu and Yang, 1999; Bolund and Hunhammar, 1999; Wen, 2005). To reflect this cost, this item was calculated to reflect the amount required to compensate Chinese citizens for the accumulated area of lost agriculture land.

To achieve this, it was assumed that the value of agricultural land – i.e., the sum of its productivity and ecological services – was 15 000 yuan per hectare in 1995 (Liu and Yang, 1999). This was adjusted to 2005 prices. The annual loss of agricultural land was sourced from the *National Resource Communiqué* (Ministry of Land Resources). The final cost of lost agricultural land was calculated using the following equation:

$$Ag = C_{Ag} \times L_{C} \tag{9.16}$$

where Ag = total cost of lost agricultural land; C_{Ag} = the unit cost of lost agricultural land (yuan per hectare); and L_C = the cumulative loss of agriculture land (hectares). Annual values of lost agricultural land area can be found from *Country Resource Communiqué*.

Cost of Excessive Irrigation Water Use

As mentioned earlier in the chapter, China is subject to severe water shortages and gross water use inefficiencies. As a consequence, the amount of water used for irrigation dramatically exceeds actual need, thus placing greater stress on already scarce water supplies. For this study, the cost of excessive irrigation use was assumed to equal the value of water wasted through inefficient and excessive irrigation practices. It was calculated by multiplying the average water price for irrigation by the volume of water used for irrigation purposes which was then multiplied by the percentage of water wasted through inefficiency. That is:

$$I = P_W \times V_W \times (1 - \eta) \quad (9.17)$$

where I = cost of excessive irrigation water use; P_W = average water price for irrigation (yuan per cubic metre); V_W = volume of water used for irrigation; and η = irrigation effectiveness. According to the *Water Resource Statistic Communiqué* (Ministry of Water Resources), irrigation efficiency in 2001 and 2005 was 43 per cent and 45 per cent respectively. It was assumed that irrigation efficiency in 1970 was 35 per cent. The efficiency rate of the intervening years was acquired through interpolation.

Cost of Timber Depletion

Timber resources dwindle whenever the rate of harvest exceeds the regenerative capacity of timber stocks. Unlike non-renewable resources, timber stocks can be augmented either through natural regeneration or reforestation programs. Between 1970 and 1975, China's timber stocks actually rose. They have declined ever since, although the rate of decline in 2005 was considerably less than the peak of 63 million cubic metres of timber in 1996.

To calculate the true cost of timber depletion, the average price (rent) per cubic metre of timber was multiplied by the difference between timber output (roundwood production volume) and the natural growth rate of forest stocks. In the years where timber stocks declined, the El Serafy (1989) user cost formula was applied.[6] Based on the same assumptions used to calculate the cost of non-renewable resource depletion, it was estimated that the user cost of timber stocks was 80 per cent of the total value of timber depletion. The remaining 20 per cent was legitimate income. The data on timber prices was sourced directly from the *National Forest Yearbook*, while timber prices were drawn from the World Bank.[7]

All up, the following equations were used to calculate the cost of timber depletion:

$$TIMB = \left[2 \times \left(1 - \frac{1}{(1.01)^{51}}\right)\right] \times \left[\left(Q_{RWOOD} - Q_G\right) \times P_{TIMB}\right] \quad (9.18)$$

or

$$TIMB = 0.8 \times \left[\left(Q_{RWOOD} - Q_G\right) \times P_{TIMB}\right] \quad (9.19)$$

where $TIMB$ = cost of timber depletion; Q_{RWOOD} = volume of roundwood production (cubic metres); Q_G = forest growth; P_{TIMB} = average price (rent) of timber (yuan per cubic metre).

Cost of Urban Waste-Water Pollution

Despite the rapid modernisation of many urban areas in China, especially along the eastern seaboard, urban waste-water management systems are inadequate to deal with the growing quantity of discharged waste-water. The cost of urban waste-water pollution was therefore calculated by summing municipal and industrial waste-water treatment expenditures, the cost of urban sewage system construction, and the impact of water pollution on human health (i.e., cost of premature death, lost working days, and the medical expenses incurred to treat hepatitis, dysentery, and water pollution-induced forms of cancer).

Since many of the costs of urban waste-water pollution are reflected in other GPI items (e.g., lost working days and poorer health outcomes reduce productivity and therefore consumption expenditure), and to avoid double-counting, it was assumed that the direct cost of urban waste-water pollution was 50 per cent of the total cost. That is:

$$0.5 \times WWP \quad (9.20)$$

where

$$WWP = WW_I + WW_H \quad (9.21)$$

and where WWP = cost of urban waste-water pollution; WW_I = investment costs for implementation of waste-water treatment; and WW_H = cost of impact on human health. The important parameters used to determine the various costs related to urban waste-water pollution can be found in Wen and Chen (forthcoming).

Cost of Air Pollution

Earlier in the chapter, it was revealed that a World Bank report had estimated the cost of air pollution in China to be 3.8 per cent of its GDP (World Bank, 2007). This percentage was therefore used in the estimation of the cost of air pollution for each year over the study period. However, not unlike waste-water pollution, the total cost of air pollution includes the indirect impact on labour productivity and impacts reflected by other GPI items. It was therefore assumed that the direct cost of air pollution was 50 per cent of the total cost.

Cost of Long-Term Environmental Damage

In recent times, many national governments have placed great emphasis on the need to manage the root causes of climate change (e.g., CO_2 emissions). The increased urgency is due largely to compelling evidence regarding the long-term environmental implications of climate change (IPPC, 2007) and the potential economic cost of not taking immediate action (Stern, 2006). China's massive, coal-oriented economy contributes no small part to this problem. In order to estimate the long-term environmental cost of China's economic activity, two pollutants were taken into account: CO_2 and ozone-depleting substances (ODS).

In calculating this item, it was assumed, firstly, that the long-term cost of CO_2 emissions equals a given percentage of a nation's GNI, as demonstrated by Hamilton (2005). Secondly, it was assumed that ozone depletion damage equates to US$15.26 per kilogram of ODS produced (Anielski et al., 1999). This price was adjusted to reflect its equivalent value in Chinese yuan at 2005 prices.

Once again, it was assumed that an element of the long-term cost of environmental damage is currently being reflected in other GPI items. The direct cost of long-term environmental damage was therefore assumed to be 50 per cent of the total cost and was subsequently estimated by adhering to the following equation:

$$LTED = 0.5 \times \left[\left(C_{CO2} \times GNI \right) + \left(C_{ODS} \times Q_{ODS} \right) \right] \tag{9.22}$$

where $LTED$ = cost of long-term environmental damage; C_{CO2} = cost of CO_2 emissions as a percentage of GNI; GNI = Gross National Income; C_{ODS} = damage cost per kilogram of ozone-depleting substances (ODS); Q_{ODS} = cumulative quantity of ODS produced.

RESULTS OF THE CHINESE GPI STUDY

Analysis of the Component Items

The results of the GPI study on China are revealed in Table 9.2. The values of some GPI items have been aggregated into specific categories to simplify the interpretation of the results. Thus, to begin with, column *A* (weighted consumption) represents the welfare contribution made by durable and non-durable consumption goods that has been weighted by the Distribution Index (DI). Column *A* indicates that the welfare contribution from China's weighted consumption increased dramatically from 312.3 billion yuan in 1970 to 3680.4 billion yuan by 2005. This constitutes a massive rise of 1078.5 per cent over the study period or an average rate of increase of 7.3 per cent per annum. Having said this, in 2005, the welfare contribution from consumption was just 52.2 per cent of the adjusted consumption value due to the enormous 91.2 per cent deterioration in the distribution of income over the study period.

Column *B* in Table 9.2 reveals that the welfare generated by publicly-provided infrastructural assets (WPPI) grew nearly 32-fold from 7.4 billion yuan in 1970 to 236.3 billion yuan in 2005. Indeed, such was the magnitude of this rise that the contribution made by WPPI towards the GPI increased over the study period from 0.5 per cent to 5.5 per cent. This reflects a significant increase in the Chinese Government's investment in public infrastructure. Given the projected growth of the Chinese economy, the demands placed on the Chinese Government to maintain if not boost infrastructural spending are likely to remain for some time to come.

The values of non-paid household labour and volunteer labour have been combined to create the non-paid labour category revealed in column *C* in Table 9.2. Caused largely by China's increasing population, the

Table 9.2 Genuine Progress Indicator (GPI) and real GDP for China, 1970–2005

	Weighted CON_{ADJ} (yuan)	WPPI (yuan)	Non-paid labour (yuan)	Social costs (yuan)	LNCS (yuan)	GPI (yuan)	Real GDP (yuan)	China's pop. (millions)	GPI p.c. (yuan)	GDP p.c. (yuan)	GPI p.c. (yuan)	GDP p.c. (yuan)
Year	*A*	*B*	*C*	*D*	*E*	*F*	*G*	*H*	*I*	*J*	*K*	*L*
1970	312	7	1 486	-88	-176	1 542	965	829 920	1 858	1 163	100.0	100.0
1971	345	7	1 510	-86	-188	1 589	1 033	852 290	1 864	1 212	100.3	104.2
1972	372	8	1 530	-85	-187	1 638	1 072	871 770	1 879	1 230	101.1	105.7
1973	424	9	1 549	-83	-198	1 702	1 157	892 110	1 908	1 297	102.7	111.5
1974	437	9	1 575	-83	-240	1 699	1 184	908 590	1 869	1 303	100.6	112.0
1975	487	12	1 609	-81	-299	1 728	1 287	924 200	1 870	1 392	100.6	119.7
1976	489	10	1 641	-82	-325	1 733	1 266	937 170	1 849	1 351	99.5	116.1
1977	536	10	1 667	-81	-352	1 781	1 362	949 740	1 875	1 434	100.9	123.3
1978	629	18	1 697	-86	-454	1 805	1 522	962 590	1 875	1 581	100.9	135.9
1979	680	22	1 732	-89	-526	1 818	1 637	975 420	1 864	1 678	100.3	144.3
1980	744	23	1 757	-91	-578	1 855	1 765	987 050	1 880	1 788	101.2	153.7
1981	802	18	1 802	-92	-636	1 895	1 857	1 000 720	1 893	1 855	101.9	159.5
1982	870	20	1 830	-88	-655	1 978	2 026	1 016 540	1 946	1 993	104.7	171.3
1983	942	24	1 871	-92	-558	2 188	2 246	1 030 080	2 124	2 181	114.3	187.5
1984	993	28	1 918	-102	-595	2 241	2 588	1 043 570	2 148	2 480	115.6	213.2
1985	1 106	35	1 965	-107	-659	2 341	2 937	1 058 510	2 212	2 775	119.0	238.5
1986	1 082	36	2 021	-125	-607	2 407	3 196	1 075 070	2 239	2 972	120.5	255.5
1987	1 203	34	2 076	-145	-719	2 450	3 566	1 093 000	2 242	3 263	120.6	280.5

Table 9.2 (continued)

	Weighted CON_{ADJ} (yuan)	WPPI (yuan)	Non-paid labour (yuan)	Social costs (yuan)	LNCS (yuan)	GPI (yuan)	Real GDP (yuan)	China's pop. (millions)	GPI p.c. (yuan)	GDP p.c. (yuan)	GPI p.c. (yuan)	GDP p.c. (yuan)
Year	*A*	*B*	*C*	*D*	*E*	*F*	*G*	*H*	*I*	*J*	*K*	*L*
1988	1 384	31	2 127	-152	- 743	2 647	3 969	1 110 260	2 384	3 575	128.3	307.3
1989	1 318	32	2 177	-170	- 805	2 552	4 132	1 127 040	2 264	3 666	121.9	315.2
1990	1 368	38	2 227	-191	- 901	2 541	4 289	1 143 330	2 222	3 751	119.6	322.5
1991	1 414	48	2 282	-187	- 915	2 641	4 684	1 158 230	2 280	4 044	122.7	347.6
1992	1 481	49	2 338	-193	- 961	2 713	5 349	1 171 710	2 316	4 565	124.6	392.4
1993	1 506	70	2 390	-201	- 999	2 766	6 098	1 185 170	2 334	5 145	125.6	442.3
1994	1 631	71	2 447	-232	- 988	2 929	6 896	1 198 500	2 444	5 754	131.5	494.7
1995	1 919	80	2 515	-231	-1 075	3 207	7 648	1 211 210	2 648	6 314	142.5	542.8
1996	2 294	93	2 574	-224	-1 161	3 576	8 413	1 223 890	2 922	6 874	157.2	590.9
1997	2 464	115	2 620	-240	-1 165	3 794	9 195	1 236 260	3 069	7 438	165.2	639.4
1998	2 568	155	2 642	-230	-1 098	4 037	9 912	1 247 610	3 235	7 945	174.1	683.0
1999	2 604	174	2 680	-268	-1 122	4 069	10 666	1 257 860	3 234	8 479	174.1	729.0
2000	2 754	191	2 721	-260	-1 353	4 053	11 562	1 267 430	3 198	9 122	172.1	784.2
2001	2 912	214	2 739	-308	-1 337	4 220	12 521	1 276 270	3 307	9 811	178.0	843.4
2002	3 047	230	2 756	-331	-1 436	4 267	13 661	1 284 530	3 322	10 635	178.8	914.3
2003	3 145	232	2 777	-381	-1 614	4 157	15 027	1 292 270	3 217	11 628	173.1	999.7
2004	3 512	234	2 802	-493	-1 776	4 280	16 545	1 299 880	3 292	12 728	177.2	1 094.2
2005	3 680	236	2 829	-557	-1 921	4 268	18 232	1 307 560	3 264	13 944	175.7	1 198.7

Note: Values in columns *A* to *G* are in billions of 2005 yuan; values in columns *I* and *J* are single 2005 yuan; values in columns *K* and *L* are index numbers starting from 1970 = 100.

value of all non-paid labour increased steadily over the study period from 1486.1 billion yuan in 1970 to 2828.9 billion yuan in 2005. However, its relative importance diminished. For example, in 1970, the welfare generated from non-paid labour was 4.8 times that of weighted consumption, but it was only 76.9 per cent of the contribution made by weighted consumption in 2005. As a percentage of China's GPI, the contribution of non-paid labour fell from 96.4 per cent to 66.3 per cent over the study period.

The social cost category represented by column *D* in Table 9.2 includes the cost of unemployment, crime, family breakdown, and the change in net foreign debt.[8] Column *D* reveals that China's social costs increased enormously from just 87.7 billion yuan in 1970 to 557.2 billion yuan in 2005. This represents a 635.3 per cent increase over the study period or an average rate of increase of 5.4 per cent per annum. The most significant social costs were the cost of crime, which increased from 73.4 to 339.2 billion yuan over the study period, and the change in net foreign debt, which rose significantly in magnitude during the 1980s and again between 2000 and 2005. The cost of unemployment was not nearly as large but, at 31 billion yuan in 2005, remains a pressing social issue that no doubt contributes to the deepening income inequality in China.

Of greater concern must be the magnitude and the extent of the increase in China's environmental costs. In Table 9.2 (column *E*), China's environmental costs appear as the cost of lost natural capital services (LNCS).[9] Column *E* reveals that China's environmental costs increased steadily between 1970 and 1981; stagnated between 1981 and 1986; grew steadily again between 1986 and 1993; increased marginally between 1993 and 1999; and grew very rapidly between 1999 and 2005. Overall, China's environmental costs increased elevenfold from 176 billion yuan in 1970 to 1920.9 billion yuan in 2005. This constitutes an average rate of increase over the study period of 7.1 per cent per annum. Interestingly, this rate of increase was almost the same as the average rise over the study period of China's per capita GDP (7.4 per cent per annum).

Contributing most to the growth in China's environmental costs was the cost of non-renewable resource depletion (particularly between 1970 and 1981), land degradation (which grew steadily over the entire study period), urban waste-water pollution (the most significant environmental cost in the early 1970s), air pollution, and long-term environmental damage (particularly since 1995). Timber depletion played virtually no part in the rapid growth of China's environmental costs.

Per Capita GPI versus Per Capita GDP

To assess the rate of genuine progress in China, Figure 9.3 presents a comparison between China's per capita GPI and per capita GDP (columns *I* and *J* in Table 9.2). The most startling aspect of Figure 9.3 is the exponential-like increase in per capita GPI yet the more modest overall rise in per capita GPI. Indeed, as columns *K* and *L* in Table 9.2 reveal, China's per capita GPI increased by 75.7 per cent over the study period (average increase of 1.6 per cent per annum), whilst its per capita GDP increased by 1098.7 per cent (average increase of 7.4 per cent per annum).

The other interesting feature of Figure 9.3 is how China's per capita GPI was overtaken by its per capita GDP having begun the study period at a much higher value. In 1970, for example, the per capita GPI was 159.7 per cent higher than the per capita GDP, but was just 23.4 per cent of per capita GDP by the end of the study period. Figure 9.3 shows that the point when China's per capita GDP surpassed its per capita GPI was 1981–82 which, as we shall see, was a pivotal moment in China's economic development.

Whilst China's per capita GPI varied considerably between 1970 and 2005, it is possible to divide the entire study period into five key development periods. The relationship between the component items and China's per capita GPI can then be examined to explain the rate of genuine progress specific to each development phase. This not only provides some insight as to which factors had the greatest impact on China's genuine progress over the 35-year study period, it can also provide future policy guidance.

To assist the assessment process, consider Figure 9.4 which presents China's per capita GPI and the per capita values of the major benefit and cost categories appearing in Table 9.2. Through careful examination of the per capita GPI curve and the values appearing in column *I* of Table 9.2, the following five development phases were identified:

1. Steady per capita GPI phase (industrialisation phase): 1970–81
2. Modest per capita GPI growth phase (industrialisation take-off phase): 1982–88
3. Steady but fluctuating per capita GPI phase (globalisation phase): 1989–93

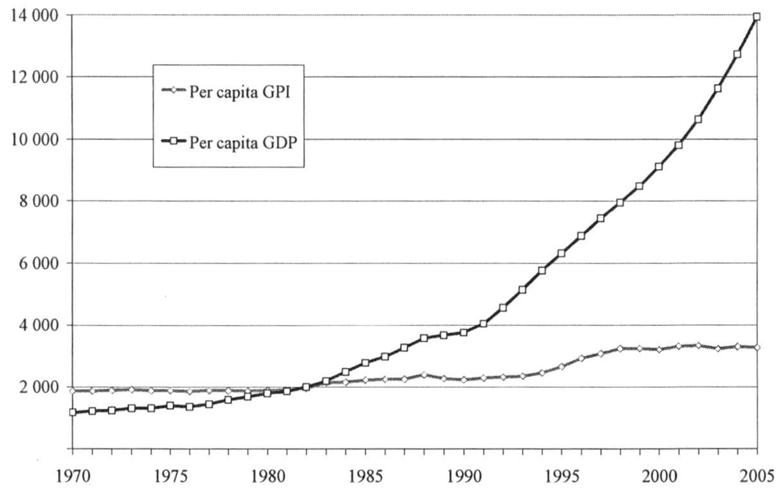

Note: Valued in Chinese yuan at 2005 prices.

Figure 9.3 *Per capita GPI versus per capita GDP: China, 1970–2005*

4. Rapid per capita GPI growth phase (globalisation take-off phase): 1994–98
5. Decelerating per capita GPI growth phase (high externality cost phase): 1999–2005.

Steady per capita GPI phase (industrialisation phase): 1970–81

The first period can be considered China's *industrialisation* phase since it was during the 1970s that China began the transformation from an agrarian economy to an economy with a substantial industrial base. During this period, China's per capita GPI remained remarkably steady with no major fluctuations evident. For example, in 1970, China's per capita GPI was 1858.1 yuan but it was only slightly higher at 1893.4 yuan in 1981. Furthermore, the per capita GPI never fell below 1849.4 yuan, nor did it rise above 1907.6 yuan.

The process of industrialisation between 1970 and 1981 is very much reflected in Figure 9.4 by the rise in per capita weighted consumption – the consequence of a much larger output of consumer goods – and the rapid increase in per capita environmental costs. In addition, it can be seen why there was no growth in China's per capita GPI. Effectively, the

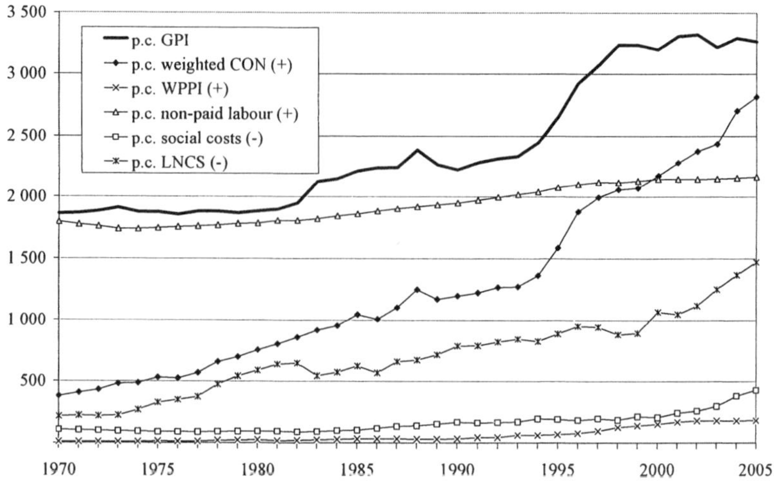

Note: Valued in Chinese yuan at 2005 prices.

Figure 9.4 Per capita GPI and its major component categories: China, 1970–2005

growth in environmental costs offset the welfare benefits generated by the additional consumption.

Although urban waste-water pollution was a significant environmental cost during this industrialisation phase, the most critical environmental cost factor was the cost of non-renewable resource depletion which increased from just 6.4 billion yuan in 1970 to 400.3 billion yuan in 1981. This reflects the massive rise in non-renewable resource depletion that took place in order to fuel the expansion in infrastructure and capital goods typical of any industrialisation process.

The per capita value of non-paid labour varied little during this development phase and thus had virtually no impact on the trend change in the per capita GPI. Having said this, the sheer magnitude of non-paid labour meant that it was instrumental behind the overall value of China's per capita GPI during the 1970s. This was very much the case throughout the entire study period although, as explained earlier, the relative contribution of non-paid labour progressively declined. Hence, what has been said here in relation to the per capita value of non-paid labour applies almost equally to the remaining development phases.

There is little point, therefore, in discussing the impact of non-paid labour during the remainder of this sub-section.

Modest per capita GPI growth phase (industrialisation take-off phase): 1982–88

The second development period is what we have described as the *industrialisation take-off* phase. By the early 1980s, China had established a strong industrial base upon which it could now enjoy the economic spoils. Thus, between 1982 and 1988, China's per capita GPI grew moderately from 1946 yuan in 1982 to 2384.3 yuan in 1988.

This short period of genuine progress was characterised by a number of key factors. Firstly, as Figure 9.4 illustrates, there was a very large rise in China's per capita weighted consumption, although this increase was dampened somewhat by a considerable deterioration in the distribution of income. Secondly, there was little if any increase in China's per capita environmental costs. Despite some growth in the cost of land degradation, urban waste-water pollution, air pollution, and long-term environmental damage, there was a significant fall in the cost of non-renewable resource depletion. Indeed, the decline in the latter virtually offset the rise in the remaining environmental costs.

But the fall in the cost of non-renewable resource depletion came at a price. How? The third major feature of this period was the rise in per capita social costs which, if anything, had fallen slightly during the initial industrialisation phase. Included in this cost category is the change in net foreign debt. Between 1982 and 1988, China's net foreign debt grew dramatically and was predominantly caused by the rapid rise in China's importation of non-renewable resources. In other words, domestically sourced mineral and energy resources were failing to keep pace with the resource demands of China's growing economy.

Overall, China experienced a moderate increase in per capita GPI during this development phase because the welfare contribution of China's per capita weighted consumption exceeded the combined increase in per capita social and environmental costs. This, however, was very shortly to come to an end as China moved into the next development phase.

Steady but fluctuating per capita GPI phase (globalisation phase): 1989–93

The third period between 1989 and 1993 is China's *globalisation* phase. Whether by design or circumstance, it was during the early 1990s that

China became fully integrated into the global economy. Since the world economy was in a recession at this time, the initial impact of globalisation was not at all beneficial.[10] After nearly a decade of annual rises, China's per capita GPI fell in both 1989 and 1990 (see Figure 9.4). It increased once more in 1991, 1992, and 1993, but not substantially. Having ended the previous development phase at 2384.3 yuan in 1988, China's per capita GPI was slightly lower at 2334 yuan in 1993.

During this brief development phase, China's per capita weighted consumption increased at its lowest rate of the three development phases so far discussed. It also suffered its biggest one-year decline in 1989. This was due to a slowing-down in consumption expenditure and the continuing growth in the income disparity between China's rich and poor. On a positive note, the welfare from publicly-provided infrastructure (WPPI) more than doubled. However, it was too small to have any major impact on China's per capita GPI.

As for China's per capita social and environmental costs, the former increased by 23.4 per cent and the latter by 25.9 per cent during this development phase. The rise in per capita social costs was again principally due to the increase in net foreign debt, although the cost of crime made a strong presence for the first time in the study period. Per capita environmental costs increased during this development phase, in part because of a rise in the cost in non-renewable resource depletion in 1989 and 1990, but more so as a consequence of steep rises in the cost of long-term environmental damage, air pollution, and urban waste-water pollution.

Rapid per capita GPI growth phase (globalisation take-off phase): 1994–98

We now come to what might be described as China's *globalisation take-off* phase. It was during this short period that the entrenched integration of China into the global economy led to a massive 54.4 per cent rise in its per capita GDP in just five years. As Figure 9.4 shows, it also corresponded to a large rise in China's per capita GPI. Indeed, over the same five–year period, China's per capita GPI increased by 38.6 per cent or at an average rate of 6.7 per cent per annum.

The considerable rate of genuine progress experienced during this development phase can be attributed, firstly, to the very steep rise in per capita weighted consumption that resulted from an increase in consumption expenditure and a slight improvement in the distribution of income. While probably still too small to have had any major impact on China's per capita GPI, it is worth pointing out that the welfare from publicly-provided infrastructure (WPPI) again more than doubled. Secondly, China's per capita social costs increased only minimally, thanks almost entirely to a decline in the rate of increase in China's net foreign debt. Having said this, the cost of crime and unemployment grew significantly. Thirdly, China's per capita environmental costs scarcely changed over the five-year period – a consequence of a massive decline in the cost of non-renewable resource depletion that largely offset the small increases in land degradation, urban waste-water pollution, air pollution, and long-term environmental damage.

Decelerating per capita GPI growth phase (high externality cost phase): 1999–2005

The final development phase of the study period is the *high externality cost* phase. Whilst the globalised nature of the Chinese economy contributed to the healthy growth in consumption, many of the social and environmental costs of GDP growth – what might be deemed 'scale-related' externalities – grew dramatically. Furthermore, the deterioration in the distribution of income resurfaced.

Taking as a starting point the per capita GPI at the end of the previous development phase, China's per capita GPI increased negligibly from 3235.4 yuan in 1998 to 3263.8 yuan in 2005. Yet, as Figure 9.4 reveals, per capita weighted consumption increased at a greater rate than almost any time prior to 1994 (i.e., prior to the globalisation take-off phase). Thus, the economic benefits of globalisation continued to grow unabated.

Unfortunately, the social costs of crime, family breakdown, and net foreign debt also grew, but at previously unseen rates. The same can also be said in relation to the environmental costs of land degradation, air pollution, and long-term environmental damage. Whilst the rise in the cost of non-renewable resource depletion did not match the huge increase experienced during the industrialisation phase (1970–81), it was still very substantial.

Overall, having swiftly undergone the transformation from agrarian economy to a globalised industrial giant, it would appear that the sheer weight of expansion in the scale of the Chinese economy is now placing enormous pressure on China's social and natural (environmental) capital. It is now incumbent upon Chinese policy-makers to take some bold steps to alleviate this scale-related stress. Should they fail to do so, there is every possibility that the genuine progress forged in China since 1970 may eventually be put at risk.

CONCLUSION

China has experienced the most extraordinary rate of economic transformation of any country in the world. Having begun in 1970 with an economy largely dominated by agricultural production, the Chinese economy has undergone what we believe to be five development phases in the space of just 35 years. In addition, per capita GDP has increased nearly twelvefold over the same period.

Whilst the transformation of the Chinese economy has brought with it substantial economic benefits, the results of this study indicate that the rate of genuine progress, as conventionally indicated by the increase in per capita real GDP, has been greatly overstated. Furthermore, it would appear that the rapid growth in China's real GDP is resulting in a massive increase in scale-related externalities which is being reflected by the recent huge rises in social and environmental costs.

There is little doubt, therefore, that China must undergo a new development phase with a heavy emphasis on improving the quality of the growth in its real GDP. Not unlike India, China's future growth desperately needs to be characterised by a more equitable distribution of income; value-adding in production (better rather than necessarily more goods); a substantial increase in resource use efficiency; the development and application of renewable energy and resource-saving technology; and, wherever possible, minimal depletion of natural capital stocks, including critical ecosystems.

China has already taken steps to deal with population stabilisation and is therefore in a more fortunate position than India in this regard. Exactly what measures Chinese policy-makers should introduce to facilitate an improved form of growth will not be discussed here. Suffice to say, they would be very similar to those prescribed in Chapter 8 for India, although they would need to be specifically designed to accommodate a vastly different institutional setting. Similar to India, China will inevitably need to consider when best to make the transition to a steady-state economy, although this is probably some decades away. Again, China will be better positioned to make such a transition given that its population is expected to peak around the year 2030 whereas India's population is still expected to be rising in 2050 (WRI, Earthtrends).

For now, however, Chinese policy-makers need to focus all their energies on improving the quality of China's growth over the coming decades. As for the remainder of the industrialised world, it needs to put aside any fears it may have of a rich and powerful China and assist it, in every way possible, in achieving a sustainable, just, and efficient economy.

NOTES

1. As at 2007, China was ranked 109th in the world in per capita GDP terms (Central Intelligence Agency, 2007).
2. The values were calculated by the author.
3. The ratio ranged between 8 and 12 per cent over the study period.
4. As an indication, the adjustment resulted in the number of hours per day being 2.72 in 1970 and 2.28 in 2005.
5. The 1992 value was adjusted to 2005 prices.
6. In years where timber stocks rose, the full value was added.
7. See http://faostat.fao.org/site/381/default.aspx.
8. The change in foreign debt was included as a social cost because China's foreign debt increased in each year from 1970 and 2005. The value of this item was therefore negative over the study period.
9. Column *E* thus equates to the sum of the cost of non-renewable resource depletion, land degradation, excessive irrigation water use, timber depletion, urban waste-water pollution, air pollution, and long-term environmental damage.
10. This in no way suggests that a recession, from the point of view of real GDP growth, necessarily leads a low rate of increase in a nation's per capita GPI. Nor does it suggest that real GDP growth is required to boost the per capita GPI.

REFERENCES

Anielski, M. and Rowe, J. (1999), *The Genuine Progress Indicator – 1998 Update*, San Francisco, CA: Redefining Progress.

Bolund, P. and Hunhammar, S. (1999), 'Analysis of ecosystem services in urban areas', *Ecological Economics*, **29**, 293–301.

Central Intelligence Agency (2007), *The World Fact Book 2007*, https://www.cia.gov/cia/publications/factbook/_rankorder/_2004rank.html.

El Serafy, S. (1989), 'The proper calculation of income from depletable natural resources', in Y. Ahmad, S. El Serafy and E. Lutz (eds),

Environmental Accounting for Sustainable Development, World Bank, Washington, DC: World Bank, pp. 10–18.

Hamilton, K. (2005), 'Testing genuine saving', World Bank Policy Research Working Paper 3577, April.

International Panel on Climate Change (IPCC) (2007), *IPCC Fourth Assessment Report: Climate Change 2007*, Geneva: World Meteorological Organisation.

Jiang, A.L. (2003), 'The basic judgment of China's industrial development state', *Journal of Shantou University (Social Science Edition)*, **19(2)**, 1–11.

Li, H.T., Shang, R.B. and Zhai, Q. (2003), 'The calculation and application of the GINI coefficient based on the Lorenz Curve', *Journal of Gansu Science*, **15(1)**, 89–94.

Liu, L. and Yang, T. (1999), 'Case study on the economic cost evaluation of farmland loss in Hebei Province', *Agriculture Technological Economics*, **5**, 51–53.

Lu, J.R. and Peng, C. (1999), 'The trend state and life-time of urban residents in China', *China Soft Science*, **6**, 90–93.

Ministry of Forestry (various), *National Forest Resource Statistics*, Beijing: Ministry of Forestry.

Ministry of Land and Resources (MLR) (various), *National Resource Communiqué*, Beijing: MLR.

Ministry of Water Resources (MWR) (2003), *The Report on China's Water Resources*, Beijing: MWR.

Ministry of Water Resources (MWR) (2004), *The Statistical Report of China's Water Resources*, Beijing: MWR.

Ministry of Water Resources (MWR) (various), *Water Resource Statistic Communiqué*, Beijing: MWR.

National Bureau of Statistics of China (NBSC) (various), *China Statistical Yearbook*, Beijing: China Statistical Publishing House.

Stern, N. (2006), *Stern Review on the Economics of Climate Change*, London: HM Treasury.

Wen, Z.G. (2005), 'Capital extension methodology: the simulation study into policy alternatives towards sustainable development', dissertation submitted to Tsinghua University in partial fulfillment of the requirement for the degree of Doctor of Engineering, Library of Tsinghua University.

Wen, Z. and Chen, J. (forthcoming), 'A cost-benefit analysis for the economic growth in China', *Ecological Economics*.

World Bank (2006), *Little Green Data Book*, Washington, DC: World Bank.

World Bank (2007), *Cost of Pollution in China: Economic Estimates of Physical Damages*, Washington, DC: World Bank.

World Resources Institute (2005), *World Resources 2005: The Wealth of the Poor – Managing Ecosystems to Fight Poverty*, in collaboration with

United Nations Development Programme, Washington, DC: United Nations Environment Programme and World Bank.

World Resources Institute (WRI) (various), *Earthtrends*, http://www.earthtrends.wri.org.

World Volunteer Web, 'China strengthens national volunteer campaign', www.worldvolunteerweb.org, accessed 7 August 2007.

Xu, A.Q. and Ye, W.Z. (2001), 'The impact of family breakdown on children and the constraint factors: a survey in Shanghai', *China Social Science*, **6**, 137–149.

10. Genuine progress in Thailand: a systems-analysis approach

Matthew Clarke and Judith Shaw

INTRODUCTION

Thailand, like all countries, is unique with its own distinct history shaped by its specific geography, political experiences, and social interactions. Thailand was never colonised, is a Buddhist country, has low levels of urbanisation, and possesses an abundance of land. Yet, despite this distinctiveness, Thailand can be considered representative of many developing countries in that it has a dualistic economy, significant rural–urban migration, a large income gap between the rich and poor, and political instability. Whilst its history is unique, Thailand is a member of a large group of low-middle income countries, all of which are seeking to increase their national income in order to reduce the incidence of poverty and increase living standards.

Thailand's recent economic experience is widely judged as successful, having regularly outperformed many developing (and developed) countries in terms of its annual growth in real Gross Domestic Product (GDP) (World Bank, 2006). Indeed, some observers have argued that Thailand is a potential role model for much of the Third World (Watkins, 1998; World Bank, 1999; Vines and Warr, 2000). However, before such a conclusion can be made, attention must be paid to the costs as well as the benefits associated with Thailand's growing economy. This chapter will help clarify the extent to which genuine progress has been achieved in Thailand by presenting a Genuine Progress Indicator (GPI) for Thailand for the period 1975–2004.

To achieve its aims, this chapter is structured as follows. Firstly, the general features of the Thai economy are outlined along with some of Thailand's recent economic developments. Secondly, the methods used to calculate the Thai GPI are described. Also explained in this section is the rationale for the inclusion of some GPI items unique to Thailand (e.g., cost of corruption and commercial sex work). The GPI results are presented in the following section, while the final section includes a brief discussion on the relevance of the GPI results for Thailand.

THE THAI ECONOMY

Growth of Thailand's real GDP has been strong for more than three decades. During the 1970s, the growth in per capita GDP averaged 7 per cent per annum. Given the 1973 and 1979 oil price shocks, the consequent slowdown of the world economy, the withdrawal of the US military from South-East Asia, and the considerable domestic political instability in Thailand, 'the growth of the Thai economy during the period 1971 to 1978 was remarkable' (Dixon, 1999, p. 108).

It was during the 1970s that the Thai economy, like the economy of China (see Chapter 9), was transformed from an agricultural to a primarily industrial economy, at least in terms of the composition of Thailand's real GDP. Yet, interestingly, this transformation occurred despite, rather than because of, explicit government policies and interventions. High levels of protection for domestic industries in the form or tariffs and fuel subsidies, together with protracted and violent political upheaval, did little to boost investor confidence. Meanwhile, Thailand's current account deficit was uncomfortably large and mounting, inflation was high, and rising government expenditure was resulting in a growing fiscal deficit. Furthermore, overseas debt (whilst comparatively low) also increased substantially during the 1970s (Dixon, 1996).

Despite the presence of these negative economic factors, the Thai economy was literally in the right place at the right time. As the 1970s unfolded, Japan and other newly industrialising countries (NICs) began to shed their low-level manufacturing operations in response to rising domestic labour costs. Thailand was well positioned to assume these industries given its relatively low labour costs, its well-educated workforce, and the fact that the labour movement, though once strong, was under attack from the government.

In the first half of the 1980s, Thailand's annual rate of growth in real GDP slowed to just over 3 per cent. However, this growth was quite strong when compared to most of the countries in the Asia-Pacific region that were experiencing a recession at this time. Then, in the late 1980s,

Thailand experienced what many have termed a 'golden age' with real GDP resurging to a growth rate of 11 per cent in 1987. Between 1982 and 1993, real GDP effectively doubled, making the Thai economy one of the fastest growing in the world during this period (Jansen, 1997; Vines and Warr, 2000).

As the Asia-Pacific region and world economy emerged from the early 1980s recession, Thailand continued to attract the industries that, because of relatively higher labour costs, the NICs were still shedding (Dixon, 1999). Continuing strong growth in the manufacturing sector was underpinned by an expansion in primary exports, a rapidly growing tourism sector, and labour migration (with the subsequent repatriation of income). But, again, Thailand's economic expansion appeared not to be the result of carefully developed economic policy. As Dixon (1999, p. 128) explains:

> [T]here is in all of this a clustering of favourable global, regional, and national circumstances that Thailand was able to take advantage of, rather than any particular policies or strategies that could be isolated and applied elsewhere.

By the mid-1990s, the so-called golden age had ended. In 1996, the Thai economy was characterised by the zero growth in export earnings, an increasing balance-of-payments deficit, rising private sector debt levels, and, most critically, an expansion in short-term speculative capital movements that was accompanied by an overheating of the property and financial markets. The 1997 financial crisis that struck down many Asian economies brought Thailand's decade of rapid growth in real GDP to an abrupt halt (Dixon, 1999). Fortunately, the Thai economy quickly recovered from the financial crisis and again recorded high GDP growth rates in the range of 5 per cent per annum between 1999 and 2004.

In view of the recent free trade agreements that Thailand has signed or negotiated with its large trading partners, it is likely that Thailand's real GDP will continue to grow for some time to come. Even the 2006 political coup appears not to have altered the view that Thailand is a lucrative country for foreign investors to operate within.

Over the past three decades, economic growth (as conventionally indicated by the growth in real GDP) has been the explicitly stated priority of the Thai government (NESDB, 1996 and 2000). Regrettably, this narrow policy emphasis has often been at the exclusion of other economic, social, and environmental goals. Indeed, as Phongpaichit and Baker (1995) have highlighted, it would seem that the government effectively abandoned a number of policies in the early 1990s in order to focus its entire attention on planning the direction and outcome of economic growth. As such, there have been concerns that the high priority assigned to GDP growth has been at the expense of wider welfare concerns and principles of social justice (Parnwell, 1996; Schmidt, 1996).

For example, whilst the higher tax revenue generated by the growth in Thailand's real GDP has permitted large increases in government expenditure, many observers believe that the additional government spending has been poorly directed. Their belief is predicated on statistical evidence indicating that government programmes have clearly failed to alleviate the high rates of poverty experienced by many of Thailand's poorest citizens (Kakwani and Krongkaew, 1997).

At the same time, a number of environmental concerns have also been inadequately dealt with. Between 1985 and 2002, per capita CO_2 emissions in Thailand increased dramatically from 0.88 tonnes to 3.25 tonnes per person while, more alarmingly, Thailand's ecological footprint grew beyond its biocapacity (WRI, 2005).[1] As at 2003, Thailand's ecological footprint stood at 1.4 hectares per person compared to its biocapacity of 1 hectare per person (Global Footprint Network, 2006). Having previously enjoyed an ecological surplus, Thailand now suffers from an ecological deficit of –0.4 hectares per person. The disconcerting aspect of this statistic is that an ecological deficit is widely regarded as an indication that a nation's natural capital is being eroded. In Thailand's case, this is no better exemplified than the evidence revealing widespread land degradation and the continuing decline in Thailand's forest stocks.

Given, therefore, the reduced policy emphasis in Thailand on broader social and environmental concerns, the question that remains is this: Whilst the Thai economy has been successful in terms of achieving high GDP growth rates over an extended period, has this brought about correspondingly high rates of genuine progress? That is, just how much has the sustainable welfare of the average Thai citizen increased over recent decades?

MEASURING THAILAND'S GENUINE PROGRESS

From a systems-analysis perspective, genuine progress can be viewed as a function of a number of domains or sub-systems interacting within a larger ecological system (see Clarke, 2006). These domains can be described as economic, social, political, spiritual, and environmental systems that, when taken together, are fundamental to the sustainable welfare of a nation.[2] Determining the level of genuine progress in Thailand thus requires some estimate of the beneficial and negative impacts that an increase in economic output has upon these various systems. Numerous monetary estimates of the benefits and costs associated with a greater volume of economic activity are therefore necessary. Table 10.1, which essentially follows the GPI methodology outlined in Chapter 3, lists these items and provides a brief description of the valuation methods used in their calculation. The GPI items are also grouped within the various interacting domains to facilitate discussion on Thailand's genuine progress later in the chapter.

Economic Domain

Consumption expenditure (CON)

Private sector consumption expenditure (Item *a*) was drawn directly from the National Statistics Office (NSO) *Statistical Yearbook*. In this particular study on Thailand, welfare adjustments were made to expenditure on tobacco products and alcoholic beverages, but no adjustment was made in relation to defensive and rehabilitative expenditures. The latter was adopted given data constraints and Thailand's low consumption base.

Expenditure on consumer durables (ECD) and the service from the existing stock of consumer durables (SCD)

Under the GPI methodology, current expenditure on consumer durables (ECD) (Item *b*) is not considered to be welfare-increasing in the present and is therefore subtracted. Expenditure on consumer durables was identified by examining the various consumption expenditure categories contained within the National Statistics Office (NSO) *Statistical Yearbook*.

The service derived from consumer durables (SCD) (Item *c*), which is added when calculating the GPI, is generally regarded as the depreciation

Table 10.1 Items and valuation methods used to calculate the GPI for Thailand, 1975–2004

Item	Welfare contribution	Method of valuation
Economic domain (*A*)		
Item *a*: Consumption expenditure (*CON*)	+	*CON* = private sector consumption expenditure *less* all spending on cigarettes and tobacco *less* 0.5 × spending on alcoholic beverages
Item *b*: Expenditure on consumer durables (*ECD*)	–	*ECD* equals the sum of all household expenditure on consumer durables
Item *c*: Service from consumer durables (*SCD*)	+	SCD equals the depreciation value of the existing stock of consumer durables (assumed that stock endures for 10 years) • *SCD* = 0.1 × value of consumer durables
Item *d*: Adjusted consumption	+	Timing adjustment to consumption benefits • *Adjusted CON = CON – ECD + SCD*
Item *e*: Distribution Index (*DI*)	+/–	*DI* based on the change in income distribution over the study period as measured by the Gini coefficient (1975 = 100)
Item *f*: Adjusted consumption (weighted)	+	Adjusted CON weighted by the Distribution Index adjustment to consumption benefits • *Adjusted CON ÷ DI × 100*
Item *g*: Welfare generated by publicly-provided service capital (*WPPSC*)	+	Welfare from infrastructural capital assumed to equal the depreciation value of the existing stock of non-dwelling capital assets provided by the private sector, publicly-owned corporations, and general government

Table 10.1 (continued)

Item	Welfare contribution	Method of valuation
Social domain (*B*)		
Item *h*: Welfare from public expenditure on health	+	Equal to 75% of public expenditure on health (i.e., 25% deemed defensive)
Item *i*: Welfare from public expenditure on education	+	Equal to 75% of public expenditure on education (i.e., 25% deemed defensive)
Item *j*: Cost of commuting	–	Equal to $US219 per new car registration each year in Bongkok (Tanaboorboon, 1990) converted to Thai baht
Item *k*: Cost of urbanisation	–	Equal to 18% of the income of Bangkok residents required to overcome air pollution from growing urban congestion and to access safe drinking water (World Bank, 1999)
Item *l*: Cost of noise pollution	–	Equal to 1% of real GDP (World Health Organisation, cited in Daly and Cobb, 1989)
Political domain (*C*)		
Item *m*: Welfare from public expenditure on roads and highways	+	Equal to 50% of public expenditure on roads and highways
Item *n*: Cost of corruption	–	Cost of corruption = $GDP_{1975\text{-}81}(0.0088) + GDP_{1982\text{-}88}(0.0074) + GDP_{1989\text{-}99}(0.007) + GDP_{2000\text{-}04}(0.007)$
Item *o*: Change in net foreign debt	+/–	Annual cost (benefit) equal to the change in net foreign liabilities

Table 10.1 (continued)

Item	Welfare contribution	Method of valuation
Spiritual domain (*D*)		
Item *p*: Value of non-paid household labour	+	Benefit of non-paid household labour = $CW_{1975*(0.75)} + CW_{1976*(0.74)} + \ldots CW_{2004*(0.46)}$ where CW denotes compensation for non-paid household wages
Item *q*: Cost of commercial sex work	–	Equal to 3% of real GDP (Phongpaichit et al., 1998)
Environmental domain (*E*)		
Item *r*: Cost of timber depletion	–	Calculated to reflect the opportunity cost of lower timber stocks brought about by harvesting rates exceeding the rate of timber regeneration and plantation establishment • Using El Serafy (1989) user cost method, the cost of timber depletion = value of timber depletion × 0.44
Item *s*: Cost of land degradation	–	Equal to 1% of total agricultural production each year. This annual loss is added cumulatively to reflect the strong sustainability stance of having to keep natural capital intact
Item *t*: Cost of air pollution	–	Equivalent to the cost of pollution abatement from CO_2, CO, NO_X, SO_X, and SPM sources
Item *u*: Cost of urban waste-water pollution	–	Equal to the cost of rehabilitating polluted urban waste-water cleaning water. Assumed to equal 7.5 baht per kilogram of biochemical oxygen demand (BOD) (Department of Industrial Works, 1986). Multiplied by two to account for non-point sources of waste-water pollution
Item *v*: Cost of long-term environmental damage	–	Estimated damage assumed to equal 21.59 baht per tonne of carbon emissions. Cost was accumulated but weighted downwards by 1% recovery factor

value of the existing stock of consumer durables. For this study, the depreciation value was assumed to be 10 per cent of the total value of all consumer durables (i.e., the average serviceable lifetime of a consumer durable was assumed to be ten years).

Adjusted consumption

The adjusted consumption item (Item *d*) was calculated by following equation (3.6) from Chapter 3.

Distribution index (DI)

The distribution of income has fluctuated considerably in Thailand over the past three decades (Krongkaew, 1993). Rather than make an assumption as to the ideal level of income equality, we simply took the income gap between rich and poor in 1975, the first year of the study period, as a given. We then assumed that any improvement/deterioration in the distribution of income since 1975 had a positive/negative impact on the welfare contribution of the adjusted consumption item. To determine the welfare impact of the changing distribution of income, we prepared a distribution index (DI) (Item *e*) based on the change over the study period in the Gini coefficient for Thailand. The DI was then applied to weight the adjusted consumption item (Item *f*).

Initially, the DI had virtually no welfare impact on the Thai GPI. However, an increase in income inequality led to a 5–10 per cent downward weighting of Thailand's consumption-related expenditure during the 1990s. An improvement in the distribution of income after 1996 led eventually to a slight upward weighting of consumption-related expenditure by the end of the study period.

Welfare generated by publicly-provided service capital (WPPSC)

Welfare not only flows from government consumption expenditure, but is also generated from the stock of government-funded capital goods such as roads, bridges, schools, hospitals, and museums. These infrastructural assets increase welfare not unlike the way in which services flow from the stock of consumer durables. However, like consumer durables, it is erroneous to count current expenditure on publicly-provided service capital as if it were enhancing current welfare.

Having said this, it is necessary to estimate the welfare flowing from past expenditure on publicly-provided service capital (Item *g*). To do this, we assumed that 75 per cent of all government investment spending is devoted to service capital rather than producer goods (plant, machinery, and equipment). The welfare from publicly-provided service capital therefore equals the public sector consumption of fixed capital (i.e., the depreciation of existing capital goods) multiplied by the 75 per cent share of government investment expenditure allocated to the accumulation of service capital. The data required to calculate this item was extracted from the National Statistics Office (NSO) *Statistical Yearbook.*

Social Domain

Benefit of public expenditure on health

It is generally acknowledged that when public expenditure on health begins from a low base, any additional expenditure can dramatically increase welfare (Item *h*). One clear indication of the benefit that increased public expenditure can have on health outcomes is in terms of the increase in life expectancy. Within Thailand, life expectancy increased from around 60 to 70 years of age between 1975 and 1999. Since the increase in medical expenditure in Thailand: (a) has begun from such a low base; and (b) has generated significant health benefits, it was assumed that 75 per cent of public health expenditure should be added when calculating the Thai GPI (i.e., 25 per cent of expenditure was deemed as defensive).

Benefit of public expenditure on education

Within developing countries, the need to invest in human capital is critical since a lack of education and skills often impedes economic development (OECD, 2001). Despite the skewing of government funding towards tertiary education, often at the expense of the more important secondary education, the welfare impact of additional education expenditure in developing countries is generally greater than that of developed countries (i.e., less can be considered defensive).

In Daly and Cobb's (1989) initial study on the USA, it was assumed that only 50 per cent of public expenditure on education should be added as a welfare benefit. This has been increased to 75 per cent in the case of the Thai GPI (Item *i*).

Cost of commuting

Rising commuting costs are a negative side-effect of the growth in real GDP. As the economy grows and cities become increasingly overpopulated, roads become clogged with increased numbers of private and public vehicles attempting to move large numbers of people. The end result is increased levels of wasted time spent commuting to and from work.

A study by Tanaborrboon (1990) estimated the cost of commuting in Bangkok to be approximately US$400 million per year in 1988. This constitutes a commuting cost of US$219 per registered car in Bangkok. This figure was then converted to Thai baht and multiplied by the number of registered cars each year to calculate the cost of commuting over the study period (Item *j*).[3] Using this approach, the cost of commuting increased from 0.49 per cent of GDP in 1975 to 0.59 per cent in 2004. This is consistent with similar estimates by Dixon (1991), Martin and Schuumann (1997), and Khomnamol (1999).

Cost of urbanisation

It has been recognised for some time that one of the major costs of a growing economy is the cost of urbanisation (Mishan, 1977; Dhiratayakinant, 1993). Urbanisation can be defined as 'an increase in the proportion of a country's population in communities above a specific size, the term community implying a concentration of people within a small area' (Kuznets, 1968, p. 97). For the purposes of this GPI study, the cost of urbanisation (Item *k*) was based on a World Bank (1999) study which estimated that, as a consequence of increased urbanisation, the average Bangkok citizen is required to spend 8 per cent of their income on overcoming air pollution, and 10 per cent of their income to access safe drinking water.

Cost of noise pollution

The cost of noise pollution was included in the initial GPI study conducted by Daly and Cobb (1989) on the USA but has generally been disregarded in most GPI studies. In Bangkok, noise pollution is a considerable problem given the high population density and the many thousands of small motor-scooters and motor-cycles used in confined spaces and on narrow roads. For this reason, it was decided that the cost of noise pollution was particularly relevant to Thailand (Item *l*).

Unlike air pollution, noise pollution is not suitably reflected by associated health costs. Therefore, estimates of the cost of noise pollution must focus on the loss of amenity rather than its health impact. The method used in this study to estimate the cost of noise pollution was based on a report released by the World Health Organization on the USA some three decades ago (see Daly and Cobb, 1989). Whilst this study is obviously dated, it is assumed that it remains a relevant estimate of noise pollution for Bangkok today. Since the increased volume of traffic and industrial activities has accompanied the growth in economic activity, it was assumed that noise pollution has increased proportionately with the rise in Thailand's real GDP (Dhiratayakinant, 1993; Hamilton, 1998). Hence, the cost of noise pollution was estimated to be 1 per cent of real GDP over the study period.

Political Domain

Benefit of public expenditure on roads and highways

Given the poor state of most roads in Thailand, and the important transport role that roads and highways play in a nation's development, it was assumed that one-half of all public expenditure on new roads (including maintenance costs) contributes as a welfare benefit (Diefenbacher, 1994). It was therefore added in the calculation of the GPI for Thailand (Item *m*).

Cost of corruption

Corruption exists at most levels of public office in nearly all countries (Elliott, 1997). However, corruption is usually more prevalent in the Third World where modern political systems have been introduced to subsume traditional systems based on paternalism and patronism. Since these political systems are often hastily and poorly conceived rather than naturally evolved, they are more vulnerable to corruption. In addition, as economies rapidly grow, the financial rewards from corruption increase. So too does the competition between officials to obtain such rewards. As Phongpaichit and Piriyarangsan (1994, p. 5) have observed: 'Competition to secure the corruption revenue that accrues from the command of high office is a key theme in Thai politics.'

To calculate the welfare cost of corruption-related activities (Item *n*), corruption was divided into two categories: (a) corruption undertaken by bureaucrats (including the military and police); and (b) corruption undertaken by politicians. In both cases, an estimate was made of the cost of corruption as a percentage of GDP. The two estimates were then added to determine an approximate total cost of corruption as a percentage of GDP.

To calculate the cost of the first corruption category, Phongpaichit and Piriyarangsan (1994) reviewed a number of publicly accessible corruption cases and focused on the two main mechanisms that exist in Thailand to investigate alleged corruption activities – namely, the Office of the Auditor General (OAG) and the Counter Corruption Commission (CCC). Based on known and prosecuted cases of corruption, it was assumed that 20 per cent of all ministry budgets allocated for the purchase of materials or to finance government-contracted construction work are misappropriated through corruption. This can be considered a conservative figure since it has been suggested that it could be as high as 50 per cent (Morell, 1975; quoted in Phongpaichit and Piriyarangsan, 1994, p. 3).

Using the 20 per cent assumption, it was possible to estimate the approximate cost of bureaucratic-related corruption during three government administrations during the study period. Converted to a percentage of GDP, the average annual corruption costs were 0.48 per cent of GDP per annum during the Sanya–Kriangsak administration (1974–81), 0.34 per cent of GDP per annum during the Prem administration (1982–88), and 0.3 per cent of GDP per annum during the Chatchai administration (1989–99). Since the three administrations do not encompass the entire study period, it was assumed that the cost of bureaucratic-related corruption between 2000 and 2004 (i.e., since the demise of the Chatchai administration in 1999) was 0.3 per cent of GDP per annum.

As for the second category of corruption that is related directly to politicians, the estimated cost was based on assets seized following departure from office. For the period 2000–04 and the three administrative periods listed above, this form of corruption was assumed to be 0.4 per cent of GDP. Not unlike the first corruption category, this is likely to be a conservative estimate since it does not take into account of the embezzled wealth never seized by authorities. In all, the total corruption cost as a percentage of real GDP was assumed to be:

- 0.88 per cent of GDP per annum during the Sanya–Kriangsak administration (1974–81);

- 0.74 per cent of GDP per annum during the Prem administration (1982–88);
- 0.70 per cent of GDP per annum during the Chatchai administration (1989–99);
- 0.70 per cent of GDP per annum between 2000 and 2004.

Change in net foreign debt

Foreign debt has long been recognised as a major impediment to the sustainable development of countries (George, 1999; Watkins, 1998). This is because a nation's long-term capacity to sustain the welfare generated by its economic activity depends largely upon the extent to which the natural and human-made capital within its borders is domestically or foreign owned.

In line with the standard GPI accounting practice, any increase in net foreign debt was subtracted as a cost, while any decline in net foreign debt was treated as a benefit. The data required to calculate this item (Item *o*) was drawn straight from the data found in *National Income of Thailand* (NSO, various). Based on a five-year rolling average, Thailand's net foreign debt increased every year between 1975 and 1999 but fell between 2000 and 2004.

Spiritual Domain

Non-paid household labour

In a study on the value of household labour, Chiswick (1983) found that when non-paid household labour (including household production) was taken into consideration for the year 1975, total household income was effectively 70–80 per cent higher than household income earned from money wages alone. Given that the modernisation of the Thai economy since 1975 has increased money wages and thus reduced the incentive for Thais to undertake substantial home production, it is fairly safe to assume that the additional household income generated by household labour has fallen by 1 per cent per year over the study period. It was therefore estimated that the value of non-paid household labour (Item *p*) in 1975 was equal to 75 per cent of equivalent wage compensation which declined to 46 per cent of equivalent wage compensation by 2004.

Cost of commercial sex work

Commercial sex work is now considered a part of the Thai culture (Packard-Winkler, 2000; Lyttleton, 2000). Within Thailand, sex tourism has virtually become part of the official government tourism industry (Phongpaichit and Chiasakul, 1993). Unfortunately, most commercial sex workers are forced to endure slave-like conditions, while exploitation is increasingly being extended to include children and ethnic minorities (Paul, 1995; Phongpaichit et al., 1998; Clarke, 2001). Also, the negative consequences of commercial sex work extend well beyond the costs borne by clients and workers. In addition to the societal consequences of infidelity, significant health-related costs have emerged through the spread of sexually transmitted diseases, such as HIV/AIDS.

Phongpaichit et al. (1998) have estimated that the value of commercial sex work in Thailand was approximately 3 per cent of GDP between 1993 and 1995. Treated as a spiritual cost rather than a benefit, 3 per cent of GDP was subtracted each year to take account of the negative impact of commercial sex work in Thailand (Item *q*).

Environmental Domain (lost natural capital services: LNCS)

Cost of timber depletion

Within many developing countries, such as Thailand, the majority of the population are heavily reliant upon agriculture and subsistence farming for their livelihood (Dixon, 1996). With the rise in economic activity over time, a nation's demand for land increases which, in turn, intensifies the pressure exerted on wetlands and forests. In the case of Thailand's forests, more continue to disappear each year (Tingsabadh, 1989).

Based on a study undertaken by Panayotou and Parasuk (1990), the value per hectare of forest lost was estimated at 886 baht.[4] Using the El Serafy (1989) user cost approach with an assumed discount (regeneration) rate of 2 per cent per annum and exhaustion time of 40 years under current harvesting rates, the total value of lost forest per year was multiplied by 0.44 to obtain the annual depletion cost of Thailand's forest resources (Item *r*).

Cost of land degradation

Land degradation poses a serious threat to the future welfare of Thailand. A healthy agrarian sector is necessary to underpin Thailand's rapidly expanding manufacturing and services sectors. Based on previous studies (see Lawn and Clarke, 2006), it was assumed that the cost of unsustainable farming practices equates to 1 per cent of total agricultural production each year. To compensate future generations for the cost of land degradation (Item *s*), and in view of our adoption of the strong sustainability need to keep natural capital intact (see Chapter 4), the annual cost was added cumulatively.[5]

Cost of air pollution

Air pollution reflects a loss of the ecosystem's sink function that impacts negatively on social welfare (NESDB, 1996 and 2000). Five major pollutants are regularly measured in Bangkok and assessed against World Health Organization (WHO) standards (Tiwari, 1997). These include carbon dioxide (CO_2), carbon monoxide (CO), nitrogen oxide (NO_X), sulphur oxide (SO_X) and suspended particulate matter (SPM). Each pollutant is a by-product of production processes and other human activities arising from the increase in consumption levels.

One means of estimating the cost of air pollution is to determine how much it would cost to reduce or abate pollutant levels to minimum WHO standards. This has previously been undertaken by Agotini and Col (1992; cited in Guenno and Tiezzi, 1998). Converted to Thai baht (1988 prices), the respective abatement costs for each of the five pollutants are:

- 0.03335 baht per kilogram of carbon dioxide and carbon monoxide;
- 2.84 baht per kilogram of nitrogen oxide;
- 7.4 baht per kilogram of sulphur oxide;
- 4.15 baht per kilogram of suspended particulate matter.

To determine the emissions levels for each of the five pollutants, data from the Department of Energy Development and Promotion (DEDP) (1990) on the transportation, electricity, industry, household, and commercial sectors – the main polluting sectors in Thailand – was closely analysed. The emission levels of each pollutant were subsequently multiplied by the per kilogram abatement cost to obtain the total cost of air pollution (Item *t*).

Cost of urban waste-water pollution

The growth in economic activity increases the pressure on water resources in terms of both water use and the generation of water-related pollution. A study conducted in the mid-1980s found that 514 381 tonnes of biochemical oxygen demand (BOD) was added to Thailand's rivers and canals in 1986 (Phansawas, 1987). It was also revealed in this study that the food, drink, paper, chemical, and textile industries in Thailand contributed to 99.6 per cent of all waste-water pollution. By calculating the growth of each of these industries as a percentage of real GDP, it was possible to extrapolate the 1986 load of BOD both forward and backward to estimate the total amount of waste-water pollution generated each year over the study period (TESCO, 1993).

The cost of waste-water pollution (Item *u*) was then made firstly by multiplying the BOD load for each year by the estimated per kilogram cost of restoring the water to an acceptable discharge condition. A value of 7.5 baht per kilogram of BOD (1988 prices) was used based on a report issued by the Department of Industrial Works (1986). Secondly, the cost was doubled to account for non-point sources of pollution (i.e., sources not captured by the 1986 waste-water pollution survey).

Cost of long-term environmental damage

As is the case with most GPI studies, the cost of long-term environmental damage (Item *v*) was included to account in some way for the loss of the natural environment's life-support function. To do this, we estimated the long-term environmental impact of increasing greenhouse gas emissions and the projected change in global climate patterns.

There are three factors that contribute most to the annual rise in greenhouse gas emissions in Thailand – deforestation, wet-rice farming, and fossil fuel consumption (Chongpeerapien et al., 1990). In the case of deforestation, it has been estimated that 246 tonnes of carbon dioxide are released per hectare of forest destroyed. As for wet-rice farming, 9.216 kilograms of methane are released per year for every 400 square metres of rice paddy under cultivation. This latter estimate of methane was converted to carbon equivalents as per the method used by Israngakurn (2001). The annual quantity of carbon dioxide released from fossil fuel consumption was based directly on the quantity of fossil fuel consumed each year in Thailand.

After summing the total carbon emissions from each main source, the annual emissions levels were multiplied by an estimated cost of 21.59 baht per tonne of carbon emissions. This cost is based on a study conducted by Nordhaus (1991) on the USA in 1981. The American cost was converted to Thai baht by making adjustments for inflation, the relative difference in real GDP levels, and the shadow exchange rate between the two countries in 1981.

Not unlike the cost of land degradation, the cost of long-term environmental damage was annually accumulated to conform to the strong sustainability stance adopted for this study. However, in the case of this item, the cumulative cost was weighted downwards by a recovery factor of 1 per cent per annum.

RESULTS OF THE THAI GPI, 1975–2004

Comparing Thailand's Per Capita GPI and Per Capita GDP

The results of the GPI study on Thailand are presented in Table 10.2 (valued at 1988 prices). The table reveals the values of each GPI item as well as the overall value of each interacting domain. Also revealed in monetary and index forms are the per capita values of Thailand's GPI and real GDP. By presenting the results in this way, it can be seen how the changing influences and feedbacks from the various domains or sub-systems impact on the rate of genuine progress experienced in Thailand.

The monetary values of Thailand's per capita GPI and GDP values (columns *I* and *J* in Table 10.2) are graphically illustrated in Figure 10.1. As can be seen from Figure 10.1, Thailand's per capita GPI not only grew at a slower rate over the study period, it also declined in some years when the per capita GDP increased. Moreover, despite a 3.7-fold increase in per capita GDP between 1975 and 2004 (14 662 baht to 54 671 baht), the per capita GPI grew by a more moderate 94.3 per cent (10 511 baht to 20 426 baht). There was virtually no gain in the per capita GPI between 1981 and 1990, while the per capita GPI fell in the last three years of the study period after peaking at 22 476 baht in 2001. During the last decade of the study period (1994–2004), the per capita GPI declined in four of the ten years and was marginally lower in 2004 than it was in 1997. Conversely, Thailand's per capita GDP fell twice only – in 1997 and 1998 – and was 20 per cent higher in 2004 than it was in 1994.

Although the GPI and GDP are money-metric, they are not essentially cardinal in nature. What can best be inferred from a time series of both indices is the variation and divergence in their two trend lines. This is more easily gleaned from Figure 10.2 which compares, over the study

Table 10.2 Genuine Progress Indicator (GPI) and real GDP for Thailand, 1975–2004

	Economic Domain					
	CON	ECD	SCD	Adjusted CON (*a* - *b* + *c*)	DI 1975 = 100	CON_{ADJ} (weighted) (*d/e*) / *100*
Year	*a*	*b*	*c*	*d*	*e*	*f*
1975	480 741	65 248	42 491	457 984	100.0	457 984
1976	523 101	70 082	46 418	499 437	99.9	499 826
1977	563 732	79 979	50 607	534 360	99.8	535 194
1978	604 069	85 244	55 308	574 133	99.8	575 477
1979	647 883	95 477	60 250	612 655	99.7	614 570
1980	714 164	109 392	66 213	670 985	99.6	673 608
1981	743 453	115 810	72 529	700 172	99.5	703 459
1982	758 931	120 485	79 181	717 627	100.6	713 626
1983	813 628	134 995	86 119	764 752	101.6	752 792
1984	854 543	139 274	93 823	809 092	102.6	788 459
1985	874 451	139 434	101 599	836 616	103.6	807 195
1986	899 104	147 616	109 017	860 505	104.7	822 090
1987	964 420	172 097	116 771	909 094	102.2	889 353
1988	1 041 718	197 822	125 982	969 878	99.8	972 150
1989	1 145 006	234 471	137 240	1 047 775	105.3	995 445
1990	1 282 879	280 615	151 140	1 153 404	110.7	1 041 470
1991	1 353 753	296 497	168 262	1 225 518	102.3	1 197 538
1992	1 467 307	336 115	186 331	1 317 523	105.1	1 253 110
1993	1 584 415	344 218	207 894	1 448 091	106.2	1 363 658
1994	1 707 043	368 675	228 816	1 567 184	107.2	1 461 339
1995	1 834 150	414 972	251 756	1 670 934	107.7	1 551 323
1996	1 954 914	435 229	279 310	1 798 995	108.2	1 663 002
1997	1 924 278	398 537	308 071	1 833 812	105.8	1 732 608
1998	1 741 747	308 924	330 715	1 763 538	103.5	1 703 825
1999	1 813 528	329 105	341 825	1 826 248	104.2	1 752 543
2000	1 896 366	350 705	351 289	1 896 950	104.7	1 812 264
2001	1 974 670	353 303	358 298	1 979 665	99.8	1 984 301
2002	2 068 707	384 544	363 978	2 048 141	100.4	2 040 988
2003	2 085 846	428 655	368 821	2 026 012	99.3	2 040 794
2004	2 143 917	460 475	377 265	2 060 707	98.2	2 098 459

Table 10.2 (continued)

	Social Domain					
	WPPSC	*Economic domain* (*a* to *g*)	Public health	Public education	Cost of commuting	Cost of urbanisation
Year	*g*	*A*	*h*	*i*	*j*	*k*
1975	6 814	*464 798*	2 407	12 240	-3 066	-18 084
1976	9 878	*509 704*	3 457	13 372	-3 466	-20 164
1977	10 336	*545 530*	3 753	13 683	-3 829	-22 255
1978	11 759	*587 237*	4 003	16 883	-3 939	-24 634
1979	12 461	*627 031*	4 530	18 427	-3 787	-25 712
1980	9 622	*683 230*	4 708	21 455	-3 560	-27 382
1981	9 868	*713 327*	5 217	21 614	-4 704	-29 172
1982	11 581	*725 207*	6 252	26 855	-5 441	-31 258
1983	12 546	*765 339*	7 153	28 274	-6 171	-30 869
1984	15 731	*804 191*	7 673	31 239	-7 192	-32 420
1985	19 286	*826 481*	8 555	32 788	-9 141	-33 843
1986	20 649	*842 739*	8 584	34 871	-9 710	-35 177
1987	19 088	*908 441*	8 686	34 274	-10 012	-37 963
1988	17 109	*989 259*	8 765	34 634	-10 164	-41 374
1989	19 400	*1 014 845*	9 788	38 198	-9 133	-48 611
1990	21 120	*1 062 590*	10 372	42 148	-10 218	-53 538
1991	26 980	*1 224 518*	11 045	44 793	-9 947	-62 459
1992	34 787	*1 287 897*	13 297	52 041	-10 647	-70 775
1993	39 200	*1 402 858*	16 749	59 305	-11 497	-70 927
1994	48 100	*1 509 440*	17 914	60 327	-12 107	-70 560
1995	53 415	*1 604 737*	21 208	69 457	-12 406	-81 507
1996	69 771	*1 732 773*	22 562	73 176	-13 289	-90 561
1997	105 707	*1 838 316*	25 904	74 579	-17 099	-93 200
1998	130 571	*1 834 396*	26 532	79 595	-22 264	-87 740
1999	145 703	*1 898 247*	25 868	81 549	-22 495	-98 231
2000	123 523	*1 935 787*	25 817	81 713	-18 959	-99 008
2001	114 504	*2 098 805*	27 005	85 014	-19 730	-103 068
2002	106 975	*2 147 963*	28 193	88 314	-20 501	-107 128
2003	98 133	*2 138 927*	29 382	91 615	-21 273	-111 189
2004	94 763	*2 193 222*	30 570	94 915	-22 044	-115 249

Table 10.2 (continued)

	Political Domain					
	Cost of noise poll.	*Social domain (h to l)*	Public roads	Cost of corruption	Change in foreign debt	*Political domain (m to o)*
Year	*l*	*B*	*m*	*n*	*o*	*C*
1975	-6 216	*-12 719*	3 216	-5 470	-1 944	*-4 198*
1976	-6 808	*-13 609*	4 114	-5 991	-3 131	*-5 008*
1977	-7 501	*-16 149*	2 412	-6 600	-5 705	*-9 893*
1978	-8 247	*-15 934*	4 157	-7 257	-10 776	*-13 876*
1979	-8 678	*-15 220*	3 824	-7 637	-13 391	*-17 204*
1980	-9 138	*-13 917*	4 091	-8 041	-15 891	*-19 841*
1981	-9 674	*-16 719*	4 523	-8 513	-19 123	*-23 113*
1982	-10 201	*-13 793*	3 845	-7 549	-17 774	*-21 478*
1983	-10 759	*-12 372*	3 692	-7 962	-15 684	*-19 954*
1984	-11 383	*-12 083*	3 884	-8 424	-13 307	*-17 847*
1985	-11 911	*-13 552*	4 546	-8 814	-14 847	*-19 115*
1986	-12 565	*-13 997*	4 354	-9 298	-11 544	*-16 488*
1987	-13 770	*-18 785*	4 554	-10 190	-12 548	*-18 184*
1988	-15 598	*-23 737*	4 970	-11 543	-11 187	*-17 760*
1989	-17 520	*-27 278*	5 387	-12 252	-11 734	*-18 599*
1990	-19 462	*-30 698*	6 351	-13 623	-14 129	*-21 401*
1991	-21 117	*-37 685*	6 757	-14 782	-28 389	*-36 414*
1992	-22 830	*-38 914*	7 841	-15 981	-31 285	*-39 425*
1993	-24 947	*-31 317*	8 560	-17 463	-46 931	*-55 834*
1994	-26 696	*-31 122*	9 123	-18 687	-64 933	*-74 497*
1995	-28 845	*-32 093*	10 126	-20 191	-112 797	*-122 862*
1996	-30 953	*-39 065*	11 041	-21 667	-114 919	*-125 545*
1997	-30 520	*-40 336*	10 752	-24 514	-101 262	*-115 024*
1998	-27 874	*-31 751*	10 544	-19 512	-74 791	*-83 759*
1999	-28 234	*-41 543*	11 082	-19 764	-39 930	*-48 612*
2000	-30 047	*-40 483*	11 509	-21 033	43 961	*34 438*
2001	-30 736	*-41 515*	11 958	-21 515	83 057	*73 500*
2002	-32 370	*-43 493*	12 406	-22 659	88 081	*77 828*
2003	-34 647	*-46 112*	12 855	-24 253	91 070	*79 672*
2004	-36 785	*-48 593*	13 303	-25 750	78 630	*66 184*

Table 10.2 (continued)

	Spiritual Domain			**Environmental Domain**		
	Non-paid h/h labour	Cost of sex work	*Spiritual domain (p to q)*	Timber depletion	Land degradation	Air pollution
Year	*p*	*q*	*D*	*r*	*s*	*t*
1975	93 148	-18 646	*74 502*	-62 013	-1 616	-4 117
1976	104 024	-20 371	*83 653*	-58 844	-3 370	-4 509
1977	113 173	-22 430	*90 743*	-113 162	-5 160	-4 913
1978	126 698	-24 558	*102 140*	-113 162	-7 116	-5 515
1979	140 806	-25 744	*115 062*	-33 949	-9 133	-5 758
1980	165 639	-27 190	*138 449*	-33 949	-11 257	-6 046
1981	174 027	-28 562	*145 465*	-33 949	-13 323	-6 069
1982	192 132	-30 133	*161 999*	-33 949	-15 214	-6 302
1983	204 889	-32 043	*172 846*	-30 327	-17 374	-6 774
1984	210 818	-33 754	*177 064*	-30 327	-19 374	-7 382
1985	216 101	-35 137	*180 964*	-29 875	-21 258	-7 930
1986	219 921	-36 950	*182 971*	-11 316	-23 227	-8 030
1987	229 481	-40 599	*188 882*	-11 316	-25 393	-9 299
1988	243 711	-46 051	*197 660*	-11 316	-27 916	-10 508
1989	262 429	-51 838	*210 591*	-11 316	-30 555	-12 146
1990	289 588	-57 650	*231 938*	-25 348	-32 986	-14 244
1991	311 564	-62 420	*249 144*	-25 348	-35 658	-16 144
1992	344 906	-66 967	*277 939*	-24 896	-38 465	-17 521
1993	393 552	-72 808	*320 744*	-25 348	-40 963	-19 479
1994	420 811	-79 645	*341 166*	-24 869	-43 806	-21 880
1995	470 155	-86 771	*383 384*	-25 348	-47 032	-24 307
1996	493 609	-91 513	*402 096*	-24 869	-50 444	-27 105
1997	493 280	-89 590	*403 690*	-25 348	-53 347	-29 257
1998	445 100	-79 414	*365 686*	-24 869	-56 310	-31 657
1999	458 715	-82 165	*376 550*	-4 526	-59 010	-34 056
2000	472 612	-90 140	*382 472*	-4 526	-61 731	-31 816
2001	466 880	-92 280	*374 600*	-4 526	-64 539	-33 340
2002	481 672	-97 111	*384 561*	-4 526	-67 593	-34 865
2003	504 807	-103 941	*400 866*	-4 526	-71 145	-36 390
2004	524 556	-110 355	*414 201*	-4 526	-74 849	-37 914

Table 10.2 (continued)

	GPI results					
	Urban w/w pollution	L-T env damage	*Env. domain (LNCS) (r to v)*	GPI	Real GDP	Population (000s)
Year	*u*	*v*	*E*	*F*	*G*	*H*
1975	-4 067	-4 960	*-76 773*	445 610	621 555	42 393
1976	-4 454	-10 873	*-82 050*	492 690	680 778	43 213
1977	-4 956	-17 697	*-145 888*	464 343	750 053	44 271
1978	-5 362	-31 097	*-162 252*	497 315	824 706	45 223
1979	-5 503	-47 682	*-102 025*	607 644	867 796	46 113
1980	-6 143	-67 297	*-124 692*	663 228	913 733	46 961
1981	-6 854	-89 806	*-150 001*	668 960	967 706	47 876
1982	-7 151	-115 087	*-177 702*	674 233	1 019 501	48 846
1983	-7 583	-142 202	*-204 260*	701 598	1 076 432	49 516
1984	-8 336	-171 138	*-236 557*	714 767	1 138 353	50 582
1985	-8 033	-201 872	*-268 968*	705 809	1 191 255	51 796
1986	-8 364	-234 371	*-285 308*	709 917	1 257 177	52 968
1987	-8 833	-267 703	*-322 545*	737 809	1 376 847	53 874
1988	-10 213	-302 815	*-362 768*	782 654	1 559 804	54 962
1989	-11 533	-338 798	*-404 348*	775 210	1 749 952	55 888
1990	-12 145	-377 357	*-462 080*	780 350	1 945 372	56 303
1991	-13 528	-418 469	*-509 147*	890 416	2 111 862	56 961
1992	-14 443	-461 373	*-556 698*	930 800	2 282 572	57 790
1993	-15 060	-505 999	*-606 849*	1 029 602	2 470 908	58 336
1994	-16 733	-552 258	*-659 546*	1 085 441	2 692 973	59 096
1995	-18 422	-600 250	*-715 359*	1 117 807	2 941 736	59 460
1996	-19 493	-650 513	*-772 424*	1 197 835	3 115 338	60 116
1997	-20 033	-702 282	*-830 267*	1 256 378	3 072 615	60 816
1998	-18 296	-755 798	*-886 930*	1 197 642	2 749 684	61 465
1999	-18 533	-811 042	*-927 167*	1 257 475	2 871 521	61 662
2000	-20 797	-867 510	*-986 380*	1 325 834	3 004 659	63 937
2001	-21 589	-925 596	*-1 049 590*	1 455 799	3 073 601	64 774
2002	-22 380	-985 284	*-1 114 649*	1 452 210	3 237 042	65 611
2003	-23 172	-1046 560	*-1 181 792*	1 391 560	3 464 701	66 448
2004	-23 963	-1109 405	*-1 250 658*	1 374 356	3 678 511	67 285

Table 10.2 (continued)

	GPI results			
	Per capita GPI (*F/H*)	Per capita GDP (*G/H*)	Per capita GPI	Per capita real GDP
Year	*I*	*J*	*K*	*L*
1975	10 511	14 662	100.0	100.0
1976	11 402	15 754	108.5	107.5
1977	10 489	16 942	99.8	115.6
1978	10 997	18 237	104.6	124.4
1979	13 177	18 819	125.4	128.4
1980	14 123	19 457	134.4	132.7
1981	13 973	20 213	132.9	137.9
1982	13 803	20 872	131.3	142.4
1983	14 169	21 739	134.8	148.3
1984	14 131	22 505	134.4	153.5
1985	13 627	22 999	129.6	156.9
1986	13 403	23 735	127.5	161.9
1987	13 695	25 557	130.3	174.3
1988	14 240	28 380	135.5	193.6
1989	13 871	31 312	132.0	213.6
1990	13 860	34 552	131.9	235.7
1991	15 632	37 076	148.7	252.9
1992	16 107	39 498	153.2	269.4
1993	17 649	42 356	167.9	288.9
1994	18 367	45 569	174.7	310.8
1995	18 799	49 474	178.8	337.4
1996	19 925	51 822	189.6	353.5
1997	20 659	50 523	196.5	344.6
1998	19 484	44 736	185.4	305.1
1999	20 393	46 569	194.0	317.6
2000	20 736	46 994	197.3	320.5
2001	22 476	47 451	213.8	323.6
2002	22 134	49 337	210.6	336.5
2003	20 942	52 142	199.2	355.6
2004	20 426	54 671	194.3	372.9

Note: All values in millions of Thai baht except columns *I* and *J*, which are in single baht, and where indicated.

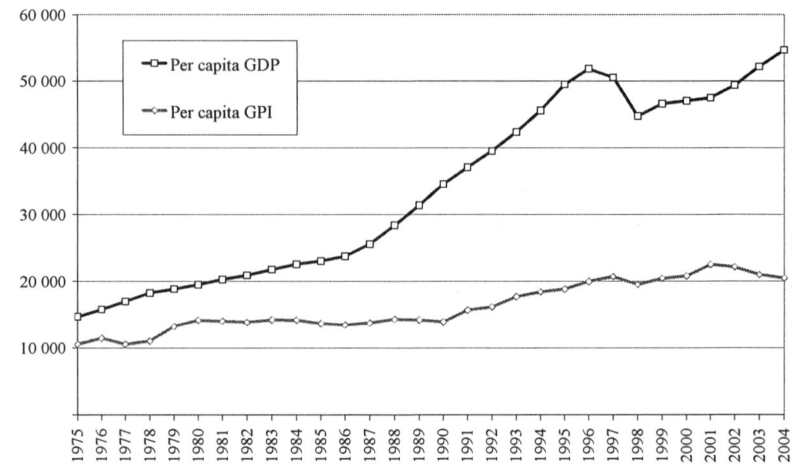

Note: Thai baht valued at 1988 prices.

Figure 10.1 Per capita GPI versus per capita GDP: Thailand, 1975–2004

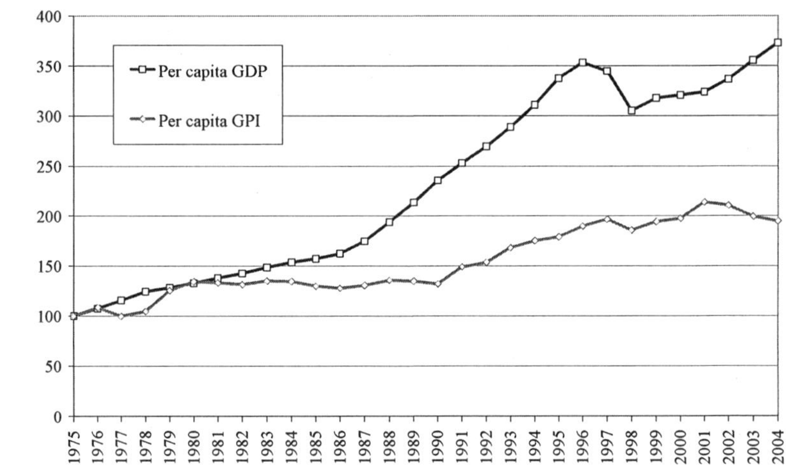

Note: 1975 = 100.

Figure 10.2 Index values of per capita GPI and per capita GDP: Thailand, 1975–2004

period, the index values of Thailand's per capita GPI and per capita GDP (columns *K* and *L* in Table 10.2).

The trend line of the per capita GDP index in Figure 10.2 can be divided into four main phases: the initial steady rise to 1986, the accelerated growth phase between 1987 and 1996, the brief but steep decline in 1997 and 1998, and the recovery phase between 1999 and 2004. Whilst there were also four main phases applicable to the per capita GPI index, the pattern of change was quite different. Not unlike the per capita GDP, there was an initial growth phase. However, it was much weaker and considerably shorter (1975–80). The second phase involved a stagnant period that occurred between 1981 and 1990. This was followed by an accelerated growth period between 1991 and 1997 which, it must be said, was not as strong as the growth spurt in per capita GDP. Finally, there was an overall decline in the per capita GPI index between 1997 and 2004 that occurred despite the rapid recovery of Thailand's per capita GDP.

The growing divergence between the two indices following the 1997 financial crisis is clearly of greatest concern since it implies, at best, that the relationship between Thailand's per capita GDP and per capita GPI is weakening over time. At worst, it implies that the increase in per capita GDP is beginning to impact negatively on Thailand's sustainable welfare. Whilst it is possible that the decline in Thailand's per capita GPI over the last three years of the study period had more to do with the quality of Thailand's GDP growth than the growth of GDP itself, the evidence revealed here casts considerable doubt over the long-term desirability of having GDP growth as the primary goal of Thailand's development policy. Moreover, it highlights an important question in relation to the 'threshold hypothesis' raised in Chapter 1.

To recall, Max-Neef (1995) examined the relationship between the per capita GPI and per capita GDP of a number of wealthy European and North American countries and discovered that once a nation's per capita GDP reached a certain 'threshold' level, the additional costs associated with a higher level of economic activity appeared to outweigh the additional benefits. As a consequence, the sustainable welfare in each case declined. To make matters worse, Max-Neef suggested that sustainable welfare was only likely to increase again through income redistribution, greater resource use efficiency, improved institutional arrangements, and better rather than more production.

As it turns out, the consideration of something akin to a threshold level of real GDP is not new within the development literature (Hicks, 1940; Pigou, 1962; Ng and Ng, 2001). Indeed, it has been argued for more than 30 years that a threshold point has probably been transgressed by a number of countries (see Daly, 1971 and 1999; Barkely and Seckler, 1972; Zolatas, 1981; Hamilton, 1998). Empirical evidence also supports these claims. A relatively common finding has been the fall in the per capita GPI of wealthy nations during the mid-1970s and mid-1980s as the per capita GDP passes through the US$20 000–25 000 level (see Daly and Cobb, 1989; Diefenbacher, 1994; Jackson and Marks, 1994; Stockhammer et al., 1997; Lawn and Sanders, 1999).

Given the results presented here on Thailand, could the threshold point at which the per capita GPI declines for some developing countries exist at a much lower per capita level of GDP? That is, could the threshold level of per capita GDP be contracting as the global economy as a whole expands, thereby penalising the growth 'late-comers' in the sense that they will have difficulty attaining the per capita GPI levels currently enjoyed by wealthy nations? This issue will be explored in greater detail in Chapter 12. Suffice to say, the apparent lower threshold point in the case of Thailand suggests that an entirely new approach to its economic development may be required.

Policy Consequences of the GPI Results

As previously mentioned, sustainable welfare is a function of the various interacting domains co-evolving within the larger ecological system upon which their sustainability depends (Dopfer, 1979; Capra, 1982; Norgaard, 1988; Clayton and Radcliffe, 1996; Clarke and Islam, 2004; Clarke, 2006). This so-called systems-analysis approach to sustainable welfare is depicted in Figure 10.3. It can be seen from Figure 10.3 that the various domains or sub-systems not only impact directly on human welfare but also indirectly as each domain feeds back and influences the total system as a whole.

The GPI results were deliberately presented in Table 10.2 to reveal the monetary value of the various domains depicted in Figure 10.3. Hence, this GPI study of Thailand is consistent with the systems-analysis view of sustainable welfare. It thus provides a better understanding of the interaction of the various domains which can lay the foundation for improved policy recommendations. For example, as the five domains

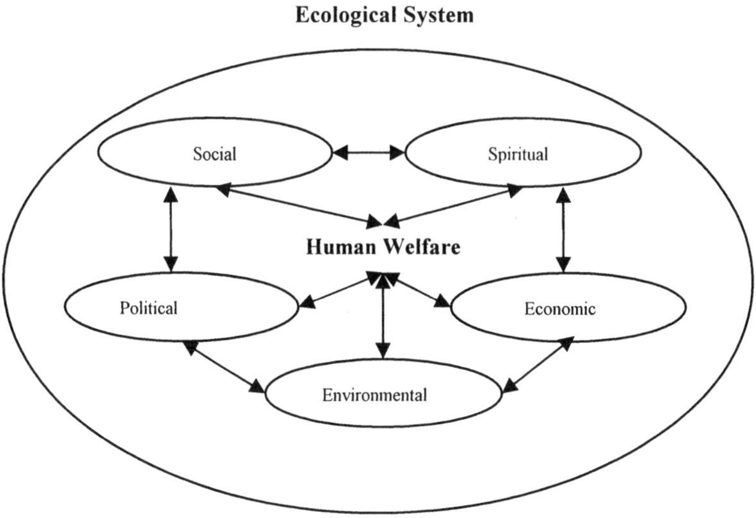

Figure 10.3 *Interacting sub-systems (domains) which affect sustainable welfare*

interact, one aspect contained within a particular domain (e.g., public health expenditure in the social domain) can generate a positive impact in another domain (e.g., increased consumption in the economic domain through higher labour productivity). This can lead to an altered view on the impact of public health expenditure and a subsequent reformulation of government health policy. Similarly, aspects can feed back and have negative implications for an alternative domain.

Policies related to the economic domain

To assist further in the policy assessment process, Figure 10.4 provides a graphical illustration of Thailand's per capita GPI and the per capita values of the five interacting domains. It can be clearly seen from the figure that the per capita value of the *economic* domain – which consists of the welfare contribution of consumption expenditure and publicly-provided service capital – was the main positive component of Thailand's per capita GPI. Of particular note is the gap that began to emerge between the per capita GPI and the per capita value of the

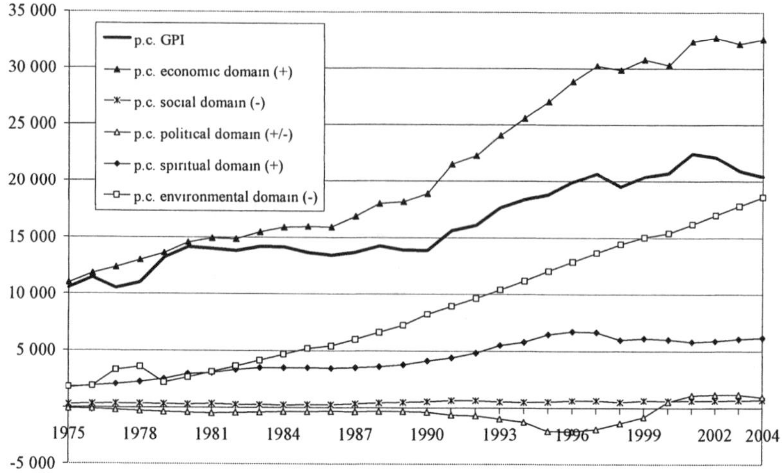

Note: Thai baht valued at 1988 prices.

Figure 10.4 Per capita GPI and component sub-systems (domains): Thailand, 1975–2004

economic domain in the early 1980s. This gap continued to grow until 1990, but remained largely unchanged between 1990 and 1995. From 1997 onwards, the disparity between the two values grew dramatically. This disturbing development after 1997 was due, initially, to the decline in consumption expenditure in the years just following the Asian financial crisis. Beyond 1999, it was due largely to the significant fall in the welfare generated by publicly-provided service capital. This indicates that the Thai Government should do more to maintain if not boost its investment in vital infrastructural assets.

One of the main impediments to the contribution made by the economic domain to Thailand's sustainable welfare was the continuing high rate of absolute poverty (i.e., around 20 per cent of the Thai population survive on US$2 or less per day). Although the redistribution of income through a more comprehensive tax and transfer system would help appreciably in this regard, Thailand clearly needs a dose of pro-poor GDP growth. By pro-poor, we mean GDP growth that is directed specifically at the poorest citizens and the regions of Thailand with the highest concentrations of absolute poverty (e.g., north-east Thailand).[6]

One of the major benefits of a pro-poor growth policy is that, by reducing income inequality, it lowers the poverty elasticity of future growth. In other words, it reduces the amount of GDP growth needed to lower absolute poverty in the future (World Bank, 2000; Deolalikar, 2002).

In suggesting a pro-poor growth policy, we feel it is important to qualify our recommendation by emphasising that the growth will need to be as resource efficient and ecologically sensitive as possible. Since GDP growth relates directly to the economic domain, a pro-poor policy must also account for the impact that growth has on the remaining domains. Only then will it be a form of growth which adheres to the systems-analysis view of sustainable welfare. And only then will it contribute to a lasting form of genuine progress for Thailand.

Policies related to the social domain

The *social* domain differs from the economic domain in that it includes a number of benefits and costs. Despite a dramatic rise in the social benefits of public health and education expenditure, the social costs of commuting, increased urbanisation, and noise pollution were sufficiently large to ensure a negative per capita value of the social domain throughout the study period. This negative value can be interpreted many ways. As we see it, it reflects the Thai Government's preoccupation with real GDP growth at the expense of broader social concerns.

In order to increase the positive contribution of the social domain, more emphasis should be placed on minimising the social costs of economic activity; in particular, the cost of urbanisation. Some of the policy measures that ought to be considered here include the decentralisation of many government departments, incentives to encourage the relocation of businesses and expanding industries to non-urban areas, improved services and infrastructural capital in rural regions, and greater pecuniary rewards and tax breaks for people living in remote regions of Thailand.

From a systems-analysis perspective, the reduction in rural poverty which ought to emerge from improved rural services and a more equitable distribution of income should also help to minimise the rate of land degradation and other forms of environmental damage. Evidence indicates that rural poverty is a major factor behind the use of unsustainable land use practices (Daly, 1996, Chapter 8). As such, policies aimed at improving the economic and social domains are likely, if well targeted, to benefit the environmental domain.

Policies related to the political domain

The *political* domain incorporates the welfare benefit of government expenditure on roads and highways plus the cost of corruption and the change in net foreign debt. As a result of the growing cost of corruption and the steep rise in Thailand's net foreign debt between 1990 and 1997, the per capita value of the political domain was negative from 1975 to 1999. However, from 2000 to 2004, the per capita value of this domain was in positive territory. This change from a negative to a positive value was the result of a decline in net foreign debt, a stabilisation in the cost of corruption, and a marginal rise in the welfare benefit of government expenditure on roads and highways.

As desirable as the shift in value was for the political domain, there is little doubt that its positive contribution would be much greater in future if reforms were introduced to reduce the incidence of political and bureaucratic corruption (Phongpaichit and Piriyarangsan, 1994; Parnwell, 1996; Linter, 1998). Of course, this is probably the most difficult policy to implement because anti-corruption reforms must be designed and enforced by those at the root of the problem who also have the most to lose from the reform process. External organisations, such as Transparency International, may be required to assist in monitoring the effectiveness of anti-corruption initiatives.

Policies related to the spiritual domain

The two items contained within the *spiritual* domain had a considerable impact on Thailand's per capita GPI. The first is the value of non-paid household labour – the second-largest positive item – which represents the moral commitment made to the family unit that comes at the expense of forgone money wages. The second spiritual item is the cost of commercial sex work. This item reflects, in a very real sense, a loss of mutual respect and community kinship. Although the cost of commercial sex work was significant in magnitude and grew throughout most of the study period, it was outweighed by the value of non-paid household work.

In view of the large positive contribution made by the spiritual domain towards the GPI, Thai policy-makers need to establish more family-friendly institutional arrangements and discourage the growth in the commercial sex work industry. The latter can be achieved, in large part, by improving the distribution of income and making available, to those in most need, basic government services. This again shows that policies aimed at particular domains (e.g., the economic and social domains) can have major welfare benefits for another domain (e.g., the spiritual domain), and vice versa.

Policies related to the environmental domain

The *environmental* domain includes the cost of the source, sink, and life-support services provided by natural capital which are lost as a consequence of a growing national economy. Figure 10.4 shows that the per capita value of Thailand's environmental domain increased steadily after 1978. Why was this so? Although the cost of timber depletion fell significantly during the latter stages of the study period, the remaining environmental costs increased dramatically. Indeed, so much so, that the environmental domain was most responsible for the decline in Thailand's per capita GPI towards the end of the study period.

The overwhelming impact of the rise in environmental costs is consistent with most studies revealing a decline in a nation's per capita GPI. The reason for this is quite straightforward. Of all the domains affecting sustainable welfare, the environmental domain is perhaps the least understood in terms of its positive impact on the remaining four domains depicted in Figure 10.3. There is often a belief that a trade-off exists between 'development' needs and the need to maintain a healthy natural environment. To the contrary, a healthy environmental domain underpins the 'sustainability' of the welfare enjoyed by a nation. It also provides the foundation upon which the welfare benefits flow from the economic and social domains.

With this in mind, there is an urgent need for policy-makers to introduce environmental policy initiatives that are consistent with the strong sustainability stance of having to keep the stock of natural capital intact. We therefore strongly recommend policies which aim to: (a) facilitate increases in resource use efficiency; (b) encourage the development and uptake of resource-saving technology (thereby reducing the environmental pressure per unit of economic activity); (c) minimise and eventually halt the diminution of natural capital and critical ecosystems; and (d) encourage investment in natural capital as well as human-made capital. The Thai Government would be well advised to consider some of the policy measures recommended in the policy section of Chapter 8 on India.

CONCLUSION

This chapter has involved an empirical application of the GPI to Thailand over a 30-year period (1975–2004). The results of the study suggest that Thailand's per capita GDP overstated its sustainable welfare as well as the rate of genuine progress it made over those 30 years. Indeed, towards the end of the study period (1997–2004), it would appear that the increase in per capita GDP impacted negatively on Thailand's sustainable welfare.

This raises three serious concerns. Firstly, Thailand may have already reached a 'threshold' level of per capita GDP. Secondly, and assuming the first assertion is correct, the threshold point for Thailand would appear to have occurred at a much lower per capita GDP than the level experienced by wealthy nations in the 1970s and 1980s. Thirdly, one must question the Thai Government's preoccupation with real GDP growth as the centrepiece of its development policy.

Despite our third concern, we have not ruled out the need for further GDP growth in Thailand. What we have recommended is a pro-poor growth policy that is deliberately directed at Thailand's poorest citizens and regions, is resource efficient, and aims to minimise the rate of natural capital degradation. To achieve this, we have put forward a range of policies that we believe would impact positively on the economic domain as well as enhance the remaining four domains (sub-systems) critical to Thailand's sustainable welfare. One can dispute the nature of the policies we have recommended. However, in view of the GPI results revealed in this chapter, one cannot dispute the need for a new development approach for Thailand. Just how well conceived the response is will undoubtedly determine the level of sustainable welfare that Thailand enjoys in the distant future. But an appropriate response is required soon, for there is little time to waste.

NOTES

1. For more on what constitutes a nation's ecological footprint and biocapacity, see the explanations of both in Chapter 1.
2. While the economic, political, social, and environmental domains are self-explanatory, further explanation of the spiritual domain may be required. The spiritual domain is not concerned with religious belief or faith in some sort of deity, but rather is concerned with the interactions between humans. It could just as easily be labelled the moral domain or humanity domain. A healthy spiritual domain is characterised by mutual respect and a common bond of humanity. A failing spiritual domain is characterised by the dehumanising of others and exploitation. The breakdown of society, as evidenced by recent events in the Balkans, Rwanda, and terrorist attacks in the United States and South-east Asia, is characterised by a dehumanisation of others. Spiritual sustainability requires this shared humanity to withstand external pressures such as ecological destruction, political insecurity, and economic collapse.
3. The cost of commuting was confined to Bangkok on the premise that other cities in Thailand have relatively low levels of urbanisation and, as such, commuting costs would be relatively minor and have a limited impact on the GPI (Dixon, 1999).
4. Apart from the loss of timber, deforestation causes soil erosion and regional flooding, and contributes to continental and global climate change. Since this estimate was based solely on the costs associated with soil erosion, it can be considered conservative.
5. Unlike timber resources, there is no substitute for agricultural land and so it is necessary to cumulatively add the cost of land degradation.
6. The north-east region of Thailand has traditionally been the poorest with poverty rates similar to parts of sub-Saharan Africa (Watkins, 1998). In many rural areas of Thailand, the large majority of the population have benefited little from the GDP growth over the past 30 years but have experienced more than their fair share of the associated costs (Dixon, 1999; Warr, 2001).

REFERENCES

Barkley, P. and Seckler, D. (1972), *Economic Growth and Environmental Decay: The Solution Becomes the Problem*, New York: Harcourt Brace Jovanovich.

Capra, F. (1982), *The Turning Point*, London: Fontana.

Chiswick, C. (1983), 'Analysis of earnings from household enterprises: methodology and application to Thailand', *Review of Economics and Statistics*, **65(4)**, 658–662.

Chongpeerapien, T., Sungsuwan, S., Kritiporn, P., Buranasajja, S. and Resource Management Associates (1990), 'Energy and environment:

choosing the right mix', Research report presented at the 1990 TDRI Year-End Conference, 8–9 December, Chon Buri.

Clarke, M. (2001), 'Case studies: learning from experience, Thailand', in D. Brandt (ed.), *The Approaching Storm*, Monrovia: World Vision International, pp. 25–30.

Clarke, M. (2006), 'Policy implications of the ISEW: Thailand as a case study', in P. Lawn (ed.), *Sustainable Development Indicators in Ecological Economics*, Cheltenham, UK and Northamption, MA, USA: Edward Elgar, pp. 166–185.

Clarke, M. and Islam, S. (2004), *Economic Growth and Social Welfare*, Amsterdam: North Holland.

Clayton, A. and Radcliffe, N. (1996), *Sustainability: A Systems Approach*, London: Earthscan.

Daly, H. (1971), 'Towards a new economics – questioning growth', in W. Johnson and J. Hardesty (eds), *Economic Growth Versus the Environment*, Belmont, CA: Wadsworth Publishing.

Daly, H. (1996), *Beyond Growth: The Economics of Sustainable Development*, Boston: Beacon Press.

Daly, H. (1999), *Ecological Economics and the Ecology of Economics*, Cheltenham: Edward Elgar.

Daly, H. and Cobb J. (1989), *For the Common Good*, Boston, MA: Beacon Press.

Deolalikar, A. (2002), 'Poverty, growth, and inequality in Thailand', ERD Working Paper Series No. 8, Asia Development Bank, Manila.

Department of Energy Development and Promotion (1990), *Industry Survey*, Bangkok: DEDP (in Thai).

Department of Industrial Works (1986), *Industry Survey – 1985*, Bangkok: DIW (in Thai).

Dhiratayakinant, K. (1993), 'Urbanization, inefficient urban management and income inequality', paper presented at the 'Fifth International Conference on Thai Studies', School of Oriental and African Studies, University of London, 5–12 July.

Diefenbacher, H. (1994), 'The index of sustainable economic welfare in Germany', in C. Cobb and J. Cobb (eds.), *The Green National Product*, New York: University Press of America, pp. 215–245.

Dixon, C. (1991), *South East Asia in the World Economy*, New York: Cambridge University Press.

Dixon, C. (1996), 'Thailand's rapid economic growth: causes, sustainability and lessons', in M. Parnwell (ed.), *Uneven Development in Thailand*, Aldershot: Avebury, chapter 2.

Dixon, C. (1999), *The Thai Economy: Uneven Development and Internationalism*, London: Routledge.

Dopfer, K. (1979), *The New Political Economy of Development: Integrated Theory and Asian Experiment*, Melbourne: Macmillian.

El Serafy, S. (1989), 'The proper calculation of income from depletable resources', in Y. Ahmad, S. El Serafy and E. Lutz (eds), *Environmental Accounting for Sustainable Development*, Washington, DC: World Bank, pp. 10–18.

Elliott, K. (1997), *Corruption and the Global Economy*, Washington, DC: Institute for International Economics.

George, S. (1999), *The Debt Boomerang*, London: Pluto Press.

Global Footprint Network (2006), *Ecological Footprint and Biocapacity*, Oakland, CA: Global Footprint Network.

Guenno, G. and Tiezzi, S. (1998), 'An Index of Sustainable Economic Welfare for Italy', Working Paper 5/98, Milan: Fondazione Eni Enrico Mattei.

Hamilton, C. (1998), 'Measuring changes in economic welfare', in R. Eckersley (ed.), *Measuring Progress*, Melbourne: CSIRO Publishing, pp. 69–92.

Hicks, J. (1940), 'The valuation of social income', *Economica*, 7: 104–124.

Israngakurn, A. (2001), personal communication, July.

Jackson, T. and Marks, N. (1994), *Measuring Sustainable Economic Welfare*, Stockholm: Stockholm Environment Institute in cooperation with The New Economics Foundation.

Jansen, K. (1997), *External Finance in Thailand's Development*, London: Macmillan.

Kakwani, N. and Krongkaew, M. (1997), 'Thailand's generational accounts', Discussion Paper 14, School of Economics, University of New South Wales, Sydney.

Khomnamol, N. (1999), 'A vision of new Bangkok in the next century', Office of the Commission for the Management of Land Traffic, Bangkok.

Krongkaew, M. (1993), 'Poverty and income distribution', in P. Warr (ed.), *The Thai Economy in Transition*, Cambridge: Cambridge University Press, pp. 401–437.

Kuznets, S. (1968), *Toward a Theory of Economic Growth*, New York: W.W. Norton and Co.

Lawn, P. and Clarke, M. (2006), *Measuring Genuine Progress: Application of the Genuine Progress Indicator*, New York: Nova Science.

Lawn, P. and Sanders, R. (1999), 'Has Australia surpassed its optimal macroeconomic scale? Finding out with the aid of benefit and cost accounts and a sustainable net benefit index', *Ecological Economics*, **28(2)**, 213–229.

Linter, D. (1998), 'Thailand's illicit GNP', *Far Eastern Economic Review*, **161(45)**, 48–49.

Lyttleton, C. (2000), *Endangered Relationships*, Amsterdam: Harwood Academic Publishers.

Martin, H. and Schuumann, H. (1997), *The Global Trap*, London: Zed Books.

Max-Neef, M. (1995), 'Economic growth and quality of life: a threshold hypothesis', *Ecological Economics*, **15(2)**, 115–118.

Mishan, E. (1977), *The Economic Growth Debate*, London: George Allen & Unwin.

National Economic and Social Development Board (NESDB) (1996), *Eighth Five Year Plan*, Bangkok: NESDB.

National Economic and Social Development Board (NESDB) (2000), *Ninth Five Year Plan*, Bangkok: NESDB.

National Statistical Office (NSO) (various), *National Income of Thailand*, Bangkok: NESDB.

National Statistical Office (NSO) (various), *Statistical Yearbook Thailand*, Bangkok: NESDB.

Ng, S. and Ng, Y. (2001), 'Welfare-reducing growth despite individual and government optimalisation', *Social Choice and Welfare*, **18**, 497–506.

Nordhaus, W. (1991), 'To slow or not to slow: the economics of the Greenhouse Effect', *Economic Journal*, **101**, 920–937.

Norgaard, R. (1988), 'Sustainable development: a co-evolutionary view', *Futures*, **December**, 606–620.

Organisation for Economic Co-operation and Development (OECD) (2001), *The Well-being of Nations: The Role of Human and Social Capital*, Paris: OECD.

Packard-Winkler, M. (2000), *Knowledge, Sex and Marriage in Modern Bangkok: Cultural Negotiation in the Time of AIDS*, Ann Arbor, MI: University of Michigan Press.

Panayotou, T. and Parasuk, C. (1990), *Land and Forest: Projecting Demand and Managing Encroachment*, Bangkok: TDRI.

Parnwell, M. (1996), 'Conclusion: future paths toward development in Thailand', in M. Parnwell (ed.), *Uneven Development in Thailand*, Aldershot: Avebury, pp. 282–291.

Paul, D. (1995), *Child Labour in Context*, Melbourne: World Vision Australia.

Phansawas, T. (1987), *Community Wastewater Pollution in the Bangkok Metropolitan Area*, Bangkok: ONED (in Thai).

Phongpaichit, P. and Baker, C. (1995), *Thailand: Economy and Politics*, Oxford: Oxford University Press.

Phongpaichit, P. and Chiasakul, S. (1993), 'Services', in P. Warr (ed.), *The Thai Economy in Transition*, Cambridge: Cambridge University Press, pp. 151–171.

Phongpaichit, P. and Piriyarangsan, S. (1994), *Corruption and Democracy in Thailand*, Chiang Mai: Silkworm Books.

Phongpaichit, P., Piriyarangsan, S. and Treerat, N. (1998), *Guns, Girls, Gambling, Ganja: Thailand's Illegal Economy and Public Policy*, Chiang Mai: Silkworm Books.

Pigou, A. (1962), *The Economics of Welfare*, 4th edition, London: Macmillan.

Schmidt, J. (1996), 'Paternalism and planning in Thailand: facilitating growth without social benefits', in M. Parnwell (ed.), *Uneven Development in Thailand*, Aldershot: Avebury.

Stockhammer, L., Hochrieter, F., Obermayer, B. and Steiner, K. (1997), 'The Index of Sustainable Economic Welfare: the results of the Austrian (revised) ISEW calculations 1955–1992', *Ecological Economics*, **21**, 19–34.

Tanaborrboon, Y. (1990), 'Recommendations for relieving traffic problems in Bangkok', *Proceedings of the First Conference on Environment and Natural Resources Conservation in Thailand*, Bangkok: TDRI.

TESCO (1993), 'Environment plan for development in Bangkok and central areas', presented to the Pollution Control Department, Ministry of Science, Technology and Environment, Bangkok (in Thai).

Tingsabadh, C. (1989), 'Economic systems and the environment in Thailand', *Culture and the Environment in Thailand*, Bangkok: Siam Society.

Tiwari, D. (1997), *Economic Valuation of the Health Effects of Air Pollution and Implications for Environmental Tax Reform in the Bangkok Metropolitan Area*, Singapore: EEPSEA.

Vines, D. and Warr, P. (2000), 'Thailand's investment-driven boom and crisis', Working Paper No. 00/11, Asia Pacific School of Economics and Management, Australian National University, Canberra.

Warr, P. (2001), 'Poverty reduction and sectoral growth: evidence from Southeast Asia', paper presented for the WIDER Development Conference on 'Growth and Development' in Helsinki, 25–26 May.

Watkins, K. (1998). *Economic Growth with Equity: Lessons from Asia*, Oxford: Oxfam.

World Bank (1999), *Thailand Social Monitor: Challenge for Social Reform*, Bangkok: World Bank.

World Bank (2000), *World Development Report 2000/2001: Attacking Poverty*, New York: Oxford University Press.

World Bank (2006), *World Development Indicators*, Washington, DC: World Bank.

World Resources Institute (WRI) (2005), *Climate Analysis Indicators Tool (CAIT) Version 3.0*, Washington, DC: WRI.

Zolotas (1981), *Economic Growth and Declining Social Welfare*, New York: New York University Press.

11. Genuine progress in Vietnam: the impact of the Doi Moi reforms

Vu Xuan Nguyet Hong, Matthew Clarke, and Philip Lawn

INTRODUCTION

This chapter involves a genuine progress study of Vietnam which, like Thailand in the previous chapter, has only recently begun a process of industrialisation. However, unlike Thailand, Vietnam has been forced to fashion its development path in the wake of two devastating wars between 1947 and 1975.

Possessing a largely agrarian economy organised around communist principles, Vietnam has recently introduced a number of economic liberalisation policies to confer a more prominent role for the market in the allocation of resources. As a result of the economic reforms, there has been a huge upsurge in the number of foreign investors taking advantage of Vietnam's low cost of production. Indeed, while many neighbouring economies have been forced to shed their intermediate manufacturing industries in response to their higher relative production costs, Vietnam has been able to attract significant inflows of foreign investment capital. The major upshot of the economic reform measures has thus been the significant growth of Vietnam's real Gross Domestic Product (GDP) over the past two decades. However, as we shall soon see, this has not necessarily equated to genuine progress.

In order to examine Vietnam's genuine progress more closely, this chapter is organised as follows. The first major section provides a brief historical background of Vietnam, including a thumbnail sketch of the Doi Moi economic reforms introduced in 1986. In the next section, the various adjustments undertaken to calculate Vietnam's Genuine Progress Indicator (GPI) are outlined and explained. This is followed by a section analysing the GPI results. The chapter concludes with a section detailing some of the policy implications of the GPI results for Vietnam.

VIETNAM'S ECONOMIC DEVELOPMENT: HISTORICAL BACKGROUND AND RECENT DEVELOPMENTS

Early History of Vietnam

Legendary tales date the beginning of what we now know as Vietnam as far back as 2000 BC. More reliable evidence suggests that the Vietnamese people originated from minority ethnic groups in southern China who, during times of repression, sought sanctuary to the south. A century after the Chinese establishment of a military garrison in northern Vietnam in 214 BC, most of present-day northern Vietnam was annexed as the Chinese province of Giao Cha. From 111 BC to AD 938, Vietnam was essentially under the direct rule of successive Chinese dynasties (Vinh, 1992).

Despite gaining independence in AD 939, Vietnam remained a tributary state of China. On numerous occasions Vietnam fought off Chinese attempts to reinstate it as an official part of the Chinese Empire (Williams, 1992). Originally confined to the Red River Delta region, Vietnam gradually expanded southward and by the eighteenth century had encompassed the majority of the Mekong Delta.

Whilst European involvement in Vietnam can be traced back to the arrival of Roman merchants in 166 BC, no major European influence occurred in Vietnam until the seventeenth century (Tucker, 1999). It was during this time that a sizeable Catholic community was established following an increase in Christian missionary activity, most particularly by the French. It was also during the seventeenth century that the battle between the Trinh and Nguyen Lords provided European traders with an opportunity to support both sides with weapons and new technology. While the Portuguese assisted the Nguyen Lords in the south, the Dutch were instrumental in arming the Trinh Lords in the north (Watt, 1968).

In 1784, a French Catholic bishop named Pigneaux de Behaine returned to France to garner military support for Nguyen Anh, a surviving heir of the Nguyen Lords, in his battle against the Tay Son Dynasty. Unfortunately for Pigneaux, the strategy was thwarted by the outbreak of the French Revolution. Not to be discouraged, Pigneaux secured two ships and a regiment of Indian soldiers from the French territory of Pondicherry (Vinh, 1992). Returning to Vietnam in 1788 to support a reorganised Nguyen Anh navy, Tay Son was defeated at Qui Nhon in 1792. This enabled Nguyen Anh's forces to capture Hanoi a few years later (Watt, 1968).

Western Colonisation of Vietnam

After establishing the Nguyen Dynasty in 1802, Nguyen Anh agreed to tolerate Catholicism as a mark of appreciation of Pigneaux's assistance. Nevertheless, as a conservative Confucian, Nguyen Anh resisted the Europeanisation of Vietnam. Future Nguyen emperors would not be as accommodating as their predecessor and, as such, openly engaged in the brutal suppression of Catholicism. Many thousands of Vietnamese and foreign-born Christians were religiously persecuted, while trade with Europe also began to slow significantly in the wake of Vietnam's anti-Western policy (Vinh, 1992). The French viewed these acts as a pretext for armed intervention into Vietnam.

In 1859, the French army captured Saigon and, by 1867, had conquered all of southern Vietnam. A short time later, after securing Hanoi, Annam, and Tonkin in the north, France assumed control over Vietnam and established French Indochina in 1887 (Tucker, 1999). United under a single Governor-General, the French created a rail and road network as a means of providing the first physical links between the north and south of Vietnam.

Resistance to French control continued in vain until 1916, generally under the leadership of imperial family members and Vietnam's mandarin class. A number of underground nationalist organisations emerged during the 1920s whilst, in 1930, Ho Chi Minh founded the Indochinese Communist Party (Tucker, 1999). It was also in 1930 that a nationalist uprising took place in Tonkin that was closely followed by a peasant revolt under communist leadership (Williams, 1992). Both forms of resistance were successfully extinguished by the French (Vinh, 1992).

During World War II, Japan assumed control over French Indochina. Eventually, in March 1945, the Japanese ousted the French authorities and installed a puppet regime under the former Annamite emperor, Bao Dai (Vinh, 1992). Following the Japanese surrender to the Allied forces in August 1945, the Viet Minh – an Independence League established by Ho Chi Minh in 1941 – briefly took over Hanoi and Saigon. Emperor Bao Dai abdicated on 25 August and the Democratic Republic of Vietnam (DRV) was declared on 2 September with Ho Chi Minh as President and Hanoi as the nation's capital (Watt, 1968).

Post-World War II

Independence for Vietnam was short-lived. Under the Potsdam Agreement between the USA, Britain, and the Soviet Union, the north was occupied by the Chinese and the south by British troops (Tucker, 1999). Although China recognised the Hanoi Government, the British rearmed the French who proceeded to regain control of Saigon. A compromise agreement between the French and Vietnamese Governments was signed in March 1946 recognising the Democratic Republic of Vietnam (DRV) as a free state within the French Union (Tucker, 1999). However, this only served to fuel clashes between the French and Vietnamese forces. By December 1946, a full-scale war had broken out between France and the Viet Minh (Williams, 1992).

France eventually proposed a new unified government under the leadership of Bao Dai – a plan accepted by Cochin-China and Annam but rejected outright by Ho Chi Minh and the Viet Minh. Undaunted, the French established the 'State of Vietnam' Government in June 1948 with Bao Dai as the Chief of State (Vinh, 1992). The new state was recognised by Western nations but not by the world's communist countries which instead opted to officially recognise the DRV in 1950. With the assistance of China, the Viet Minh forces grew considerably in strength and, by 1954, had gained control of most rural regions within Tonkin and Amman as well as large expanses of Cochin-China. Following a decisive battle at Dien Bien Phu in north-west Tonkin, French troops surrendered to the Viet Minh on 7 May 1954 (Tucker, 1999). By July of the same year, a Geneva Accord was signed between France and the Viet Minh paving the way for the French to exit Vietnam.

Whilst the Accord left Vietnam divided between the Ho Chi Minh Government in the north and the Bao Dai administration in the south, the plan was to reunite both sides in lieu of elections in July 1956. Unfortunately, the promised elections and Vietnamese reunification did not eventuate (Williams, 1992). In the belief that the communists would obstruct legitimate elections, Ngo Dinh Diem deposed Bao Dai in 1955 and subsequently declared South Vietnam an autonomous republic (Tucker, 1999). Vietnam thus remained split between the communist north and a US-supported south.

The new Diem administration immediately stamped its authority by introducing a range of oppressive security measures (Tucker, 1999). By 1959, the intensification of Diem's oppression had led to a significant rise in communist-led guerrilla warfare. In order to maximise their military impact, the various southern-based guerrilla groups merged in 1960 to form the National Liberation Front (NLF or Viet Cong) (Tucker, 1999). Concerned about accelerated activity by the North Vietnam-supplied NLF, the USA increased its economic and military assistance to the Diem administration in 1961 (Vinh, 1992).

In late 1963, conflict between the Diem Government and the persecuted Buddhist community intensified. This brought about a major political crisis in South Vietnam which culminated in a military coup and the ousting of the Diem administration in November of the same year. Until the establishment of a military regime in February 1965, political instability would result in 12 changes of government in 15 months (Tucker, 1999).

Meanwhile, in 1964, the USA launched air assaults on North Vietnam following claims that the North Vietnamese had attacked US vessels patrolling the Gulf of Tonkin. The US Congress responded by passing a resolution to sanction the use of US forces in the region, thus formally beginning America's protracted involvement in the Vietnam War. In early 1965, the USA initiated a sustained bombing attack on North Vietnam (Williams, 1992). By the end of the year, 185 000 American troops were deployed in Vietnam. US troop numbers grew over the following years to eventually peak at 543 000 in early 1969 (Tucker, 1999). In time, US forces would also be reinforced by smaller armed contingents from South Korea, Thailand, the Philippines, Australia, and New Zealand.

After years of bloodshed and political instability, North and South Vietnam and their respective allies agreed to a ceasefire in January 1973 (the Paris Peace Agreement). However, fighting continued. Eventually, southern forces succumbed to a massive northern offensive with the Vietnam War finally ending with the fall of Saigon (now Ho Chi Minh City) and the de facto reunification of Vietnam on 30 April 1975 (Tucker, 1999). By now, hundreds of thousands of civilians on both sides were dead, millions more had been displaced, and the Vietnamese economy was reduced to tatters.

Post-Vietnam War

In 1976, Vietnam was officially unified and renamed the Socialist Republic of Vietnam (SRV) with Hanoi as its capital. The former South Vietnam was reorganised along communist principles and the new SRV government, under Pham Van Dong, emphasised the development of heavy industry and the collectivisation of agriculture. For the next few years, private enterprises were seized by the government and farmers incorporated into state-controlled co-operatives (Tri, 1990). Except for government activities, a prohibition was imposed on the interprovincial movement of goods. Compounded by natural disasters, Vietnam was struck down by severe food shortages with the Mekong Delta, once a heavy rice-producing region, threatened with famine.

In terms of foreign relations, Vietnam was forced to contend with border disputes with neighbouring Cambodia which eventually escalated into open warfare by the end of 1977. In late 1978, Vietnam overthrew Pol Pot's Khmer Rouge regime and established a pro-Hanoi government. A short time later, China launched a punitive but short-lived attack in northern Vietnam in response to the invasion of Cambodia and the continuing persecution of ethnic Chinese in northern regions of Vietnam (Tucker, 1999). In addition, normalised relations with the USA failed to materialise, thus denying Vietnam vital US trade links and American aid. However, Vietnam was able to secure substantial economic and military support from the Soviet Union in the early 1980s. Furthermore, it was now able to conduct its international trade through the USSR and many Eastern European countries (Tucker, 1999).

The 1986 Doi Moi Reforms

Following the death of Le Duan in 1986, efforts were made to reconstruct the still war-ravaged Vietnamese economy and improve the efficiency of state-owned enterprises. Under the new leadership of Nguyen Van Linh, the Doi Moi reforms were introduced to stimulate the economy, liberalise foreign investment laws, and grant limited freedom to private enterprise, education, and the arts (Williams, 1992; Than and Tan, 1993; Masina, 2006).

In 1991, in the wake of the collapse of communism in the Soviet Union and Eastern Europe, the Vietnamese Government reaffirmed the Doi Moi reforms by embracing a state-controlled market economy similar to the

Chinese model (Masina, 2006). In other words, Vietnam was to remain a communist political state but with greater private ownership, the decollectivisation of state farms, fewer price controls, a reduced number of government employees, and the public–private development of export-processing zones.

In the two decades since the implementation of the Doi Moi reforms, Vietnam's real GDP has grown at a dramatic rate. Between 1992 and 2004, per capita real GDP increased by 99.3 per cent or at an average rate of 5.9 per cent per annum. This growth has been fuelled by the recent escalation in foreign direct investment (FDI) into Vietnam. In the 15-year period from 1990 to 2005, the total stock of FDI increased from US$1.6 billion to US$31.1 billion (UNCTAD, 2006). In 2005 alone, just over US$2 billion was invested into the Vietnamese economy – up from US$1.4 billion in 2003.

Because of the nature of the FDI into Vietnam, the manufacturing and service sectors have expanded considerably. As a consequence, the relative shares of the major sectors of the Vietnamese economy have altered radically. For example, at the time of the Doi Moi reforms in 1986, agriculture was responsible for nearly half of Vietnam's real GDP and employment for the majority of the population. Following two decades of the manufacturing and service sectors outpacing the growth of agriculture, the agricultural sector now accounts for just 20 per cent of Vietnam's real GDP. On the other hand, the manufacturing and service sectors each account for around 40 per cent of the nation's output (WRI, http://earthtrends.wri.org). Having said this, Vietnam remains the world's second-largest rice exporter and a nation heavily reliant upon agricultural output as a source of export revenue. Furthermore, despite significant changes in the relative output contribution of each key sector of the Vietnamese economy, the majority of the labour force continues to be employed in the agricultural sector with less than 10 per cent employed in the service sector (Abrami and Henaff, 2004).

One of the apparent downsides of the Doi Moi reforms has been the deterioration in the distribution of income from the poor to the rich. According to the Vietnam Living Standards Surveys undertaken between 1992 and 2004, the level of income inequality, as measured by the Gini coefficient, worsened by nearly 30 per cent over this period. In 1992, the value of the Gini coefficient was 0.330 which, by any standards, represents a relatively equal distribution of income across the nation. This figure progressively deteriorated to 0.423 by 2004. Much of this inequality can be apportioned to the move away from public to private ownership and the reduction in state welfare support. The increasing marginalisation of Vietnam's poor is also reflected by the fact that, in 2002, the poverty rate (i.e., the percentage of the population living on less than US$1 per day) was still a disconcertingly high 29 per cent (UNDP, 2006).

The net benefits of the Doi Moi reforms can also be considered mixed when judged against the Millennium Development Goals (MDGs) (Feeny and Clarke, 2006). The MDGs are a set of eight internationally agreed goals emanating from a number of development-related conferences held during the 1990s. Designed to improve the welfare of the poor in developing countries, the MDGs include: (a) eradicating extreme poverty and hunger; (b) achieving universal primary education; (c) promoting gender equality; (d) reducing child mortality; (e) improving maternal health; (f) combating HIV/AIDS, malaria, and other diseases; (g) ensuring environmental sustainability; and (h) developing a global partnership for development. In addition to the eight MDGs, 18 Targets and 48 Indicators have also been codified as a means of national performance assessment.

To Vietnam's credit, it has significantly reduced the proportion of its population that is undernourished from 31 per cent in 1991 to 19 per cent in 2001 (UNDP, 2005). In addition, the rate of under-five mortality has improved from 53 per 1000 live births in 1990 to 23 per 1000 live births in 2003. Levels of gender representation in primary and secondary schools are also approaching equality. However, it is unlikely that, on present trends, Vietnam will achieve a desired reduction in maternal morality, having reduced the rate only slightly from 160 per 100 000 live births in 1990 to 130 per 100 000 live births in 2000. Nor is Vietnam likely to achieve targets in terms of access to clean water and sanitation, with no improved access for around one-quarter of the population since 1990.

As for any progress reflected by the Human Development Index (HDI), Vietnam has steadily improved its HDI from 0.617 in 1990 to 0.709 in 2006 as well as its overall ranking from 120th to 108th in the world over the same period (UNDP, 2006). But while there has been a noticeable decline in political repression in Vietnam, corruption levels have risen, and the latter has no doubt impacted negatively on the productivity and sustainability of the Vietnamese economy (Beresford, 2004).

Clearly, despite rapid expansion of the Vietnamese economy over the past two decades, the social and environmental costs associated with this growth have not been fully considered. As explained in Chapter 2, GDP fails to explicitly incorporate the many externalities of growth that may impact negatively, or in some instances positively, on the economic, social, and/or environmental spheres pertaining to a nation's sustainable welfare. It is for this reason that a GPI needs to be estimated for Vietnam to assess whether the recently recorded growth of the Vietnamese economy has increased its sustainable welfare and, if so, the extent to which this has been the case.

THE GENUINE PROGRESS INDICATOR FOR VIETNAM, 1992–2004

Introduction

The GPI that has been calculated for Vietnam relates to the period from 1992 to 2004.[1] It is therefore restricted to the post-Doi Moi reform era, thus making it difficult to draw conclusions about the full impact of the reforms on Vietnam's genuine progress. The truncated nature of the study period was due entirely to data constraints. While data on macroeconomic indicators was available, disaggregated data was difficult to access. As for social and environmental data, in many instances it did not exist, particularly pre-1990.

In order to calculate GPI for Vietnam, data was drawn largely from the Government Statistics Office (GSO) and the Ministry of Natural Resources and Environment (MONRE). Where data could not be located from these official sources, alternative independent research sources were used. The items and the various valuation methods used to estimate Vietnam's GPI are set out in Table 11.1. The methodology and rationale for the items included in the GPI are essentially the same as those explained in Chapter 3.

The Calculation of the GPI Items

Consumption expenditure (private and public) and defensive and rehabilitative expenditure (DRE)

Aggregated data for private and public consumption expenditure (Item *a*) was drawn straight from the national accounts published by the GSO of Vietnam (GSO, various). Defensive, rehabilitative, and non-welfare-contributing expenditure (DRE) (Item *b*) was assumed to be 10 per cent of total consumption expenditure. This is a very conservative estimate when compared to most GPI studies.[2]

Table 11.1 Items and valuation methods used to calculate the GPI for Vietnam, 1992–2004

Item	Welfare contribution	Method of valuation
Item *a*: Consumption expenditure (*CON*)	+	*CON* = private sector + public sector consumption expenditure
Item *b*: Defensive and rehabilitative expenditures (*DRE*)	–	*DRE* was assumed to equal 10% of all consumption expenditure
Item *c*: Expenditure on consumer durables (*ECD*)	–	*ECD* equals the sum of all household expenditure on consumer durables
Item *d*: Service from consumer durables (*SCD*)	+	Equal to the net present depreciation value of the existing stock of consumer durables (assumed that stock endures for 10 years; discount rate of 7%) • *SCD* = 0.142 × value of consumer durables
Item *e*: Adjusted consumption	+	Timing adjustment to consumption benefits • *Adjusted CON* = *CON* – *DRE* – *ECD* + *SCD*
Item *f*: Distribution Index (*DI*)	+/–	*DI* based on the change in income distribution over the study period as measured by the Gini co-efficient (first year of study period has an index value of 100)
Item *g*: Adjusted consumption (weighted) (**)	+	Adjusted CON weighted by the Distribution Index • *Adjusted CON* ÷ *DI* × 100
Item *h*: Welfare generated by publicly-provided infrastructure (*WPPI*) (**)	+	Welfare assumed to equal 75% of public sector consumption of fixed capital

Table 11.1 (continued)

Item	Welfare contribution	Method of valuation
Item *i*: Value of non-paid household labour (**)	+	Non-paid labour is valued using the net opportunity cost method • Equal to the number of non-paid labour hours × average wage valued at 1994 prices
Item *j*: Value of volunteer labour (**)	+	Volunteer labour is valued using the net opportunity cost method • Equal to the number of volunteer hours × exclusion fee to avoid compulsory community service
Item *k*: Cost of unemployment and underemployment (**)	–	Calculated by multiplying the total number of unworked hours pertaining to unemployed and underemployed labour by the minimum wage rate (GSO, various)
Item *l*: Cost of corruption (**)	–	The direct cost of corruption is assumed to be worth 2.5% of Vietnam's real GDP (i.e., *real GDP* × 0.025)
Item *m*: Change in net foreign debt position (**)	+/–	Annual cost (benefit) is equal to the average change in net foreign liabilities over the previous five-year period
Item *n*: Cost of non-renewable resource depletion (*)	–	Calculated by using the El Serafy (1989) 'user cost' formula to determine the amount to set aside to sustain a flow of income equal to that generated by the exhausted resource • Equal to value of non-renewable resource extraction × 0.89
Item *o*: Cost of lost agricultural land (*)	–	Calculated to reflect the amount required to compensate citizens for the cumulative impact of past and present agricultural practices • Annual cost equal to 7% of the value of agricultural output (Khor, n.d.). The annual cost is accumulated to satisfy the strong sustainability condition that: (a) human-made capital is not a substitute for natural capital; and (b) agricultural land has no natural capital replacement

Table 11.1 (continued)

Item	Welfare contribution	Method of valuation
Item *p*: Cost of timber depletion (*)	–	Calculated by using the El Serafy (1989) 'user cost' formula to reflect the opportunity cost of lower timber stocks brought about by harvesting rates exceeding the rate of timber regeneration and plantation establishment • Equal to value of timber depletion × 0.64 (based on assumption that timber stocks would be fully exhausted in 50 years at current harvesting rates; and the regeneration rate of timber stocks is 2% per annum)
Item *q*: Cost of air pollution (*)	–	Calculated by multiplying the annual expenditure on air pollution mitigation by a factor of five
Item *r*: Cost of urban waste-water pollution (*)	–	Calculated by multiplying the annual cost associated with the mitigation of urban waste-water pollution by a factor of five
Item *s*: Cost of long-term environmental damage (*)	–	Calculated to reflect the amount required to compensate citizens for the long-term environmental impact of energy consumption
Item *t*: Lost natural capital services (*LNCS*) (**)	–	Sum of (*) items. The *LNCS* sub-total reflects the cost of the sacrificed source, sink, and life-support services provided by natural capital
Item *u*: Genuine Progress Indicator (GPI)	+	Sum of (**) items beginning with Adjusted CON (weighted)
Item *v*: Population		Population of Vietnam
Item *w*: Per capita GPI	+	GPI ÷ population

Expenditure on consumer durables (ECD) and the service from the existing stock of consumer durables (SCD)

The expenditure on consumer durables (ECD) (Item *c*) was estimated using data drawn from the Vietnam Living Standards Surveys (VLSS, various). Four of these surveys have been conducted in Vietnam in recent times – in 1992–93, 1997–98, 2002, and 2003–04. Since there were only four surveys during the study period, the value of each expenditure category in the intervening years was estimated by assuming that the share of the corresponding commodity structure was the same as the most recent prior survey.

The service derived from the existing stock of consumer durables (SCD) (Item *d*) was calculated by multiplying the start-of-year stock value by 0.142. This approach was based on a discount rate of 7 per cent and the assumption that the average consumer durable has a life of ten years (see Chapter 2 for an explanation).

The Distribution Index (DI)

The Distribution Index (DI) (Item *f*) was estimated for Vietnam utilising the Gini coefficient calculated from the Vietnam Living Standards Surveys (VLSS, various). Because there were only four surveys during the study period, it was assumed that the income distribution (Gini coefficient) between the survey years remained unchanged.

Based on the method outlined in Chapter 3, the DI was assigned a value of 100 for 1992, the first year of the study period. It was then weighted by the change in the Gini coefficient so that a rise/fall in the DI signified a growing/diminishing disparity between the incomes of Vietnam's rich and poor.

Welfare from publicly-provided infrastructure (WPPI)

The welfare from publicly-provided infrastructure (WPPI) (Item *h*) was estimated firstly by multiplying the consumption of fixed capital (i.e., depreciation of human-made capital) by the ratio of public to private sector investment. This was done on the assumption that the ratio of public to private sector investment reflects the relative difference between the public sector and private sector ownership of human-made capital. The value obtained was then multiplied by 0.75 on the assumption that 75 per cent of all government investment spending is on infrastructural capital and the remaining 25 per cent on producer goods.

Social benefits: the value of non-paid household labour and volunteer labour

The value of non-paid household labour (Item *i*) was determined by a four-stage process. The first stage involved the estimation of the average number of non-paid household labour hours undertaken by one person in a week. This was obtained directly from the Vietnam Living Standards Surveys (VLSS, various).[3] The second stage involved the multiplication of the per capita weekly number by 52 to obtain the per capita annual number. Since most non-paid household work is undertaken by active adults, the third stage involved the multiplication of the per capita annual number by the Vietnamese population aged above 15 years. The final stage involved the multiplication of the total annual number of non-paid household labour hours by the average wage.

To estimate the value of volunteer labour (Item *j*), an innovative method was used. Within Vietnam, there are a specified number of hours that all citizens must legally perform. Widely understood as 'work for public benefit', there is, within the system, an option to pay an annual fee to exclude oneself from this compulsory community service. The 'exclusion fee' can thus be used as a proxy for the value of volunteer work. To estimate the annual value of volunteer labour in Vietnam, the number of people required to work for public benefit, as set out in the regulation, was multiplied by the exclusion fee.

Social costs: the cost of unemployment, underemployment, and corruption

The cost of unemployment (Item *k*) was estimated by multiplying the number of unemployed workers (based on the official unemployment rate as defined by the GSO) with the minimum wage rate. As for calculating the cost of underemployment – the difference between the number of hours employees would like to work and the number actually worked – the same method was adopted. In other words, the number of unemployed hours was multiplied by the minimum wage rate.

Two items traditionally included in the GPI are the cost of crime and family breakdown. Unfortunately, the data related to these two social cost categories does not exist in Vietnam. Both items have consequently been replaced by an item to reflect the cost of corruption (Item *l*). This item was included because, as explained earlier, corruption is a growing social issue in Vietnam with significant productivity and sustainability implications for the Vietnamese economy.

To calculate an appropriate value for this item, it was assumed that the total cost of corruption is equivalent to 10 per cent of Vietnam's real GDP. However, it was also recognised that the total cost of corruption is reflected, to a large extent, by a number of other GPI items. For example, any constraints that corruption imposes on the efficiency and productivity improvements of the Vietnamese economy are borne out in terms of a lower than expected consumption level. Similarly, corruption that permits pollutive and ecologically destructive forms of production is borne out in terms of higher than expected environmental costs. To avoid double-counting, it was assumed that 75 per cent of the total cost of corruption is reflected in other GPI items. This implies that the direct cost of corruption is equivalent to 2.5 per cent of real GDP (i.e., equal to *real GDP* × 0.025).

Change in net foreign debt

The change in the net foreign debt position of Vietnam (Item *m*) was drawn straight from the national accounting data (GSO, various).

Cost of non-renewable resource depletion

The cost of non-renewable resource depletion (Item *n*) was calculated using the El Serafy 'user cost' formula from Chapter 3 (equation 3.12). In order to employ the formula, it was assumed that the appropriate discount rate was 2 per cent (i.e., based on strong sustainability) and that the average life of each non-renewable resource type was 40 years. It was also assumed that markets undervalue resource prices by 50 per cent. Hence, the cost of non-renewable resource depletion was equal to 88.8 per cent of the total value of all mining production. The data on mining production was extracted from the GSO annual statistical year books (GSO, various).

Cost of lost agricultural land and timber depletion

In Vietnam, significant areas of agricultural land have been lost as a result of industrialisation, urbanisation, and unsustainable land use practices. There has, unfortunately, been no reliable study on the cost of soil erosion in Vietnam to date. However, Khor (n.d.) has argued that annual soil degradation losses across the East Asia region amount to around 7 per cent of agricultural output. This study has therefore been used to estimate the cost of lost agricultural land (Item *o*) over the study period.

Assuming a strong sustainability stance and given that no substitute resource exists for agricultural land, the annual cost was accumulated. It was assumed that the cumulative cost at the end of 1991 (beginning of the study period in 1992) was 5000 billion VND. The annual cost was then added to obtain the accumulated cost for each year over the study period.

The cost of timber depletion for Vietnam (Item *p*) was calculated by multiplying the annual value of lost timber production due to deforestation by 0.64. The value of 0.64 was derived using the El Serafy user cost formula and by assuming: (a) the discount rate or natural regeneration rate of timber stocks is 2 per cent (strong sustainability stance); and (b) that unreserved timber stocks will be fully exhausted in 50 years at current harvesting rates despite recent reforestation measures.[4]

Cost of air pollution and urban waste water pollution

The lack of information about air pollution in Vietnam prevents any direct calculation of the cost of air pollution. As a substitute means of estimation, the annual private and public sector expenditure on air pollution mitigation was utilised. Based on the approach used in some GPI studies, it was assumed that the total cost of air pollution was five times the mitigation cost.

A similar approach was adopted to estimate the cost of urban waste-water pollution. However, a further step was required given that the base line data on urban waste-water pollution expenditure was confined to the period between 1996 and 2004. To estimate the urban waste-water pollution expenditure for each year between 1992 and 1996, it was assumed that the change in expenditure over this period was equal to the average annual change in expenditure between 1996 and 2004. The annual values were then multiplied by a factor of five.

Cost of long-term environmental damage

The cost of long-term environmental damage was calculated by converting Vietnam's annual energy consumption (in thousands of tonnes of oil equivalent) to Petajoules (WRI, http://earthtrends.wri.org). This was then converted to millions of crude oil barrels and multiplied by 2500 VND to yield the yearly environmental cost. To obtain the annual cumulative long-term environmental cost, it was assumed that the cumulative cost at the end of 1991 (beginning of the study period in 1992) was 10 000 billion VND.

RESULTS OF THE VIETNAMESE GPI STUDY

The results of the GPI study on Vietnam are summarised in Table 11.2 (valued at 1994 prices). Columns *Y* and *Z* reveal the values of Vietnam's per capita GPI and per capita GDP over the study period. Both are also illustrated in Figure 11.1. Table 11.2 and Figure 11.1 show that Vietnam's per capita GDP began at a value of 2.22 million VND in 1992. It then rose quite significantly in every year to be 4.42 million VND by 2004. Altogether, Vietnam's per capita GDP increased by 99.3 per cent over the study period.

Vietnam's per capita GPI, on the other hand, began in 1992 at 1.78 million VND and grew overall by 26.4 per cent to be 2.26 million VND by 2004. Apart from being much lower and rising at a much reduced rate than per capita GDP, Vietnam's per capita GPI fell in four years over the study period – namely, 1997, 1998, 1999, and 2001. Importantly, per capita GPI was only marginally higher in 2004 (2.26 million VND) than it was in 1996 (2.15 million VND). From this information, it can be quite safely concluded that Vietnam's per capita GDP overstated the genuine progress experienced in Vietnam over the study period and that the growth in economic activity fostered by the Doi Moi reforms and recent economic liberalisation policies has translated poorly in terms of Vietnam's sustainable welfare.

The decelerated increase in Vietnam's per capita GPI after 1996 is even more starkly revealed in Figure 11.2 where a comparison is drawn between the index values of per capita GPI and per capita GDP (columns *AA* and *BB* in Table 11.2). It can clearly be seen from the figure that the trend rate of change in both index values was very similar between 1992 and 1996. From 1996 onwards, there was a significant departure in the trend values of both indexes. Whilst the index of per capita GDP continued to rise, the index of per capita GPI declined from a value of 120.6 in 1996 to a value of 110.7 in 2001. The per capita GPI index recovered thereafter to reach a value of 126.4 in 2004. Overall, Figures 11.1 and 11.2 indicate an emerging break in the nexus between Vietnam's per capita volume of economic activity and the rate of its genuine progress.

Table 11.2 Genuine Progress Indicator (GPI) and real GDP for Vietnam, 1992–2004

Year	CON (bill.VND) *A*	DRE (bill.VND) *B*	ECD (bill.VND) *C*	Consumer durables (bill.VND) *D*	SCD (bill.VND) *E*	Adjusted CON (bill.VND) *(A + B + C + E)* *F*	Distribution Index (DI) 1992 = 100 *G*	Weighted Adj.CON (bill.VND) *(F/G) x 100* *H*	WPPI (bill.VND) *I*	Non-paid h/h labour (bill.VND) *J*
1991	-	-	-	147 174.5	-	-	-	-	-	-
1992	130 884.7	-13 088.5	-18 167.6	153 447.5	20 898.8	120 527.4	100.0	120 527.4	3 376.1	48 507.6
1993	136 512.3	-13 651.2	-18 794.9	159 720.5	21 789.5	125 855.7	101.5	124 056.9	4 932.8	49 439.9
1994	148 037.0	-14 803.7	-20 341.4	166 912.7	22 680.3	135 572.2	102.9	131 738.6	9 943.1	50 372.3
1995	159 973.3	-15 997.3	-21 974.0	175 110.2	23 701.6	145 703.6	104.4	139 616.3	14 464.2	51 299.4
1996	177 040.6	-17 704.1	-24 397.3	185 103.7	24 865.6	159 804.9	105.8	151 015.8	18 276.6	52 214.9
1997	184 778.0	-18 477.8	-27 543.1	197 615.7	26 284.7	165 041.8	107.3	153 856.5	22 247.4	53 122.2
1998	192 037.8	-19 203.8	-28 646.1	210 603.4	28 061.4	172 249.3	111.3	154 803.0	23 495.2	54 037.6
1999	193 314.8	-19 331.5	-29 009.1	223 326.8	29 905.7	174 879.9	115.3	151 713.3	24 743.0	54 981.5
2000	199 436.3	-19 943.6	-29 896.6	236 310.4	31 712.4	181 308.5	119.3	152 015.2	29 601.9	55 965.5
2001	208 239.3	-20 823.9	-31 150.2	249 920.3	33 556.1	189 821.2	123.3	153 988.2	30 064.2	56 989.3
2002	223 053.8	-22 305.4	-26 393.3	258 146.0	35 488.7	209 843.8	127.3	164 880.8	30 114.9	58 041.1
2003	244 035.7	-24 403.6	-30 423.0	269 774.1	36 656.7	225 865.9	128.2	176 209.9	32 996.6	59 104.9
2004	259 027.8	-25 902.8	-32 242.9	281 675.6	38 307.9	239 190.0	129.1	185 289.4	36 460.0	60 163.0

Table 11.2 (continued)

	Volunteer labour (bill.VND)	Cost of unemp. (bill.VND)	Cost of corruption (bill.VND)	Change in foreign debt (bill.VND)	Non-renew. R depletion (bill.VND)	Land degradation (bill.VND)	Timber depletion (bill.VND)	Air pollution (bill.VND)	Urban w/w pollution (bill.VND)	L-T env. damage (bill.VND)
Year	*K*	*L*	*M*	*N*	*O*	*P*	*Q*	*R*	*S*	*T*
1991	-	-	-	-	-	-	-	-	-	-
1992	1 202.6	-5 434.4	-3 794.6	-17 185.9	-6 470.1	-5 310.7	-1 629.9	- 146.9	- 958.5	-10 457.4
1993	1 042.2	-4 709.4	-4 101.1	-15 024.9	-7 493.4	-5 601.4	-1 525.8	- 125.1	- 884.1	-10 935.4
1994	906.2	-3 365.6	-4 463.4	-14 737.3	-8 093.2	-5 888.4	-1 440.0	- 107.0	-4 361.7	-11 434.2
1995	787.0	-2 923.1	-4 889.2	-15 032.9	-8 352.7	-6 202.5	-1 543.8	- 91.4	-5 591.6	-11 953.6
1996	735.7	-2 677.9	-5 345.8	-14 535.9	-10 666.9	-6 557.2	-2 346.2	- 84.1	-9 981.2	-12 493.8
1997	701.0	-3 129.7	-6 221.0	-13 368.0	-12 944.1	-6 909.9	-2 256.4	- 256.1	-14 966.6	-13 054.6
1998	654.1	-3 328.2	-5 870.3	-13 171.4	-14 557.1	-7 283.2	-2 284.6	- 252.9	-14 834.9	-13 636.1
1999	628.0	-3 144.0	-6 406.8	-12 184.7	-19 177.2	-7 666.8	-2 337.1	- 641.4	-14 178.1	-14 238.2
2000	615.5	-3 669.1	-6 568.0	-10 032.0	-23 443.9	-8 060.2	-2 329.5	- 686.1	-14 116.2	-14 878.3
2001	611.9	-4 162.8	-7 313.4	-10 187.4	-23 934.5	-8 455.5	-2 354.5	-2 348.0	-11 855.6	-15 557.2
2002	596.4	-3 882.9	-7 204.7	-7 895.7	-23 962.3	-8 876.1	-2 416.1	-1 869.8	-13 121.5	-16 274.9
2003	567.4	-4 905.8	-7 733.6	-7 052.0	-27 902.5	-9 317.8	-2 709.4	-2 167.0	-13 610.9	-17 031.4
2004	531.8	-4 455.1	-9 060.9	-6 669.2	-32 616.8	-9 778.6	-3 031.8	-1 590.1	-12 206.2	-17 826.8

Table 11.2 (continued)

Year	LNCS (bill.VND)	GPI (bill.VND)	Real GDP (bill.VND)	Population (000s)	Per capita GPI (000s VND) *(V/X)*	Per capita GDP (000s VND) *(W/X)*	Per capita GPI 1992 = 100	Per capita GDP 1992 = 100	Growth rate of p.c. GPI (%)	Growth rate of p.c. GDP (%)
	U	*V*	*W*	X	*Y*	*Z*	*AA*	*BB*	*CC*	*DD*
1991	-	-	-	-	-	-	-	-	-	-
1992	-24 973.5	122 225.4	151 782.0	68 450.1	1 785.6	2 217.4	100.0	100.0	-	-
1993	-26 565.3	129 071.2	164 043.0	69 644.5	1 853.3	2 355.4	103.8	106.2	3.8	6.2
1994	-31 324.5	139 069.5	178 534.0	70 824.5	1 963.6	2 520.8	110.0	113.7	6.0	7.0
1995	-33 735.6	149 586.2	195 567.0	71 995.5	2 077.7	2 716.4	116.4	122.5	5.8	7.8
1996	-42 129.3	157 554.2	213 832.0	73 156.7	2 153.7	2 922.9	120.6	131.8	3.7	7.6
1997	-50 387.6	156 820.9	231 263.0	74 306.9	2 110.4	3 112.3	118.2	140.4	-2.0	6.5
1998	-52 848.8	157 771.3	244 594.0	75 456.3	2 090.9	3 241.5	117.1	146.2	-0.9	4.2
1999	-58 238.8	152 091.5	256 272.0	76 596.7	1 985.6	3 345.7	111.2	150.9	-5.0	3.2
2000	-63 514.1	154 414.8	273 666.0	77 635.4	1 989.0	3 525.0	111.4	159.0	0.2	5.4
2001	-64 505.2	155 484.7	292 535.0	78 685.8	1 976.0	3 717.8	110.7	167.7	-0.7	5.5
2002	-66 520.7	168 129.2	313 247.0	79 727.4	2 108.8	3 929.0	118.1	177.2	6.7	5.7
2003	-72 739.1	176 448.4	336 242.0	80 902.4	2 181.0	4 156.1	122.1	187.4	3.4	5.8
2004	-77 050.3	185 208.7	362 435.0	82 031.7	2 257.8	4 418.2	126.4	199.3	3.5	6.3

Note: Values are in billions of Vietnamese dong (VND) at 1994 prices unless otherwise stated.

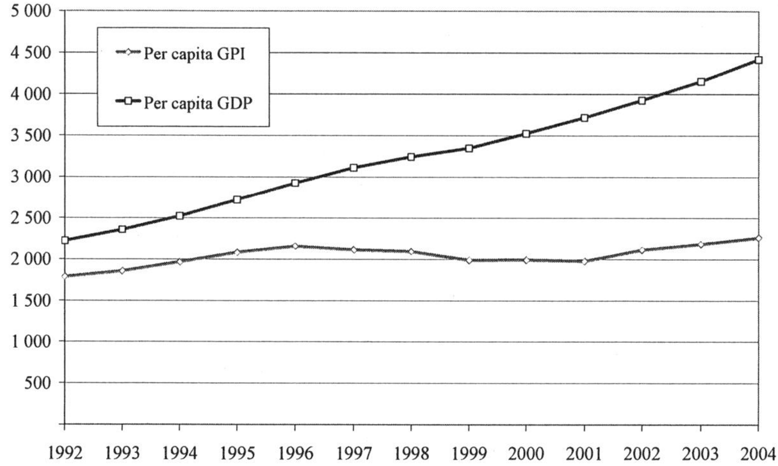

Note: Valued in thousands of Vietnamese dong at 1994 prices.

Figure 11.1 Per capita GPI versus per capita GDP: Vietnam, 1992–2004

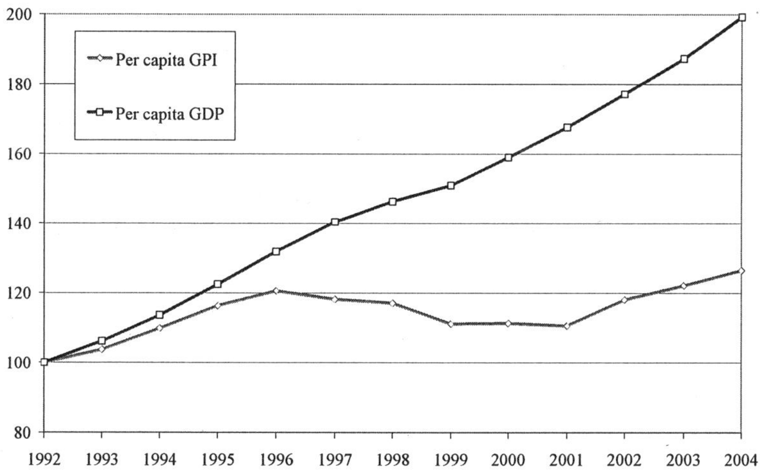

Note: 1992 = 100.

Figure 11.2 Index values of per capita GPI and per capita GDP: Vietnam, 1992–2004

UNDERSTANDING VIETNAM'S GPI AND ITS POLICY IMPLICATIONS

In this section, we aim to explain the reasons for the fluctuations in Vietnam's per capita GPI and the main factors impeding the rise in Vietnam's per capita GPI after 1996. To do so, we will examine the component items that make up the GPI to determine which had the greatest impact on the overall trend movement of Vietnam's per capita GPI. Understanding the reasons for the divergence between the two indices can assist greatly in determining the policy implications that emerge from this GPI study on Vietnam.

Analysis of Vietnam's GPI

Consumption-related welfare

As explained in Chapter 3, various adjustments are made to the sum total of private and public consumption expenditure to determine its genuine welfare contribution (Items *a–g* in Table 11.1). To recall, these adjustments include the subtraction of defensive and rehabilitative expenditures (DRE), the subtraction of all current expenditure on consumer durables (ECD), and the addition of the services from the existing stock of consumer durables (SCD) (equation 3.6). Once these adjustments have been made, the adjusted consumption value is then weighted by a Distribution Index (DI) (equation 3.7).

Columns *F* and *H* in Table 11.2 reveal a growing disparity between the unweighted and weighted consumption values that is particularly evident from 1997 onwards. This divergence suggests a weakening in the relationship between the level of consumption and its overall welfare contribution. There are two main reasons for this. The first and most obvious factor is the rise in the DI (column *G* in Table 11.2). Over the study period, the DI increased from 100 to 129.1 which implies that the distribution of income in Vietnam deteriorated by 29.1 per cent between 1992 and 2004 (i.e., income inequality increased). This had a significant negative impact on the weighted value of adjusted consumption. For example, while the value in 2004 of Vietnam's adjusted consumption expenditure was 239 190 billion VND, its welfare contribution was a much lower 185 289 billion VND.

The second major influence can be attributed to the change in Vietnamese consumption patterns. Towards the end of the study period, a much greater proportion of private consumption involved expenditure on such commodities as energy, private vehicles, the hospitality industry, and transportation services. There was, as a consequence, an increasing level of defensive expenditure that did not directly contribute to a rise in human welfare.

Welfare from publicly-provided infrastructure

The welfare from publicly-provided infrastructure (WPPI) rose rapidly during the study period (column *I* in Table 11.2). Overall, the value of this item increased from 3376 to 36 460 billion VND suggesting that the increase in the government provision of infrastructural capital played a significant positive role in the genuine progress experienced in Vietnam between 1992 and 2004.

Two additional measures highlight the growing contribution of WPPI towards Vietnam's GPI. In the first instance, Vietnam's WPPI began in 1992 at just 16.2 per cent of the service provided by the existing stock of consumer durables (SCD). By 2004, it had grown to be 95.2 per cent of SCD. Secondly, the ratio of Vietnam's WPPI to GPI increased from a paltry 2.8 per cent in 1992 to 19.7 per cent by 2004. While, as we shall soon see, the rise in this ratio had much to do with the dramatic increase in many costs that consequently impeded the rise in Vietnam's GPI, it undoubtedly reflected the increase in the Vietnam Government's willingness to invest in vital public assets, such as health and education facilities.

The value of non-paid labour

The value of non-paid household labour increased gradually over the entire study period while the contribution from volunteer labour declined (columns *J* and *K* from Table 11.2).[5] Given that the value of volunteer labour was comparatively smaller in magnitude – just 1–2 per cent of the value of household labour – the overall value of non-paid labour rose steadily over the study period. It began at a value of 49 710 billion VND in 1992 and increased to be 60 695 billion VND by 2004. Non-paid labour thus constituted a major component of Vietnam's GPI, yet reflects a significant dimension of Vietnam's shadow economy that generally goes unrecognised. Given the projected rise in Vietnam's population, the value of non-paid labour is likely to continue rising into the future, although its relative contribution to Vietnam's genuine progress will more than likely decline, having already fallen from 41 per cent of the GPI in 1992 to 33 per cent in 2004.

Social costs of unemployment, underemployment, and corruption

Collectively, the cost of unemployment and underemployment had little bearing on the trend movement of Vietnam's GPI (column *L* in Table 11.2). After declining from 5434 billion VND in 1992 to 2678 billion VND in 1996, the cost of unemployment (broadly defined) increased in most years to be 4455 billion VND in 2004. However, at never more than 4.5 per cent of the value of Vietnam's GPI, the cost of unemployment and underemployment was too small to play a significant role in the latter's fluctuating fortunes.

This in no way suggests that unemployment and underemployment are not important social issues in Vietnam. Indeed, much of the poverty existing in pockets of various urban centres can very much be blamed on a lack of employment opportunities. Since unemployment has also contributed to the widening income gap between Vietnam's rich and poor, it is a social cost requiring the constant attention of policy-makers.

The overall impact of corruption in Vietnam (column *M* in Table 11.2) is a more difficult problem to assess since it has been assumed that the direct cost of corruption constitutes just 25 per cent of the total cost of corruption. To recall, this approach was adopted to avoid some degree of double counting on the basis that 75 per cent of the total cost of corruption (i.e., the indirect cost of corruption) is reflected by other GPI items. This aside, the direct cost of corruption rose from 3795 billion VND in 1992 to 9061 billion VND by 2004, which amounts to a 238.8 per cent increase over the study period.

Not unlike the cost of unemployment (broadly defined), the direct cost of corruption had very little impact on the overall trend value of Vietnam's GPI. However, given the magnitude of its increase and its broader implications, there is little doubt that corruption has greatly reduced the extent of Vietnam's genuine progress and has also impeded its rate of increase. There is, therefore, an urgent need for Vietnamese policy-makers to implement a range of anti-corruption measures to enhance Vietnam's future progress.

Change in net foreign debt

Vietnam's net foreign debt grew throughout the study period (column *N* in Table 11.2). This indicates a rise in the foreign ownership of Vietnam's productive capital that, in turn, represents a reduction in Vietnam's long-term capacity to sustain its welfare into the future. Having said this, the extent of the increase in net foreign debt diminished in each year during the study period except in 1994 and 2001. Overall, the increase in Vietnam's net foreign debt declined from a high of 17 186 billion VND in 1992 to a low of 6669 billion VND in 2004. This decline had a minor positive impact on the trend change in Vietnam's GPI in the sense that the deduction made for this particular item in the calculation of the GPI decreased in all but the two just mentioned years during the study period. The positive impact occurred primarily because of the recent growth in Vietnam's export revenue.

Cost of non-renewable resource depletion, lost agricultural land, and timber depletion

Over the last 15 years, Vietnam has taken measures to protect its natural forests as well as to undertake a national reforestation programme. Regrettably, deforestation still continues although not nearly as intensely as it did during the 1980s. Nevertheless, the cost of timber depletion grew from 1630 billion VND in 1992 to 3032 billion VND in 2004 (column *Q* in Table 11.2). This increase was not, however, sufficient in size to have any major impact on the trend movement in Vietnam's GPI.

More disconcertingly, Vietnam experienced a fivefold increase in the cost of its non-renewable resource depletion (column *O* in Table 11.2). By 2004, this item amounted to 32 617 billion VND, by far the largest of Vietnam's environmental costs. Given that there has been no significant expansion of Vietnam's renewable resource stocks to offset these losses, Vietnam is clearly failing to meet the strong sustainability condition of having to keep its natural capital intact.

This stark conclusion is compounded by the constant rise in land degradation in Vietnam over the study period (column *P* in Table 11.2). While not nearly as significant in magnitude as the cost of non-renewable resource depletion (9779 billion VND in 2004), the losses emanating from land degradation are large enough to pose a significant threat to Vietnam's future prosperity in view of the agricultural sector's 20 per cent contribution towards the nation's total economic output. Although the recently reduced rates of deforestation and the use of previously idle land for agricultural activities should offset some of the recent impacts of land degradation, considerably more needs to be done to encourage the uptake of sustainable land use practices.

Cost of air pollution, urban waste-water pollution, and long-term environmental damage

The cost of air and urban waste-water pollution in Vietnam has grown rapidly as a result of accelerated industrialisation and urbanisation following the 1986 Doi Moi reforms (columns *R* and *S* in Table 11.2). The statistics, however, show that the cost of air pollution increased at a much slower rate over the study period than the cost of waste-water pollution. It is highly conceivable that this discrepancy could be the result of the estimation method used in this study to calculate the cost of both forms of pollution which involved a reliance on pollution control expenditure as an indicator of pollution costs. As it turned out, the expenditure on waste-water pollution control in urban centres accounted for a major proportion of total environmental expenditure in Vietnam. Statistics reveal that the expenditure on waste-water pollution accounted for 85 per cent and 62 per cent of total environmental expenditure during the periods of 1996–2000 and 2001–04 respectively. Meanwhile, expenditure on air pollution constituted only 3 per cent and 10 per cent of total environmental expenditure during the same periods.

This aside, the rising cost of urban waste-water pollution was significant enough to have a considerable negative impact on Vietnam's GPI, particularly between 1993 and 1997 when the cost rose from 884 to 14 967 billion VND. Following 1997, the cost of urban waste-water pollution fell annually to be 11 856 billion VND in 2001 before rising again to 13 611 billion VND in 2003. In 2004, the final year of the study period, the cost of urban waste-water pollution fell once more to 12 206 billion VND.

Whilst the cost of air pollution fluctuated more wildly over the study period than waster-water pollution, its highest value was a mere 2348 billion VND in 2001. In all, the cost of air pollution was too small to have had any bearing on the trend change in Vietnam's GPI.

As for the cost of long-term environmental damage (column *T* in Table 11.2), it increased gradually but significantly over the study period. Beginning at a value of 10 457 billion VND in 1992, it grew to 17 827 billion VND by 2004. Being one of the larger environmental costs, it had a major negative impact on Vietnam's GPI. With Vietnam's real GDP expected to increase at similar rates to those experienced over the past decade, there is an urgent need for policy-makers to quell the rise in Vietnam's energy consumption and CO_2 emissions in order to limit future increases in the cost of long-term environmental damage.

Policy Implications of the Vietnamese GPI Study

Some basic policy conclusions can now be drawn from the preceding discussion as well as Figure 11.3 showing Vietnam's per capita GPI and the per capita values of its major aggregated components. As can be seen from Figure 11.3, per capita weighted consumption was almost identical to the value of Vietnam's per capita GPI. This indicates that the remaining benefits and costs of economic activity effectively offset each other over the course of the study period.[6] This does not mean that the remaining benefits and costs were irrelevant since, for example, a less significant rise in per capita lost natural capital services (LNCS) would have resulted in a much higher per capita GPI. Furthermore, there would have been a marked divergence between Vietnam's per capita GPI and per capita weighted consumption.

Nevertheless, in view of its sheer magnitude, per capita weighted consumption had a major influence on both the value of Vietnam's per capita GPI and its trend movement over the study period. One can therefore conclude that the distribution of income in Vietnam was also a key factor in the rate of Vietnam's genuine progress. Earlier in the chapter, it was explained that a 29.1 per cent deterioration in the distribution of income over the study period significantly reduced the welfare contribution of Vietnam's consumption expenditure. Had the distribution of income remained much as it was at the beginning of the study period, the per capita GPI of Vietnam would probably have been at least 20 per cent higher in the 2004.

To some extent, the deterioration in the distribution of income can be attributed to the initial Doi Moi reforms and the continuing economic liberalisation of the Vietnamese economy. This poses a dilemma for the Vietnamese Government – on the one hand, the economic reforms have played a key role in boosting Vietnam's consumption expenditure; on the other hand, they have also led to a widening gap between rich and poor. Without imposing a burden on the Vietnamese economy, policy-makers need to do more to improve the existing distribution of income as well as ensure future economic gains are more equitably shared amongst the Vietnamese population.

Figure 11.3 reveals that per capita non-paid labour remained almost unchanged over the study period. Beginning at a value of 726 225 VND per person in 1992, it increased marginally to a value of 739 894 VND per person by 2004. Whilst it clearly had a major impact on the absolute value of Vietnam's per capita GPI, it had no bearing at all on its trend

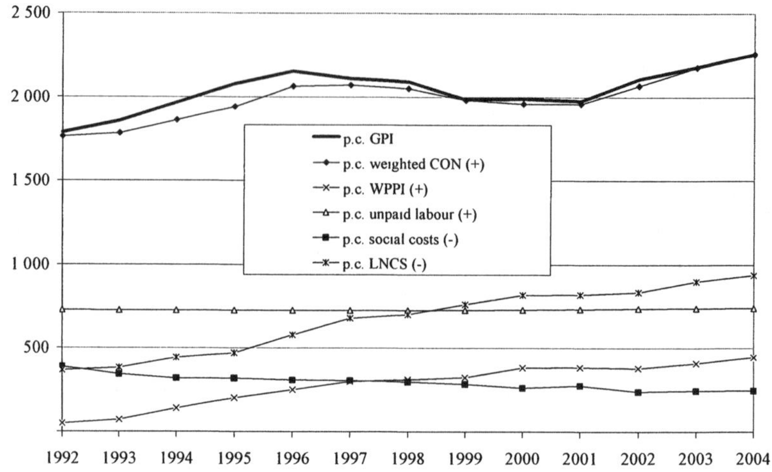

Note: Valued in thousands of Vietnamese dong at 1994 prices.

Figure 11.3 Per capita GPI and its major component categories: Vietnam, 1992–2004

movement over the study period. The same cannot be said of the per capita welfare from publicly-provided infrastructure (WPPI). It rose from a value of just 49 322 VND per person in 1992 to a value of 444 462 VND per person in 2004. Given the massive increase in the positive contribution of this item, the Vietnamese Government would be best advised to continue the strong investment in public infrastructure. Such a policy would not only generate future welfare benefits directly, it would presumably boost productivity rates throughout the economy. Moreover, if the public investment programme was well targeted, it would provide an ideal opportunity for the Vietnamese Government to take a lead on the establishment of resource-saving or 'green' infrastructural capital and technology.

In many GPI studies (e.g., Chapters 5 and 8), the net foreign debt item is included when assessing the impact of social costs on a nation's per capita GPI. The same approach has been adopted for this study given the continued rise in Vietnam's net foreign debt between 1992 and 2004. The per capita social cost curve in Figure 11.3 therefore represents the per capita value of all the major social costs incurred in Vietnam over the study period (Items *k–m* in Table 11.1). The curve indicates that Vietnam's per capita social costs declined in each year between 1992 and 2000. Per capita social costs subsequently increased in three of the last four years of the study period. However, at 231 411 VND per person in 2004, Vietnam's per capita social costs were considerably lower than they were in 1992 at 385 902 VND per person.

Despite the general fall in Vietnam's per capita social costs over the study period – due principally to the declining increase in net foreign debt – social costs constitute a policy domain that should be of significant concern and one where appropriate policy measures could do a great deal to improve Vietnam's future genuine progress. Without doubt, a further escalation in Vietnam's export revenue would assist in this regard, but it should not be forgotten that a fall in import spending arising from an import-replacement policy would have the same immediate accounting effect. So which is the better option? We believe an import-replacement policy of the kind outlined in Chapter 8 is the superior alternative since it is likely to generate more equitable and lasting gains than the archetypical export-growth policy widely recommended by most international organisations and institutions.

To better appreciate the impact of environmental degradation on Vietnam's GPI, Table 11.2 includes a sub-total (column *U*) referred to as the cost of lost natural capital services (LNCS) (sum of Items *n–s* in Table 11.1). The annual value of this column is divided by the population for the corresponding year to obtain a value of Vietnam's per capita cost of lost natural capital services (LNCS). It is this which forms the basis for the final curve to be discussed from Figure 11.3. As the curve clearly shows, Vietnam's per capita LNCS not only increased every year, but grew dramatically from 364 842 VND per person in 1992 to 939 275 VND per person in 2004. This constitutes a 257.4 per cent increase in per capita environmental costs over the study period.

Given the magnitude of this value and the extent of the increase, it is clear that the rise in Vietnam's environmental costs was instrumental in the subdued rise and, at times fall, in Vietnam's per capita GPI over the study period, particularly after 1996. It also sends a candid message that Vietnam's future rate of genuine progress will depend largely on how well it can restrict the rise in its environmental costs when, for the next two decades at least, it will require further growth of its real GDP simply to alleviate the poverty that currently exists.

To achieve this, Vietnam will need to minimise the depletion of its remaining natural capital stocks and do more to promote and facilitate increases in resource use efficiency, since the latter can reduce the environmental impact of each additional unit of economic activity. Of course, this can simply be undone by rapid population growth. Although Vietnam's population numbers are dwarfed by those of India, the projected 40 per cent rise in Vietnam's population between 2004 and 2050 (if no additional measures are taken) should ring alarm bells and indicate that Vietnam, like India, must do more to rapidly stabilise its population numbers.[7]

CONCLUDING REMARKS

This GPI study conducted on Vietnam has revealed that Vietnam's per capita GDP significantly overstated the genuine progress experienced in Vietnam over the study period (1992–2004). Moreover, any nexus that may have existed between Vietnam's per capita GDP and its rate of genuine progress appears to have been severed. The most significant reason for this appears to be the rapid rise in Vietnam's environmental costs, both at an aggregate and per capita level. A deterioration in the distribution of income has also played a key role in Vietnam's subdued performance over the study period.

Given its high poverty rate, Vietnam is a country requiring further growth of its real GDP. However, in order to gain the most from any future rises in economic activity, Vietnam will require growth that is more equitably distributed, more efficiently generated, and of superior quality (i.e., characterised by the generation of better goods rather than, in some cases, more goods). It will also need to be a form of growth that minimises the rate of natural capital depletion. This can be achieved by increasing the efficiency of natural resource use and by reinvesting a portion of Vietnam's resource depletion profits into the cultivation of suitable renewable resource assets.

In a number of chapters in this book, reference has been made of the need for countries to consider growing real GDP at a much lower rate and to eventually make the full transition to a steady-state economy. Vietnam is no exception, although it need not have to consider this for some time. Having said this, policies which bring about a more just, efficient, and 'green' economy – as we have recommended – would not only permit any future growth to translate better into genuine progress, it would also lay the foundations for a smooth transition to a steady-state economy, when the appropriate time arrives. As we see it, the benefits of this cannot be underestimated.

NOTES

1. The authors wish to thank Miss Nguyen Phuong Pien of CIEM who assisted with the data collection and estimation of adjustments.
2. In most GPI studies, defensive and rehabilitative expenditures are much nearer to 20 per cent of total consumption expenditure.
3. Because there were only four surveys during the study period, the number of non-paid household labour hours in each intervening year was estimated by assuming a straight-line change between the survey years.
4. By unreserved forests, we are referring to all timber stocks that lie outside existing National Parks and other conservation areas.
5. The fall in the value of volunteer labour does not reflect a reduced desire on the part of Vietnamese citizens to engage in volunteer work, but can instead be attributed to recent economic reforms which have reduced the compulsory form of 'volunteer work'.
6. This, we might add, is coincidental rather than something of any significance.
7. See Chapter 8 for more detail on the population stabilisation policies recommended for India.

REFERENCES

Abrami, R. and Henaff, N. (2004), 'The city and the countryside: economy, state, and socialist legacies in the Vietnamese labour market', in M. Beresford and T. Angie (eds), *Reaching for the Dream: Challenges of Sustainable Development in Vietnam*, Singapore: NIAS Press, pp. 95–134.

Beresford, M. (2004), 'Lessons from the Asian crisis for the sustainability of Vietnamese economic development', in M. Beresford and T. Angie (eds), *Reaching for the Dream: Challenges of Sustainable Development in Vietnam*, Singapore: NIAS Press, pp. 51–94.

Feeny, S. and Clarke, M. (2006), 'Will the MDGs be achieved in the Asia-Pacific region?', presented at the Education and End of Poverty Conference, RMIT University – World Vision Australia, Melbourne, 28 April.

GSO (various), *National Accounts of Vietnam*, Ha Noi: General Statistics Office of Vietnam.

Khor, M. (n.d.), 'Land degradation causes $10 billion loss to South Asia annually', http://www.twnside.org.sg/title/land-ch.htm, accessed 20 June 2006.

Masina, P. (2006), *Vietnam's Development Strategies*, Abingdon: Routledge.

Rosenberg, D., and Oegema, T. (1995), *A Pilot Index of Sustainable Economic Welfare for the Netherlands, 1952 to 1992*, Amsterdam: Institute for Environment and Systems Analysis.

Than, M. and Tan, J. (1993), 'The Vietnamese economy in transition: Introductory overview', in M. Than and J. Tan (eds), *Vietnam's Dilemmas and Options*, Singapore: Institute of Southeast Asian Studies, pp. 1–21.

Tri, V.H. (1990), *Vietnam's Economic Policy Since 1975*, Singapore: Institute of Southeast Asian Studies.

Tucker, S. (1999), *Vietnam*, London: UCL Press.

United Nations Conference on Trade and Development (UNCTAD) (2006), *World Investment Report 2006: FDI from Developing and Transition Economies: Implications for Development*, New York: United Nations.

United Nations Development Program (UNDP) (2005), *Human Development Report 2005*, New York: UNDP.

United Nations Development Program (UNDP) (2006), *Human Development Report 2006: Beyond Scarcity – Power, Poverty and the Global Water Crisis*, New York: Palgrave Macmillan.

Vinh, P.K. (1992), *Vietnam: A Comprehensive History*, San Diego, CA: The Pham Kim Vinh Research Institute.

VLSS (various), *Vietnam Living Standards Survey*, Vietnam: General Statistics Office.

Watt, A. (1968), *Vietnam: An Australian Analysis*, Melbourne: Cheshire.

Williams, M. (1992), *Vietnam at the Crossroads*, New York: Council on Foreign Relations Press.

World Resources Institute (WRI), Earthtrends Searchable Database Results, http://earthtrends.wri.org.

PART III

Genuine progress across the Asia-Pacific region

12. Genuine progress across the Asia-Pacific region: comparisons, trends, and policy implications

Philip Lawn and Matthew Clarke

INTRODUCTION

This book began by questioning whether sustainable welfare has progressed across the Asia-Pacific region at the rapid rate claimed by most development commentators. We expressed this doubt because of a concern – supported by the conflicting data revealed in Chapter 1 – that conventional macroeconomic indicators fail to reveal the full impact of a growing economy on sustainable welfare. Upon explaining why real GDP is an inadequate indicator of sustainable welfare (Chapter 2) and how the GPI overcomes the deficiencies of conventional macroeconomic indicators (Chapters 3 and 4), seven GPI case studies were presented on countries from across the Asia-Pacific region. Since these case studies include countries still in the process of industrialisation and others which have long been industrialised, we believe they provide a good overall picture of the pattern of development that has taken place within the Asia-Pacific region over the past 20 to 30 years.

Having said this, one of the weaknesses of the GPI raised in Chapter 4 was the lack of a standardised set of items and valuation techniques used in its calculation. Most readers will have detected the subtle variations between the GPI methodologies adopted for each case study and the difference in the valuation methods used to estimate the monetary values of particular items. These differences no doubt limit the conclusions that can be drawn from direct GPI comparisons of each country. For example, it is not strictly correct to say that New Zealand categorically enjoys a higher level of sustainable welfare than Japan or that India is unquestionably better off than Vietnam. It would also be misleading to suggest that the per capita GPI provides a definitive measure of a nation's sustainable welfare. But nor does the per capita GDP, and we are of the strong opinion that as imperfect as the GPI might be at this stage of its methodological development, it constitutes a far superior indicator of genuine progress.

Given this, we are prepared, at this stage, to make two bold declarations. Firstly, the case studies presented in this book indicate that a nation's per capita GDP invariably overstates the sustainable welfare it enjoys. Secondly, the rate of genuine progress experienced across the Asia-Pacific region over recent decades, while commendable, was not nearly as spectacular as the rise in per capita GDP would suggest.

Based on these premises and upfront declarations, we believe it is possible to undertake at least some form of comparative analysis and make general albeit tentative conclusions. To be clear again, we are not proposing that direct comparisons be made between all countries to determine which nation has experienced the greatest rate of genuine progress. Rather, we seek to draw some cautious lessons from the general pattern of development across the Asia-Pacific region and the relationship between the per capita GDP and the rate of genuine progress experienced by each of the studied countries. From these lessons, some basic policy recommendations and an overall course of action for the Asia-Pacific region can be deduced.

THE THRESHOLD HYPOTHESIS AND ITS IMPLICATIONS FOR THE ASIA-PACIFIC REGION

The Per Capita GPI across the Asia-Pacific Region

To assist in the upcoming discussion, we have converted the per capita GPI of the seven case study nations to 2004 International dollars (Int$).[1] The annual values are revealed in Table 12.1 and are diagrammatically presented in Figure 12.1. Figure 12.1 reveals an enormous disparity between the per capita GPI values of the wealthy countries (Australia, New Zealand, and Japan) and the poorer countries (China, India, Thailand, and Vietnam). Despite the danger associated with GPI comparisons, it would be difficult not to conclude that the sustainable welfare enjoyed by the wealthy trio far exceeds the sustainable welfare experienced by their poorer inter-regional neighbours.

Table 12.1 Per capita GPI and per capita GDP of the seven case study countries

	Australia		*New Zealand*		*Japan*		*India*		*China*		*Thailand*		*Vietnam*	
Year	p.c. GPI	p.c. GDP	p.c. GPI	p.c. GDP	p.c. GPI	p.c. GDP	p.c. GPI	p.c. GDP	p.c. GPI	p.c. GDP	p.c. GPI	p.c. GDP	p.c. GPI	p.c. GDP
1967	19 842	14 519	—	—	—	—	—	—	—	—	—	—	—	—
1968	20 167	14 999	—	—	—	—	—	—	—	—	—	—	—	—
1969	20 275	15 722	—	—	—	—	—	—	—	—	—	—	—	—
1970	20 590	16 519	13 109	12 827	5 143	12 550	—	—	861	539	—	—	—	—
1971	20 516	16 446	13 894	13 069	6 208	12 893	—	—	863	561	—	—	—	—
1972	20 788	16 790	14 026	13 164	7 337	13 784	—	—	871	570	—	—	—	—
1973	21 233	16 981	14 534	13 503	7 949	14 690	—	—	884	601	—	—	—	—
1974	**21 583**	17 386	13 948	14 216	7 232	14 336	—	—	866	603	—	—	—	—
1975	21 082	17 379	14 969	14 530	7 343	14 583	—	—	866	645	1 633	2 278	—	—
1976	20 649	17 671	15 266	14 761	7 762	15 023	—	—	857	626	1 772	2 448	—	—
1977	19 982	18 078	15 101	14 758	7 963	15 538	—	—	869	664	1 630	2 632	—	—
1978	19 256	18 028	15 281	14 341	8 569	16 202	—	—	869	732	1 709	2 834	—	—
1979	18 636	18 580	15 714	14 754	8 318	16 949	—	—	863	777	2 047	2 924	—	—
1980	18 256	18 929	15 312	15 117	7 967	18 232	—	—	871	828	2 194	3 023	—	—
1981	18 117	19 271	**16 040**	15 166	8 503	18 561	—	—	877	859	2 171	3 141	—	—
1982	17 853	19 540	15 623	15 792	8 824	18 830	—	—	901	923	2 145	3 243	—	—
1983	17 621	18 817	15 165	15 775	9 482	18 992	—	—	984	1 010	2 202	3 378	—	—
1984	17 616	19 462	14 488	16 560	10 272	19 549	—	—	995	1 149	2 196	3 497	—	—
1985	17 733	20 227	14 510	17 297	10 915	20 509	—	—	1 025	1 285	2 117	3 574	—	—
1986	17 390	20 823	14 879	17 144	11 330	21 193	—	—	1 037	1 377	2 082	3 688	—	—

Table 12.1 (continued)

Year	*Australia*		*New Zealand*		*Japan*		*India*		*China*		*Thailand*		*Vietnam*	
	p.c. GPI	p.c. GDP	p.c. GPI	p.c. GDP	p.c. GPI	p.c. GDP	p.c. GPI	p.c. GDP	p.c. GPI	p.c. GDP	p.c. GPI	p.c. GDP	p.c. GPI	p.c. GDP
1987	16 675	21 004	14 511	17 590	11 633	21 832	1 280	1 618	1 038	1 511	2 128	3 971	—	—
1988	17 170	21 729	14 192	17 748	11 678	23 209	1 299	1 740	1 105	1 656	2 213	4 410	—	—
1989	16 988	22 155	14 175	17 661	11 988	24 367	1 222	1 814	1 049	1 698	2 155	4 865	—	—
1990	17 093	22 690	13 502	17 566	12 276	25 475	1 295	1 880	1 029	1 738	2 153	5 368	—	—
1991	16 979	22 259	12 836	17 132	12 522	26 273	1 179	1 859	1 056	1 873	2 429	5 761	—	—
1992	16 918	22 009	14 185	17 086	13 121	26 452	1 287	1 919	1 073	2 115	2 503	6 137	996	1 240
1993	16 551	22 591	9 840	17 899	13 484	26 313	1 237	1 969	1 081	2 383	2 742	6 581	1 034	1 317
1994	16 722	23 271	11 879	18 570	13 310	26 425	1 341	2 076	1 132	2 666	2 854	7 080	1 096	1 410
1995	16 862	24 022	12 130	19 026	13 660	26 888	1 367	2 192	1 227	2 925	2 921	7 687	1 160	1 519
1996	17 065	24 685	12 963	19 507	13 439	27 772	1 403	2 306	1 353	3 184	3 096	8 052	1 202	1 634
1997	17 072	25 368	10 962	19 959	13 724	28 192	1 350	2 364	1 422	3 446	3 210	7 850	1 178	1 740
1998	17 051	26 230	11 857	20 058	**14 075**	27 806	1 406	2 460	1 499	3 681	3 027	6 951	1 167	1 813
1999	17 305	27 274	14 237	20 963	13 539	27 743	1 478	2 587	1 498	3 928	3 169	7 236	1 108	1 871
2000	17 573	28 022	14 208	21 344	13 427	28 337	1 439	2 639	1 481	4 226	3 222	7 302	1 110	1 971
2001	17 711	28 185	14 206	21 821	13 408	28 313	1 517	2 726	1 532	4 545	**3 492**	7 373	1 102	2 079
2002	17 949	28 907	12 911	22 457	13 518	28 209	1 460	2 790	**1 539**	4 926	3 439	7 666	1 177	2 197
2003	17 580	29 471	13 925	22 979	13 955	**28 525**	**1 562**	**2 981**	1 490	5 387	3 254	8 102	1 217	2 324
2004	18 185	30 331	14 286	23 413	—	—	—	—	1 525	5 896	3 174	**8 495**	**1 259**	**2 470**
2005	18 102	30 763	14 462	**23 537**	—	—	—	—	1 512	**6 459**	—	—	—	—
2006	18 161	**31 219**	—	—	—	—	—	—	—	—	—	—	—	—

Note: All currencies valued in International dollars (Int$) at 2004 prices.

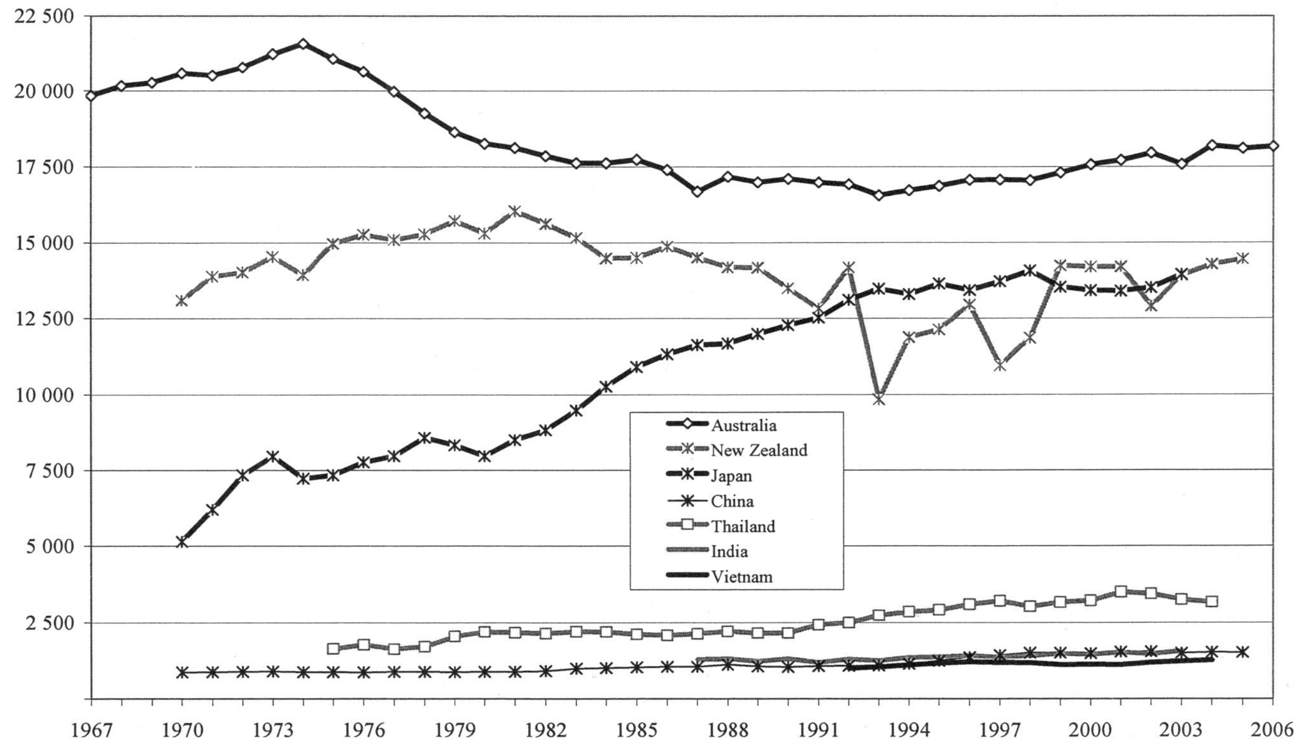

Note: Per capita GPI valued in International dollars (Int$) at 2004 prices.

Figure 12.1 Per capita GPI of selected Asia-Pacific countries

Looking specifically at the group of wealthy nations, Table 12.1 reveals that the per capita GPI of Australia and New Zealand declined for an extended period after peaking in 1974 and 1981 at Int$21 583 and Int$16 040 respectively. In both instances, the per capita GPI recovered towards the end of the study period. However, the final per capita GPI values were still well short of their peak levels; 15.8 per cent lower in the case of Australia and 9.8 per cent lower for New Zealand.

Japan began with a much inferior per capita GPI compared to Australia and New Zealand. Its per capita GPI rose quite considerably in most years but, like Australia and New Zealand, peaked prior to the end of the study period. Unlike Australia and New Zealand, Japan's per capita GPI reached its zenith of Int$14 075 much later in the study period (1998). Although Japan's per capita GPI declined overall between 1998 and 2003, it was only 0.9 per cent lower at the end of the study period than its 1998 peak value.

Turning now to the four poorer nations, Table 12.1 reveals that Thailand's per capita GPI, whilst much lower than that of Australia, New Zealand, and Japan, was at all times significantly higher than the per capita GPI of China, India, and Vietnam. As weak as conclusions drawn from GPI comparisons are when disparities between values are relatively small, it is probably safe to conclude that Thailand enjoyed a higher level of sustainable welfare over the study period than China, India, and Vietnam. However, Figure 12.1 suggests that all four poorer nations at no stage achieved the same *rate* of genuine progress that Japan experienced between 1970 and 1993, or that Australia achieved between 1967 and 1974 and New Zealand likewise between 1970 and 1981.

Of significant interest and potential importance is the evidence showing that the per capita GPI of India and Vietnam was still on the rise at the end of the study period (Int$1562 and Int$1259 respectively), but had peaked early for China in 2002 (Int$1539) and Thailand in 2001 (Int$3492). As intimated in Chapters 9 and 10, this could indicate that China and Thailand have reached a threshold level of per capita GDP where the additional costs associated with the growth of their economies are now exceeding the additional benefits.

The Relationship Between the Per Capita GPI and Per capita GDP

In order to consider the threshold hypothesis issue more closely, we have plotted the annual per capita GPI values of each surveyed country against the corresponding per capita GDP values. They appear in Figure 12.2 along with a superimposed 'line of best fit' to indicate the trend change in the relationship between the per capita GDP and the sustainable welfare experienced by each of the studied countries.[2]

Figure 12.2 reveals that Australia, New Zealand, and Japan have all reached a threshold level of per capita GDP. Despite a slight recovery in Australia and New Zealand beyond the Int$20 000 level of per capita GDP, the end-of-period trend in the relationship between per capita GDP growth and sustainable welfare was weakly negative for Australia and neutral for New Zealand. What also stands out is that Australia's per capita GPI was significantly lower in 2006 than its 1974 peak value despite its per capita GDP being much higher in 2006 at Int$31 219 compared to Int$17 386 in 1974. The same applies to New Zealand where the per capita GPI in 2005 was also much lower than its 1981 peak value even though its per capita GDP was considerably higher at Int$23 573 in 2005 compared to Int$15 166 in 1981.

Whilst Japan eventually reached a threshold level of per capita GDP, it appears to have avoided the threshold point for a considerably longer time than Australia and New Zealand. This can be attributed to two main factors. Firstly, in 1970, Japan was still completing the process of industrialisation as part of its post-war reconstruction. Unscathed by World War II, Australia and New Zealand were already fully industrialised at the beginning of their respective study periods. In a sense, Japan was still 'catching up' on Australia and New Zealand and logically took longer to reach a threshold level of per capita GDP.

Secondly, unlike Australia and New Zealand, Japan is not richly endowed with huge quantities of natural resources. It therefore relies heavily upon the importation of raw materials of which the cost is largely financed by Japan's extensive exports of manufactured products and services. Because of this pattern of trade, Japan has managed to offload many of the environmental costs associated with the growth of its economy onto other countries.[3] This is very much evidenced by the massive decline in Japan's environmental costs from ¥30 293 billion in 1970 to ¥12 377 billion in 2003. Conversely, the environmental costs of Australia and New Zealand increased over the study period.

In Chapter 7, Makino argued for the establishment of an open economy GPI on the basis that the long-term cost of satisfying the demands of a resource-importing country is borne by the extracting (exporting) country but not by the consuming (importing) country. Hence, via international

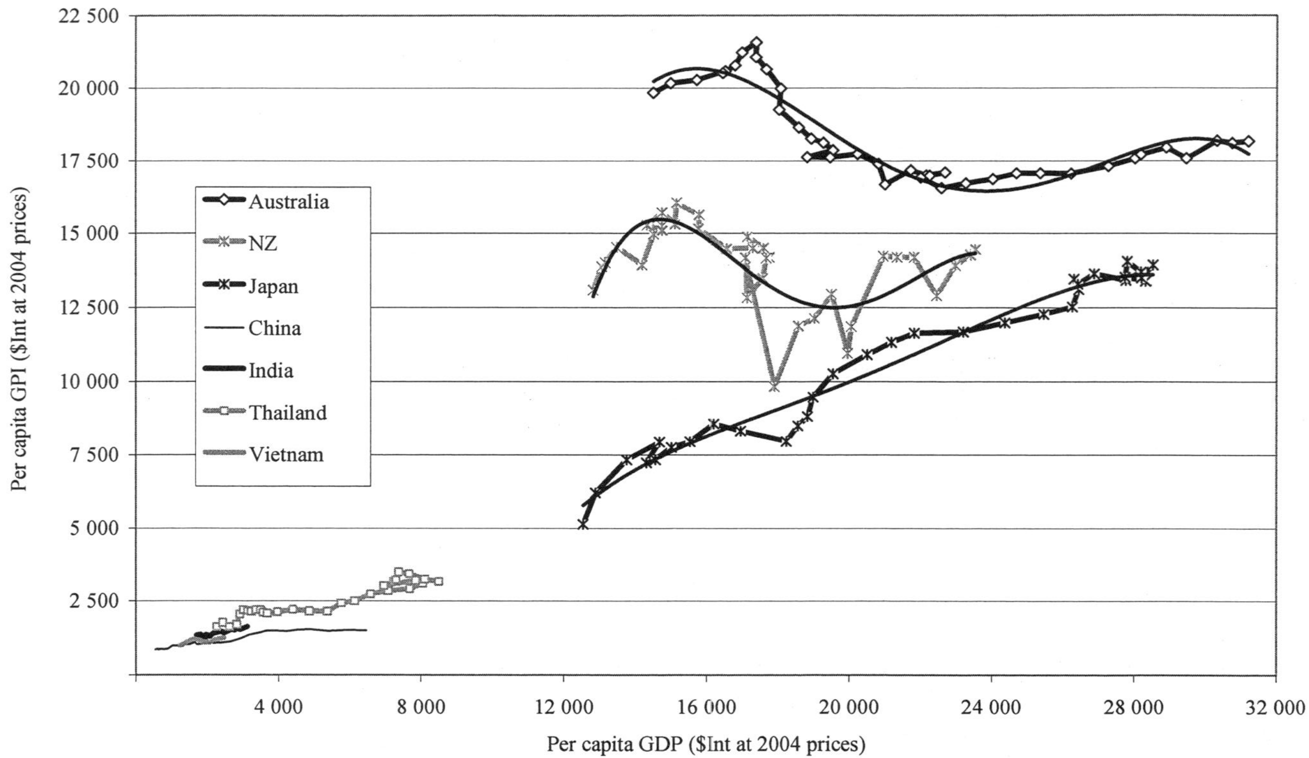

Figure 12.2 Per capita GPI versus per capita GDP of selected Asia-Pacific countries

trade, it is possible for the GPI of a resource-importing country to remain artificially inflated. This could well have happened in the case of Japan. If so, Japan's pattern of trade has enabled its sustainable welfare to appear higher than it would otherwise have been, thereby extending its threshold level of per capita GDP while at the same time contracting the threshold point of other nations.

Table 12.1 and Figure 12.2 appear to confirm the earlier apprehension regarding China and Thailand's premature arrival at a threshold level of per capita GDP. Of even greater concern to China is that its threshold point was reached at a per capita GDP in the order of Int$5000 whereas it was reached by Thailand at a per capita GDP closer to Int$7500. Either way, both fall far short of the Int$15 000–$25 000 threshold range experienced by Australia, New Zealand, and Japan.

A New 'Contracting Threshold' Hypothesis

Given what has occurred to China and Thailand, it begs the question as to what the level of per capita GDP will be for India and Vietnam when both countries arrive at their respective threshold points. The trend revealed by Figure 12.2 suggests it will be less than Int$5000. If this is correct, one is left pondering whether India, with an end-of-period per capita GDP of around Int$3000, is on the verge of reaching its peak per capita GPI value. If so, one can only assume that Vietnam, with a per capita GDP of around Int$2500, will follow closely in India's footsteps.

These disconcerting reflections are premised on two main observations. To begin with, it appears that the later a nation experiences an initial GDP growth phase (i.e., the later it undergoes an initial period of rapid economic expansion), the lower is the per capita GDP when its per capita GPI begins to stagnate or decline. This is no better exemplified than in Figure 12.2 by the tunnelling of the per capita GPI-GDP curve of each nation below the corresponding curve of its growth predecessor.

Secondly, and largely as a result of the first factor, the peak per capita GPI values of the growth latecomers – in effect, China, Thailand, India, and Vietnam – are considerably less than the peak per capita GPI values of their wealthier inter-regional neighbours. This brings forth the possibility that the poorer countries in the Asia-Pacific region (and throughout the world generally), may never attain the per capita GPI levels currently enjoyed by wealthy nations.

Assuming these observations are real and not simply an empirical artifact, what could be the structural factors behind them? Leading ecological economist, Herman Daly, has frequently expressed his concerns about a 'full' world in the sense of a world increasingly ladened with more human beings and more physical goods created via the physical transformation of natural capital to human-made capital (Daly, 1991, 1996, and 1999). As Daly points out, economic logic informs us that the marginal costs of an increment of GDP growth in a full world are likely to be substantially higher than in an 'empty' world.[4] Thus, in a full world, we can expect the marginal costs of economic expansion to more rapidly approach the associated marginal benefits – meaning, of course, that if expansion continues, the former will quickly exceed the latter, thereby causing sustainable welfare to decline early on in a nation's development process.

Despite the fact that the GPI does not, as noted several times, take account of many transboundary influences, a significant proportion of a nation's environmental costs are a function of what is happening elsewhere in the world if only because environmental impacts do not confine themselves to international borders. Indeed, the health of a nation's natural capital is inextricably related to the state of the natural capital located in neighbouring countries. The GPI is therefore likely to capture at least some of the spillover costs imposed on a nation by the past and present economic expansion of other nations. With this in mind, it would appear that the decline over time in the threshold level of per capita GDP is in part due to growth latecomers having to contend with economic expansion in a world already considerably full. For countries like Australia and New Zealand, initial economic expansion took place at a time when the world was much emptier and thus when the marginal costs of expansion were considerably less.[5]

The next explanatory factor is undeniably more controversial. Within the international trade literature, there is growing support for what is generally termed the 'pollution haven hypothesis'. The pollution haven hypothesis is based on the view that since international trade in a globalised world is governed by the principle of absolute advantage – a consequence of the free international mobility of capital (Daly and Cobb, 1989; Daly, 1996; Lawn, 2000) – many transnational corporations have progressively shifted their operations to countries with low wages, low corporate tax rates, feeble workplace laws, and deficient environmental regulations.[6] Virtually all such nations have a low per capita GDP. Not surprisingly, it has been claimed that many poor countries have become a haven for polluting industries and for firms generally seeking to enjoy a competitive advantage from the lower associated cost of production.

One of the major fallouts from the shift in location of 'dirty', low-wage production is the rapid increase in the excessive rates of resource depletion and industrial pollution in poorer nations. Conversely, there is a significant relative decline in the cost of environmental degradation in wealthier countries (i.e., a fall in depletion and pollution costs as a proportion of real GDP).[7] From the social perspective of poor nations, supporters of the pollution haven hypothesis claim that industrial flight – the relocation of capital to countries with weaker workplace and environmental standards – has also contributed significantly to rising income inequality, rural underdevelopment, urban overpopulation, and the loss of previously self-reliant communities.

In as much as industrial flight, if it has occurred, has boosted the volume of economic activity in the poorer nations of the Asia-Pacific region, it has almost certainly forced them to bear a disproportionately large burden of the social and environmental costs of regional, if not global, GDP growth. In doing so, it has brought forward their threshold level of per capita GDP yet more than likely extended the threshold point of many rich countries. This might explain why Australia and New Zealand, after respectively reaching a threshold level of per capita GDP in 1974 and 1981, managed to stage a minor GPI recovery in the decade following 1993. We have already commented on Japan's pattern of trade and the likely impact it has had on Japan's own threshold point and those of other nations.

We now, of course, come to a critical point in the debate. That is, how valid is the pollution haven hypothesis that we believe is underpinning the apparent decline over time in the threshold level of per capita GDP? A number of empirical studies have been undertaken to verify or repudiate the theory that capital moves to locations with weaker workplace and environmental regulations. The majority of these studies support the position that differences in labour costs account for numerous instances of industrial flight (Leonard, 1988; Hodge, 1995; Garrod, 1998; Ratnayake and Wydeveld, 1998). However, the position in relation to environmental regulations is not as clear cut. Most of the studies initially conducted in the late-1980s and the 1990s came to the conclusion that environmental stringency had had very little impact on the choice of production location (Dean, 1992; Pearce and Warford,

1993; Jaffe et al., 1995; Garrod, 1998). The reason for this early conclusion was that the cost of adjusting to environmental standards appeared to be small for all but a few highly pollutive industries, and avoiding such costs through relocation was almost always absorbed by the cost of relocation itself (Leonard, 1988; Stevens, 1993; Goodstein, 2008).

Since these initial studies were conducted, the availability of data and the models used to test the pollution haven hypothesis have improved considerably in terms of both their depth of coverage and degree of sophistication. As a consequence, the great majority of recent studies have produced vastly different conclusions in relation to the impact of environmental standards on production location. Indeed, they now show that disparate environmental regulations do result in capital flight to countries with weaker environmental standards (Wilson et al., 2002; Cole, 2004; Grether et al., 2006; MacDermott, 2006; Akbostanci et al., 2007; Levinson and Taylor, 2008). What's more, it has been shown that regional trade agreements can intensify the pollution haven effect (MacDermott, 2006). We will say nothing in relation to this last point other than to stress the need for further investigation into this claim which, if verified, should be borne in mind prior to any future trade negotiations at the Asia-Pacific regional level.

Overall, we believe the weight of evidence revealed by the more credible recent studies on the pollution haven hypothesis validates its fundamental proposition that weaker workplace and environmental regulations lead to industrial flight. By combining this verdict with the earlier conclusion regarding the increase in marginal costs in a full world, we are prepared to put forward a new 'contracting threshold hypothesis'. The hypothesis is essentially this: as the economies of the Asia-Pacific region and the world collectively expand in a globalised economic environment, there is a contraction over time in the threshold level of per capita GDP. Worse still, the threshold point confronting growth latecomers occurs at a much reduced level of sustainable welfare (i.e., at a lower per capita GPI).

Clearly, the implications of the contracting threshold hypothesis, if valid, are both concerning and far-reaching. All the same, we believe there is much hope for further genuine progress across the Asia-Pacific region. The hope lies with the opportunity to extend the threshold level of per capita GDP. But there are two considerations worth bearing in mind. Firstly, and this applies equally to all nations, there is an inevitable social and biophysical limit to the extension of the threshold level of per capita GDP (Hirsch, 1976; Daly, 1996). As it is, we believe that when artificial globalisation benefits accruing to wealthier nations are taken into account, the threshold limits for countries such as Australia, New Zealand, and Japan have already been reached. May we say that this in no way implies that these countries have reached the limit of their per capita GPI.

Secondly, we believe that any extension of the threshold level of per capita GDP currently confronting poorer nations depends entirely upon the adoption of a new course of action or development approach within the Asia-Pacific region. A slight variation on the business-as-usual approach is unlikely to succeed and is therefore bound to end in disappointment for the region's wealthy as well as poor nations.

A NEW DEVELOPMENT APPROACH FOR THE REGION'S POORER NATIONS

Although the course of action we are about to recommend involves a different development approach for the rich and the poor nations of the Asia-Pacific region, many of the policies we believe should be implemented apply to all countries regardless of their current state of development. A great majority of these policies have already been recommended in previous chapters. We will therefore avoid repeating most of the policy details and confine ourselves to a general overview of what is necessary to increase sustainable welfare across the Asia-Pacific region.

Population Stabilisation

If there is one thing that separates the richer and poorer nations of the Asia-Pacific region, it is the extent of the absolute poverty in the latter which is not found in the former (See Table 1.7). For some time to come, the poorer nations of the Asia-Pacific region will unquestionably require a development approach based on GDP growth. But it will need to be a form of growth vastly different to what has been undertaken in the past.

The first feature of this qualitatively new form of GDP growth stands out clearly from the rest. In view of current population projections, many of the region's poorer countries will need to take immediate action to stabilise their population numbers. This applies particularly to India, Cambodia, Indonesia, Malaysia, Pakistan, the Philippines, Thailand, and Vietnam. Population growth not only makes it more difficult to alleviate absolute poverty, it also leads to 'unnecessary' GDP growth in the sense that additional economic output is required merely to meet the basic needs of a larger population.

Distributional Equity

Even if population stabilisation can be successfully achieved, future GDP growth must be characterised by a more equitable distribution of future economic gains. Distributional equity is not only a moral imperative; it is necessary to maintain the social capital that underpins a healthy society and economy. In addition, a more equitable distribution of income and wealth increases the aggregate welfare contribution of a given level of consumption. Since this reduces the GDP growth needed to alleviate poverty, it further lessens any unnecessary GDP growth and thus brings with it obvious benefits in terms of lower environmental and social costs. All in all, a more equitable distribution of income and wealth has the potential to both increase the per capita GPI for a given per capita GDP and extend the threshold level of per capita GDP confronting poor nations in the Asia-Pacific region.

Self-Sufficiency

We shall say something soon about the predilection that many poor nations have for export-led growth strategies but, for now, we would like to say something about the mix of goods that poor nations ought to be producing. Export-led growth requires a significant proportion of a nation's output to meet the consumer demands of relatively wealthier people living elsewhere in the world. The types of goods produced are usually at odds with the consumer demands, if not basic needs, of the impoverished. Whilst export-led growth generates some domestic employment benefits, it benefits the wealthy owners of export-producing capital significantly more, who need not concern themselves with the purchasing power within poorer countries but only that within wealthier nations.

We believe that the governments of the region's poorer countries should provide inducements to encourage the production of goods more specifically aimed at meeting their citizens' basic needs. This does not mean that exporting should be discouraged altogether, only that export programmes are probably best confined to the production and exportation of goods where a nation: (a) has a clear natural production advantage (e.g., the production of particular agricultural commodities due to geography and climate); and (b) can efficiently generate surplus output above domestic requirements.

Apart from tax incentives, some of the inducements required to achieve a 'self-sufficiency' growth strategy would include policies which strengthen the purchasing power of a nation's citizens. As explained in Chapter 8, this requires healthy levels of domestically generated employment, a decent minimum wage, and an equitable distribution of income and wealth – all of which would boost the per capita GPI and further extend the threshold level of per capita GDP.

Increased Efficiency: Reducing the Resource Use Intensity of Economic Activity

In each of the case studies revealed in this book, one of the most notable impacts of economic expansion is the rising cost of environmental degradation. Given that further GDP growth in the region's poorer nations will involve the production of more goods, these countries must do all they can to reduce the environmental impact per unit of economic activity. Whether this would lessen the overall impact on the natural environment is a moot point since it would require the percentage reduction in the resource use intensity of economic output to exceed the percentage increase in the volume of economic activity. As explained in Chapter 4, progress with respect to the former is subject to severe biophysical and thermodynamic limits. Complicating matters is the fact that, even within these limits, the lowering of the resource use intensity of economic output is not a simple, steady, and resource-free process.

Of course, the ramifications of failing to limit any rises in the environmental impact per unit of economic activity are grave. It is highly probable that the environmental costs of GDP growth would soon exceed the associated benefits, thereby reducing rather than increasing sustainable welfare (e.g., China and Thailand). We are not suggesting that further rises in environmental costs can and must be entirely averted. However, if rises occur, they must be kept to an absolute minimum to ensure any economic expansion in the immediate future is not rendered futile.

There are many ways to lower the resource use intensity of economic activity. Perhaps the simplest means is to increase the efficiency of resource allocation within the economy. This can be achieved by internalising the environmental spillover costs of production that are regularly overlooked by markets. Depletion and pollution taxes of the type proposed in earlier chapters would greatly assist in this regard as would well-designed systems of tradeable depletion and pollution permits. Given that efficiency is also facilitated by ensuring markets are suitably contestable (Baumol et al., 1982), governments of the Asia-Pacific's poorer nations should establish appropriate institutional mechanisms to preclude anti-competitive corporate mergers. They should also be mindful of the potential anti-contestable impact on domestic industries from having large transnational corporations relocate within their economies.

As any economist would attest, efficiency gains generated via the market reallocation of resources are eventually exhausted.[8] To bring about greater resource use efficiency over time, it is necessary to encourage the development and application of resource-saving technology. The previously recommended internalisation of environmental spillover costs would no doubt be of assistance since it would induce firms to employ new technologies in order to avoid the additional resource-related costs they would otherwise incur.

One of the potential problems with internalising environmental spillover costs in poorer countries is that, prior to the introduction of any resource-saving technology, many local firms are likely to have difficulty absorbing the higher resource costs and/or pollution charges. Other firms will simply find the cost of investing in resource-saving technology prohibitively expensive. This could result in an unhealthy number of business closures. An alternative approach worth considering is the introduction of subsidies (grants) or a system of tax rebates to reward firms that develop and employ resource-saving technology. Thus, rather than trying to increase the uptake of resource-saving technology by penalising firms, governments would offer a financial inducement to encourage firms to make a socially desirable form of investment. In recommending this alternative approach, we are mindful of the fact that the full internalisation of environmental spillover costs (i.e., full cost pricing) is necessary to promote genuine efficiency in the long run. We therefore believe that the use of subsidies and tax rebates is a potentially useful means of initiating the resource-saving process, but not a long-run policy solution.

Natural Capital Investment and the Preservation of Critical Ecosystems

Take the time to study the development history of any country and it soon becomes evident that the great majority of investment spending is directed towards the accumulation of human-made capital (plant, machinery, and equipment). Very little is directed towards the maintenance, let alone accumulation, of natural capital. Indeed, one could argue that the history of GDP growth has been overwhelmingly characterised by the conversion of natural capital to human-made capital.[9] In Chapter 4, it was pointed out that natural capital maintenance is required to achieve strong sustainability. Since GDP growth will almost certainly result in resource throughput growth, the regenerative and waste-assimilative capacities of some existing forms of natural capital are likely to be exceeded.[10] This will inevitably lead to some depletion of the natural capital stock.

In order to minimise natural capital depletion, the governments of the Asia-Pacific's poorer nations must encourage greater natural capital investment. Governments themselves can play a leading role by undertaking extensive reforestation programmes, restocking rivers and lakes with fish, and restoring and rehabilitating important wetlands. As for non-renewable resources, governments should consider introducing legislation to compel all resource liquidators (e.g., mining companies) to set aside a certain portion of their depletion profits into capital replacement accounts (see Chapters 5 and 8). The funds could then be used to cultivate renewable resources that, in turn, would offset the decline in non-renewable resource assets.

Unlike the natural resources used directly for economic purposes, it is very difficult to restore important ecosystems once they have been significantly disturbed. For example, better soil management can restore the fertility of agricultural land, but a radically modified ecosystem is often irreparably damaged. Given this and the fact that ecosystems generate non-substitutable services that are vital to the successful functioning of economic systems, we believe the exploitation of natural capital in the Asia-Pacific's poorer countries should be confined to areas already significantly modified by previous human activity. In addition, all critical ecosystems should be preserved via the establishment of an extensive National Park system of the type that exists in the majority of wealthy nations.

An Import-Replacement Policy

At present, poor nations are encouraged by international development agencies to engage in a form of GDP growth underpinned by a rapid rise in exports. We believe the poorer nations of the Asia-Pacific region should abandon export-oriented strategies – as opposed to abandoning the exportation of goods altogether – in favour of import-replacement policies. Import replacement occurs when, instead of focusing on the need to boost exports, a country focuses on reducing its imports. This can be achieved when a nation increases the efficiency of its production to such an extent that it is able to produce a variety of goods at a lower cost than it previously cost to import them. There are a number of benefits to be had from an import-replacement strategy. These were discussed in Chapter 8 and will not be repeated here. What we will do is outline two major drawbacks of an export-oriented strategy that are particularly applicable to poor nations.

To begin with, export-oriented strategies often lead to overspecialisation and export revenue dependence. This locks countries into international trade, thereby reducing their freedom not to trade.[11] It also renders them particularly vulnerable to fluctuating international market forces which, in the past, has led to serious debt consequences (see Table 1.2).

Secondly, to attract the foreign investment necessary to establish and expand export-oriented industries, poor nations are often forced to engage in a standards-lowering form of competition (Wilson et al., 2002). In a globalised world of free capital mobility, this leads, in many cases, to lower minimum wages and the dilution of workplace and environmental standards. In some instances, it results in governments withholding the enactment of cost-internalising regulations. Hence, rather than promoting genuine efficiency, the imperatives of export-oriented growth often force the governments of poor nations to adopt a policy stance that reduces efficiency – ironically, the very efficiency that needs to be increased to extend the threshold level of per capita GDP they confront. It almost goes without saying that an export-oriented strategy can seriously undermine attempts to increase distributional equity and minimise the depletion of natural capital.

Eventual Transition to a Steady-State Economy

As mentioned earlier in the chapter, there are inevitable social and biophysical limits to the extension of the threshold level of per capita GDP. Once this threshold point is reached, the poorer nations of the Asia-Pacific region which, by then, ought to be experiencing a higher level of sustainable welfare, will need to move towards a steady-state economy. Exactly what this entails will not be detailed here, but will be briefly outlined in the following section on the region's rich nations.

A NEW DEVELOPMENT APPROACH FOR THE REGION'S RICHER NATIONS

It is our belief that all the rich countries of the Asia-Pacific region have probably reached their threshold level of per capita GDP. In addition, we believe there is little or no capacity for wealthy countries to extend their respective threshold points without diminishing the threshold level of per capita GDP confronted by each of the region's poorer nations. For this reason, the region's wealthy countries must *immediately* initiate the transition to a steady-state economy. Not only would such a transition provide 'space' for the poorer nations to grow into, it would also prevent the decline in their own sustainable welfare.

An immediate move towards a steady-state economy is unlikely to involve an immediate cessation of GDP growth. Like all interdependent systems, economies are 'path dependent' and subject to structural inertia (David, 1985; Silverberg, 1988; Hodgson, 1991). Thus, any abrupt cessation of GDP growth would give rise to significant net costs that could jeopardise the transitional process itself. This aside, the entire process will need to be as truncated as possible and involve a very rapid shift to a low rate of growth prior to a further rapid shift to the non-growth scenario.

Distributional Equity

Making the transition to a steady-state economy to prevent a decline in sustainable welfare is one thing. To go one step further and increase sustainable welfare, the region's wealthy countries will need to focus their development strategy entirely on qualitative improvement rather than quantitative expansion (growth). Not unlike the region's poorer nations, this new development approach must be based on improving the distribution of income and wealth. Even in the presence of GDP growth, the detrimental impact of growing inequality is clearly evident from the GPI results on Australia, New Zealand, and Japan. The benefits generated by a more equitable distribution of income and wealth will unquestionably be of greater significance in a steady-state economy.

Internalisation of Externalities: Increasing Efficiency and Preparing Countries for the Movement to a Steady-State Economy

Despite the widespread deregulation of markets in recent years, we believe the allocation of resources in most wealthy nations is anything but efficient (see Lawn, 2007, Chapter 9). Gross inefficiencies are largely the consequence of environmental spillover costs continuing to remain unpriced. The region's wealthy nations therefore need to internalise environmental externalities just as urgently as their poorer inter-regional neighbours. Full cost internalisation would lead to greater product durability, increased recycling rates, and the more rapid development and uptake of resource-saving technology. In turn, this would reduce the environmental costs associated with the ongoing maintenance of a given quantity of human-made capital which, presumably, would increase the GPI of any wealthy country in possession of a steady-state economy.

Having said this, a steady-state economy is, by definition, a sustainable economy. To achieve strong sustainability over the long term, it is necessary to keep the stock of natural capital intact. Apart from the preservation of critical ecosystems, natural capital maintenance requires the rate of material and energy throughput to remain within the environment's regenerative and waste assimilative capacities. As explained in Chapters 5 and 8, the depletion and pollution taxes commonly used to internalise environmental externalities are unable to ensure that the rate of resource throughput is restricted in the manner necessary to achieve strong sustainability (Daly, 1992; Lawn, 2007). This can only be achieved via the direct imposition of resource throughput constraints which are probably best introduced in the form of tradeable resource use permits (see Chapter 5 for a full explanation).

It is here, however, that the governments of the region's wealthy nations must proceed with caution. If resource use constraints were immediately imposed at the maximum sustainable rate of throughput, it would bring the growth of many economies to an abrupt halt.[12] In some cases, it would result in economic contraction. Because of the path-dependent feature of economic systems, an overly aggressive approach could endanger the smooth transition to a steady-state economy. We therefore believe that depletion and pollution taxes are an ideal means of preparing economies for the eventual imposition of much harsher throughput constraints. However, tradeable permit systems will need to be introduced promptly and the throughput constraints embodied within them speedily tightened.[13]

Natural Capital Investment

Whilst throughput constraints and greater resource use efficiency are necessary to achieve strong sustainability, they are insufficient. Neither guarantees the integrity of critical ecosystems nor deals with the fact that a major proportion of exploited natural capital exists in a non-renewable form. Additionally, some wealthy nations, having experienced a prolonged period of economic expansion, are now bereft of the natural capital required to sustain their own economic activity (e.g., Japan). They therefore depend heavily upon the natural capital of other countries, many of which are poor and currently engaged in a growth process of their own. But even where rich countries are well endowed with non-renewable resource assets (e.g., Australia), they very much rely on the exportation of these resources to finance their own consumption.

To the extent that many of the Asia-Pacific's wealthy nations continue to invest in human-made capital at the expense of their own natural capital, this conversion process must cease. Given, also, that many forms of natural capital possess public goods characteristics, the governments of wealthy nations have a crucial role to play as natural capital investors. To boost the contribution made by the private sector, governments should provide greater tax incentives to increase the attractiveness of investment in natural capital *vis-à-vis* other forms of investment. As previously argued, governments should also compel non-renewable resource liquidators to set aside a certain portion of their depletion profits to establish renewable resource replacements, thereby keeping the total stock of natural capital intact.

Of course, not all non-renewable resources have a readily available renewable resource substitute. In these instances, the non-renewable resource in question should be used sparingly with the depletion rate controlled via the use of depletion permits. This would not only be more equitable from an intergenerational perspective, it would also provide additional time for a nation to overcome any reliance upon the resource or, if possible, to establish a suitable resource replacement.

Value-Adding in Production and Ecological Tax Reform

In a steady-state economy, the stock of human-made capital remains constant over time. That is, the quantity of new goods produced over a given year effectively equals the quantity of goods directly consumed or fully depreciated over the same year. To increase the welfare generated by a non-growing stock of human-made capital, it is necessary to augment the use value added to all newly produced goods. To achieve this, the governments of the region's wealthy nations must reduce the tax impost on the financial rewards that emanate from successful value-adding – namely, the income from productive ventures, wages, and profits. Whilst this would reduce a source of government tax revenue, it would largely be offset by an increase in the tax revenue arising from depletion and pollution taxes and the sale of tradeable resource use permits (assuming the latter are introduced as recommended).

This policy of reducing taxes on 'desirables' and increasing taxes on 'undesirables' is an example of what is widely referred to as ecological tax reform (Lawn, 2007). We believe that all wealthy nations in the Asia-Pacific region should undertake tax reform of this nature, not only because of the benefits revealed above, but because it can lead to higher wages, increased leisure time, job sharing, and lower rates of unemployment. In doing so, it can help reduce the cost of overwork, crime, and family breakdown – all of which have generally increased in wealthy nations in recent decades and thus contributed significantly to the disappointing GPI performance of Australia, New Zealand, and Japan.

Increased Foreign Aid to the Region's Poorer Nations

As explained earlier, the Asia-Pacific's richer countries are in the privileged position of having undergone an initial expansion phase in a relatively empty world. In recognition of this good fortune, wealthy nations should increase the financial aid they provide to the region's poorer countries. At present, foreign aid spending averages 0.3 per cent of GDP per wealthy nation (OECD, www.oecd.org/statistics). We believe this is woefully inadequate. A target foreign aid rate of at least 0.7 per cent of GDP would, in our opinion, be more appropriate and eminently more just.[14]

There are five main areas where the increased aid money should be directed. Firstly, aid money should be used to provide basic goods and services to people suffering from extreme poverty, famine, war, and the impact of natural disasters. Although wealthy countries administer ongoing aid programmes to deal with these circumstances, increased financial aid would greatly alleviate the suffering that continues at levels we consider to be morally indefensible. Secondly, in view of the need for many poorer nations to control their population numbers, aid money should be used to fund population stabilisation programmes in circumstances where governments lack the necessary fiscal capacity.

Thirdly, many of the region's critical ecosystems (e.g., rainforests, wetlands, and coral reefs) exist in the poorer nations where further GDP growth is required. These ecosystems are likely to come under intense pressure at a time when preservation is more urgent than ever. While the preservation of ecosystems generates non-direct use benefits for all nations, it denies the host country any direct use benefits. To promote ecosystem preservation, the governments of wealthier nations should distribute aid money to compensate poorer countries for the direct use benefits they would subsequently forego. The aid money could then be redistributed by the recipient country to the citizens most affected by the lack of direct ecosystem access, and might take the form of direct compensation or, more productively, the establishment of a substitute industry (e.g., tourism to replace logging).

Fourthly, we have shown that ecosystem preservation will not, by itself, minimise the rate of natural capital depletion in the region's poorer nations. Aid money should therefore be distributed to poor nations to boost their investment in natural capital – in particular, to augment reforestation programmes, promote wetland restoration and rehabilitation, and assist in the adoption of sustainable land management practices. Finally, since rich countries would indirectly benefit from a reduction in resource use intensity in the region's poorer nations, the former should establish a transfer programme to assist the latter in the uptake of resource-saving technology. This might best be achieved by allocating foreign aid money to subsidise and thus lower the purchasing price of expensive new technology.

CONCLUSION

In view of the GPI results revealed in this book, we began this chapter by making two bold declarations: (a) the per capita GDP of any given nation generally overstates the sustainable welfare it enjoys; and (b) the recent rate of genuine progress across the Asia-Pacific region has not been as marked as the rise in per capita GDP would indicate. Upon close examination of the relationship between the per capita GPI and per capita GDP, we believe we have made an important new discovery. That is, the threshold level of per capita GDP (i.e., the point where the additional costs of GDP growth exceed the additional benefits) contracts over time as economies collectively expand. As a consequence, the threshold point of growth latecomers is reached at a significantly lower per capita GDP than wealthier nations. This suggests that poorer countries (e.g., India, China, Thailand, and Vietnam) may never experience the per capita GPI levels currently enjoyed by wealthy nations (e.g., Australia, New Zealand, and Japan).

Fortunately, there is hope in the form of an extension of the threshold level of per capita GDP. For this to occur, it will require, at least for some time, a new form of GDP growth to be undertaken by the region's poorer nations – namely, GDP growth that is clean, efficient, equitable, minimises natural capital depletion, emphasises natural capital investment, and includes an import-replacement strategy that increases national self-sufficiency and avoids standards-lowering competition. Population stabilisation must also be the centrepiece of this new form of GDP growth.

The wealthy countries of the Asia-Pacific region, if not the world over, also have a part to play in extending the threshold point of poorer nations. To play their role successfully, they must immediately begin the transition to a steady-state economy. However, in order to increase their own sustainable welfare, wealthy nations must undertake a development approach based, not unlike the strategy required by poorer countries, on increasing the efficiency of resource use and improving the distribution of income. But it must also be based on keeping natural capital intact, augmenting the use value added to goods in production (i.e., improving the quality of goods), and better organising the production process so as to generate more fulfilling forms of employment and provide more time for engagement in non-economic pursuits.

Rich nations will also need to lend greater support to the poorer countries in the form of increased foreign aid. Apart from providing basic goods and services to those in most need, the aid money should also be used to preserve critical ecosystems (i.e., compensate poor nations for the direct use values forgone), finance population stabilisation programmes, and assist with the uptake of resource-saving technology. In return, and since the threshold level of per capita GDP cannot be extended forever, poorer nations must be prepared eventually to move to a steady-state economy. When this time comes, which will differ depending on the country in question, the development approach currently required of the region's wealthier nations will need to be fully embraced by the region's poorer nations.

Provided the warning signs conveyed by the GPI results in this book are heeded and an appropriate course of action is undertaken, there is no reason why the sustainable welfare currently being enjoyed across the Asia-Pacific region should not rise in coming decades. Nor is there any reason why the huge gap between the sustainable welfare enjoyed by the region's poor and wealthy nations ought not to narrow. However, we are convinced that if the warning signs are ignored and a business-as-usual approach continues, the future of the Asia-Pacific region is grim. In our opinion, it would be a future characterised by gross overpopulation, high poverty rates, enormous disparities between rich and poor, social unrest, unimaginable pollution levels, and eventual ecological collapse.[15]

With this image in mind, let us hope that the policy-makers in the Asia-Pacific region take greater notice of the growing evidence now seriously questioning the efficacy of indiscriminate GDP growth. Let us also hope that any recognition of the impending calamity translates into the policy solutions required to bring about a lasting and sustainable rate of genuine progress across the entire Asia-Pacific region. Despite the enormous philosophical, political, and institutional barriers that stand in the way, we see no reason why the outcome should not be a positive one. Only time will tell whether a positive outcome eventuates.

NOTES

1. An international dollar (Int$) is a fictitious monetary unit which represents the equivalent purchasing power of a nation's currency over its GDP as the purchasing power of a US dollar in the United States. It thus indicates an equivalent quantity of goods or services that can be purchased irrespective of the country in question.
2. A line of best fit was not superimposed over the curves for China, India, Thailand, and Vietnam owing to the shortness of their length and their close proximity.
3. This may have occurred as a result of a deliberate policy on the part of Japan. We are more inclined to believe it was the inadvertent result of a pattern of trade that evolved following the gradual increase in the international mobility of financial capital (see Daly, 1996; Lawn, 2007). If the latter is correct, Japan cannot be held solely responsible for whatever environmental costs have occurred elsewhere in the Asia-Pacific region and the world generally.
4. This principle applies mainly in microeconomics where it is assumed that the marginal costs associated with higher production levels for a single firm increase as the firm nears 100 per cent production capacity. This principle applies equally well to macroeconomic systems, whether they be conceived at the national or global level.
5. As a means of illustration, the economies of Australia and New Zealand grew rapidly in the early post-World War II period of the 1960s and 1970s. In 1961, the ecological footprint of the world was 50 per cent of the world's biocapacity (Global Footprint Network, 2006). It is reasonable to assume that the world was 'half full' at that point in time. By 1970, when Australia and New Zealand had fully industrialised, the ecological footprint of the world had grown significantly but was still just 65 per cent of the world's biocapacity. For many of the poorer case study nations, their initial expansion phase did not occur until the 1980s and 1990s. In 1987, the ecological footprint of the world caught up with the world's biocapacity. The world was, in effect, '100 per cent full'. It is therefore clear that the conditions under which Australia and New Zealand engaged in a rapid initial phase of economic expansion differed greatly to the conditions confronted by countries like China, India, and Vietnam.
6. The use of the term 'pollution haven' clearly has connotations that go well beyond transnational corporations simply avoiding the cost of pollution abatement. It is an expression used more broadly to describe any instance involving the relocation of capital induced by cost savings arising from disparate regulations between countries.
7. Of course, in an aggregate sense, depletion and pollution costs have risen for the majority of rich countries. For example, the cost of lost natural capital services

(total environmental costs) for Australia increased by 149.9 per cent between 1967 and 2006. However, as a percentage of real GDP, the cost fell from 26.7 per cent to 17.7 per cent over the same period. In the case of Japan, the aggregate environmental cost declined as well as the cost as a percentage of real GDP.

8. This exhaustion point is often referred to as *Pareto efficiency* – a situation where it is impossible, through reallocation alone, to make one person better off without making another worse off.
9. This was a logical course of action in an empty world where there was abundant natural capital and very little human-made capital. Since we are now moving to a world where natural capital is becoming the limiting production factor, this conversion and subsequent running–down of natural capital no longer makes sense.
10. This will, of course, depend on the rate of increases in resource efficiency over time.
11. One of the fundamental conditions required for trade to be mutually beneficial is that it is and remains voluntary. This condition is compromised if the freedom not to trade is lost.
12. Given the potential to miscalculate the maximum sustainable rate of throughput and the complexity of ecosystems, it would be sensible to set the throughput constraint at something much less than the estimated maximum. This is often referred to as the 'precautionary principle'.
13. We also believe that assurance bonds should be introduced to deal with the qualitative nature of pollution and waste (see Costanza and Perrings, 1990; Lawn, 2007).
14. 0.7 per cent of GDP was the figure agreed to by wealthy donor countries at the UN General Assembly in 1970. The respective foreign aid contribution of Australia, New Zealand, and Japan is 0.3 per cent, 0.27 per cent, and 0.25 per cent of GDP (OECD, www.oecd.org/statistics).
15. Although wealthy nations would suffer, these dire circumstances apply more particularly to poorer nations.

REFERENCES

Akbostanci, E., Ipek Tunç, G. and Türüt-Aşik, E. (2007), 'Pollution haven hypothesis and the role of dirty industries in Turkey's exports', *Environment and Development Economics*, **12**, 297–322.

Baumol, W., Panzar, J. and Willig, R. (1982), *Contestable Markets and the Theory of Industry Structure*, San Diego, CA: Harcourt Brace Jovanovich.

Cole, M. (2004), 'US environmental load displacement: examining consumption, regulations, and the role of NAFTA', *Ecological Economics*, **48(4)**, 430–450.

Costanza, R. and Perrings, C. (1990), 'A flexible assurance bonding system for improved environmental management', *Ecological Economics*, **2**, 57–76.

Daly, H. (1991), *Steady-State Economics: Second Edition with New Essays*, Washington, DC: Island Press.

Daly, H. (1992), 'Allocation, distribution, and scale: towards an economics that is efficient, just, and sustainable', *Ecological Economics*, **6**, 185–193.

Daly, H. (1996), *Beyond Growth: The Economics of Sustainable Development*, Boston, MA: Beacon Press.

Daly, H. (1999), *Ecological Economics and the Ecology of Economics*, Cheltenham, UK and Northampton, MA, USA: Edward Elgar.

Daly, H. and Cobb, J. (1989), *For the Common Good: Redirecting the Economy Toward Community, the Environment, and a Sustainable Future*, Boston, MA: Beacon Press.

David, P. (1985), 'Clio and the economics of QWERTY', *American Economic Review*, **75 (2)**, 332–337.

Dean, J. (1992), 'Trade and the environment: a survey of the literature', in P. Low (ed.), *International Trade and the Environment*, Washington, DC: World Bank, pp. 15-28.

Garrod, B. (1998), 'Are economic globalization and sustainable development compatible? Business strategy and the role of the multinational enterprise', *International Journal of Sustainable Development*, **1**, 43–62.

Global Footprint Network (2006), *Ecological Footprint and Biocapacity*, 2006 edition, Oakland, CA: Global Footprint Network.

Goodstein, E. (2008), *Economics and the Environment*, Hoboken, NJ: John Wiley & Sons.

Grether, J.-M., Mathys, N. and de Melo, J. (2006), 'Unraveling the world-wide pollution haven effect', World Bank Policy Research Working Paper 4047, Washington, DC: World Bank.

Hirsch, F. (1976), *The Social Limits to Growth*, London: Routledge & Kegan Paul.

Hodge, I. (1995), *Environmental Economics*, London: MacMillan Press.

Hodgson, G. (1991), 'Evolution and intention in economic theory', in P. Saviotti and J. Metcalfe (eds), *Evolutionary Theories of Economic and Technological Change*, Reading: Harwood Academic Publishers, pp. 108–132.

Jaffe, A., Peterson, S., Portney, P. and Stavins, R. (1995), 'Environmental regulation and the competitiveness of US manufacturing: what does the evidence tell us?', *Journal of Economic Literature*, **33**, 132–163.

Lawn, P. (2000), *Toward Sustainable Development: An Ecological Economics Approach*, Boca Raton: CRC Press.

Lawn, P. (2007), *Frontier Issues in Ecological Economics*, Cheltenham, UK and Northampton, MA, USA: Edward Elgar.
Leonard, H. (1988), *Pollution and the Struggle for the World Product: Multinational Corporations, Environment, and International Comparative Advantage*, Cambridge: Cambridge University Press.
Levinson, A. and Taylor, M. (2008), 'Unmasking the pollution haven effect', *International Economic Review*, **49(1)**, 223-254.
MacDermott, R. (2006), 'Trade agreements and the environment: an industry level study for NAFTA', *Global Economy Journal*, **6(3)**, Article 3.
Organisation for Economic Co-operation and Development (OECD), *OECD Development Statistics Online*, www.oecd.org/statistics, accessed 12 September 2007.
Pearce, D. and Warford, J. (1993), *World Without End: Economics, Environment, and Sustainable Development*, New York: Oxford University Press.
Ratnayake, R. and Wydeveld, M. (1998), 'The multinational corporation and the environment: testing the pollution haven hypothesis', Department of Economics Working Paper Series No. 179, University of Auckland.
Silverberg, G. (1988), 'Modelling economic dynamics and technical change: mathematical approaches to self-organisation and evolution', in G. Dosi, C. Freeman, R. Nelson, G. Silverberg and L. Soete (eds), *Technical Change and Economic Theory*, London: Pinter Publishers, pp. 531–559.
Stevens, C. (1993), 'Do environmental policies affect competitiveness?', *OECD Observer*, **183**, 22–25.
Wilson, J., Otsuki, T. and Sewadeh, M. (2002), 'Dirty exports and environmental regulation: do standards matter to trade?', World Bank Policy Research Working Paper 2806, Washington, DC: World Bank.

Index